WE'RE GOING TO
WIN THIS THING

WE'RE GOING TO WIN THIS THING

WIN THIS THING

The Shocking Frame-Up
of a Mafia Crime Buster

LIN DeVECCHIO
AND CHARLES BRANDT

B

BERKLEY BOOKS, NEW YORK

THE BERKLEY PUBLISHING GROUP
Published by the Penguin Group
Penguin Group (USA) Inc.
375 Hudson Street, New York, New York 10014, USA
Penguin Group (Canada), 90 Eglinton Avenue East, Suite 700, Toronto, Ontario M4P 2Y3, Canada
(a division of Pearson Penguin Canada Inc.)
Penguin Books Ltd., 80 Strand, London WC2R 0RL, England
Penguin Group Ireland, 25 St. Stephen's Green, Dublin 2, Ireland (a division of Penguin Books Ltd.)
Penguin Group (Australia), 250 Camberwell Road, Camberwell, Victoria 3124, Australia
(a division of Pearson Australia Group Pty. Ltd.)
Penguin Books India Pvt. Ltd., 11 Community Centre, Panchsheel Park, New Delhi—110 017, India
Penguin Group (NZ), 67 Apollo Drive, Rosedale, Auckland 0632, New Zealand
(a division of Pearson New Zealand Ltd.)
Penguin Books (South Africa) (Pty.) Ltd., 24 Sturdee Avenue, Rosebank, Johannesburg 2196,
South Africa

Penguin Books Ltd., Registered Offices: 80 Strand, London WC2R 0RL, England

The publisher does not have any control over and does not assume any responsibility for author or
third-party websites or their content.

WE'RE GOING TO WIN THIS THING

A Berkley Book / published by arrangement with the authors

PRINTING HISTORY
Berkley hardcover edition / March 2011
Berkley premium edition / February 2012

Copyright © 2011 by Lin DeVecchio and Charles Brandt.
Cover photos: *Lin DeVecchio* by Robert Stolark; *Judge's Gavel* by Tetra Images/Getty Images.
Cover design by Diana Kolsky.
Interior text design by Laura Corless.

ISBN: 978-0-425-24609-2

BERKLEY®
Berkley Books are published by The Berkley Publishing Group,
a division of Penguin Group (USA) Inc.,
375 Hudson Street, New York, New York 10014.
BERKLEY® is a registered trademark of Penguin Group (USA) Inc.
The "B" design is a trademark of Penguin Group (USA) Inc.

PRINTED IN THE UNITED STATES OF AMERICA

10 9 8 7 6 5 4 3 2 1

Most Berkley Books are available at special quantity discounts for bulk purchases for sales,
promotions, premiums, fund-raising, or educational use. Special books, or book excerpts, can also
be created to fit specific needs.

For details, write: Special Markets, The Berkley Publishing Group, 375 Hudson Street, New York,
New York 10014.

This book is dedicated to all the outstanding men and women in the FBI, past and present, who made and continue to make our world a much better and safer place in which to live.

ACKNOWLEDGMENTS

The person who stood by my side and gave me the strength to persevere through a very difficult period in my life is my wife, Carolyn. Without her love and encouragement I would have suffered far more than I did. Similarly, my daughter, Ann, and my brother, Jay, provided love, understanding, and financial and legal assistance that was without precedent. These three were the finest support team anyone could have desired.

Significantly and equally valuable was my defense team of Doug Grover, Mark Bederow, and Ginnine Fried, who, with an unshakeable belief in my innocence, gave tirelessly of their time, expertise, and good office. To Jim Kossler, Andy Kurins, and Chris Mattiace I have nothing but the highest praise and admiration. They provided unselfishly of their time and know-how to make my trips to New York bearable. They conducted effective interviews of potential witnesses; got accurate and truthful information out to the public; and generated financial support to help with my legal costs. Long before my legal problems, these are men that I would go through any door with and literally trust with my life.

To Charlie Brandt, who watched every minute of the trial and believed in me from the start. Without his guidance and writing skills my time in the FBI and subsequent ill-conceived indictment could not have been so eloquently presented.

To two other writers whose significance and valor will become clear to the reader, thank you Jerry Capeci and Tom Robbins.

My heartfelt gratitude for their assistance in countless ways, and for their moral and financial support goes out to Geoff Doyle, Lou Stephens, Brian Taylor, Bill Carden, Joe Pistone, Pat Marshall, Bill Doran, Tom French, Denis Collins, Warren Flagg, Doug Corrigan, Tom Vinton, Craig Dotlo, Ken Brown, Jim Brennan, Dave Stone, Ken Steiger, Joe Fanning, and more than a thousand former and current FBI special agents—you know who you are. Finally, to Kathleen Karelis, who provided additional legal counsel to my fine defense team and to longtime NYO Administrative Officer Nick Sacco, who tirelessly worked unseen defending my innocence.

—RLD

Our literary agent, Frank Weimann, introduced me to Joe Pistone and we became friends for life. Nine months before Lin's trial, Joe and I criticized Lin's murder charges in three chapters in Joe's book *Donnie Brasco: Unfinished Business.* Joe recommended me to Lin for his book and I added another friend for life. Like Joe, Lin is a true American hero and one of the bravest and finest men I've ever been privileged to know. No one can truly know what Lin has gone through or how magnificently he has handled it. I echo Lin's thoughts about Carolyn. Her good humor and support helped make the trial bearable for everyone. I echo Lin's comments regarding Capeci, Robbins, his outstanding legal team, and especially his former FBI colleagues who were indispensable to Lin's cause and to the writing of this book. This was truly a Shakespearean "band of brothers" in action. Working on this book with Lin, his legal team, and his "brothers" was an honor. Our goal was to give Lin back his reputation.

Our editor, Denise Silvestro, and her assistant, Meredith Giordan, were top-notch and had their hearts in everything they did.

Finally, and as always to Nancy, my wife, and first line editor in my writing and in my life, and to our children and grandchildren.

—CB

THE JOB INTERVIEW

Mary Bari leaned right up to her mirror. Was she wearing too much eye shadow and eyeliner? Mary didn't want her eye makeup to rob attention from the all-natural glow of her large brown eyes. But as she knew too well, for a girl to work in a social club the made men in the Colombo Family expected the cosmetic works. The hippy look never caught on past a certain age, at least not in Bensonhurst, Brooklyn. All the young Italian girls in the neighborhood got made up and took good care of their hair. She smiled at her image and dabbed My Sin perfume behind each ear.

Mary touched her hands to her petite hips and swiveled sideways. She was satisfied with the way her black halter top snugly clung to her shapely breasts and how her studded wide leather belt accented her slim waist and drew attention to her shapely legs in designer jeans. Thirty-one-year-

old Mary was stunning, way better looking than Allie Boy's middle-aged wife.

I'm not being catty, Mary thought, but that woman had her day, and even in her day she wasn't exactly worth bragging about. I'm not getting any younger either, for that matter. Even though everybody says I look the youngest of anybody out there. Her and me both gave Allie Boy the best years of our lives. But no way she's ending up with him.

I'll raise holy hell, Mary thought. You know what? You can push me only so far. It's about time these people did something for me. They can afford it.

In a flash Mary imagined that "For Sale" sign planted in the front lawn of her boyfriend Allie Boy and his wife's house. Ever since she first heard that Allie Boy Persico's house was going up for sale, the image of a Cantalupo Realty sign haunted her like crazy. She got the story about them selling the house from her girlfriend who got it from her second cousin who worked right inside the Colombo Family real estate agency that controlled Bensonhurst. The Colombo Family made it so you had to be Italian to buy a house in their territory.

Mary Bari had lived her whole life in Bensonhurst in Colombo Family territory.

You know what, Mary thought, I know for a fact what she's up to. I should have told his brother Junior everything. She's selling their house and moving someplace out of the way like Florida. That way he can sneak in and be with her. And like what do I get out of the deal? He'll spend all his time on the lam in Florida—with her and their precious grandchildren with their Confirmations and Communions. And who's the one who's been putting up with him being on the lam for four years already?

So what, I got some jewelry. Swag jewelry! Big deal. I'm sure his wife gets the best swag. His goddamn crew used to bring me to see him, at least. Big deal. He has his fun. Then what? They bring me right back to the neighborhood. To nothing and nobody. I should have told Junior that.

I should have told his brother Junior everything. I should have told Junior I'm scared, too, you know, of Allie being sent back to jail.

When she first met him in 1969, Allie Boy was out of jail about two years. Mary was sixteen. Big, strapping, good-looking Allie Boy Persico spotted her and at once took a fancy to her. Allie Boy was forty, and he'd been a made man in what they call "the life" his whole adult life. He'd spent eighteen years of "the life" in jail on a card game murder. The night's big winner made the mistake of falling asleep at the table—no doubt so he could stop playing and preserve his winnings. The guy stayed asleep at the table permanently.

Allie Boy had a youthfulness that comes from not drinking and carousing too much for eighteen years while you're in jail, and then from not having to work and get worn out when you're out of jail and from getting up whenever you feel like it. Allie Boy had the big-shot flair that goes with being a made man and the adviser, the consigliere, to his kid brother, Junior, the big Boss of the whole Colombo Family. Junior Persico was a puny man compared to his older brother. Junior had perpetual bags under his eyes and his whole face seemed to sag from the weight of his responsibili-

ties. But in their world in Bensonhurst you didn't get any
bigger than Junior Persico. Maybe if Allie Boy hadn't been
in jail all those years he would have been Boss of the Colombos. After all, he was the older brother. Don't let the name
fool you. In Bensonhurst, if your name was the same as an
older relative or family friend, you stood a good chance of
having "Boy" attached to your name. Junior Persico named
one of his sons after his brother Allie Boy and that son
had become known as Little Allie Boy. He would be Boss
someday—Junior planned.

Junior Persico had just gotten out of jail on parole for
an old hijacking charge when Mary went to see him to talk
about the "For Sale" sign planted in her head and about
her future with Allie Boy.

The door buzzer sounded and Mary Bari took one long
last look in the mirror. At least Junior got me this job, she
thought as she picked up her bag—the real thing, not a
knockoff—and headed for the front door.

It was the driver and he was here with a borrowed car to
take Mary to a formality of a job interview with Carmine
Sessa at his new social club, Occasions. Even though Mary
had never met him, she knew Carmine Sessa would hire
her. In fact, he'd do whatever he was told by Junior Persico
without blinking. Carmine Sessa would be easy to work for.
Mary heard he had a nice smile and a nice wife, even though
he's been known to beat her. Carmine Sessa was under Greg
Scarpa's crew, but it was all under Junior Persico. It was
like Amway. Whatever anybody earned out in the street,
they kicked a big cut of it upstairs.

Mary and her friends always thought that Greg Scarpa

stood out. He had animal magnetism, charisma, and a really deep voice. He always handled his personal affairs like a gentleman. Greg Scarpa kept his wife and their grown kids in New Jersey, but he lived in a nice house in Bensonhurst with Linda Schiro and their two younger kids together, common law. Like Mary when she met Allie Boy, Linda Schiro was sixteen when she met Greg Scarpa. He was thirty-five. Greg Scarpa had four kids already in New Jersey with the Communions and Confirmations, but it didn't stop him from doing the right thing by Linda. Greg Scarpa and Linda Schiro were a precedent for the life Mary always had in mind for her and Allie Boy.

All of that had been on Mary Bari's mind when she went to see Junior Persico at his own social club the other day.

"This whole thing is ridiculous," Mary said to Junior. "I got no life like this. Nobody'll even date me. They're petrified on account of Allie. I ended up goin' on a date with a cop to a preview of Once Upon a Time in America."

"Stay away from the cop," Junior said. "You want people talkin'?"

"Just platonic, but it goes to show you what I'm up against. Allie cut me off of my support he was givin' me. I got no job. I'm goin' around puttin' in applications. I don't want to start no trouble. I just want what's right. I'm fifteen years standin' in the wings, but you know what, I'm standin' by Allie all the time. Maybe if I could talk to Allie myself. Maybe if he could see me . . ."

That gave the diminutive Junior Persico an idea that settled behind the bags under his eyes. Junior said to her: "Just stay away from the cop. I'll see what I can do. Mean-

time, you need to get outta the house. Have some fun. And yez need a little cash flow. I'll put you in a job—cocktail hostess in a new club. Carmine Sessa's club. Carmine lives upstairs from his own club. That way you'll be around people, minglin', till we can work things out."

"Just think about it, please, if there's some way I could see Allie myself."

"You tryin' to say I know where he is?"

"No, no, I'm just sayin'. There's precedent. Not to change the subject but there's a big lie goin' around that I had a beef with Allie's children, which is not true. I assure you. Personally."

"I don't know nothin' about nothin'. Yez better get outta here before I change my mind."

On the way over to the job interview, Mary and her driver talked about how Hollywood discriminates against Italian-American women. They don't have any glamour stars that are Italian, except maybe if they come from Italy itself, like Sofia Loren or Gina Lollabrigida used to be, but that was twenty years ago. It's 1984 now. They both agreed Madonna didn't count.

"They didn't even use an Italian girl to play the Italian girl in Saturday Night Fever," *Mary Bari pointed out. "They used some American girl. Nobody knows her name even."*

"The old former Boss, Joe Colombo, was right with that Italian-American Civil Rights League," the driver said. "Too bad that nigger clipped him."

"I was at that rally at Columbus Circle," Mary said. "It was awful. Poor Joe Colombo, rest his soul, laid in a coma

for seven years like a vegetable till he died. What a tragedy for the family."

"I wasn't with the family, then."

"No, I mean his wife and kids and all, his real family."

"Oh."

The driver dropped Mary Bari off in front of Carmine Sessa's club and drove off.

Greg Scarpa's legitimate grown son from Connie in New Jersey, Gregory Jr., unlocked the front door and let Mary in. He locked the door behind her. It was a private club. Members only or a search warrant.

"Don't you look foxy," Gregory Jr. said. He was Gregory Jr., not Greg Boy. Junior did not have his father's strong good looks, but he did get respect. He wholesaled a lot of marijuana.

"The foxy lady," Joe "Brewster" DeDomenico said. Joe Brewster was more Gregory Jr.'s age than Greg Scarpa's. He always had jewelry from burglaries.

Mary flashed a smile, satisfied that her outfit and makeup were camera ready. She waved hi to Greg Scarpa, the father, who was standing with Carmine Sessa, towering over tiny Carmine, who must have been about five foot four. Greg Scarpa was some sexy-looking man, Mary always thought from afar—solid, powerful, dressed sharp, nice mustache, a born leader.

"Hi, honey," Greg Scarpa said in his baritone voice, smiled, and waved back. Like a lion, Greg Scarpa was king of all he surveyed.

Next Mary waved hi to Carmine Sessa and said, "You must be Carmine." While this was Carmine Sessa's club, it was Greg Scarpa's business that Carmine Sessa would be conducting in it. And they couldn't just have anybody working here. They had to have somebody they could trust to hear things and keep her mouth shut.

"Hi, Mary," Carmine Sessa said. "Ready for your interview?"

"I'm ready for my close-up, Mr. DeMille," Mary said.

With that, Gregory Jr. put his arm around Mary, kidding around playfully.

Oh brother, Mary thought, it's starting already. If Allie Boy was still around here where he belongs, Gregory Jr. would never think of being so handy with his hands.

"Whoa," Mary scolded as Gregory Jr. suddenly pulled her to the floor and held her down tightly. "Whoa, there." Mary was mad.

Greg Scarpa, the father, was now standing over Mary and he fired a .38 into her face twice.

Who knows what Mary thought when she saw the gun or if she even had time to think about what she might have done wrong.

Carmine Sessa would later say he was sorry that this was being done, but in the meantime he and Joe Brewster rolled Mary Bari up in movers' blankets and cleaned her blood from his club's floor. Carmine Sessa didn't like killing a woman. Neither did Joe Brewster. Nobody did. That's why Greg Scarpa did it himself. Greg Scarpa was known as the Grim Reaper.

Carmine Sessa and Gregory Jr. put Mary's rolled-up body into a car trunk, drove off, and dumped her on a street

*in Bensonhurst, not all that far from the house that shortly
would have a "For Sale" sign on it.*

This is from my FBI Form 209 report of a meeting with
my Top Echelon (TE) confidential informant Greg
Scarpa, number 3461:

> "On November 21, 1984, NY3461-TE advised Super-
> visory Special Agent R. LINDLEY DE VECCHIO
> that the wife of ALPHONSE "Allie Boy" PERSICO is
> moving to Florida, and the house in Brooklyn is up for
> sale. The source said it is probable that Allie Boy is now
> in the South Florida area, or at least meets his wife
> there on a regular basis."

CHAPTER ONE

INTO THE COLD

MARCH 29, 2006

I sat alone, stuck in a chair in a nine-by-twelve room in the Brooklyn D.A.'s Office. It was late at night, March 29, 2006. I was impatient and, looking back, maybe a little anxious about where I would spend the years I had left. One thing that made me impatient was that the room was ice cold. Maybe it was because I'd just flown up from Florida that day that the room felt so cold. Or maybe it was the coldness of the metal chair I sat on. There was ice in my heart, too.

The room was way too bright, an institutional fluorescent lighting that sucks out the warmth. The lighting bounced off the room's closed door and glistened off the floor. Occasionally I shut my eyes to the glare.

I'd been retired from the FBI for almost ten years. I'd flown up from Sarasota at my own expense alone that very day to report to the D.A.'s Office and meet a 10 p.m. deadline.

More times than I care to remember during my retirement years, I kept getting reminded by something new out of the blue that certain decisions I'd made in the FBI were never going to rest in peace. In all its injustice, since the day I retired following my first scandal, this was the reality. It was a reality I had no choice but to accept and to keep on accepting with each new barrage of incoming fire.

At the same time, many of the events of the past couple of weeks during this second scandal seemed surreal. Was this really happening to me? Was it happening exactly as it seemed to be happening? Why was it happening? And what was going to happen next?

Like Mary Bari, what had I done wrong to make it happen to me?

On the other side of the locked door of my room, young D.A. detectives were going about their business. They were doing the kinds of things I'd done. They were taking the risks I'd thrived on in my thirty-three years with the Bureau, just about all of it spent here studying and fighting the Mafia crime families in the streets of Brooklyn.

I couldn't make out the detectives' words, but their chatter was a familiar hum. Some were no doubt getting set to hit the bricks to make arrests in the dead of night so as to avoid harm to bystanders; to stare at doors of Mafia social clubs until dawn writing down the comings and goings; and to sit in vans wearing headphones, patiently waiting for bugs to reveal dark secrets, all the while sipping dark coffee.

Others were bitching about the reports they were writing; checking in with their supervisor; and taking calls from confidential informants with good or bad information, such information being the lifeblood of any investigation, and all of it having to be taken seriously, followed up on, and corroborated.

Whenever the D.A.'s phone rang it should have triggered a memory—that for many years before my first scandal, I used to get sent down from New York to the FBI Academy at Quantico, Virginia, to teach classes in informant development to other agents and police. Maybe one of these D.A. detectives had been in my class and was applying what he'd learned from me on the phone with his confidential informant. Simple nostalgic thoughts like that were stolen from me when I retired, as if deleted from my memory bank. Any thought about informant development during my retirement would only leave ashes in my mouth.

Despite these two scandals, my thirty-three-year career in the FBI had fulfilled my wildest dreams. It was one mighty adventure after another, shoulder to shoulder with dynamite agents, very sharp, very ballsy guys. By whatever means at our disposal we had gone toe-to-toe with the Mafia, attempting to expose its secrets to the sunlight. We knew that like a vampire it would die from the exposure to the sun. Some of the work we did was dangerous; some of it was downright hilarious. Our heyday was during the 1980s. It was like a championship season for us. We worked hard and we played hard. I like to think we did a lot of good for law-abiding people.

The Mafia was probed and poked at on all fronts by my colleagues in Organized Crime in the New York FBI Office, men I call the New Untouchables. Fighting alongside us in this war were special agents in other Bureau offices throughout the country and agents and police in other law enforcement agencies. We never let up for a second until the Mafia became fully exposed. Under unceasing pressure from increased exposure, the Mafia in the 1990s began cannibalizing itself, fighting internal street wars for power, and becoming more and more paranoid. As it killed more and more of its own soldiers, it forced other soldiers to roll over, expose more secrets, and seek out the FBI for protection. That was the plan and it's still working, thanks to those who understood the importance of shining a bright light on the secret society of the American Mafia. And thanks to all our paid confidential informants, our personal unsung heroes behind all the exposing we did.

But a black fog now clouded those memories of our championship season for me. It was my best informant who had been used against me in my first scandal and was now being used against me in this second scandal. Informant development, I always taught, presents lots of personal hazards for the agent handling the confidential informant. As the joke goes: If you have an informant who can't get you in trouble he couldn't be much of an informant.

Now even the Informant Program that J. Edgar

Hoover instituted in 1961 was under a black cloud and was being reduced to almost nothing due to media pressure and ignorance.

If I were to prevail in this second scandal of mine, maybe those irreplaceable memories of what we accomplished at a significant point in history could be exciting tales to tell my two toddler grandsons when they grew older. If God were to give me the chance, maybe they could be reminiscences for me whenever retired agents and cops who had fought together got together at a retirement party or a funeral, with some of us taking credit for more than we did.

For now, every bit of my focus had to be on trying to figure out what people were saying what things about me this second time around. The FBI's Office of Professional Responsibility (OPR) had cleared me in the first scandal, which happened in 1994—the mutiny fomented by an overly ambitious young agent in the Colombo Family squad I supervised named Chris Favo (pronounced *Fay*-vo.)

To prevail in this second scandal, my lawyers and I were going to have to uncover the personal profit motives of the witnesses against me. We already knew the personal profit motives of the Brooklyn D.A. and his prosecutors in swallowing the lies these witnesses were saying about me. The D.A. and his prosecutors were motivated by book deals and publicity.

My first scandal—the 1994 Chris Favo OPR investigation—took a real toll on me—mentally, emotionally, financially, and physically. Among other things,

I developed high blood pressure. Sitting locked in this room, I felt my pressure rising. I needed to walk around a bit in my nine-by-twelve room; maybe that would calm me down. Mechanically I rose from my chair and began pacing. The handcuff on my left wrist gave me about eight inches from the arm of the chair that I was cuffed to. This made me have to slide the chair along as I paced. I moved like an old man with a walker, which I guessed I would be in the not-too-distant future. Against one wall there was a metal bench bolted to the floor. Earlier I'd tried to lie down on it, with my ball and chain of a chair beside me. But its metal mesh was really cold and hard—no pillow, no blanket—and the room was so bright that sleep had no chance with me.

The grand jury that heard the D.A.'s arguments and the evidence it cherry-picked to present decided that in my close relationship with my high-placed confidential informant in the Mafia I'd gone more than native, I'd drifted over the line.

Going native is something I did growing up as my family moved from country to country in the military. I had to learn how to adapt and assimilate. That ability to go native was a valuable trait of mine in informant development, or so I thought.

Now it was being claimed that I'd been intimate with the Mafia for so many years, working so closely with paid Mafia informants, that I'd gotten seduced by "the life." I had adapted and assimilated and morphed by degrees into one of them.

The Brooklyn grand jury found that I was selling FBI

secrets to the Mafia for a weekly stream of cash. The made man paying me these bribes in his kitchen each week in Bensonhurst, Brooklyn, was supposed to have been getting Bureau cash from me for informing on the Mafia. But instead it was the other way around. He paid me cash, and on top of that, I pocketed the cash I was supposed to be paying him. This supposed cash cow of mine was not just a confidential informant, he was a Top Echelon confidential informant. He was the Colombo Family's powerful murderer Greg "The Grim Reaper" Scarpa. The grand jury also found that on three occasions I ordered Scarpa to do hits and on a fourth occasion I provided the home address and daily routine of a Scarpa Colombo Family war enemy so Scarpa could do that hit. The grand jury found that following that last hit, I celebrated in my office in front of Chris Favo.

This four-count murder indictment made the original Chris Favo OPR allegations look like a parking ticket. This much I already knew: The principal witness against me was likely to be Scarpa's common-law wife for thirty years, Linda Schiro. From illegal leaks out of the Brooklyn D.A.'s Office to the press, leaks of what by state law is secret testimony, it was apparent that Linda Schiro testified at the grand jury that she had sat in their kitchen and witnessed it all.

Greg Scarpa couldn't testify for me in my trial even if he wanted to. Scarpa had died of AIDS in 1994 at the beginning of my first scandal.

The murders covered the period from 1984 to 1992. The first murder victim was Mary Bari in 1984, at a time when I was simultaneously supervisor of both the Mafia Commission Case and the Bonanno Family Squad. While I knew of the city of Bari in southern Italy, I'd never even heard of Mary Bari until I was indicted for ordering her murder, allegedly because I'd heard she was going to cause trouble for Allie Boy Persico. My other three alleged victims were: (1) Patrick Porco, a teenage eyewitness to a drive-by murder committed by Joey Schiro, the illegitimate son of Linda Schiro and Greg Scarpa; (2) Joseph "Joe Brewster" DeDomenico, a forty-something-year-old Mafia soldier, a made member of the Colombo Family who was suspected of becoming a born-again Christian and who helped dispose of Mary Bari's body; and (3) Lorenzo "Larry Lamps" Lampasi, a senior-citizen soldier, a made member of the Colombo Family who was believed to be an enemy of Greg Scarpa during the Colombo Family War of 1991 to 1992.

Based on whatever it was that the grand jurors heard from the D.A.'s witnesses, whoever they all were, the good citizens of the Brooklyn grand jury had voted a few days earlier to indict me on every one of these murders as if I'd pulled the trigger myself.

The next day at 2 p.m., at my arraignment, I would plead not guilty. I had two outstanding trial lawyers, Doug Grover, a former federal prosecutor I'd worked with on Mafia cases, the lawyer I'd chosen to represent me years earlier in the Chris Favo scandal; and Mark Bederow, a former state prosecutor in the prestigious Manhattan District Attorney's Office. They would go through the motions of asking that I be released on reasonable bail that I could afford. But the Brooklyn D.A. planned on insisting that because of the seriousness of the charges— organized crime murders—and because of my betrayal of my FBI oath, I be held without bail in Rikers Island jail until trial, which would take place a year or two later. Rikers was a zoo run by the inmates, a place especially dangerous for a former law enforcement officer. Whoever heard of a man charged with four Mafia murders being allowed out on bail? Because we anticipated that I was going to Rikers and not returning to Florida, we decided that my wife, Carolyn, should remain at home in Sarasota. The ordeal of seeing me leaving the courtroom in handcuffs under an armed guard to be taken to Rikers would break her heart. It was a memory she didn't need to carry.

Meanwhile, before I learned my immediate fate at the arraignment, I had to sit and wait or pace and try to keep my faith in a system that had turned on me twice.

Like the perfect storm, this one had been the perfect frame, the piling on of forces, and each one had made the frame tighter and tighter.

In my opinion, the 2006 frame began in 1994 when my first scandal was leaked to the press by my enemies. It stained me with permanent ink and made me an easy target.

Although the identities of all the witnesses and much of the evidence was unknown to me as I sat in the lockup, deep down I suspected it was members of the Colombo Family who were framing me from their jail cells in order to advance their legal appeals. I had been at war against the Mafia. I'd turned one of their fiercest men, Greg Scarpa, into what they would call "a rat," a rat that exposed their activities and helped capture and imprison a great many of them. Twenty years after our championship season, with the help of their allies on the outside, they had now captured me. I was their hostage. They had turned my relationship with Greg Scarpa against me. It was poetic justice for the damage I'd done to them with Greg Scarpa's help. Under a strange and new legal theory, my alleged murderous corruption in league with Greg Scarpa would put the keys to the jailhouse in their hands. On appeal of their convictions they would trade places with me, and walk out free while I walked in.

But isn't this what they all say? "I wuz framed!!!" And I'm sure there were those saying, "If there's smoke, isn't there fire? How does lightning strike the same man twice? And wasn't the first scandal based on allegations from one of his own agents and two other agents corroborating him? Didn't the FBI cover up for him in the first scandal? Wasn't he accused of giving Scarpa sensitive information in the first scandal, too?"

In announcing my indictment and arrest at his press conference, the powerful Brooklyn D.A. Charles J. "Joe" Hynes called this "the most stunning example of official corruption I have ever seen." Hynes assigned his toughest high-profile prosecutor, Michael Vecchione, chief of the investigations division, to nail me in court. He was going to be the good Italian and I was going to be the bad Italian.

A conviction of DeVecchio by Vecchione on any one

of the four counts would put me in Attica prison for life. For a man of sixty-six, life really would be life. Would I ever see my two grandsons again? My wife, Carolyn, and I joked about buying a condo near Attica in upstate New York so she could visit me.

But black humor and steeled nerves provided scant comfort. The only thing that really comforted my heart and soul as I paced back and forth, pushing my chair, in that room was that I had a legion of retired FBI agents covering my back—men and women, my friends and colleagues from our championship season. They'd started an organization to help relieve some of the pressure of my hundreds of thousands in legal fees: Friends of Lin DeVecchio.

Among these friends were: Andris Kurins, who helped bring down Big Paul Castellano and chronicled it in the book *Boss of Bosses*, and who would help with any investigating Doug Grover and Mark Bederow might need. Chris Mattiace (pronounced Mat*tee*se), who grew up in New York's Hell's Kitchen and served in Vietnam, and who helped bring down the Colombo Family, would serve as a liaison keeping other retired agents informed. Joe Pistone, the real Donnie Brasco, would lend his fame and prestige to my cause. Joe would devote three chapters on my innocence in his book *Donnie Brasco: Unfinished Business*, which came out nine months before my trial. Jim Kossler, the master strategist of our championship season, indispensable to our defeat of the Mafia, would lend his unparalleled expertise to the defense and would create a Web site for our organization: www.lindevecchio.com, which kept my supporters informed. Jim Kossler said, "This prosecution of Lin DeVecchio is the most outrageous abuse of prosecutorial authority that I have seen in my career." Jim Kallstrom, our former big boss, our former technical genius at bugging and wiretapping, and at the time of my arrest a top adviser to the New York governor, immediately declared to the press: "Lin DeVecchio is not guilty and did not partake in what he's being charged with. It's as simple as that." My former supervisor, our Special Agent in Charge, Bill Doran wrote a fund-raising letter stating that "our brother is in a very difficult and costly bind—one in which but for the grace of God, any one of us could have found ourselves."

To a man, my over-the-hill gang of supporters believed in my innocence, and to a man they also knew that an innocent man could get framed and die in jail.

After pushing and dragging the chair for a while in my confined space, I had to go to the bathroom, so I called out: "Gotta whiz."

A couple of the D.A.'s detectives unlocked the door and came into the room. I could tell both men were uncomfortable; their hearts weren't in it. One of them took out his key, uncuffed me, and escorted me down the hall to the bathroom. When we got back to my bright cold storage room and he cuffed me to my chair again, he squeezed my arm and said, "I'm sorry."

"I understand," I said. "You've got a job to do." Except for fooling around with handcuffs in FBI training in 1965, I'd never before been in them. But I'd slapped plenty of them on the thick wrists of Italian bad guys. And when I did, I never said, "I'm sorry." Can you imagine apologizing for cuffing a man your office has just charged with four counts of organized crime murder? Their treatment of me was class.

As they headed toward the door, the other detective stopped and said, "Why don't we put the light out?"

I got my hopes up that I might get some sleep.

The one who had apologized said, "I don't want to take that chance. If Vecchione comes in tonight, he'll go nuts if we do that."

"That's all right," I said. "The light's the least of my problems."

This long night was nothing compared to a few days earlier when I had to call my daughter, Ann, to tell her that her father had just been indicted for murder and his picture would be splashed all over the news.

CHAPTER TWO

THE FIG TREE

How did I end up sitting in a frigid room under indictment for ordering Greg Scarpa to murder Mary Bari and for conspiring with him to commit three other murders?

While all my troubles came out of my thirty-three years in the Bureau, there's a lot more here than meets the FBI, if you'll excuse the pun. Ironically, in the opinion of most of the men I worked with, I did my best work with Greg Scarpa. My fellow FBI supervisor Chris Mattiace cheered me up after my arrest: "If you don't get in trouble from time to time, it means you're not doing your job."

Although of Italian descent on my father's side, I didn't come from a world anything like Bensonhurst. I was assigned to that world.

"You're Italian. You shouldn't be doing this." Because of my last name and because I look Italian, on two or three occasions a wiseguy I handcuffed asked me how I could be a traitor to my own people by working for the FBI against the Mafia.

"I'm only half Italian," I would say.

"Yeah, and the other half is a rat."

And they were serious, almost pained. They truly believed that I was working against my people. The first time I was asked that question I thought it was a put-on. How could someone seriously think like that? But when you get to know certain Mafia-controlled neighborhoods like Bensonhurst, you understand. In Bensonhurst, it was all about loyalty to family, and anyone who was Italian was considered family. These people didn't know any other way. Some of them had never been to another borough. This is all that these people knew. In *Saturday Night Fever*, John Travolta's character, Tony Manero, wanted to break out from his Brooklyn neighborhood and his job in a Bensonhurst paint store. The four bridges leading out of Brooklyn served as a metaphor for Manero's quest to escape to a better life. While many Italians from neighborhoods like Bensonhurst have gone on to great things, the cards are stacked from childhood. "Stayin' Alive" by the Bee Gees was an appropriate theme song for that 1977 movie.

I had it so much easier.

Sunny Fresno, California, where I was born, is nearly three thousand miles from Brooklyn. It's a salad bowl in the San Joaquin Valley, midway between L.A. and San Francisco. It's a fertile land of fruit and vegetable growers. It has a large Armenian population living side by side with a large number of hardworking Italians.

My grandmother's brother prospered as an artichoke grower. We got reunited after forty years when he picked up a *Newsweek* in a dentist's office and was shocked to read that his grandnephew was under indictment for murder.

It gets brutally hot in the summer. In order to beat the heat before the days of air-conditioning, a resourceful Italian immigrant, Baldo Forestieri, took his pick and shovel and built a cool underground summer retreat. It's a tourist attraction today. He built it so sunlight could get in to grow his garden.

My grandfather Angelo DeVecchio came over on a boat from Tuscany at the turn of the last century. What a trip, what guts. My grandmother Vermiglia Barsotti, one of nine children, also came from Tuscany, sailing out of Genoa by way of Argentina in 1904. Her oldest sister was already in Fresno to welcome the family. This was often the drill. An older son or daughter would come first and earn the American dollars needed to bring over the rest of *la famiglia*.

"Did you just get off the boat?" was, and still is, an expression of derision for the newly arrived.

My grandparents met in their teens shortly after my grandmother got "off the boat." To court her, my grandfather biked twenty miles each way from Madera to Fresno. They wed in 1904 when my grandfather was seventeen and my grandmother was sixteen.

My grandfather had very little English. My grandmother had a little more. Both spoke with a heavy accent.

My grandfather, a thick, stocky, muscular man with salt-and-pepper hair, made spaghetti in the Borelli spaghetti factory in Fresno. My grandmother, a big-boned and big-chested woman of five feet seven inches, was a supervisor in a fig-packaging plant. They lived in a modest house, very clean and well kept. He took care of their flourishing garden and she canned their fruits and vegetables. They were delightful, affable, very pleasant to be around. As long as you ate. God forbid if you didn't eat. And you were always too thin, pronounced "teen-a." To this day I can't leave a scrap of food on my plate in a restaurant for fear that it will be wasted. At home, I put the table scraps in the refrigerator and eat them later.

My earliest memory is of my grandfather's typical Italian garden on a quarter acre of land. Not a square inch of that land was wasted. There was a fruit or a vegetable growing on all of it at all times, even a kumquat tree. The best place for me was high up in the fig tree, pronounced "feeg-a." During my childhood, the feeg-a tree was easy to climb and it held my small frame without breaking a branch. I picked figs warmed by the sun and ate them on my perch, swaying with the breeze, with the California sunshine on my face and looking out on the fragrant pure world provided for us by my grandparents. To this day I adore dark figs. I love Fig Newtons. I think of that tree every time I have a feeg-a.

My grandparents also had a grape trellis that ran straight back from the garage. It was about thirty yards long with a red grape arbor. My grandfather had a wine-press he kept in the garage and he made the best wine I ever tasted. When I was a boy, they gave it to me Italian-style for kids—a little bit of wine mixed with water.

Their first child was a son who died when he was one year old, which was not uncommon in those days. Then came my aunt Evelyn in 1906. Four years later, in 1910, my father, Roy DeVecchio, was born. There seemed to be a pattern of increased height with each new Italian generation growing up in America. While my grandfather was about five seven, my father grew to about five eleven and I'm six feet. My kid brother, Jay, twelve years my junior, is an inch taller than me, and his two sons are bruisers.

Unlike his parents, my father went to high school. There he played football. And thanks to his parents' hard work and his own hard work, he went on to Fresno State College. Lucky for me, because that's where he met my mother, a fellow student. Lois Lindley was blond and beautiful, but always "too teen-a." It was quite an achievement for the son of Italian immigrants to marry a blond American, much less a slim, talented beauty. She even had a lovely American name and I got part of it.

Lois Lindley had come to Fresno to college from Pittsburgh, Kansas—with family across the line in Missouri. It was rural America, more nineteenth than twentieth century. My mother's mother died from TB when she was two, then her father left her in the care of her aunt and uncle and drifted off. My mother's aunt and uncle raised her. I viewed them as my other, faraway grandparents.

But I was raised Italian and called my grandfather "Nono," which my grandsons now call me, and I called my grandmother "Nona." We were so traditional that my mother converted to Catholicism for their marriage. We lived a block and a half from my grandparents' house in a mixed neighborhood of Italians and Armenians. Italians don't move too far from family, whether it's Bensonhurst or Fresno.

An Italian immigrant in San Francisco, Amadeo Pietro Giannini, founded the Bank of America. He would make loans to immigrants, who, while they had no credit rating, believed they would die of shame and burn in hell if they ever defaulted on a loan. They had spiritual collateral. The bank was small in those days and had a branch in Fresno. On graduation from college, my father went to work for the bank. Later, in the 1930s, he joined the army reserve. There was no peacetime draft. But he was, like so many Italians, fiercely patriotic, as was my mother, like so many rural Americans. Nono was very proud of his son in the military—an American officer.

I was born on April 18, 1940. I was named after both my parents, Roy Lindley DeVecchio. To distinguish me from my father, Roy, my parents called me "Lin" and it stuck. Roy Boy would have been a disaster. The only other Lin I know of died in China almost two hundred years ago.

There's a statue in Chinatown in Manhattan of Commissioner Lin, a legendary and martyred law enforcement officer from the Canton province. In the early 1800s Commissioner Lin cleaned up China's opium addiction problem. The Brits were growing the drug in India and pushing it in China. In reaction to Commissioner Lin's success in seizing opium and treating the addicts with Chinese medicine, the Brits started the First Opium War. The Brits crushed the Chinese and forced China to permit opium sales.

I was almost two when World War II broke out. My father was called up to the regular army as a lieutenant in the financial branch. As a finance officer, he was kept stateside for the duration. The only time I remember my father leaving us during the war years was when he was ordered to Los Alamos for what he later told me was a highly secretive A-bomb test—before they dropped the two bombs on Japan.

When I was two and a half, my dad got his orders for the Presidio in San Francisco. So we moved to a rental house on Divisadero in the Marina district. We lived upstairs in a two-family house. The elderly Italian owners lived downstairs. I remember blackout curtains. For a long time people figured the Japanese were going to attack the coast. At night my parents would put up dark colored cloth to block out the light.

I went to kindergarten down the street. I walked myself. Alone. San Francisco was as safe as Fresno. My father came home from work every day like any other father, but in a uniform. On most weekends we went to Fresno and stayed with Nono and Nona. Every Sunday we went to church as a family.

We were extremely close. I was very close to my mother, but I had an excellent relationship with my father. He was a military man and he laid down the law. He was a very fair man, but I didn't step out of line too much. When you're brought up in a military household, I guess you know instinctively that everything you do could have consequences on your father's career. But kids generally didn't disobey their fathers in those days, especially Italian kids. If he told you to do something, you did it. You didn't know what the consequences were, but you didn't want to find out. All the kids were that way, civilian and military. My father would never disobey his father.

Like they do with the FBI, some people today disparage the military, but not then. People in uniform were looked up to. And boy, did I look up to my father.

My father had dark wavy hair and was a handsome, well-built 180 pounds. He was always a very charming guy—smooth, outgoing, gregarious, well spoken. You admire everything about your father as a boy, at least I did. Your father knows everything. You assume there's no question he can't answer. Except for his father's wine, my father rarely drank, but he smoked Chesterfield cigarettes and I assumed I would, too, when I grew up. I never did smoke Chesterfields, but Dad's people skills were in my genes and they helped me enormously when I handled Mafia informants.

Still, in hindsight, my mother was the more special one of the two. She was very athletic, a terrific tennis player. She was so good at bridge that she had to give it up because the other army husbands and wives wouldn't play with her. She won all the tournaments. My mother loved to read and loved the arts. She knew more about Michelangelo than any other kid's mother, that's for sure. She had a flair for interior decorating and gradually over the years developed a word-of-mouth reputation that brought her a nice side business. If my parents argued, it was over a purchase of my mother's. My father was old-style Italian: careful with a dime. And being a finance officer, he tried to keep a tight grip on the family budget. My mother would usually win, and we'd get the new whatever to replace the old whatever.

We were all ecstatic when the war ended. Since as a family we enjoyed army life as we knew it, my father decided to make a career out of it. And for me, as good as it was in San Francisco and Fresno, the best was yet to come.

"We're going to Bermuda," my father announced one afternoon.

My father's first peacetime orders were for us to report to Bermuda in late '45.

We were eager to go, but I knew I would miss my grandparents and my fig tree. By the time I returned, I was too big and too heavy for its branches to support me.

CHAPTER THREE

THE SECRET SOCIETY

To understand my journey from that boy in a fig tree to a Mafia fighter under indictment for murder—accused of going native—it might help to glance back at the journey of the Mafia in America. From its beginning, the Mafia was a dangerous creature that needed to be handled with care. It was a unique creature that needed to be fought with unique weapons.

"Mary Bari," my lawyer Doug Grover said in his opening statement on the first day of my trial on October 15, 2007, "was the victim of Mafia gang violence, which has plagued the streets of Brooklyn for seventy-five years."

In 1924 when my father was fourteen, President Calvin Coolidge signed a law that reduced Italian immigration quotas from two hundred thousand men, women, and children a year, all of them squeezing through Ellis Island like cattle, to four thousand a year. America already had a sufficient amount of cheap Italian labor. Fifteen percent of New York's population consisted of Italians shoehorned into Little Italy, East Harlem, and Brooklyn. As a member of the FBI's first SWAT team, I trained on a vacant and decayed Ellis Island before private donors restored it.

Not only did America have enough Italian factory workers, coal miners, gravediggers, laborers, and street sweepers, but America had more than enough headlines about Italian criminals.

While my grandfather made wine for his family, notorious Italian bootleggers like Al Capone were exploiting the Prohibition laws. They were using tommy guns against each other, and against Jewish and Irish rivals. Their rat-a-tat-tat was making noisy headlines. By 1924 the notion that Italian immigrants were murderous criminals was a given.

Years earlier, around 1900, when Teddy Roosevelt was the police commissioner of the NYPD, the problem of Italian criminals was mostly that of Italian on Italian.

"Mama," the Italian grocer would call, clutching a piece of paper to his chest.

"Oh Di, oh God," his wife would moan, crossing herself when she saw the Black Hand reproduced on the paper.

Soon after, a stranger would arrive.

"A friend of mine—who could be a friend of yours—told me you maybe need protection," the stranger would say. "I give to you. Don't you worry."

With his hand shaking, the grocer and his wife knew he had to either pay a monthly extortion or die. If he wasn't thrown down a flight of stairs tied to a chair so his arms and legs couldn't break the fall, his grocery store and anyone in it would be blown to bits. The grocer had no place to go for help. He didn't speak the language the Irish policeman on the beat spoke and he didn't trust the police to understand this special breed of criminal.

Teddy Roosevelt, as New York's police commissioner, devised a plan to help the Italian immigrant fight back against the Black Hand gangs. He created the Italian branch of the NYPD. Roosevelt promoted his department's first Italian-speaking cop, the immigrant and former shoeshine boy Joe Petrosino, and put him in charge.

With the same carte blanche Commissioner Lin had been granted by the Chinese emperor, Teddy Roosevelt gave Petrosino complete authority to concentrate on the Italian gangster. Petrosino rounded up members of the Black Hand gangs, interrogated them in their own language, convicted over five hundred, and deported many others. Ernest Borgnine portrayed the heroic Petrosino in a 1960 movie aptly titled *Pay or Die*.

In 1909, Lieutenant Joe Petrosino took an ocean voyage to Palermo, Sicily. He'd gone with a list of immigrants he suspected had criminal records in the old country. If Lieutenant Petrosino could find a rap sheet for anyone on his list, he could deport him back to Sicily. On the day Petrosino arrived in Palermo, around the time Angelo De-Vecchio and Vermiglia Barsotti were expecting the birth of my father in Fresno, he visited a public square to admire a statue of the Italian unifier Giuseppe Garibaldi. Lieutenant Petrosino's own first name was Giuseppe and he was proud that Garibaldi had once lived in New York City. While Petrosino soaked in the sights and sounds of a Sicilian square, a Sicilian Mafia member walked up from behind and shot him three times in the head. His funeral in New York was very big—250,000 mourners lined up at St. Patrick's Cathedral. A small square in Little Italy was named after him. A plaque in his memory stands in Petrosino Square.

Lieutenant Petrosino's plaque is almost directly across town from Commissioner Lin's statue. I think of the lieutenant every time a cop is shot.

I recall the first cop-shooting case I was involved in. It was during some very dangerous years when police "pigs" were slaughtered for no reason. It was the 1971 murders of NYPD Patrolman Waverly Jones and his partner, Patrolman Joseph Piagentini. They'd responded to a routine domestic disturbance at a Harlem housing project that occupied the old site of the New York Giants baseball field, the Polo Grounds. As they walked back to their police car from the building, they were both shot in the back.

Through informants, the NYPD quickly identified the killers as members of the Black Liberation Army (BLA). Squads were formed to follow leads from informants to try to capture them. After an assassination of a fellow law enforcement officer, we all band together to try to do whatever we can. Because I was a crack shot, I was pulled out of Organized Crime to help.

We knew our .357 revolvers left us dangerously out-gunned. The BLA was known to have an arsenal of automatics. We also knew that most of us would stand out as the white enemy and the black agents among us would stand out the way the black officer Waverly Jones had as the "pig" enemy. This was most true in the areas of Harlem that we would be going into, hotbeds of murderous rage. We never knew if a door we knocked on would be answered by high-powered gunfire.

"We need to be carrying shotguns," I said to our squad supervisor.

"Headquarters advised no shotguns," the supervisor said. "No automatics either. Service revolvers only. That's firm."

So we smuggled in weapons from home. I wore a rain-coat that concealed a .45 automatic in my belt and a sawed-off shotgun in a sling over my shoulder. Thank God we had no need to use them or we'd have been fired. Alive, but fired.

A young agent on another squad told me about a BLA arrest he'd made with an old-time NYPD detective. By the time they reached the sidewalk with their arrestee, there was a dangerous crowd in the street demanding the release of the "political prisoner."

"Grab the prisoner and follow my lead," the older detective barked.

"Got him," the young agent replied.

The older detective walked straight toward the crowd and grabbed the closest militant to him. He put his gun in the militant's mouth and walked with the man in tow.

"Anybody moves toward us, this asshole gets his brains blown out."

They continued on to their car and they left with their prisoner.

In 1924 Italian immigration in America got an unexpected boost from Benito Mussolini, the new prime minister of Italy. In that year Mussolini began rounding up Italian Mafia members and tossing them into iron cages in courtrooms. He convicted them on the charge of "banding together for criminal purposes."

Coincidentally, also in 1924, J. Edgar Hoover was named director of the FBI. The 1924 anti-Italian immigration laws in America kept boatloads of law-abiding Italian immigrants out, like my relatives in Tuscany, but they did nothing to stop Italian Mafia members from illegally pouring in to escape Mussolini's Mafia trials.

Until its end in 1933, Prohibition provided a welcome mat for this influx. Mafia-connected illegal aliens knew bootlegging could be their ticket to riches. If they survived the tommy guns' rat-a-tat-tat during turf warfare, they would soon have lots of money and power.

The Mafia illegals had chosen wisely. In Italy they would have been jailed for "banding together for criminal purposes." We never did get the iron cages here, but in the 1980s we got new unique laws designed specifically to fight the American Mafia using a charge similar to Mussolini's—that of being a member of a "criminal enterprise."

To use these laws in court we needed to be able to prove that an American Mafia "criminal enterprise" had come into being and show exactly what it was.

CHAPTER FOUR

LUCIANO'S BUSINESS PLAN

In 1931 the American Mafia "criminal enterprise" was created.

The Bosses of the five most prominent Italian gangs in New York City secretly gathered in Chicago with Al Capone and other Italian Bosses from around the country. The purpose of this sit-down—the brainchild of New York's Lucky Luciano—was to create a plan that would put an end to the noisy headlines and the rat-a-tat-tat.

Its main result was the creation of a commission to lay down the law, arbitrate disputes, and supervise the orderly succession of Bosses.

Since any single New York gang—including the two I would spend my career concentrating on: the Bonanno Family and later the Colombo Family, the family that got me in trouble—was much stronger than any other in the country, all five New York Bosses were placed on the ruling commission. The Bosses of Chicago and Buffalo made it seven. By creating a ruling commission, the sit-down successfully created the "organized" part of a national organized crime network. With members from the Italian criminal gangs of America, there now was a secret American Mafia "criminal enterprise."

It would be 1986 before the Commission would be fully exposed and proven to be a criminal enterprise in Rudy Giuliani's Mafia Commission Case, which I was very proud to have served on as the FBI case supervisor. When I testified in countless trials as an expert on the Mafia, I emphasized its secrecy and our need to expose it.

Above all, Luciano's plan was to keep the organization a secret. He knew that if anyone found out about their secret society, something would be done about it, something similar to what Mussolini did in Sicily. Secrecy was, by design, the indispensable element. All the other rules were intended to bolster secrecy. Without secrecy, the new American Mafia would fail. Secrecy was its secret weapon.

Secrecy was so valued and so carefully nurtured that it would take over half a century for law enforcement, Congress, and the media to completely expose the American Mafia: its existence; its structure; its membership; its methods; its victims; its activities; and its scope.

In the 1980s, when my colleagues and I were working hard to expose the American Mafia, an old-time Sicilian Mafia Boss, Tommaso Buscetta, rolled over. He became a cooperating witness and testified for the prosecution in

Rudy Giuliani's Pizza Connection heroin smuggling trial. Tommaso Buscetta observed that secrecy, not violence, is what gave the Mafia its power.

The law of *omertà*, sealed lips and absolute silence, was strictly enforced; breaking this code was punishable by torture and death. Under the rules of secrecy, use of the word *Mafia* was strictly forbidden, even among made men. Made men were required to deny the American Mafia's existence to everyone all the time, even to their wives and parents.

Soldiers were "made" in a secret ritual whose oath further emphasized secrecy. To become a soldier, a man had to be sponsored by a capo who would personally vouch for the inductee's ability to remain silent no matter what pressure was brought to bear on him.

Only a Boss could sanction the murder of a made man. No one, not even another made man, could so much as lay hands on a made man. Providing such physical security removed resentments and vendettas that could lead to loose lips.

Further security was provided to the made man by the influence the Bosses had over judges and local law enforcement. In exchange for this protection, the made man passed a portion of everything he earned or stole up the chain to his capo, who took half and passed the remainder up to the Boss.

In the first generation of the American Mafia's existence, only Italian was spoken, and the language was laced with secret meanings. When English inevitably became more common, the secret meanings remained. To get "paraded out" meant to get made. To be introduced as a "friend of *ours*" meant you were in the Mafia. You were a full-fledged "wiseguy." "A friend of *mine*" was merely an associate member.

Membership was for life. There would be no walking out and turning one's back on the secret society, because once a member was out, there was no way to control his tongue.

If you were the victim of an attempted hit, you were never to finger your assailant. Mere suspicion of cooperating with authorities, even against someone who tried to kill you, meant instant death. Being in a position where you might be tempted to cooperate, such as facing a long jail sentence, meant instant death. Failure to report an unauthorized contact with law enforcement meant instant death. As the well-placed Mafia associate Frank "The Irishman" Sheeran expressed it to my cowriter Charles Brandt in *I Heard You Paint Houses*: "When in doubt have no doubt."

Members' real names and addresses were often kept secret even from other made members. When Joe Pistone was "under" as Donnie the Jeweler, very few knew Donnie's last name, Brasco. Joe's mentor, "Lefty Guns" Ruggiero, didn't learn the last name until he needed it to fill out his marriage certificate since Donnie Brasco was Lefty's best man. (This is why one of my murder counts included the accusation of providing an address of the intended victim.)

Omertà would be bolstered by court rulings beginning in the 1960s that made it more difficult to penetrate the Mafia's veil of secrecy. In what came to be called the Criminal Law Revolution, the requirements for getting a search warrant became harder and harder as new decisions came down from countless courts on a daily basis. Many of these court rulings tied the hands of law enforcement the way the British tied the hands of Commissioner Lin in his anti-opium operation in China.

With their new secret "criminal enterprise" now ruled by a commission and protected by a tangle of deadly rules designed to ensure secrecy, this supremely secret and organized Mafia began to quietly take over as much of America as it could. The list of what the Mafia silently seized for itself is staggering.

The Mafia put whole police departments on the payroll—"the pad"—in exchange for leaving their gambling operations alone. Into the 1970s, before the scandals in the NYPD depicted in *Serpico* and *Prince of the City*, it was a common sight to see a cop in uniform with his tie loosened sitting in a booth in an East Harlem luncheonette sipping espresso with a local Mafia member. Cops used organized crime bribe money to send their kids to college. What was the harm, they figured; it was only gambling money.

The Mafia had mayors, governors, and senators in its pocket and it handpicked judges. In New York it selected members of grand juries. For decades Boss Frank Costello aka Frank Castiglia openly controlled the city's Democratic Party, which meant Costello controlled New York City government. Chicago Boss Sam Giancana was heard on an illegal bug saying about his city: "This is the safest place in the world for a big meet . . . The cops don't bother us here."

The Mafia played an occasional secret role in foreign affairs. For example, in 1943, while my father and millions of Italians were serving our country, the American Mafia murdered New York anti-Mussolini journalist Carlo Tresca on behalf of Benito Mussolini, then our nation's wartime enemy. In the early 1960s, the CIA recruited Mafia Bosses Sam Giancana of Chicago and Russell Bufalino of northeastern Pennsylvania for Operation Mongoose, an aborted conspiracy to assassinate Fidel Castro.

The Mafia accomplished all this and more as a consequence of its ability to remain a secret society. While bits and pieces were exposed from time to time, nobody in authority or in the public gleaned anything close to the full extent of its territory for over half a century.

In 1977, Top Echelon confidential informant Greg Scarpa's FBI handler for years, the retired agent Tony Villano, wrote a book about his experiences called *Brick Agent*. In it he described an informant to whom he gave the name Rico Conte. Tony wrote that in 1952 Conte had described the secret structure and inner workings of the American Mafia to his then handlers. But they thought it was Conte's imagination running wild and dismissed it as a tall tale. Tony died a few years ago, so I can't ask him now, but I always suspected that the character of Rico Conte was based on Greg Scarpa.

During my career I taught organized crime to agents, the NYPD, and other police agencies and to foreign police. In the 1980s and 1990s I testified in dozens of trials as an expert witness on the nature of the secret society. But Lucky Luciano's business plan worked so well for so long that it took decades for any of us to gain any expertise at all.

How did we come to understand this very unique breed of criminal? How did we gradually develop our expertise? I know where I got mine. From countless conversations with my Mafia informants, whether made men or wannabes. I listened and I learned their ways. I penetrated their psyches. At times I spoke, thought, and acted like them. I blended in the way I had been doing my whole life.

CHAPTER FIVE

THE ARMY BRAT

I have no idea what Dad did in Bermuda in 1945. It had something to do with finance. It was grown-up stuff and I was just a kid, so I didn't pay attention. Besides, I was living on the island of Bermuda!

The local British school was a mile away, and at six years old I walked it. You walked everywhere in Bermuda. I dove right in and made friends. When you move around a lot, if you don't make friends readily, you don't have any. Out of necessity, military kids are a lot more gregarious than local kids.

In the 1940s Bermuda was not the tourist attraction it has become. It was more of a natural paradise. They had a lot of old forts there that my pals and I could play in. There were concrete fortifications with guns in place, outdated artillery pieces with barbed wire, to add to the fun. We played war games, of course, and if you were caught, you ended up a prisoner in an antique fort.

We swam in beautiful blue waters. We walked in very quaint towns with cobblestone streets. It really was paradise.

"We've got orders to Italy," my father said.

My father's assignment was to furnish the Italians money to rebuild from the devastation caused by years of fighting. It was late 1946, a year after the war ended. I was almost seven and I was on my way to being a world citizen.

My mother and I boarded a converted military transport in New York City. We went over in the Spartan way our fighting men had. It took a hell of a long time, almost thirty days. There's not a lot to do on a transport ship, no shuffleboard on deck; it's unlike anything you'd see today. For us it was like that song "Slow Boat to China."

We docked in Livorno, south of Pisa, and Dad was waiting on the dock. He had a military car and driver. We were whisked to a hotel in a town called Viareggio. Across the street was the Mediterranean Sea, where the sun set in all its glory. In front of the hotel was a double-lane road and in the center were islands. On these islands every so many yards there were small boxlike Nazi pillboxes for machine gunners that were then being jackhammered out.

We lived in Italy four years and the rebuilding was still in full swing when we left. I remember going up in a jeep to the top of Monte Cassino, the site of one of the longest and most ferocious battles between the Allies and the Nazis—the Battle for Rome. From their vantage place on top of the small mountain, the Nazis held the line trying to prevent the Allies from marching north eighty miles to Rome and eventually to Germany. There were commanding views overlooking the valley. We had to be extremely careful to avoid unexploded bombs and shells that might explode if disturbed. Coming down the mountain, I remember seeing a skull in a shelled hole in the battlefield.

We stayed in Viareggio several months, then went on to Rome. It was exciting to see bullet holes in the tomb of King Victor Emmanuel. We had a beautiful apartment in Rome. I visited the place the last time Carolyn and I were in Rome. We were on a tour bus and I noticed the building where I went to school, a large villa converted by the British. We went back and I retraced my school route on foot to the apartment we lived in. It was more beautiful than I'd remembered.

It had been a privilege to attend that British-run school. It was situated on acres of land and was a great place to play—like walling off a piece of Central Park. The budding postwar Italian cinema industry used to make movies on the grounds. For one movie they bussed a bunch of us kids to a set at the famous Cinecittà studio to portray a choir. We sang Italian songs. I'd love to know the name of that movie that I appeared in.

My classmates were mostly American and British, but my playmates where I lived were Italians. At school I was "Lindley"; among my neighborhood friends I was "Leen." I learned to speak fluent Italian just from being there.

Mussolini had made the dialect of Tuscany the official language of Italy. My dad grew up speaking that dialect and helped me learn it. I played soccer, which was a problem when I returned to the States. I had no baseball, basketball, or football skills, and in America soccer was unknown.

There was a local brother and sister who worked for us, Vincenzo and Paola. Vincenzo lived with us in a back room and worked as a houseboy.

"Andiamo, Leen," he would say holding his little pouch up.

"Si, Vincenzo," I would reply. "Let's go." I knew it was time to scour the streets of Rome for cigarette butts. We'd strip them and put the tobacco in his pouch. Later we'd roll the tobacco into cigarettes. Vincenzo would sell them in the street. I think he invented recycling.

I used to go to Italian black-and-white movies with Paola, a girl in her midtwenties. I remember seeing a war movie and something disparaging was said about America. I shouted out: *"Non è vero"*—That's not true! Paola was taken aback by it, embarrassed that I would blurt something out in the middle of a movie. The Italians seemed to lack self-confidence after all they'd been through in the war.

We visited the small Tuscan town where my grandfather was from: Marlia. We met truckloads of *Di*Vecchio relatives whose name had not been changed in the process of emigrating to America. The *paisans* distributed flyers announcing that the son of Angelo DeVecchio had returned as a colonel. As a boy, you get tired of meeting

all the relatives, but I wish I could do it over again today.
It was a real big deal to the relatives to have my dad come
back as a conquering hero. That was a proud moment.
He wore a uniform all the time until he retired as a full
colonel.

My mother adored Italy. She learned to speak enough
Italian to get by and to cook, and she drank in all the art
she could get. Michelangelo became her passion. When
we returned to the States, she incorporated Italian themes
into her interior decorating.

The cold war was starting while we were abroad. You
don't hear much about the Berlin Airlift now, but it was
a fairly big deal during the early days of the cold war. In
1948 Russia instituted the Berlin Blockade, refusing to
allow trucks to pass through the Russian sector of Germany to get food and other supplies to the free sector of
West Berlin. To counter this, the United States instituted
a massive airlift, which succeeded in putting an end to the
blockade. It was the subject of a 1950 feature film starring
Montgomery Clift called *The Big Lift*, which was filmed
on location. My mother got to help out and fly in one of
the planes bringing in food and supplies to the West Ber-
liners. The Communists in Italy were very prominent and
vocal. They would picket with red banners and red flags
trying to foment a Marxist revolution. It didn't faze me,
though. You don't give politics a thought at that age and
my parents didn't make a big deal out of it.

My father was fairly conservative, as military people
tend to be, but he kept his views to himself. My mother
was a bit of a political wonk. My father retired in 1965

and that freed her to become active in politics. Mom was a delegate to the Republican National Convention that nominated George H. W. Bush. My only child, my daughter Ann, was a page at the convention, but Mom's politics didn't stick with her.

Dad died of esophageal cancer at seventy in 1980, the year I met Greg Scarpa on a street in Brooklyn. Mom unexpectedly died from a heart attack in her sleep in 1999 at eighty-five. This was following Favo's allegations against me and their terrible consequences. My parents and I were very close and I think of them often, but I take comfort in knowing that they were not here to see me indicted for murder. It was bad enough for my great-uncle to see it in *Newsweek*.

While in Italy I saw almost all of Europe. As tourists before tourism was revived in Europe, we saw Germany, France, Greece, Switzerland, Holland, Turkey. Who doesn't fall in love with Paris, at any age?

My parents took me to the opera a lot. And of course, I understood the words, which made it more pleasurable. I developed a deep passion for grand opera that hasn't left me. I asked to take violin lessons. My parents didn't push me into anything. Don't ask me why, but I switched to the accordion. I don't know how I decided on the accordion, I just came to like it. I love it to this day. I still have the same Italian accordion they bought me. Dick Contino, Myron Floren, Art Van Damme are my heroes, and no one knows who they are. I know very little about baseball, but I know that future Baseball Hall of Fame pitcher John Smoltz plays the accordion. I didn't own a white puffy-sleeved silk shirt, but I could play a mean "Lady of Spain." Hey, somebody has to play the accordion. I might as well make the sacrifice.

I also started stamp collecting during our years in Italy. I still have them, four albums of stamps from the late 1940s. Many Nazi stamps with Hitler on them. Fascist stamps from Italy with Mussolini on them. Another hobby I picked up in Italy is the radio. This was before the advent of television. I had an old shortwave set and I thrived on it. Later in life I became a licensed ham radio operator. I attend conventions and keep up with the latest equipment. It's better than e-mail; you can speak live to people in distant lands, people that you would likely never meet, but have so much in common with.

It's funny to me how many people have a fear of meeting new people who are different from those they grew up with. I had agents like that under my supervision. As hard as I pushed, they just didn't have what it took to introduce themselves to Mafia wiseguys. They had a mental block when it came to grooming the wiseguys and gaining their confidence. They had no knack. Chris Favo was one such agent.

"We're going back to the States," my father announced one sunny afternoon with his new orders in hand.

When I heard we were returning to America, I was ready.

Don't get me wrong, I loved Italy. It was a great time for us. My father was highly praised by the Italians and was awarded a number of medals. We had a private audience with Pope Pius XII. Every day was an adventure. But I was ready to go home.

I was ten when we left Italy and I don't believe I had ever heard the word *Mafia* in my life up to that point. When I met the Italian wiseguys in places like Bensonhurst, they were more like foreigners to me than the Italians I had lived with in Rome.

CHAPTER SIX

SAYONARA

The ocean voyage took only ten days when we returned from Italy in 1950.

A generation removed from my grandparents' crossing of the Atlantic as human cargo, we floated into New York Harbor on a real passenger ship, not a converted troop transport. There's no more thrilling sight than nearing the Statue of Liberty.

The boat we sailed on was the *Saturnia*. I remember going with my dad to the army base at Fort Hamilton and driving on Shore Parkway. Who knew this part of Brooklyn would one day be my life? Who could imagine that someday my work fighting the Mafia tooth and nail in Brooklyn would put me "in the jackpot"; destroying my reputation with front-page headlines; bankrupting me financially; and putting me in serious danger of receiving four life sentences?

We spent a couple of days in the St. George Hotel in Brooklyn Heights. Dad had orders to head for Washington, D.C., but first he bought a new Buick and we headed west on historic Route 66. "Get your kicks on Route 66," Nat King Cole sang. Dad was like a machine as a driver. He drove and drove, but we still saw all the sights. We stayed with Mom's family in Kansas and Missouri, then drove on to Fresno to see Dad's family.

"Andiamo, Leen-a," Nona said to me with a proud look.

Before Nona took me on the rounds to visit all the friends, neighbors, and relatives, she gave me one assignment.

"Show them how you talk Italian," Nona said to me in Italian.

The America we saw on the trip back and forth across the country proved a big contrast to Europe. America was thriving, way more affluent. Leaving Europe and being in America was like going from a black-and-white movie to a Technicolor movie.

In an appliance store I saw my first TV, a twelve-inch black-and-white. We settled in an apartment in Arlington, Virginia, where they had TV reception. Something that couldn't be said of most of the rest of the country. No TV. The boy upstairs had a TV and every day at four we watched *Frontier Playhouse*. I got to revel in all the American kids' gadgetry I'd missed in Italy. Roy Rogers, my namesake, was my hero. I looked forward to the Sunday comics. I sent away for all the cereal-box gimmicks:

the Lone Ranger ring, the Straight Arrow ring, whatever Hopalong Cassidy had to offer.

Soon we had our own twelve-inch TV. Every Friday night I'd sit with my dad and watch the Friday-night fights: Ezzard Charles, Jersey Joe Walcott, Sugar Ray Robinson, Rocky Marciano. We took in Washington Senators baseball and Washington Redskins football. To this day I'm a Skins fan.

The Korean War was going on and I remember that my father was not a fan of General MacArthur. He thought MacArthur was a legitimate war hero but too much of a showboat.

Somewhere along the line, because of the superior education I'd gotten from the British in Bermuda and Italy, I was skipped a grade. That made me always younger than my classmates. But I was tall for my age. And skinny. Did I say skinny? I mean very skinny, way too *teen-a*.

"I'm going out," I'd tell my mom. I would never say where or with whom. There was no need to. We lived in Arlington from 1950 to 1953. Perpetual tourists, we saw all the sights across the bridge in D.C.

The Kefauver hearings on the Mafia were on TV, but I had my own interests, like the latest John Wayne movie. I don't remember hearing anything about the Mafia at that age.

I kept up with accordion lessons, joined the Cub Scouts, and became an altar boy. My brother, Jay, was born in 1952 and I added babysitter to my résumé. Although I'm twelve years older, my brother and I are very close, and calling Jay to tell him I'd been indicted for murder was an emotional and gruesome time for both of us. Jay is a very successful civil lawyer with a prestigious law firm in D.C.

Another thing about America that was foreign to me was race issues. In Italy I'd had black friends. The military was integrated and many of my friends were the sons of black soldiers. Race or religion was never an issue. I didn't know a thing about segregation. But in Maryland, near D.C., there was an amusement park, Glen Echo, that was segregated. I couldn't imagine that my boxing and football heroes couldn't bring their kids to go on the rides.

During my last year in D.C., I was sent to a coed Catholic school run by cruel and nasty nuns. On the first day I was late for mass and it went downhill from there. They'd rap your knuckles and embarrass you. I vowed from day one that no children of mine would ever go to a Catholic school. But I have to admit I learned a lot that year and made a lot of good friends.

"We're going to San Antonio, Texas," Dad announced one day. He had orders and that meant we were doing another of our Route 66 drives to see the relatives before we settled in Texas. I was one happy fellow.

San Antonio in 1953 was a shadow of what it is today. It was basically a military town with two air bases and an army base. The only attraction it had was the Alamo. When my parents told me I was going to an all-boys Catholic school, I was not happy. But this school was different from the one in D.C. Jesuit Brothers ran Central Catholic and they were a lot more down-to-earth than the nuns. They were good teachers and good disciplinarians. If they caught you fighting, they'd put the gloves on and challenge you. The principal was a bear. His name was Ringkamp, but we called him Ringo. You didn't want to have to fight him. Half the boys were Mexican, so I picked up a little Spanish, learning all the bad words first. There was no hostility or ethnic divide.

There wasn't any real crime either. I worked for a milkman who delivered milk, cream, and butter both on and off the base. We went from house to house in an old milk truck with the refrigerator in the back half. We did our deliveries in the dark because it got hot fast when the sun came up. At five in the morning we'd walk straight into customers' unlocked kitchens while they were asleep and put the milk right in their refrigerators. We'd have to rearrange the other items in the refrigerator to get the milk in.

I moved from the Cubs up to the Boy Scouts, remained an altar boy, took accordion lessons, got my driver's license at fifteen, and had my first girlfriend, a nice thirteen-year-old Italian girl with the body of an eighteen-year-old whose father worked on the base. We hung out at the military PX café. It was like our diner. We got great southwestern barbecue. I read all of Jack London and Zane Grey. Ike was in the White House and we all liked Ike.

"You'll never guess," Dad said. "We're off to Tokyo, Japan."

Sayonara, San Antonio. It was the same drill, a Route 66 farewell tour, then a ship out of San Francisco for Japan. Who had it better than me as a kid? I spent two carefree years in Tokyo, from 1955 to 1957.

We learned enough Japanese to get by. My parents loved it there and Mom began incorporating Japanese style into her interior designs. She became adept at Japanese flower arranging, Ikebana. She later taught it. Japan has a fascinating culture. I have a number of Japanese artifacts in my home today.

I went to an American high school, the Narimasu High School. There were about ninety of us in the graduating class of 1957 and every two years we have reunions. We come together from all over the world.

I got good grades, and I continued to be an altar boy, but I mostly learned how to goof off. Under Japanese law we weren't allowed to work, so we had lots of time for nothing but fun. We swam in a huge water tank on the Australian base. The Japanese had used the tank to test their one-man submarines. A bunch of us used to go down to the world-famous judo school—the Kodokan—in downtown Tokyo. All I remember is getting thrown around by small Japanese boys.

I wasn't serious about anything, except the next teenage party. "In the Still of the Night" by the Five Satins was my favorite song and maybe it still is. It reminds me of the junior girl I took to my senior prom.

We couldn't drive over there, but we got around Tokyo in extremely efficient trains. I was already six feet tall and I could look down the end of the car over the heads of the

Japanese. I liked Tokyo from the moment I got there—the sheer volume of people. I had great times everywhere, but Japan gave me two of the best years of my life.

"Be careful where you go. I don't want you eating on the local economy." Dad was always wary of our getting intestinal problems.

But we ignored that. In one ear and out the other. The Japanese had no legal drinking age. At fifteen we'd drink Kirin Beer and eat yakitori at the local soba shop. Soba is noodles in broth. They were small shops that sat four or five people. The Ginza was like Forty-second Street or the Block in Baltimore. We spent a lot of time on the Ginza, going in and out of the bars, talking to the girls.

Drugs in Japan were unknown. In fact, they were unknown in America at the time. They were unknown to us in college. I wouldn't have had a clue where to look for them.

I left Japan in 1957 for college at Fresno State. My parents and baby brother, Jay, stayed behind in Tokyo, but all my friends were going back to the States to attend college. I chose Fresno State because my parents went there and we had family there. I lived with my aunt Evelyn Fontes and my cousin Barbara. I was on the swim team, having practiced a lot in that Japanese submarine tank. Why I chose to study electrical engineering is anybody's guess. It was way too brutal for me. I should have picked an easier course of study. After having the time of my life in Japan, I really needed to ease back into the real world slowly.

CHAPTER SEVEN

MY ARRAIGNMENT

MARCH 30, 2006

I walked into the courtroom in handcuffs.

I shook off my tiredness from a day of travel and a night sitting wide-eyed in a chair in the D.A.'s lockup. It was 2 p.m. and I was here to find out where I would be tomorrow, and perhaps for the rest of my days.

It was embarrassing to walk into a courtroom through the door that criminals are escorted through. Cuffing me behind my back was an unnecessary humiliation, a dramatic touch stage-managed by the assistant D.A. in charge, Michael Vecchione.

Despite having never seen him, I could tell who he was right away. Dark-skinned, vacant-eyed, with an aggressive, bulky body topped by a moon face and a graying crew cut. He always seemed to be on the verge of toppling forward. He had one of those rock-star beards that never grows more than a quarter inch and endows the wearer with a degenerate look. Someone should tell him it looks ridiculous on a middle-aged man with a potbelly.

"PUT HIM AWAY"

"G-MAN BLOOD MONEY"

Those were the headlines in the morning tabloids.

In his press release that morning, D.A. Hynes said: "Four people were murdered with the help of a federal law enforcement agent who was charged with keeping them safe. Lindley DeVecchio deserves the maximum sentence of twenty-five years to life for each of these killings."

It made my blood boil.

Looking beyond Vecchione, I saw a packed house. It was full of my peers. Panning the room and seeing FBI agents everywhere lifted my anger from me. I smiled for the first time since I'd bent down and kissed my bride, Carolyn, good-bye in Sarasota.

There were forty to fifty agents and supervisors scattered throughout the courtroom, men I'd worked with my whole career. Another dozen or so waited in the hallway because there wasn't enough room inside. They had come from all over the country to be by my side, so many of them that the judge very kindly chose to arraign me in the larger, ceremonial courtroom.

I was escorted to a table where my attorneys, Doug Grover and Mark Bederow, were waiting for me and my cuffs were removed. Thin and gracious, Doug wears glasses for distance and removes them for reading, which gives him a scholarly look to match his peerless gray matter. As quarterback of the defense team, Doug takes no crap from anybody and lays it on the line all the time. I felt fortunate that Doug was available to represent me. Mark is shorter and stockier, pugnacious, with a keen, charming wit and an encyclopedic memory. They are both methodical. They were both personally outraged on my behalf. This murder case, with all their hard work to come—a lot of which could never be paid for—was a cause, a labor of love for them.

"Listen to this," I said to my lawyers. "Before I left the lockup, that assistant D.A. who conducted the grand jury . . ."

"Noel Downey," Doug said.

"Right. He shook my hand when they were getting ready to cuff me. Can you imagine that?"

Mark laughed. "That's a strange way to treat a guy you just indicted for murder."

I laughed. "Downey looked at me and said, 'I'm just doing my job.'"

"The whole thing is bizarre," Doug said. "They have no idea how to evaluate Mafia witnesses or how to handle an Organized Crime case."

"That's for damn sure," I said. "They don't have any experience with these loose cannons."

A door opened and the judge scampered in and was on the bench before the bailiff could finish saying "All rise please." We were already standing, so we sat down.

I then heard the court clerk utter the words I would hear a lot from then on, but would never get used to hearing: "Indictment Number 6825 of 2005, Roy Lind-

ley DeVecchio." Those words went right through me like
an electric shock.

So this is what it's like to be on the other side of the
fence, I thought, staring up at a judge who might end up
sending me to jail for life. He was a state court judge,
which meant I didn't know him. He looked like a nice
enough fellow, young-looking for his late fifties, light
curly hair, an informal breezy manner, wearing no robe, a
sharp light blue suit with coordinated gold tie and pocket
hankie. In later proceedings in his own courtroom, he had
a blue-and-red neon sign mounted on the wall behind his
left shoulder. It showed the scales of justice. On his bench
to his right he kept a pot of purple flowers. For almost two
years I would see a lot of this unique man, Judge Gustin
Reichbach.

"How does your client plead?"

"Not guilty as to all counts," Doug said.

How could anyone even ask us that? These charges
were such horseshit. Doug was right. Only dabblers in
Organized Crime who didn't understand the psyche of
Mafia witnesses could have presented these charges for
indictment.

Yesterday Doug, Mark, and I had begun to review the
statements that the Mafia cooperating witnesses and
Linda Schiro had given over the years.

"I stayed out of the kitchen," Linda Schiro had told
the OPR investigators twelve years ago. She said she'd
seen me at the house approximately ten times, but was
never close enough to the kitchen to hear Scarpa or me.

Now she was changing her story. Everyone on my team knew that cooperating witnesses more often than not came forward leaving a trail of lies behind them, referred to as baggage. The baggage would later be exploited during cross-examination by the defense. But prosecutors were skilled in preparing cooperating witnesses to handle being confronted by their past statements. Essentially, cooperating witnesses were free to add to or amend whatever they'd said in the past as long as they didn't overdo it and weren't all over the lot, and as long as they could supply a good reason for changing their statements.

The D.A.'s explanation for the conflicting statements was that I had bullied and intimidated Schiro into taking a know-nothing position before FBI agents interviewed her years earlier.

Our explanation was that Schiro had changed her story now in order to get a book deal.

Linda Schiro wasn't in the courtroom, but we spotted three or four book authors, along with a huge press contingent.

I already knew at least one of the members of the press corps. Somehow, illegally, she had been tipped off to my flight arrangements from Sarasota the day before. She even knew the eleventh-hour change in my itinerary. She ended up in the seat next to mine. The only comment I gave her was, "I'm surrendering tonight, but I certainly would feel better if this wasn't so." She took a photo of me with her cell phone and by the morning of my arraignment she already had a story about me in the New York *Daily News*.

After some back-and-forth on various matters, the judge got to the burning question for me. Would I go home today with an anklet monitor or would I be ferried to Rikers Island?

Vecchione stood up and asked the judge "on behalf of the people" to hold me without bail and remand me to Rikers Island prison. These were organized crime murder charges and I should get no special treatment because I had been an FBI agent. He gave what he called a "brief synopsis" of each of the four murders, but the way he droned on was hardly what you'd call brief. Essentially, he said:

"DeVecchio instructed Scarpa he must immediately eliminate Bari."

"DeVecchio instructed Scarpa to eliminate DeDomenico."

"DeVecchio telephoned Scarpa and informed Scarpa that Porco was, in fact, about to inform on Joey, his son. He instructed Scarpa, once again, that something needed to be done with regard to Porco."

"Scarpa informed Agent DeVecchio that he wanted to murder Lorenzo Lampasi . . . DeVecchio returns several days later with the following information: the location of Lampasi's residence, the fact that Lampasi left for work at 4 a.m.; most importantly, in order for Lampasi to leave his driveway, he must open and close a locked gate, thereby giving opportunity for the murder."

Vecchione added: "The likelihood of conviction, Your Honor, is very high."

Vecchione claimed that I had "no hesitancy in fingering for death individuals who provide information to law enforcement." He said that "former FBI agents" visited witnesses to "intimidate" them.

The judge asked for particulars and Vecchione had none, just a bald accusation.

The judge set Vecchione straight:

"To me, intimidation means threats or promises of harm to come, not the mere active investigation . . ."

Vecchione then argued that if not jailed, I would go on the lam.

"He has the assets to flee the country," Vecchione said with great passion, "and he has friends and associates throughout law enforcement who over the years, Your Honor, I suggest, built up contacts, not only here in the United States, but also internationally, who could easily assist him in fleeing."

There was uneasy grumbling among my FBI friends.

Doug Grover stood up and countered that reasonable bail should be set. Doug said that I "[am] and always will be a man of the law." Doug recited my accomplishments during our championship season.

"The FBI embarked on a mission to take down the five families of New York" and he said I was "in the center of everything" and "played a critical role."

"Is he angry?" Doug asked. "Yes, he is angry . . . but he is certainly not going to walk away from this."

Doug asked for electronic monitoring. Acknowledging that I lived out of state, he said: "If I had to tell this court he would stay in my house three blocks from this courthouse, I would do that, if that's what the court wishes." I got a lump in my throat on that one.

"There are forty-five retired agents in the courtroom willing to cosign the bail bond and pledge their assets."

"Can I have a show of hands?" Doug said.

All forty-five hands went up. My lump got bigger.

Vecchione jumped out of his seat and all but exploded. He told the judge that two powerful federal legislators who in the past had been critics of the FBI were monitoring these proceedings. He said that Representative William Delahunt, Democrat of Massachusetts, and Senator Charles Grassley, Republican of Iowa, had contacted him for an update.

I figured Vecchione said this as a warning in case the judge had any aspirations to go on the federal bench. I think the judge figured the same thing. He scowled.

Vecchione dragged in my OPR investigation. He cited a Favo ally, Valerie Caproni, formerly a federal prosecutor in Brooklyn who'd worked her way up since my first scandal and was now at FBI headquarters in Washington, D.C.

"The OPR . . ." Vecchione said, "was openly questioned by a federal prosecutor who is now the general counsel of the FBI, to such an extent . . . she said that the OPR investigation was itself corrupt . . ."

"I tell you, Your Honor," Vecchione boomed, "that the assembled FBI agents who are here provide a network to allow this individual to leave this country, that is what they are here for."

Boos and laughter greeted this.

What's so strange is that Vecchione made these outlandish accusations with great passion and conviction. I figured that the first scandal with Favo and his two agent followers and Valerie Caproni gave him confidence that he had support and precedence to believe he had a grand conspiracy on his hands.

I thought Doug Grover was going to call him a moron. In fact, I think he did, but in fancier words. Doug called Vecchione's accusation "truly disgraceful."

"These are the people that took down the Mob," Doug said.

Judge Reichbach listened, but he wasn't glued to every word the way I was. He'd already made up his mind before he walked into the courtroom. The judge produced paperwork that he'd prepared in advance for a million-dollar bail.

First, he explained, I needed to put up $100,000 in cash. Thank God my attorney brother, Jay, had the money for that and had deposited more than that with Doug's firm.

Second, the judge said he'd need five people to pledge cash or the equity in their homes to account for the entire remaining $900,000.

"Hey, Mark," my former supervisor and the architect of our championship season Jim Kossler called out, and showed five fingers.

Jimmy recalls, "No sooner did the judge say he needed five people to pledge $900,000 than three men immediately nodded to me and another tapped me on my back. I was the fifth."

Brian Taylor, Geoffrey Doyle, Louis Stephens, Christopher Mattiace, and James Kossler stepped up to pledge the money. (Later, for financial reasons, Dennis Collins and Tom French had to be substituted for Lou Stephens and Brian Taylor.)

I would get to kiss my wife good night.

One comment Doug made to the judge stood out for us as we left the courthouse:

"Mr. DeVecchio was a force on the Organized Crime squad, Your Honor. The district attorney . . . has no idea what they are getting into when they get into the world of organized crime."

I was a "force on the Organized Crime squad" for close to thirty years. The Brooklyn D.A. would have to drop every other case and do nothing but organized crime for years to learn what we knew about the psyche of organized crime. When I retired in 1996, I was still learning.

CHAPTER EIGHT

LEARNING THE PSYCHE OF ORGANIZED CRIME

In 1957, the year I left Japan to live in America, Lucky Luciano's secret society began to make headlines. There was a loose cannon on deck—Don Vito Genovese—and each time the loose cannon roared, the psyche of the Mafia became exposed.

That year, while I was struggling with engineering in the fall semester at Fresno State, the American Mafia held a sit-down at Apalachin, New York, a rural upstate town near the northeastern Pennsylvania border—Russell Bufalino Family territory.

In the early 1980s, with the aid of one of my informants, a petty thief, I was able to help send the powerful Boss Russell Bufalino to jail for the remainder of his life. I can reveal the informant's name now because he came forward as a cooperating witness and testified against Bufalino. His name is John Napoli.

Twenty-five years after his testimony against Bufalino, when Napoli got into some trouble on a larceny charge and was sent to jail, he surfaced again as a cooperating witness against another famous accused criminal. This time, in 2007, he was going to offer his testimony to help the Brooklyn D.A. convict me. But Napoli never made it to trial.

The date of the sit-down at Apalachin was November 14, 1957, one of the most important dates in the history of the American Mafia.

The six months preceding the Apalachin sit-down had been a major test of Luciano's business plan.

On May 2, 1957, a Vito Genovese hit man ambushed that family's Boss Frank Costello in the lobby of his luxury apartment building. Luciano's business plan had been working so well that Frank Costello never used a bodyguard. The hit man called out, "This one's for you, Frank," and Costello turned when he heard the familiar voice. The single bullet grazed his head. Naturally, Costello refused to identify the gunman, but he knew it was the former light heavyweight boxer Chin Gigante—who decades later would become the family's Boss. And Costello knew, as did everyone else inside the Mafia, that it was Vito Genovese who'd given the contract to Gigante. All the Bosses, of course, knew it was done without Commission approval.

As a young man, Vito Genovese, with his creepy and insolently toothy smile, had murdered his wife's first husband to win her for himself. It was Genovese who in 1943 ordered the hit on anti-Mussolini journalist Carlo

Tresca, leaving his body on the street as a warning to Italian Americans that they dare not criticize Il Duce.

After the attempt on his life, Costello chose not to fight Don Vito Genovese, but to retire and turn his family and his seat on the Commission over to him.

Next, Genovese took aim at Boss Albert Anastasia because Anastasia was an ally of Costello's and might retaliate for the assassination attempt. On October 25, 1957, Genovese gunmen, including future Boss of the Colombo Family Junior Persico, crept up on an unsuspecting Anastasia while he sat in a hotel barber chair with a hot towel over his face. They blew him away. I remember seeing the *Life* magazine coverage and the photo of Anastasia in the barber chair. The brazenness of it all shocked me.

Genovese then called for the Apalachin sit-down. He needed to smooth things over and explain his assassinations to all the Bosses to prevent retaliation. As things turned out, nothing got accomplished at Apalachin except the most notorious exposure the Mafia ever endured.

The secret society felt safe sitting down in the privacy of a Boss's home in the middle of nowhere. But a local cop, Sergeant Edgar Croswell, got suspicious at the activity and set up a roadblock. The attendees panicked. Fifty-eight were picked up for questioning—a police tool that was permitted by the courts before the 1960s.

"I came to visit my sick friend, Joe Barbara."

This was the uniform answer as to why these Italian men from all over the country with criminal records were congregating at Joe Barbara's mansion.

Twenty were convicted of conspiring to commit perjury and obstruction of justice. The charges were tossed out on appeal because the court could not fathom that a group as large as fifty-eight men would sit down in one place to conspire to commit a crime. The appeals court was, like the rest of America, in the dark about the existence and scope of the secret society.

In a 1958 report released after the Apalachin meeting, the brass at FBI headquarters concluded that there was an American Mafia, but in spirit only: "It exists not as a distinctly outlined, conventional organization, but as a criminal movement and a mode or way of life . . ." Ring-a-ding-ding—sounds more like the Rat Pack than a cohesive national multimillion-dollar criminal enterprise. This conclusion was a tribute to the effectiveness of Luciano's business plan.

There were many theories about what Apalachin meant. But one thing's for sure: It brought the Mafia into the national spotlight. Thanks to Vito Genovese's call for a sit-down to explain his murderous power grab, photos of the faces of American Mafia Bosses were splashed on front pages across the country.

Because so many Bosses rounded up at the sit-down claimed to be in the field of labor management, Senator John McClellan called for Senate hearings on the connection between these Italian gangsters and labor unions. Again, thanks to the loose cannon, the secret society got "paraded out" before TV cameras—if only to take the Fifth. The result was the Landrum-Griffin Act. Its criminal sanctions were to bring down scores of labor union Mafia gangsters.

Immediately, Vito Genovese got his just desserts. A Puerto Rican heroin courier in East Harlem surfaced from jail with testimony that Genovese was personally involved in drug trafficking with him. Genovese was convicted and got fifteen years—in effect, exchanging places with the cooperating witness against him.

Many Mafia experts believe the cooperator was lying, that Genovese would never have dealt hands-on with a heroin courier. And I agree. Genovese had soldiers who did that work for him. Another Mafia expert and former NYPD Mafia detective Ralph Salerno, in his book *The Crime Confederation*, wrote that "anyone who understands the protocol and insulation procedures" of a Mafia Boss would recognize that "this testimony is almost unbelievable."

Consider that the witness took this brazen step without fear of the Mafia, and it shapes up as intentional punishment by the Mafia—a frame intended to tie the loose cannon down for a stretch in a federal penitentiary. To me it has the look and feel of a Mafia frame-up.

But Genovese was not finished damaging Luciano's business plan. While in federal prison in Atlanta, Don Vito Genovese accused made man and soldier Joe Valachi of being a prison informer. In doing so, he gave Valachi the kiss of death. Now a target and armed with a length of pipe, Valachi killed the first inmate who approached him, mistaking him for a Genovese assassin. A disgruntled Valachi, facing the death penalty, rolled over and became the first made member of the Mafia to publicly reveal the inner secrets of the secret society.

Of all Genovese's many contributions to the exposure of the Mafia, the most outstanding has got to be Joe Valachi himself. The televised Valachi hearings before the U.S. Senate in 1963—the brainchild of Attorney General Bobby Kennedy—laid bare Luciano's business plan. Kennedy understood that public exposure was the greatest weapon against the Mafia's weapon of secrecy.

Valachi began his Senate testimony by announcing, "What I'm about to say, I'm doomed." Believe me, Greg Scarpa and all my other informants could have said that to me every time they talked to me.

Valachi testified against Junior Persico and landed him the lengthy sentence he had just completed when Mary Bari came to talk to him in the fall of 1984. Valachi gave us the term *Cosa Nostra*, meaning "our thing," by which made men referred to the Mafia. He also gave us the names we still use today to identify the Mafia families. For example, all the world learned that there were five New York families named by Valachi: Profaci (later Colombo), Bonanno, Genovese, Gambino, and Lucchese.

Bobby Kennedy described Valachi's virulent disobedience to the code of *omertà* as "the biggest intelligence breakthrough yet in combating organized crime and racketeering in the U.S."

Because there was no Witness Protection Program at the time, Valachi had to be housed in a special air-conditioned prison suite in El Paso, Texas. Thanks to Genovese, we now had the seeds planted for the treatment of cooperating witnesses.

Under pressure from Bobby Kennedy, J. Edgar Hoover

responded to the televised Valachi hearings by finally committing the FBI to the fight against the Mafia.

For his first foray into fighting the Mafia, Hoover established the Top Ten Hoodlum Program. Each FBI office was to identify its top ten Mafia gangsters and look for anything to convict them with—usually gambling. Although it accomplished little, the program served as an early learning tool. Amusingly, it applied to offices in Idaho as well as in New York. I wonder if Boise borrowed ten Mafia hoodlums from Cleveland.

In his next attempt, Hoover adapted to the Mafia the "black-bag" program he'd used to fight communism. Agents were to plant bugs—listening devices. Phones were to be tapped. Under federal law bugs and taps were illegal and could not be used to justify a federal arrest. But "black bags" were intended to give us a peek through the keyhole at the Mafia's secret activities. Most of these black-bag operations failed because so little was known to begin with that agents couldn't tell in which buildings to plant the bugs. President Lyndon Johnson shut them down once the anti-Mafia crusader Bobby Kennedy resigned the post of attorney general in 1964.

This left Hoover one final option and that was to concentrate on recruiting Mafia confidential informants. Soon every agent in the Organized Crime division was urged to cultivate as many Mafia confidential informants as possible, with one as a minimum. The prize catch would be the rare Top Echelon informant, a made man like Greg Scarpa or someone, even a non-Italian like Frank Sheeran, who was treated with the respect of a made man. Headquarters would have to approve the TE designation.

My career in the FBI would thrive on developing the TE. My ability to go native would be my biggest asset, and I would pay a heavy price for it.

This last gift of Genovese's power grab—his mobilizing the FBI against the Mafia—would directly lead to our championship season and the destruction we inflicted.

My loose cannon Favo's power grab would backfire and directly lead to helping the Colombo Family rebuild itself after the destruction we inflicted during our championship season.

CHAPTER NINE

WATCHING THE BORDERS

When Dad got ordered to cross the Pacific and report to Washington, D.C., I took it as an opportunity to quit Fresno State and make the trip east with the family. I enrolled at George Washington University as a political science major and practically started college all over again.

I don't recall paying much attention to the Apalachin headlines. I had my own enterprises going on: I worked as a lifeguard, had a job in a tire shop, and was the campus distributor for Ballantine Beer, pushing kegs of it to fraternity houses at George Washington, including my own Sigma Chi. One of my brothers was my biggest customer. He was a beer-guzzling weekend warrior who could drink anybody under the table, then during the week we'd never see him because he was too busy studying. Today he's an adviser to nuclear power plants.

On the side I ran the Lisner Auditorium. At that time

D.C. had two cultural venues, Constitution Hall and the Lisner Auditorium at George Washington. I booked the events a year in advance, set up the ushers, the ticket takers, the hatcheck concession, worked with the house electrician, and got the posters and tickets printed up. I was twenty and looked fourteen, tall and skinny, six feet, 135 pounds. During my tenure we had Hal Holbrook as Mark Twain, José Greco and his dance company, Andrés Segovia, Carlos Montoya, the American Ballet Theatre, the Washington Opera Society. Not only did I get to see great productions of *Carmen* and *Madame Butterfly*, but I got to hang out backstage with people like Hal Holbrook while he put on his Mark Twain makeup.

After I got my degree, I stayed on at George Washington to do graduate work in geography for a career in urban planning, but I ran out of gas. More than anything I was anxious to get "paraded out" into the real world.

In the spring of 1963 I applied to the U.S. Air Force. I wanted to fly jets. Maybe I got my taste for flying by swaying high up in the branches of Nono's fig tree. My goal was to get an officer's commission.

Around that time the American Mafia finally got my attention. I vividly recall the Valachi hearings on television. It introduced me to a world of Italians I had never known. It was terrific entertainment. Each story coming out of Valachi's mouth was more riveting than a *Sopranos* episode.

Around the same time that I applied to the air force, two fraternity brothers who had gone into the FBI told me how much they loved the work. I decided to apply. I remember telling my parents I'd applied for both the air force and the FBI. Either one would have made them proud.

First, I got a letter to report to Lackland Air Force Base in San Antonio for officer's training. Within a week, the FBI accepted me for a clerk's position at headquarters. In 1963 a law degree made you automatically eligible for new agent training, but serving as a clerk for two years took the place of a law degree. It was a program that could lead to Agent Training Class at Quantico, Virginia.

I jumped at the chance and began my two-year clerkship in November 1963, just days before President Kennedy was shot in a government limo in Dallas. I was working in the office at my desk when I heard the shocking news. Next I was in the crowd watching the funeral on Pennsylvania Avenue.

The country was then in turmoil over Ku Klux Klan terrorism in the South aimed at preventing racial integration and thwarting the will of the American people to create a just and equal society. While I was clerking I had no idea of the FBI's role in fighting the Klan. But years later I learned from a confidential source that in 1964 Top Echelon informant Greg Scarpa was enlisted in a Klan case. During Freedom Summer, three civil rights workers trying to register voters went missing in Philadelphia, Mississippi. Two days later their blue Ford station wagon was found in a swamp—torched. For forty-four days the authorities tried to find the bodies. Experienced investigators had a hunch that a local who operated an appliance store was a weak link in the secret society of the Klan. But he needed more than a smack from a telephone book upside his head to get him to talk.

This was less than a year after Joe Valachi's televised testimony. America now knew how truly murderous the Mafia was. The FBI brought Greg Scarpa to the weak link's appliance store, where Scarpa bought a TV. While it was being placed in the car the FBI had provided to Scarpa, the weak link got blackjacked. He was taken to a remote cabin where Scarpa, with his deep voice and deadly manner, convinced him to cooperate by putting a gun in his mouth and appealing to his better nature and giving him an option: "Tell me the fucking truth or I'll blow your fucking brains out."

The truth was told. The bodies were buried seventeen feet deep in a red clay dam. Seven Klan killers were convicted of civil rights violations. If I know Greg Scarpa, he got a taste of the reward money.

As a clerk from 1963 to 1965, I had the job of sorting through the files the FBI kept on certain individuals and looking for relevant information that had been requested by, for example, the White House or a federal agency for such things as a security clearance or a job interview. It was tedious work.

J. Edgar Hoover forbade the use of blue ink because that's what he used. Hoover replied to reports by making blue ink notes in the margins. His instructions in the margins were followed without question. He insisted that all reports have wide margins for this reason. On one occasion Hoover wrote in a too-narrow margin "Watch the borders," and the supervisor who had written the report immediately dispatched agents to Mexico and Canada.

Whatever we found we passed along to an agent analyst who determined whether to pass it further along. There were times I'd say to myself, "I've got a college degree what am I doing here?" but I kept my eye on the goal of becoming an agent.

I know that as many files as I looked at for two years, not one had an Italian gangster as its subject.

CHAPTER TEN

THE FNG

In the Mafia, if you're told to "get dressed" and to appear at a designated place later that day, it means that you're about to be "paraded out"—to be made.

In March 1966, after fifteen weeks of new agent training and being shuttled back and forth between the old post office building in D.C. and the Marine base at Quantico, Virginia, I reported for duty as an FBI special agent. In the FBI we had to "get dressed" in white shirts, dark suits, and conservative ties as long as they weren't red—a sign of communism—for our formal presentation to J. Edgar Hoover. We were "paraded out" one at a time to Hoover, who individually congratulated each one of us.

Before we went in, of course, we were inspected. Our hair had to be trim and neat, our nails cut. We were all worried about our appearance. It was a very proud moment and a very special occasion. Hoover was an icon, an institution.

(The J. Edgar Hoover whose hand I shook and whose name had been synonymous with the FBI for over forty years was a "Boss" who was wise enough to want me to go out in the street and make secret friends of as many made men as I could. I'd like to meet the man who can think of a better way for us to have learned all that we needed to learn about the Mafia.)

To distinguish us from regular government agents Congress called us special agents and gave us the initials SA, as in SA Roy Lindley DeVecchio. That would be me.

There were two sides in the FBI: the spy side—foreign counterintelligence including domestic revolutionaries—and the criminal side. We had little to no contact with each other. Over the years you might see agents from the spy side at the firing range, but you had no idea who they were. My strong preference was to work in the criminal side, where the action was, hopefully someday in Organized Crime. So I was elated when I was assigned to the Albany office in upstate New York for a year to learn my profession by working the smaller cases.

When you first got out of training you didn't know beans about what you really needed to do on the job. The Bureau even had a name for new guys—first office agent—FOA for short. The agents called you the FNG—the fucking new guy.

A training agent gave us an introduction at our first office, but it wasn't nearly enough. As strange as it sounds, you had to figure things out on your own. For instance, if I had to deal with, say, an auto theft, I would go back and look at an old file to see how an agent handled a similar case and what the paperwork was like.

As an FNG, I did a ton of background investigations, the menial labor a new guy could be trusted with. You went out and talked to a great many people.

I'd been an agent in Albany for two months when I was temporarily assigned to help out in Ithaca, the home of Cornell University. There were two resident agents in Ithaca, both of them real old-timers. The criminal guy was going on vacation for two weeks. I was told on a Friday to report to Ithaca on a Monday. "Okay," I said. I didn't even know how to fill out a travel request or what airline to take. I arrived and met the other Ithaca agent. He worked the spy side of the house—radical groups, everything that wasn't criminal. Cornell had a fair number of campus radicals in the late sixties. Thankfully, they were not my concern.

"Here's the key to the office. Here's the numbers you need—local police. Bye," Spy Guy said as he walked out the door. He probably went out to have coffee.

This trip to Ithaca was a trial by fire. "Here's the keys to the car. Here's where it's parked. Well, I've got some work to do. Bye." I'd never been to that area in my life. I was expected to find my own way around. The agent did show me around the office: "Here's Clyde's cases. Bye."

It was all part of being an FNG.

While there was a lot of Mafia in upstate New York at the time, controlled by Russell Bufalino's northeastern Pennsylvania family, we didn't have a clue about it. But I did make a lot of arrests in my year upstate. New agents were given the fugitive cases, mostly desertion from the military.

Normally, in order to make an arrest, you're required to have at least two agents, but often I'd make an arrest by myself. Looking back, I realize how dangerous that was, especially with military deserters. They're in shape. They do not want to go back. But I wasn't playing hero. It just sort of happened. I'd carry four or five case files and I'd be in an area where a mother lived and it would be worth a shot, and *bingo*, there's the fugitive who answers the door. You can't walk away and say, "I'll be back tomorrow."

I loved every minute of being the FNG. That's how you learn.

On April 18, 1967, after one year as an agent, I was transferred to New York City to work Organized Crime as the FNG again. It was my birthday, literally and figuratively. And for me, the rest is history—from my first day in the office to the last day of my murder trial in a Brooklyn courtroom.

Once I got assigned to the Organized Crime section, I stayed put for thirty years. I never got out of the City of New York, and as Joe Valachi had taught us, the Big Apple was the center of the Mafia's universe.

Except for the time I spent on temporary special assignments, my day-in and day-out enemy—and to a large extent my friend—was the Mafia. In addition to the time I spent getting a master's degree in criminal justice at

Long Island University in 1977, I put long hours into my work against the Mafia.

In those days the Organized Crime section of the New York office was an all-male club, a fellowship. We worked hard all week and on Friday night we got hammered. I'd gotten married to a wonderful woman in 1964, a nurse, but "the life" cost me that marriage, probably the biggest regret of my life. Divorce is rampant in law enforcement. It's always hardest on children. My daughter was ten when her mother and I divorced, and she lived with me until she left for college.

When I started in Organized Crime in April 1967 there were no courses at Quantico, no written instructions. They assigned you cases and you said, "Okay." You made a lot of mistakes, but never the same ones twice, unless you wanted to get transferred to a less active office . . . like South Bend, Indiana. My first boss was a tough guy but very fair. He'd chew your ass out, then smile and say, "Okay, you're learning."

The first case assigned to me, I had to work up my courage to go to a more experienced guy and ask for help. But mostly you kept your mouth shut and watched the seasoned guys very carefully and learned it by the seat of your pants. It was four or five months before the old-timers were satisfied with me enough to initiate conversation. As things are in any male society, the young buck had to prove himself.

I'll never forget the first few minutes of my first day in Organized Crime in New York City in the old FBI New York office on Sixty-ninth Street. I walked past a room where an old-time agent was questioning a younger man.

"For the last time, what's your name?" I overheard the agent ask with a cigar clenched in his teeth.

"I told you. I don't remember," said the man.

From out of nowhere a Manhattan telephone book batted the man in the side of the head.

"That book has a lot of names in it. Now's your chance to pick one. Don't be shy. Pick a name."

The young man did.

I was twenty-seven years old on the day I witnessed that, the youngest guy ever assigned to Organized Crime, and clearly I had a lot to learn. But I knew even then that I had a way with people that I inherited from both my parents, and I hoped that this was as good a way to unlock secrets as a phone book upside the head.

CHAPTER ELEVEN

THE "UNHEALTHY RELATIONSHIP"

In *On the Waterfront*, Rod Steiger, playing a union gangster, warns his kid brother, Terry, to break up with the anti-Mob dish played by Eva Marie Saint. Marlon Brando as Terry Malloy refuses. A frustrated Steiger explodes: "It's an unhealthy relationship."

If you're going to insist on maintaining an "unhealthy relationship" with an informant, you need to know what such relationships are about. The relationship can be more than unhealthy for the informant; it can be deadly. As well, the relationship can be unhealthy for the handler. To understand why we took these risks with our own lives and the lives of our informants, it's important to know why we needed to form these unhealthy relationships.

To begin with, most people don't know the difference between a confidential informant (CI) and a cooperating witness (CW). The difference is that the cooperating witness goes public and testifies. A CW is normally a bad guy who's been busted. Desperate to save his skin, he agrees to be debriefed and testify against his former best friends and blood brothers. But an agent has to be careful. Jurors are rightly skeptical of CWs.

Nobody needs a lesson in developing a CW. Anybody with handcuffs can do it. All you need is the arrest and the perspiration it produces. This is the hammer, a giant hammer. Most CWs volunteer for active duty.

Once they cut a deal and get out from under the hammer, some CWs subtly turn on the stand. During cross-examination they allow themselves to be used by the defense in a way that makes them appear to be lying for the prosecution.

Sometimes the CW crafts his debriefing to conceal things. The CW of all CWs, Sammy "The Bull" Gravano, took the stand against John Gotti. Later it was revealed that the Bull purposefully left Gotti's son out of his testimony, even though Junior supervised a hit squad that whacked a guy who'd been slow to come in to see Gotti when he was called. Gravano protected Gotti's son under a side deal in which Gotti agreed not to kill Gravano's son. Perjury or not, how can you blame the Bull for leaving Gotti's son out of his testimony?

Some CWs want to be super cooperators and testify to anything they think the agent wants to hear, whether true or not. They size the agent up. Does this agent want a dirty cop? Okay, coming right up. I was almost on the receiving end of that with Carmine Sessa, the man who owned the social club where Mary Bari was killed. But I'll go into that later.

Some CWs have personal motives for volunteering their lying lips for the prosecution—and these are usually tied to a big payday. Greg Scarpa's common-law wife, Linda Schiro, springs to mind. And I'll definitely go into that later.

For an agent to develop a confidential informant (CI) it takes a big set of people skills and Mafia street savvy. As Pat Marshall, my case agent in the Mafia Commission Case, put it: "Do you have any idea how hard it is to develop a really good informant? Some agents do, some don't, and some never will. Lin was, bar none, the best. What Joe Pistone was to undercover work, Lin was to informant development."

Thanks, Pat, but I know I had one failure. I could never get Chris Favo to develop a single informant. If you ask me, what Favo suffered from, to quote from the film *Cool Hand Luke*, was "a failure to communicate."

In its simplest form, a CI passes along tips in exchange for cash. A CI will never meet a Bible on a witness stand unless, somewhere along the line, he gets coaxed into becoming a CW.

Why would someone become a CI? The stakes are high: If they're found out, they're dead. There is nothing worse in the Mafia than a rat. Even someone who unintentionally violates his oath of secrecy will be killed as a risk. Except for the Top Echelon CI, most of the rest are motivated by the few hundred you have to offer depending on the quality of their information. These are guys who run through money. And this is money they don't have to pay "street tax" on to the Mafia or split with anyone. There are a handful who inform out of revenge or to weed out competition. A Top Echelon CI like Greg Scarpa usually has complicated personal motives for informing.

Everything about a confidential informant is extremely private, anonymous, and top secret, above all his identity. We even had a special filing system to ensure that no one outside the Bureau ever saw CI information. Information from a talk with a CI is put on a report called a "209." The 209 is usually three or four sentences of pertinent inside information. No one outside of the Bureau has access to 209 reports.

Information from a CW debriefing, on the other hand, is put on a "302." Whatever you write on a 302 will be read by outsiders. By law, 302s have to be turned over to criminal defense attorneys.

That system of separate reports for CIs and CWs became significant to me down the road in understanding Favo's motivation for what he did to me. But I'm getting ahead of myself again.

By the time I entered Organized Crime in 1967, the Bureau had been stockpiling 209s about the Mafia since before Valachi's testimony. But at the time there was often nowhere to go with it. You'd file your 209 for the day it might be of use.

There are many secrets to informant development, but to start you've got to dive right in and hope you come up with a pearl.

You target a guy. You do your homework on the guy. You seek him out and you catch him alone. You identify yourself. You say you know he knows a lot about how things work. You say you're trying to learn, and you'd appreciate help. Low-key, like you're asking directions to a gas station.

You ask if he'll sit down with you. You suggest a secret, out-of-the-way place that you've chosen in advance. You never mention it, but each of you knows that if he's seen with you, he risks being killed for it. You don't even think about meeting in a car in a Mafia neighborhood. If, unbeknownst to you both, he's got a contract on him, you'll go down, too.

You try to emulate his style. Your gold chains, a pinky ring, might put him at ease. It helps if you look Italian. And you've got to be a male agent, at least with the Mafia men. Female agents are at a distinct disadvantage with a wiseguy. You can't change that. It is what it is. A female agent could not go undercover in the Mafia and get anything of value.

Sometimes you'll approach a guy and he'll blow you right off. But most will at least hear you out. And if you get one out of a hundred to give you any information at all, you're a huge success.

It may take many months of grooming to develop a CI. It's like dating, courting, and marriage. Hopefully, at first he's curious. He wants to know what you know about him and that keeps his interest for a little while. Then you have to build trust and respect.

You'd better not talk down to him or patronize him.

He's street-smart. He can smell a blatant con job a mile away. He has to be able to read people just to stay alive. He has to sense when people are not a hundred percent with him because that could signal he's done something wrong. And when you do something wrong, it's called to your attention with a bullet to the brain, as it was to Mary Bari.

You tell him there can be money in it for him. All you want is historical stuff, background, and an education.

When I first met with a potential CI, I took no notes. You don't want to spook them. As soon as you get to your car, you write like crazy. When they were comfortable with me I would begin to take notes. "I can't remember all this stuff," I'd say. No one ever objected.

When you get back to the office you break down the information into separate 209s. If you had information, for example, on a hijacking, you'd do a 209 that would go to the hijacking squad and one for the particular Mafia family squad involved.

Under no circumstances would you include in a 209 the CI's name or any other identifying information. Each CI had a number, but only a few in the Bureau, such as supervisors, would know the CI's name and no one outside the FBI would ever know it. You would especially keep the CI's name from federal prosecutors, even though they often wanted names so they could clumsily try to turn a CI into a CW for use at trial.

Lawyers who work in the U.S. attorneys' offices will stay there long enough to get reputations and experience. When they leave the office many of them will join the dark side and become criminal defense attorneys. You can't have them leaving that office knowing who is or who is not an informant.

You wouldn't want an FBI file clerk to funnel valuable FBI information to the Mafia, so you would have to use discretion. From time to time you would include your own CI's criminal activity in a 209 as if he were being informed on. If your CI talked about everyone else in his crew but himself, a file clerk might figure out that he was the informant.

In the beginning I flubbed and fumbled like any rookie in the big leagues, not yet knowing how to dress, that sort of thing, but I kept at it. During our "championship season," twenty years after I'd gone on duty, I had four Top Echelon CIs, each a made man. One had risen to the position of acting underboss of his family. My four represented more than 25 percent of all the Top Echelon informants the Bureau had from coast to coast at that crucial time. In total we had fourteen CIs that were designated TE and two of the ten that I didn't have were not made men. In my thirty years in Organized Crime I had over fifty or sixty confidential informants and six of those were TE.

Over time I learned to speak their language, to use their vocabulary, and that made me more effective. Fortunately, from my childhood travel I was adept at learning new languages, not that this stuff was hard. For example, "a piece of work" means a murder. If a "guy did a lot of work" he was a stone-cold killer. If a "guy is a good earner," he's not only financially successful, but he's a favorite of the higher-ups with whom he splits his "scores." A "wiseguy," a "button," a "good fellow" is a made man. A "knock-around guy" is a guy who lives day to day by his wits—hand to mouth.

You've got to let the potential criminal informant (PCI) believe that maybe you might be in a position to give him some help down the road. That was the understanding. You tell him that early on. PCIs view it as an insurance policy. This is especially important to the TE, most of whom do not need the chump change you're authorized to pay them.

And with the CI's permission and the Bureau's, you really will help them if you can. But it's very risky. It will mean exposing their confidential informant status to a judge and to the federal prosecutor who will privately speak to the judge alone in chambers. Hopefully, the judge won't blurt out the informant's CI status in open court. Hopefully, the federal prosecutor will not share the CI's status with his colleagues in his office. Prosecutors know not to, but you never know what they'll do.

Normally, when it comes down to it, many a CI would rather take his lumps on his criminal charges than let one more human being on earth know what he's been up to. Many are afraid their own attorney might find out. A lot of these attorneys are house counsel who owe their allegiance to the family Boss and not to their client.

According to the ever-changing informant guidelines, you're required to tell them they have to pay taxes on the money you give them. But you'd better not dare follow through on that requirement or they'll immediately lose respect for you. This is a bit of bureaucracy that can't work in the real world. The hypocrisy is hilarious when you consider that these are mostly knock-around guys who do not report any of their illegal income—men without Social Security cards.

The CI is required to sign a receipt, but no truly effective TE will ever sign anything, so you're careful not to look foolish when you ask. You're required to have a backup agent to witness the handling of cash. Again, no Top Echelon worthy of the term will ever agree to meet with two of you. Top Echelon is a royal marriage and three is a crowd. You seek a waiver from the brass.

Even with my waiver in the file, the Brooklyn D.A. accused me of pocketing Scarpa's cash because he signed no receipts and no one witnessed me giving him money. But at trial we had a retired agent who became a defense attorney ready to testify that he would sometimes wait around the corner from wherever I was meeting with Scarpa. Scarpa would get the cash from me and meet the attorney and use it to pay him.

You do tell all of them, even Top Echelon, that they are not working for the Bureau. "Just because you and I sit around and bullshit, that doesn't mean the government is allowing you to commit crimes." You say this because it is required and because there's no downside to saying it. But you know and they know that you know that in the Mafia everyone is guilty of something serious at all times. It might or might not be the murder they are talking to you about, but it's some murder.

Under no circumstances do you ever come close to

verbalizing the fact that they are informants. Bite your tongue before you use the words *informing*, *stoolie*, *snitch*, or *rat* in their presence about anyone. I did not want those words in my vocabulary because I did not want any of them to ever slip out of my mouth. You'll hear agents use the word *source* to cover the field.

The biggest part is that you have to sell yourself. They admire courage, and believe it or not, they admire honesty.

Once we accomplished all of the above, the frustrating part of our job was figuring out what to do with the intelligence we gathered. How could all this clandestine work lead to arrests and convictions?

While we dove straight in and occasionally came up with a pearl, we were mostly getting our own private lessons on the subject of the secret society. We put our pearls on 209s and we disseminated what we'd learned about the Mafia to each other.

Meanwhile, violent street crime—rapes, murders, serious assaults, and robberies—began to skyrocket. From 1960 to 1965, in the wake of court rulings restricting police patrols, the rate of violent crime in America jumped 60 percent—and this, not the Mafia, was getting the daily attention of the media. To help combat the escalating crime rate, Congress passed the Omnibus Crime Control and Safe Streets Act of 1968.

A little-publicized provision of that law was to start a revolution in our anti-Mafia work. Title III of the act resurrected federal bugging and wiretapping, which had been a significant tool that was scrapped when President Johnson banned black-bag operations a few years earlier.

The beauty of Title III was that it allowed the tapes derived from taps and bugs to be used as evidence in court. To be admissible, the tapes had to come from a bug or a wire authorized by a judge. The agent had to give a sworn affidavit to the judge detailing the probable cause—the facts that would lead to the belief that crimes would be discussed on the phone line that was tapped or in the room that was bugged.

But how did the agent obtain these facts that he would swear to in the affidavit under penalty of perjury? The answer quickly became obvious. They would come from the 209s.

A further requirement of Title III was that the agent had to swear that the evidence sought could be obtained no other way than by bugging or tapping. Because of *omertà*, this part would be easy to swear to.

The 1968 Title III law was the first of Professor G. Robert Blakey's monumental contributions to American society. As a young lawyer, Blakey had been part of Bobby Kennedy's crusade against the Mafia, but he left the Justice Department in 1964 when Kennedy left. He then became a professor at Notre Dame and was asked to write the new wiretap provision by the Omnibus bill's sponsors. I hope the people who give out medals at the Kennedy Center are paying attention. Early on when Blakey worked under Bobby Kennedy, he saw up close how indispensable bugging and wiretapping were to competing with the Mafia's very sound business plan.

While a CW might get away with testifying falsely, a CI's information was always being tested. The CI had to be corroborated. If he's not being corroborated he gets closed. Sometimes information from other CIs would back up what he was saying. But now, under Title III, and without the CI's knowledge, the FBI would use the CI's gift of words to get permission to plant bugs and taps that would corroborate the CI electronically while convicting the speakers. The bugging and tapping would secure hard, irrefutable evidence from the mouths of the Mafia members themselves.

Because the Omnibus Act applied only to federal cases, soon the states followed Blakey's lead and passed their own versions of Title III.

Knowledge is king and we in Organized Crime were beginning to feel really useful. Our CIs were about to be the FBI's new best friends. But as reality set in, after listening to tapes for hours and hours, we began to see the routine quality of cases our efforts were bringing. Title III couldn't do it alone.

We needed something else, and it would take over a dozen years before we got it, another magnificent creation of Professor Blakey. But in the meantime we would have to use what we had.

CHAPTER TWELVE

THE SPECIALS

The most amazing thing, to me personally, about my career in the FBI is that they paid me to do it.

Part of the excitement was created by the special assignments. You'd be working your butt off with CIs and CWs and physical surveillances and meetings and mountains of paperwork. You'd sit in a van on a Title III wire for eight hours in three two-man shifts for thirty days and end up with a simple bookmaking case that nobody really wanted. And you'd need a break from the Mafia jungle.

Then out of the blue the Bureau would send you on an all-expenses-paid trip.

A trip to the great American West stands out vividly in my memory. I was one of the better shots in the Bureau, and in 1973 fifty of us crack shots from New York were flown to the plains of South Dakota, along with other elite agents from around the country, for a special assignment.

From the first time I fired a pistol, I loved shooting and I loved guns. In fact, I was and still am a gun collector, specializing in German Luger pistols. My interest in Lugers led to something that would add to my collection of scandals. I might as well tell you about it now:

In 1975, a fellow collector died. He was a thirty-six-year-old medical doctor who was killed in an auto crash. His grieving wife asked me to sell his collection of Lugers for her. All the proceeds went to her. I sold one to an undercover agent who was scouting the gun shows trying to buy from people who didn't file the appropriate paperwork. It was like shooting fish in a barrel because so many of the collectors didn't want to be on record in case their guns were later restricted by new gun-control statutes to the point where they couldn't resell them. And some of these people had tens of thousands of dollars tied up in their collections. Well, I was one of the fish that got shot in the barrel.

Despite protests from the revenuers that busted me, my lawyer persuaded a lawyer in the Department of Justice in Washington to drop the criminal charge. That lawyer in the Department of Justice was Rudy Giuliani. Years later, when I was arrested for murder, this incident was leaked to the media to embarrass Giuliani, who was then leading in the polls by a wide margin for the Republican nomination for president.

Anyway, back to the South Dakota trip. Falling snow

forced us to divert into Casper, Wyoming. From there, an old drafty school bus took us to the outskirts of the town of Wounded Knee on a South Dakota Oglala Sioux Indian reservation.

The town of Wounded Knee had been seized by the American Indian Movement (AIM), one of the many militant organizations of that chaotic era. There have been a lot of phony conspiracy theory books published and equally phony movies, but you can get the truth about AIM in Joseph H. Trimbach's *American Indian Mafia*. It exposes the movement for what it was—a Mafia.

The AIM siege lasted seventy-one days. Shortly after his town was taken over by radical AIM leaders and their foot soldiers, the Sioux tribal chairman called in the marshals for help. But the AIM leaders wouldn't allow the marshals to enter Wounded Knee. The marshals set up roadblocks to cordon off the town, only they didn't have enough personnel to man them. We agents were sent in to help man the roadblocks.

When the FBI contingent arrived we were greeted by an official of the Department of Justice who held a meeting.

"If you're shot at you can't return fire," he said. "There will be no deaths on our hands."

"Now, they'd be tryin' to kill us, wouldn't they?" asked an agent from Oklahoma.

"We have to assume that's so," the Justice guy said.

"If anybody so much as points a gun in my direction," I said, "you'd better dig a hole for his body."

"My men will follow the FBI manual and their training," our supervisor said. "This meeting's over. Where's the food?"

Not long after I got to my assigned roadblock, a blue Ford station wagon approached us. More than a dozen AIM foot soldiers got out, formed a battle line, and advanced slowly toward us. There were ten of us. We got our weapons ready and sought cover behind metal barriers and motor vehicles. One of the AIM leaders had a bullhorn.

"Come on out and fight, you fucking pigs," he taunted.

"Oink, oink," came our reply.

It was a standoff. By nightfall we shot flares in their direction and saw them waving their rifles overhead, about a football field away from us on a ridge. After a while they moved back below the ridge so we couldn't see them at all. And then, after an eerie silence, they began shooting at us. Bullets ricocheted off metal, pinged the dirt, and I could feel the bullets from an AK-47 whizzing overhead. We returned fire. None of us was shot. I doubt if any of the AIM guys were either because it was too dark to sight the enemy very well.

Suddenly they stopped shooting, but we could hear gunfire coming from the direction of other roadblocks. Then just as suddenly they began shooting at us again. We traded fire for about ten more minutes when the shooting stopped again. We heard over the radio that three trucks were bringing food into the besieged town. I guess the shooters were hungry and needed some chow.

Food was allowed in, but not gas, because it would be used to make Molotov cocktails. The Department of Justice employed Community Relations Service workers to help calm things down. They were allowed into the town by AIM. It turned out that the workers would drive in with full tanks of gas, allow it to be siphoned off, and then drive out with near-empty tanks.

At the end of hostilities, after nearly three months of trading gunfire, two AIM soldiers had been killed, one FBI agent wounded, and a U.S. marshal, Lloyd Grimm of Nebraska, permanently paralyzed by a bullet to his chest. Grimm later died of complications from his paralysis. I felt fortunate to come out of this alive and in one piece.

The FBI has a sworn duty to investigate serious crimes committed on Indian reservations. In 1975 I was sent out to South Dakota again. I was sent as part of a five man SWAT Team, this time to help the Bureau handle the routine FBI caseload of serious crimes. Not that any of the cases I worked on were dangerous, but to simply be on the reservation invited sniping. And if I wasn't hit by surprise, I could accurately return fire.

While I was there, the FBI was investigating the murders of agents Ron Williams, age twenty-seven, and Jack Coler, age twenty-eight, and a married father of two. The two agents were shot in the head at close range. They had been trying to find one Jimmy Eagle in connection with the robbery of two ranch hands and the theft of a pair of cowboy boots. The agents stopped behind a pickup truck when suddenly men with rifles began firing at them. They returned fire, but their .38s were no match for the AIM firepower. The desperate agents radioed for help. They were wounded. Before help could arrive, the two young FBI agents were executed. There were 125 bullet holes found in their two cars.

AIM member Leonard Peltier was convicted of the young agents' execution murders in 1977, and despite numerous appeals he remains in jail.

My early career in the FBI was exciting. Sure, some of it was dangerous, but every day I had a chance to be a part of American history.

Do you remember the movie *Dog Day Afternoon* in which Al Pacino plays a Brooklyn bank robber holding a crowd of bank patrons and employees hostage? It's based on a true story.

My partner Doug Corrigan and I were in Brooklyn keeping an eye on a wiseguy. We were in casual clothes. Suddenly a call came over the radio that there was a bank robbery in progress: "All agents respond. Call in if you're close."

We responded to the scene and parked next to the bank. We got briefed. There were two robbers inside the bank. The Al Pacino character was the ringleader, robber number one. He wanted a pilot to pick him up and drive him from the bank right onto the tarmac at Kennedy Airport. He wanted a commercial plane waiting for him, ready to go, and JFK closed to all other flights.

After being briefed, Doug and I walked back to our

car. Suddenly we heard a shot ring out from inside the bank. We looked up and fifteen shotguns were aimed at us. We were in the line of fire. No one inside the bank was actually shot, but we almost bought the farm from friendly fire.

I never saw the robber leave the bank and strut up and down shouting "Attica, Attica, Attica" as a sign of solidarity with the Attica prison rioters of 1971, but it made a good scene in the movie.

Because of my marksmanship, it was decided that I would pretend to be the copilot of the plane and sit in the passenger seat of the car that would drive the robbers to JFK. Another agent would play the role of the pilot and drive the car. On a prearranged signal I would reach under the seat for a planted gun, whirl, and shoot robber number one, the armed ringleader. That would neutralize robber number two, an unarmed, hapless follower. If it didn't, he'd get it, too.

But that plan was changed because the bank robbery squad was there and this was their case. It was decided that Jim Murphy would be the shooter. There were two Murphys on the bank robbery squad and Jim was called Murphy Number One.

Doug and I were in the car right behind Murphy Number One's car as we caravanned to JFK.

When we reached the tarmac in our cars, Murphy Number One whirled and shot robber number one. We saw the flash, and guns in hand, we rushed the car. An ambulance was there to take robber number one to the hospital. Doug jumped in the ambulance while I stayed at the crime scene . . . and stayed and stayed and stayed. I was the last car to get off the busy tarmac. Not because I had any FBI business to do. Doug had jumped into the ambulance with the car keys in his pocket.

CHAPTER THIRTEEN

TONY DEANGELO

Going undercover can get you killed.

When it happens to one of our own, those of us who have gone under pay special attention—like we did in 2006 when two NYPD undercovers, Detective James Nemorin and Detective Rodney Andrews, were executed by a drug dealer on a lonely street in Staten Island. This was nine months after my arrest. It put my troubles in perspective.

One of the most successful and well-known undercovers is my dear friend Joe Pistone. We all remain in awe of his ability to penetrate the Mafia and infiltrate their ranks as Donnie Brasco from 1975 to 1981. It was far more dangerous than the modest Joe admitted in his first book, *Donnie Brasco*, or even in the more revealing sequel, *Donnie Brasco: Unfinished Business*.

Joe surfaced from his deep cover as an extremely high-ranking associate in the Bonanno Family to kick off our championship season. What a bonanza of material and testimony Joe turned out to be. I've heard him called the wrecking ball that devastated the Mafia and I'm an eyewitness to the truth of that. He devastated the defendants in our Mafia Commission Case.

Our only complaint was with the brass that decided to pull Joe from the operation just as he was about to become a made man. Although a made man had to have committed at least one murder, Joe's capo, Sonny Black Napolitano, claimed murders Joe said he had done in the past. Joe objected to being pulled from the operation and still does. The brass said they did it for his own protection. We agents and supervisors in the field understood what a devastating blow Joe's getting made would have been to the entire Mafia. It may not sound like much to folks who don't truly understand these people, but to those of us who do, the simple act of Joe getting made would have made our job of turning the enemy a lot easier over the next few years. The allure of getting made someday is a recruitment and discipline tool. It's the Mafia Boss's casting couch. Getting Joe made would have been our reverse recruitment tool. We could have persuaded potential CIs that their sacred oath was no longer sacred, that their Bosses were fools, and that they should help themselves while they could before it all came tumbling down.

Making Joe would have been a severe blow to the image of the all-knowing and all-powerful dictators, the Bosses. Disillusionment and loss of morale from the top to the bottom would have been incalculable and instantaneous. The stain would have been permanent. And we would have milked it like crazy, rubbing their noses in it.

Of course, as it was, what Joe did accomplish helped us immensely.

As most of us did, I had some undercover special assignments. But they were of short duration—stings—and they were not against the Mafia, where you can get a bullet in the head from behind just for winning at a card game. In these targeted undercover operations I drew on my knowledge of made men, gleaned from my work with my CIs and from listening to Title III wiretaps and bugs. With my looks, and the right vocabulary and mannerisms, I made a convincing "Tony DeAngelo" and I'd get calls from fellow agents or supervisors who might need me to get into character for a particular situation.

"Lin, I need Tony DeAngelo." It was supervisor Lou Stephens.

"I'll see if he's in," I said and laughed. "Lou, what do you need? I'm yours."

"We've got a source, an Irish guy, he was approached by an IRA guy who wants to buy arms."

"He's come to the right place. I've got a nice Luger collection."

Lou laughed. "This IRA guy needs machine guns, grenade launchers, and antihelicopter missiles for the IRA in Northern Ireland. Our source is willing to introduce you to the buyer."

"Can you set up a meet for tomorrow?" I asked.

For the right price a confidential informant will sometimes do a "solid" and go that extra mile to make an introduction, as long as it doesn't involve the Mafia—that could get him killed.

I studied up on the IRA and their revolutionary cause in Northern Ireland and the next day I met with Lou and his source. At an Irish bar in Hell's Kitchen I was introduced to Colm Murphy as Tony DeAngelo, a connected guy who could help Murphy's cause.

Colm Murphy resembled an Irish version of Junior Persico, short and puny. He had an Irish brogue. We agreed to meet in my car the next day, and since he was Irish, I brought along some Irish beer.

"Fuck the Brits," I toasted.

"Fook the Brits," he replied.

"What do you need?" I asked.

"I'll be needing machine guns and some of those grenade launchers," he said. "Oh, and I'll be needing something to take down helicopters."

"I could get you twenty machine guns at five hundred apiece and I could work on the other matters."

"Twenty machine guns would be a good start, but I'll be wanting more for sure. At a hundred can you do a little better on the price?"

"No promises," I said. "I'll talk to the big boys and see what I can do."

He left and I gathered his empty beer cans so we could identify his prints.

My Ford Mustang had a bug in the console and the entire transaction was recorded. We like to give the federal prosecutors, some of whom don't have a lot of experience, as much as we can. We wanted Colm Murphy to actually take delivery of the weapons, pay the ten grand, and get caught red-handed.

Colm Murphy and I arranged to meet at a McDonald's on Queens Boulevard. He told me he would be bringing a friend. I said, "Sure thing" to his gift of a co-conspirator defendant in the future trial.

I parked my Mustang that had twenty M-16 submachine guns in the trunk and I walked into the McDonald's. A van with three agents hiding in the back was parked next to the Mustang to keep an eye on the weapons. The eating area inside the McDonald's had about ten backup agents posing as customers. Among the agents sat an unsuspecting Colm Murphy and his friend. Murphy introduced me to his accomplice, Vincent Toner, and showed me the money. The three of us walked to the door of the McDonald's to make the exchange of the guns and the money.

Just as Murphy opened the door and we got outside, the three agents inside the van burst out from the back doors with guns drawn. I thought three months of investigation was about to fizzle. I thought they'd screwed up and jumped the gun. That is, until I saw the agents run down the street and collar two punks. It turned out the punks had jimmied open the rear of the van only to be facing down the barrel of three service revolvers. The punks had panicked and the agents caught them and turned them over to the NYPD.

Meanwhile, Colm Murphy was extremely spooked. He was so spooked his Irish brogue made it difficult to follow what he said.

"Slow down," I barked at him. "I don't understand a fucking word you're saying."

"I'm gettin' the fook outta here," he said.

"Relax," I soothed him in Brooklynese. "Dis here has nuttin' to do wit' us. Fuggeddaboudit. Dis here is da freakin' land of opportunity. When McDonald's is too crowded you go to White Castle. Where da fuck were you brought up?"

We agreed to meet in an hour up the road at a White Castle. In the restaurant parking lot Colm Murphy and Vincent Toner took possession of the machine guns and I took their money. As they sat in their car waiting to exit the lot, Lou Stephens and his men yanked them from their seats and recovered the weapons.

On another undercover as Tony DeAngelo I met with a group of morons that give the word *wannabe* a bad name.

A confidential informant from Chicago had been recruited into a harebrained scheme with these "wannabes" from Staten Island. They planned to hijack the *Emerald Seas*, a cruise ship in the Caribbean, and hold it for ransom. I met with the CI and his two agent handlers from Chicago and the three of them barely kept from laughing while the CI told me the story. Of course, he agreed to bring me in and introduce me as the gun supplier. These Staten Island *stunods* didn't worry the CI from Chicago;

they were small potatoes—not made men—and they couldn't hurt him. And the CI knew the more cooperation he gave us, the more money he'd get.

Wearing a concealed wire, I met with the plotters at a diner. They no doubt got their inspiration from the movie *Assault on a Queen*. Now I'm the one who had to keep from laughing as they explained their "brilliant idea" to me and my little friend, my secret Nagra recorder.

These guys were complete morons. They made no effort to vet me, to at least ask who I was with, and made no effort to get to know me. I had a complete backstory rehearsed for them, but never had to use it. Instead, they went full bore into the details of their plot. They actually handed me four pages with all the particulars for what barely passed for a plan.

We were going to seize the vessel between Miami and Nassau. How we were going to take over a ship in the middle of the ocean they weren't so clear about. That still makes me laugh even now. We were then going to demand $6 million in American money, out of which half a million was going to me. After we somehow got the money—a detail that a guy named Tiny would handle—we were going to Bogotá, Colombia, where we would leave the ship disguised as priests and blend into the Colombian countryside. *¡Ay caramba!* Father Tony DeAngelo!

"We want you should get us six M-16 submachine guns," the main talker said. "Then we need six .45 automatics and two .38 revolvers."

"It'll cost you five grand in advance," I said.

"We don't have any money at this point," one of them said.

"But," said another of the *stunods* at the table, "if you let us borrow one .45, we'll go out and do a few scores and come back with the five thousand."

"Good thinking," I said.

We agreed to meet at two that afternoon at a Laundromat in Staten Island so I could deliver the handgun.

One thing about rank amateurs, if you don't watch yourself they can be more dangerous than the pros. They'll panic and become impulsive, so I made sure I had backup at our next meeting. When I walked into the Laundromat there were two additional men. One was Jacob Goldstein, who owned the Laundromat and doubled as the ringleader, the brains of the outfit. I chatted enough with everyone to get their voices on the recorder. You could never get that kind of chatter from real gangsters.

On a prearranged signal, the backup agents came in and arrested us all. (I was always arrested along with everyone else so I could maintain my cover.)

On another, far more serious undercover assignment, the wire I was wearing played an unexpected role.

Edwin Wilson was a six-foot six-inch giant of a man who was convicted of selling guns and explosives to Libyan leader Muammar Gadhafi for his terrorist attacks. Wilson was a former CIA operative who had lived like a sultan in a swanky estate house outside of Washington, D.C., until a federal prosecutor Larry Barcella targeted him and sent him to jail. My role in this case was re-counted in *The Death Merchant* by Joseph C. Goulden.

Later, Edwin Wilson got a reversal when his lawyers, on appeal, proved to the satisfaction of a federal judge that an affidavit admitted into evidence and used to convict him was a phony. The judge refused to credit the prosecution's claim that the inclusion of the affidavit was an honest mistake.

What wasn't a phony, for sure, was that from his jail cell, before he got his underlying convictions thrown out, Wilson had hired me—posing as hit man Tony DeAngelo—to kill a number of people on a "hit list" he'd prepared. The list was a mix of prosecutors, such as Larry Barcella, CIA officials, and the witnesses who had testified against him at the trial. I said I needed $10,000 front money before I would get started "doing the work" on the list. Wilson told the intermediary we were using, a fellow inmate who was an informant, that I should meet with Wilson's twenty-year-old son Erik in the men's room off the lobby at a Sheraton Inn near Kennedy Airport. Erik would give me the $10,000.

I arrived at the Sheraton about fifteen minutes early—wearing a wire. I kept checking the men's room. Finally, Erik showed up. In the men's room he gave me $9,800 and poor-mouthed that he had to use $200 of it as expense money. Like father like son, I thought.

Edwin Wilson was arrested for federal conspiracy to commit murder and we went to trial. I took the witness stand, told the jury my story, then the prosecutor turned on the tape recorder so the jury could listen to my rendezvous with Erik. Since the whole tape was evidence, the prosecutor had to play it from beginning to end. Naturally, there was some downtime on the tape, especially at the beginning, when I was cruising the men's room waiting for Erik. This was explained to the jury. We all sat patiently waiting for that "dead" part of the tape to end when suddenly the jurors and the judge and everyone in the courtroom began to snicker and then laugh out loud. They were listening to me urinate. And yes, I washed my hands. I have it on tape.

Edwin Wilson might have escaped his sentence on the underlying weapons-smuggling charge because he made a government official look "dirty" in preparing a phony affidavit, but my hands were clean. Edwin Wilson got twenty-five years and stayed in jail until 2004 on my charges. I hope he's not out there making lists, because I'd surely be on one.

Come to think of it, if it weren't for the tape recorder I wore throughout the time I met with Erik that captured him explaining the missing two hundred dollars, I'll bet that after my first scandal, the one involving Chris Favo, got leaked to the press in 1994, young Erik would have come forward to help his father on appeal by claiming that I palmed the money. Nothing like smearing an agent to win the heart of some judge on appeal, I would later find out.

CHAPTER FOURTEEN

THE WONDER YEARS

Like the memory of your first girlfriend, you never forget your first informant.

We didn't have individual squads for each of the five families until Jim Kossler organized them, around 1980. The first squad I supervised was the Bonanno Family squad, beginning in 1983. Prior to Jim Kossler, we just worked Organized Crime, period. We had little to no concern about which Mafia family was doing the crime we investigated. Manhattan was headquarters for Organized Crime, but there were Organized Crime squads in surrounding offices in the metropolitan area.

I broke my cherry with my first informant by innocently violating most of the rules I would later teach. One summer morning an agent in the Manhattan office came in with a tip that members of the Gambino Family frequented a particular bar in the Bronx where they met to discuss their numbers operation. The daily number came from the last three numbers of that day's daily handle (total bets placed) at a particular racetrack, as it was reported the next day in New York's daily tabloids. The number paid six hundred to one if you hit it squarely. Bet a dime and win sixty bucks. The numbers game was illegal and still is, except for the numbers-game lotteries run by the states.

The agent was thinking of going up and hanging around, but he was so Irish he might as well have had the map of Ireland on his face, and knew he wouldn't get anywhere.

I offered to go up and nose around. The next day I came in with the gold chains and the pinky ring. I'd borrowed a green Buick Riviera from a friend of mine so I wouldn't have to drive to the Bronx and be seen parking a black Crown Victoria. The bar was on Belmont Avenue. The Bronx has an Italian section very similar to Little Italy and East Harlem in Manhattan. The singing group Dion and the Belmonts, who made a big hit out of the old song "Where or When," came from that Bronx neighborhood. That song was probably playing on the jukebox when I walked into the bar about four o'clock and grabbed a bar stool. The place was empty.

What I'm about to relate is completely true, but some information is slightly altered and some held back. A part of me still protects confidential informants even when they're long dead. It's ingrained in me, like cleaning my plate when I eat.

The bartender was a giant of a man with thick lips and

a bent nose. He appeared to be in his late forties, early fifties. On the wall there were two photos side by side. One was of Il Duce, Benito Mussolini. The other was a photo of the bartender as a pro boxer taken twenty or so years earlier. He was clearly a heavyweight, both before and after.

I ordered a beer and pulled a roll of bills from my pocket. I had a hundred on the outside for show and all smaller bills, mostly ones, on the inside—a Michigan roll. I put ten on the bar.

To my surprise the bartender started talking to me. He asked me if I was there for the funeral. I assumed that a prominent figure had died and everyone was at the wake. I nodded and said, "Sort of."

He said, "Tough break."

"Tough," I said.

"If they catch the guy, forget about it."

Days later I would learn that a teenage boy had been killed in a hit-and-run.

"You got that right," I said.

I finished my beer, paid for out of my own pocket, left a two-dollar tip, and walked out.

I returned two days later at four o'clock and again the place was empty. What I should have done on the first day after I left the bar was to sit in my car and clock the regulars to see when they started to roll in. But I hadn't done that, so impulsively, I decided to dive in and try the bartender. After all, he'd likely be in a position to hear things from his perch behind the bar.

"Look," I said, "I'll level with you. I'm a federal agent.

I'm new and I'm trying to learn about how things work. I don't care if somebody runs numbers. I'm just trying to get an education."

He studied me without speaking for half a minute, then said: "What are you asking me for?"

"For one thing, I'm a big boxing fan. I loved Jersey Joe Walcott." I don't know why I tossed that name out other than that my dad and I loved the former champ's style, light on his feet and loaded with technical boxing skills. Today Jersey Joe is best known for the famous photo of his face being scrunched by a Rocky Marciano overhand right.

The bartender's face lit up. "You did your homework," he said. "I'm impressed."

The guardian angel of unprepared agents was looking out for me that day. It turned out the bartender had gone almost three rounds with Jersey Joe before hitting the canvas from what he called a "lucky punch."

"Hey, anybody can get a lucky punch in," I said.

We began meeting or talking on the phone about once a month. I introduced him to my backup agent. "This is my partner," I said. "I trust him with anything. You can always ask for him if they tell you I'm not in."

I gave him the squad number and told him to ask for Lin, and to say a friend was calling. Maybe a decade later we all had so many Mafia informants that to handle the calls we needed an empty desk in the middle of the squad with a dedicated untraceable phone. We called it a "hello" phone. Any agent could answer it, but could only say "hello." The CI calling it would ask for his handler by his first name and the phone would be passed. A call I got from Greg Scarpa on this hello phone would later get me in trouble with Chris Favo.

I told the bartender: "If anybody is passing by when you're on the phone and hears you ask to speak to Lin, it could be a woman you're asking for. Don't forget that." Later on, when I got informants that were more closely allied to one of the families, I would come up with a code name for myself, like "Mr. Dello."

I didn't always reward the bartender with cash because he didn't always have anything for me. That he didn't have anything for me from time to time was a good sign he was on the level. He wasn't making things up just to get the money. The best sign that he was on the level was when his information panned out.

I remember he called me in a big hurry one early afternoon.

"Interested in a fugazy bank robbery?" he asked.

"Why not," I said.

"This bank robber, Johnny Sabatini, is on his way up to New Haven. He's going up there to help out an old girlfriend. She's a teller. She's got her hand in the till and now she owes her account almost ten grand. Johnny's coming to the bank. He hands her a note demanding money, then he walks out without no money. That way, anybody grabs him, he's clean. She handles the rest. It was something they done one time before. Only I didn't know you then. Johnny's going up on a Greyhound. He's a wife-beatin' piece of shit."

Bank robbery is a federal offense. I quickly notified

the Connecticut FBI office to stake out the bank. One of our agents went to the New York bus depot and found the wife beater there waiting for the Greyhound. The agent followed him to Connecticut, and straight into and out of the bank. When the robber got outside, the stakeout team arrested him. It turned out there were a bunch of outstanding warrants for the guy's arrest. He didn't have any bank proceeds on him, as the girlfriend had already stolen the money. But the girlfriend rolled over as a CW, helped us nail him, and confessed to every scam they had ever done together. I assume this proved to the robber, once and for all, that no good deed goes unpunished. My partner and I ended up giving the bartender a thousand dollars for that "solid."

Confidential informants have a shelf life. At some point they begin to repeat old stories, and as they slow down and become less active, they are not as aware of the things that are going on among the younger men. I closed the bartender in the early 1970s.

But when our focus dramatically changed in 1980 with Jim Kossler's arrival as our offensive coordinator and we began our championship season with a new atom bomb of a weapon created by Professor G. Robert Blakey—the federal RICO statute—I reopened the bartender—still in the same bar—and got some good stuff from him on the Gambinos.

By the time I retired in 1996, the bartender was losing his eyesight and was down on his luck. He'd call me at home with useless information and I'd ask him to meet me in a coffee shop. I'd buy him lunch and give him a twenty out of my own pocket. Lots of agents dipped into their own pockets that way. These broken-down knock-around old-timers had no Social Security. They'd never paid taxes and never paid into Social Security to get anything out of it.

The years before Jim Kossler's arrival and his establishment of our individual family squads, I think of as the Wonder Years. During these years we were wide-eyed and learning like crazy. They weren't wasted years. We learned to obtain from our CIs the specific kind and quality of information we needed for probable-cause permission. We learned the law of probable cause. We learned how to draft affidavits and to apply for Title IIIs. We learned how to utilize the electronic bugging and tapping equipment we borrowed from the spy side. Our techies were not geeks; they were ordinary agents who sat across from you and worked cases with you. They were Vietnam veterans or ex-cops. They had no backgrounds in electronics. They just learned how to perform this wizardry. We learned how to break into places to plant the bugs and the safest and most efficient places to plant them. We learned how to monitor the taping from vans or nearby buildings or later from our own office. We learned when the law required shutting off the device— for example, if a man's lawyer called him. We learned how to handle the tapes as evidence and store them for future use. We learned how to help a prosecutor present them in a trial. And we did our learning on smaller cases that almost didn't matter if we botched them.

Of course, we also learned a lot about the Mafia from

being in the room with them or on the phone with them, listening to them talk to each other. I was often struck by how boring many of their lives were and how dumb some were. And how tough some were.

One CI that I developed was shot six times and survived. He went by the nickname "Bullets." When I made my first approach to him and asked if he would help me "get an education," his reply was blunt: "What's in it for me?"

Little Sonny from Canarsie was one of my favorite CIs. He got the "Sonny" from his plump Italian mother to whom he was devoted and the "Little" because he was a moose of a man. He was a knock-around kid and was as tough as he looked. He was the muscle for a wiseguy who was big into loan sharking. I arrested the shy and knowing I couldn't make a case against Sonny because all my evidence was against his Boss, not him, I asked the federal prosecutor to do me a solid.

"Let me have a warrant for Little Sonny to use as a hammer," I said. Luckily, I was dealing with a prosecutor who knew the score.

"Little Sonny," I said while I booked him. "Why in God's name should you go down with this shy who makes a hundred times what you make? You and I and the whole world knows, Sonny, you're a halfway honest, hardworking guy. You're just trying to make a few bucks to support your mother. Maybe I can do a solid and work something out and make this go away for you. I hate to see you going down like this."

"Not for nothing, but whatever you could do, Mr.

DeVecchio, would be . . . you know, mean a lot to me. I mean that."

It wasn't long after this that Little Sonny became one of my better sources. One night he took me out to watch *Monday Night Football* at one of the local gin mills near JFK Airport where a lot of the bad boys hung out. I went in first to make sure no one was there that I might have locked up. When I didn't come right back out, Little Sonny came in.

He introduced me as his cousin and we joined a group at a table. This guy had some set of balls. A guy at the table told me if I wanted to bet the game that night he "could get me down."

Being my father's frugal son, I said: "I'm tapped out."

Another guy had "color TVs. Zenith. I got Zenith."

"Maybe when I get back on my feet," I said.

During the evening, one guy passed by, reached down, and grabbed my arm in a viselike grip. I thought he recognized me and that Little Sonny and I were in a jackpot. This cold-looking guy pulled me to him like I belonged to him. "If you ever get behind the eight ball," he said softly to me, "and you could use a little extra cash, just ask your cousin to get a hold of me. I can help you out." I thanked him graciously.

It was all I could do to remember the names of the guys I met and what kind of action was going on that night.

I would meet Sonny at his mother's house in Canarsie, which is in the far corner of Brooklyn. She was a nice old lady with an accent. I would go at dinnertime because I knew she'd insist we eat a little something. Mamma mia, could Little Sonny's mama cook. She made the best pasta fagioli I ever tasted.

Little Sonny, like so many street guys, got himself killed over a drug deal. Informants don't ever tell you everything.

It always comes as a sad shock when you hear the news that you've lost an informant. You build a close personal relationship with the good ones. You treat them like friends, in part as a tactic and in part because you mean it.

My first made-man informant was a Colombo button who had been developed by an older street agent who got promoted to headquarters in Washington. We were on the same squad and he knew I had enough street time to know how to talk the talk, so he picked me out of the squad to take his source over. He wanted me to cut my teeth on a Top Echelon. He had prepped the informant for several weeks prior to the introduction because made men, especially Top Echelons, are paranoid about speaking to anyone other than their handling agent. Needless to say, good intentions on the part of a handler are only half of what's needed. The life of any informant, but especially the Top Echelon, literally depends on the expertise and often the flexibility of the handler.

In a room at a midtown hotel that was managed by a retired agent, I was introduced to "Blackie." He was cordial but wary. I was excited to finally be able to speak to an inducted member. It took about four months before he started giving me more than just the names of members and what crews they were in. After that, every time we met was a treasure trove of information regarding the illegal activities of the Colombo Family as well as several other Mafia families he was close to.

After about a year I felt that we were friends. Knowing that every made man was supposed to have killed someone, I felt I knew "Blackie" well enough to ask him as one friend to another: "I hope I'm not out of line, but how does it feel to do a piece of work? I mean, as far as you know."

He gave me a long silent look and then started to smile.

"The first one or two hits you get nervous," he said, "but after that it's easy."

"I can understand that." I kept a warmth in my voice.

"As far as I know," he said.

"Of course, as far as you know."

I had no idea how many kills Blackie was good for, but clearly it was more than "the first one or two." Our relationship went on for several years until one day I called the social club where he hung out.

"Blackie around?"

"He's gone."

"Okay."

My heart sank. I immediately knew what that meant. Whoever answered the phone assumed I was a friend of Blackie's and gave me the true answer. I feared that maybe someone suspected him of informing to me. I racked my brain, but we'd had no slipup.

In 1992, when the Colombo Family War was creating a bumper crop of cooperating witnesses, we learned the reason for Blackie's murder and the name of the shooter. Blackie's two brothers had been killed in a dispute over money and the shooters knew it was unsafe to leave Blackie on the street. Although I was genuinely sad about his murder, I felt better knowing it wasn't me who'd caused his death on my first Top Echelon case.

This was the first informant I was to lose in the line of duty, but not the last. Their wiseguy occupation was more dangerous than that of a logger or a coal miner.

Many of the things that motivated them to inform made them vulnerable. A man who is disillusioned with the life may show it in other ways. He might bad-mouth a superior he believes is a hypocrite. A man who uses informing as a means to eliminate competition may soon stand out as the only one in the crowd not going down. That'll get the attention of his peers. The man who is jealous or wants revenge is already saddled with character flaws that can do him in at any time. If he acts out on that jealousy or revenge in other ways and gets caught at it, "he's gone."

Other motives—fear of jail, earning some extra money, keeping law enforcement busy on other people so they don't focus on him, getting an insurance policy if he ever gets jammed and needs a friend, and so on—are less personally dangerous motives, more businesslike. I found with the smarter ones that they just like to have a conversation with someone with a brain in his head once in a while. Some actually get attached to their handler and want to please him. And vice versa. It's human nature.

Gratitude's involved in there somehow, too. It's got to be.

In your contacts with any informant you need to be aware that you face danger, too. One of the more memorable contacts for me was a time I was sitting in an informant's car in Manhattan's meatpacking district. At the time it was a hotbed of homosexual prostitution, so it was unlikely we'd run into anyone connected to the Mafia there. A man with a shopping bag passed by my passenger window.

"Did you see that?" my informant bellowed as he bolted from his car.

He caught up to the guy with the shopping bag and pushed him into the wall of a brick building. I got out and saw an obviously gay man standing near us watching.

"This cocksucker pulled a knife on that guy and took his money."

"I don't have a knife," the man with the shopping bag said.

My informant grabbed the shopping bag from the man.

"You don't have a warrant," the man said.

My informant pulled out a ten-inch carving knife from the bag and a small roll of bills. He handed the bills to the man who was watching.

"Thank you very much," the man said. "You're a gentleman."

"No problem, you better scram."

The robbery victim turned and scurried away.

My informant handed me the carving knife and began to beat the daylights out of the robber. I know he broke this guy's ribs.

"Gimme the knife," he said to me with ice in his eyes and veins bulging. He was into it. He held the robber's sagging body up with one hand and reached out to me with the other. "Gimme the fuckin' knife. This cocksucker's solicitin' these fags then he's grabbin' their fuckin' money, the cocksucker. Gimme the fuckin' knife. I'm gonna cut his nuts off."

I ignored him and walked up to the robber and let him have a couple of left hooks to his body.

"That's enough," I said, and we drove off. I took the knife with me when he dropped me off in case he had any thoughts about going back.

You can see something like a latent law-and-order streak in some of the Mafia men you deal with.

Another time, I targeted a Top Echelon who was a Genovese button. I knew this guy was on probation and I knew the time he reported to his probation officer every Thursday. I wanted to go to the probation office and be in the room when this high-ranking button showed up to report. Whenever you wanted to approach another agency you needed permission from your supervisor and from headquarters. I got the approval and my supervisor called the probation officer's supervisor and greased the wheels.

In the middle of interviewing this Genovese button, the probation officer got up and left the room. I entered and sat in the officer's chair. I introduced myself as an agent.

Before I could say another word, the irate Genovese button said: "Why are you here, and no, I don't want to talk to you."

"I understand that . . ."

"This is bullshit. If you don't leave, I will."

"It's your call," I said.

"You're goddamn fuckin'-A right it is," he shouted. "You're crossing a line here. You got some fuckin' nerve crossin' that line."

By that time in my career I'd been rejected by hundreds and was not put off. I put my name and the number of the "hello" phone on the table and left. To my shock I got a call about two weeks later on a Friday afternoon.

"Know who this is?" he asked.

I played it cool to hide my hopes. After all, he might be calling to tell me off. "Yeah, I recognize your voice," I said casually, but I didn't ask him anything. There was a pause.

"Know Cedar Lane and Garrison in Teaneck?" he asked.

"I live in Jersey," I said, "not too far."

"Be at that corner tomorrow at ten a.m."

"I'll be there." What wiseguy is up at 10 a.m. on a Saturday? I wondered.

I got there about ten minutes early to look over the area. I knew it was a predominantly Jewish neighborhood. There were a few Orthodox Jews out and about. It looked safe enough. At precisely 10 a.m. a black Lincoln limo with dark-tinted windows pulled to the curb.

The rear passenger-side window rolled down halfway. A hand waved me in. Even though I had a .38 in a holster on my ankle, I paused. I stood there and considered that despite the Mafia policy against killing law enforcement, you never know. They do a lot of things they don't do. This could be my last ride to anywhere. If my body were never found, I'd be labeled a street agent who ran off somewhere, probably with a fifteen-year-old girl who went missing from the area on the same day.

I opened the door and saw the button and another man and a driver. Not too thrilling a sight. Before I got in, the button saw my dilemma. He introduced the man to me as his lawyer and said the limo driver was just that, and that they knew nothing about anything. I sighed in relief, hoping that during the pause I had taken we had not been observed. We drove to a Sears parking lot on River Road in Hackensack, which was surprisingly deserted. The lawyer and driver got out and walked away.

"What do you want to know?" He got right to the point.

The money I could give him wouldn't even pay for the limo, much less the lawyer. I never had him long enough to understand his motives for helping me. Maybe it was insurance in case his probation officer ever wanted to violate him and send him back if he happened to get spotted in the company of men with criminal records or known Mafia figures. I had him for about a year before I closed him. And while it was all business, no friendship, he was very helpful to me. I closed him when he got killed. We never did learn why or who did it.

I guess he trusted the lawyer he had. That was his call. But over the years I learned that Mafia lawyers tend to know what's good for their health and their careers.

Yes, they were the Wonder Years. Every day it seemed I learned something new as I became comfortable moving around in a wonderland where murder was as common as lighting a cigarette.

CHAPTER FIFTEEN

KOSSLER'S BUSINESS PLAN

We in the Organized Crime unit were nowhere near as organized as organized crime itself. We had no real strategy, no real game plan. We were trying to take in as many wiseguys as we could, hoping to chip away at the crime families. During our Wonder Years we'd harvest Title III probable-cause information from our CIs for criminal acts like bank burglary, hijacking, loan sharking, or gambling. The probable cause was for individual crimes that had occurred or were about to occur. For the first three or four years after the Title III law went into effect, we were making tons of gambling cases. Our thinking was that we would get a little guy and squeeze him to get his immediate skipper, and then squeeze him to get his Boss, and so on. But after all that work, a gambling conviction would often just lead to a slap on the wrist. A revolving-door sentence squeezes nobody.

And the Bosses easily replaced the gamblers that we arrested by recruiting more crew members from the endless supply of wannabes in Italian neighborhoods. No matter how many of its operatives you sent away for a stretch, the operation itself never left home. You could close them down one day and your CI could call and make a bet the next day. Still, we plowed ahead on the assumption that gambling was the Mafia's biggest moneymaker and we were affecting their ability to make money. We simply didn't know that the secret society had a gazillion ways to take in billions of dollars. At the start of our championship season in 1980, the Mafia was by far the most profitable enterprise in America.

So, even with all our good work, we weren't making much headway. In order to cause some real damage we had to hit them at the top: We had to take down the Bosses.

To get a judge's permission for a Title III, our probable cause had to consist of facts that would prove that target's participation in a crime. And we didn't have a crime called being a Boss.

We'd listen and record and we'd get a lot of voices of little guys on tape, and an occasional made guy. But it was unlikely we'd ever get information from a CI that could get us permission to tap a Boss or another ranked guy's phone or social club. The typical CI had never even seen a Boss. Because of the spider web of Mafia rules that ensured secrecy, no Boss would ever discuss anything of a criminal nature with an underling. Believe me, a Boss was insulated from the dirty work.

Probable cause, with all its legal ins and outs, which were becoming more and more restrictive, was our "may I." And even though anyone with a brain knew that bugging a Boss's phone or social club would guarantee a load of incriminating evidence, no judge was ever going to say: "Yes, that makes sense; you may go on a fishing expedition and catch some evidence against a Boss."

Finally, in the early 1970s the federal judges threw up their hands and made it clear that they were tired of our meaningless gambling cases clogging up their court calendars.

Gambling is normally done over the phone by a bettor calling in his bet. Title III phone tapping had made us too efficient at gambling cases. We thought we were fighting the Mafia, one gambler at a time, but we could see the judges' point. We just didn't know what else to do.

Some of us sensed there was a big hole in the dike of our laws. We wanted permission to bug and tap the big boys, but our confidential informants just didn't have the ability to give us probable cause. We continued to meet with our informants, and continued in vain to try to make only big cases—whatever that meant.

Our problem all along was that we simply didn't have as strong a business plan as the Mafia had.

What we needed, without knowing it, was the capacity that Mussolini had. We needed to be able to get the Bosses for "banding together for criminal purposes." We needed the Bosses to be guilty of a very serious crime just by being a member of a "criminal enterprise" that furthered its business plan by the commission of crimes by underlings. If the Bosses could be proven guilty just by being a member of the "enterprise," then we could get permission to bug their haunts and homes and tap their phones based on evidence of their membership in the "enterprise."

We needed a one-two punch. Title III was punch number one. We did the best we could with that single tool during the Wonder Years, but to get beyond those Wonder Years we desperately needed that second punch.

In 1970 G. Robert Blakey got his old friend Senator John McClellan to pass punch number two. For all of the reasons that Blakey understood as if he were one of us, enduring, as we did, the frustrations of trying to expose the Mafia, he drafted, and McClellan assured the passage of, the RICO statute.

RICO was the centerpiece of the Organized Crime Control Act of 1970. RICO is an acronym for the Racketeer Influenced and Corrupt Organizations Act. Professor Blakey's creation made it a crime to be a member of an organization—a "criminal enterprise"—engaged in certain crimes.

The politically correct spin is that it applied to any "criminal enterprise," and while it does sometimes get used in a variety of ways, it was clearly aimed at the Mafia Bosses. After the passage of RICO, the Bosses were now committing a criminal offense by being Mafia Bosses. RICO carried gigantic potential sentences, the kind befitting a Mafia Boss.

And now, thanks to punch number two, Title III could come into play and be used against the big boys.

While he was at it, Blakey drafted and got enacted the Witness Protection Program. What a visionary Blakey was! He envisioned a weakening of *omertà* caused by the ironclad evidence that Title IIIs would harvest and by the harsh sentences that would be imposed as a result of RICO convictions. Many of those caught up in the devastation would roll over and become cooperating witnesses in order to save themselves from the embarrassment of sitting in court and hearing their own words convict them, and from fear of the ultra-long sentences they would get hammered with.

Those who rolled over and cooperated to keep from drowning would give us "may I" information to help us get more Title IIIs against still more made men. Then this new breed of Mafia CW would testify for the prosecution and ensure that any of the made men who still foolishly clung to *omertà* and who chose to go on trial did not get up from the canvas to fight another day.

The dangerous side effect for this new breed of Mafia CW and his family was the threat of vendetta and swift, deadly retribution. The safeguard Blakey created for them was to be the broom and dustpan in the cleanup of the Mafia—sweeping up the CWs from their hazardous neighborhoods and depositing them and their families in secret locations with assumed names somewhere out there beyond the blue horizon with enough income to get along.

* * *

As desperate as we were for something like RICO, during those Wonder Years of the 1970s we heard not a whisper about RICO's existence. It just sat there on the books. Blakey's 1970 RICO statute had a major flaw . . . its uniqueness. No law in our long tradition had ever made guilt by association into a crime. Would it be deemed constitutional? It was so different that it bred indifference, even a little hostility. Blakey tried like crazy to interest federal prosecutors in his baby. On one famous occasion he tried to explain RICO to a room full of federal prosecutors. The U.S. attorney in charge of the office got up and told Blakey, "You don't know what you're talking about."

From his Ivy League office at Cornell Law School in Ithaca, New York, where he was a professor, Blakey, like a missionary zealot, stepped up his visits to federal prosecutors—whom he viewed as "scalp collectors" rather than organized crime fighters. He held summer seminars for them at Cornell.

While prosecutors jumped all over Blakey's Witness Protection Program for their CWs, they yawned at RICO. By and large, the government lawyers Blakey tried to convert did not want to jeopardize the individual provable cases they had by incorporating them into a larger RICO case that added elements—such as the existence of the "criminal enterprise" and a defendant's membership and place within it—elements they'd be forced to prove in trials that would seemingly drag on forever.

RICO remained unused for nearly a decade, until 1979, when it was used by an Organized Crime strike force in Philly under the supervision of Frank Storey, a future boss of mine in New York and the man who talked me into becoming a supervisor. The RICO target was Frank "The Irishman" Sheeran, a prime suspect of Case Agent Bob Garrity in the 1975 Jimmy Hoffa murder in Detroit. Bob is now retired from the force and works for the NFL. But from 1975 to 1978 he was the Detroit agent with primary responsibility for the Hoffa investigation. Frank Sheeran's RICO trial was connected to the Hoffa murder only in the hope that when a hundred-plus-year RICO sentence slammed him, Frank Sheeran would cooperate and give up Hoffa. In this pioneering RICO indictment, Sheeran was charged with being a high-ranking associate in a "criminal enterprise"—the Russell Bufalino Family of northeast Pennsylvania. Bufalino was another on Garrity's short list of suspects in a January 1976 Garrity document called the Hoffex Memo. Sheeran's voice on the tapes made by a cooperating witness was the primary evidence. Two murders were among the underlying crimes.

Nevertheless, in 1980 one of the very first RICO trials in history ended in acquittals on all counts. The government had to learn to incorporate into our business plan anonymous juries—where names and addresses of jurors were never released to the Mafia defendants. When he testified, the enormous Irishman gave glaring looks to the jury.

But RICO caught a break in the second trial against Frank "The Irishman" Sheeran. In 1981, the more conservative jurors of Wilmington, Delaware, convicted Sheeran in another "criminal enterprise" trial and gave a real boost to RICO. This time, the "enterprise" involved more than being part of a crime family—something that might have been too vague for some people to grasp. This time it was a self-contained truck-driver leasing scheme that enabled corporations to avoid paying union wages and benefits. (It would be a year later that the Bonanno Family would be the first New York Mafia family to be convicted as a "criminal enterprise" under RICO. That conviction was obtained by the testimony of Joe Pistone, who had penetrated that tightly knit family.)

Frank Sheeran's RICO conviction had been based on the underlying crime of violating Landrum-Griffin. These were the labor laws that the loose-cannon Mafia Boss Vito Genovese inspired in the late 1950s. In reaction to the worldwide publicity generated from the 1957 Apalachin meeting of Mob Bosses Genovese called to explain his notorious killing of Albert Anastasia in a barber's chair, Senator McClellan conducted hearings on the influence Italian gangsters had on organized labor. The vast majority of those arrested at Apalachin listed their occupation as "labor organizer." The resulting Landrum-Griffin Act made a federal crime out of union corruption. Sheeran was convicted and tossed in the can. But the Irishman remained silent about Hoffa until a death-bed conversion in 2003 restored him to his Catholic faith. As Sheeran said regarding Bob Garrity's short list of suspects before he began his path to confession: "People think the FBI don't know what the fuck they're doing. The FBI knows what the fuck they're doing." A tip-off that Sheeran, a war hero, had some respect for law and order in him came immediately following the jury's verdict that convicted him. Sheeran reached out to the lead Department of Labor Agent Bob McKee, shook his hand, and said, "You did a good job."

While RICO was being experimented with against Frank Sheeran, Jim Kossler and Jules Bonavolonta, Joe Pistone's handler during the *Donnie Brasco* operation, spent two weeks at Camp Blakey in the summer of 1979 to learn about RICO.

I'll never forget the day that our coordinating supervisor of Organized Crime Squads Jim Kossler assembled us in a room and created our business plan. Before joining the FBI, Kossler had been a teacher for mentally challenged children, and he still had the same demeanor. With a pipe clenched in his mouth, he displayed patience, serenity, wisdom, and intelligence that would amaze. And rock-solid firmness.

Jim opened the meeting by asking: "What's your procedure for going about working your Organized Crime cases from start to finish?"

To a man we said: "Hominah, hominah, hominah."

"We're not going to leave this room," Jim said, "until we have a plan for investigating and prosecuting organized crime from start to finish."

Out of that room that day came the Enterprise Theory of Investigation for Organized Crime. Since it is still in use today, word for word, I need to leave it at that. It was like the discovery of a new medicine to control a disease. Organized crime damaged and killed like a disease of epidemic proportions. It was a public health issue, and this was the treatment.

Jim Kossler, with the help of his "consigliere," Bob Blakey and his operative at headquarters, Jules Bonavolonta, led us from the path of investigating, say, hijacking or a top hoodlum, to investigating a whole family all at once for any family business done by any member of that family.

And he started to re-form us into individual family squads. Man, were we inspired. I mean, we had our life's work right in our hands. It became my dream to help bring down a whole family someday—like the Colombo Family.

Jim Kossler explained the implications of all of this for our Title III probable cause "may I's." He introduced us to Professor Blakey's little friend "dynamic probable cause." As I said, the RICO statute required us to prove the existence of the "enterprise" to the jury in each and every case. Because of that extra burden of proof, we would be allowed to obtain a judge's permission to bug Bosses. This wasn't because we had CI information about a specific crime a Boss was personally involved in—an impossible thing for us to ever learn. We could get a judge's permission because we could swear that we had information that a Boss was an active member of the "enterprise." We could type into the affidavit what CI number one and CI number two and so on told us about the Boss being a Boss, and that the Boss was likely to reveal the existence of the "enterprise" and his leadership role in the "enterprise" through conversations on a specified tapped phone or in a specified bugged room.

This was a freedom to operate we'd never had. It was the freedom New York D.A. Thomas Dewey had when he bugged Lucky Luciano's brothels in the 30s—a freedom all the states had lost over the years—but were about to get back as they adopted these laws. We looked at all this legal mumbo jumbo for what it was: an excuse to bug the Bosses.

As I said, Joe Pistone was still under in 1980 as Donnie Brasco. We didn't know he was, but Jules and Jim certainly knew. And they urged Joe to keep getting the kind of "enterprise" information that would ultimately justify more bugging.

In a relatively few short years, our business plan began to outperform the Mafia's. The FBI and other law enforcement offices all over the land began to play tapes in open court and to expose the extent of the damage done to our nation by the secret society of the Mafia. As early as January 23, 1983, an editorial in the *Philadelphia Inquirer* declared: "If there is a single cancer that more fatally threatens the domestic health and security of American democracy than Organized Crime, no one has yet convincingly named it—except perhaps those who, in service to the Mob itself, deny or ignore that it exists."

Twelve years earlier, in 1971, when *The Godfather* was being filmed, the word *Mafia* was eliminated from the movie in order to appease the Colombo Family—which controlled certain movie unions that could close down filming. Also in that year, then New York Governor Nelson Rockefeller and then attorney general of the United States John Mitchell agreed to ban the use of the M-word by law enforcement officers under them. Another thing about *The Godfather* filming is that in order to assure labor peace, Colombo gangsters were handed jobs as extras. Actor James Caan fell in love with them and remained loyal. When I sat in that cold lockup cuffed to a chair in 2006, I knew from reading the *Daily News* that James Caan had written a letter to Brooklyn D.A. Hynes praising him for "undertaking such an extensive and malignant corruption case" and for "taking the time to evaluate the situation to correct the wrongs that have affected so many lives." Would those "lives" that I had "affected" by my "malignant corruption" be the families of my four alleged murder victims? No. The affected "lives" would be two of Mr. Caan's closest Colombo Family pals who were serving life for murder under RICO and who blamed me for their incarceration. Specifically, they would be Capos Jo Jo Russo and his look-alike cousin Chuckie Russo. They saw tarnishing me as a way to win their freedom on appeal.

Mr. Caan didn't beat around the bush: "Joseph Russo is a dear friend of mine." He closed with: "I cannot express enough how pleased I am that your office has taken an interest and is in pursuit of correcting this problem."

Mr. Caan had precedent for his, at best, naive attitude toward his Mafia friends. Even as late as 1985, when we had the Mafia Commission defendant Bosses under indictment for RICO and we had a Gambino Family RICO case in trial in New York and we had already proven Joe Pistone's Bonanno Family RICO case, then Governor Mario Cuomo declared at a press conference the day after the murder of Gambino Boss Paul Castellano on the sidewalk in front of Sparks Steak House on Forty-sixth Street: "You're telling me that Mafia is an organization, and I'm telling you that's a lot of baloney."

That same day after the murder of Paul Castellano I beeped Greg Scarpa to meet me so we could learn what was going on. We had just lost our Boss of Bosses in the Mafia Commission Case.

Here's my 209: "On December 17, 1985, NY3461-TE advised Supervisory Special Agent R. Lindley DeVecchio that the hit on PAUL CASTELLANO and THOMAS BILOTTI was set up by JOHN GOTTI and FRANK DE CICCO. The source said this information came from DE CICCO, and COLOMBO boss CARMINE PERSICO was aware of the plans to hit CASTELLANO. The source said PERSICO neither approved nor disapproved of the hit, but made no attempt to oppose it."

* * *

Mafia historians have surmised that the Gambino Family squad knew at once that it was Gotti because the conclusion was logical. However, that singular Top Echelon information went directly to the Gambino squad supervisor as soon as I heard it. (Information is considered "singular" when the identity of the informant would be blown instantly if the information got out.)

These three sentences in my 209 corroborated the singular information coming from one of Agent Andy Kurins's TEs and helped the Gambino squad get "may I" permission for vital taps and bugs on Gotti and his family. A few years later, when Gotti's underboss Sammy "The Bull" Gravano listened to Gotti bad-mouth him on the tapes from those bugs, Gravano rolled. In his debriefing he corroborated Scarpa's day-one information and gave all the details just like Blakey and Kossler planned it.

CHAPTER SIXTEEN

THE GRIM REAPER

How did I recruit Scarpa in the first place? While Jim Kossler was beginning to take us to school on how to investigate whole families, I figured if I went through the 209 files of closed informants I might find an old closed informant who over the years had risen in the ranks. He might bring me up-to-date on his family. I picked the thickest file. It was clear from reading that this was an informant who had provided excellent and singular information for thirteen years before he was closed in 1975. His name was "34." That's as much of a name as the other street agents were allowed to know.

"Thirty-four" was pretty famous among us street agents. I learned of him on my first day in Organized Crime. I was told: "If you need any information from a source, go to Tony." "Thirty-four" had been retired agent Tony Villano's premier source. Tony, a Brooklyn native, was one of those tough, savvy agents I learned a lot from just by watching him in action.

I showed the file to my supervisor and learned that "34" was the street legend Greg Scarpa. He was known as a man even the wiseguys feared. One time he had a beef with two capos about whether the capos were entitled to a split on a certain score. They knew they needed muscle when they confronted him even though Scarpa was merely a soldier. They took about fifty guys with them. Scarpa stood alone shouting at the capos and telling them to go fuck themselves and get out. He didn't budge an inch and the capos retreated.

If I could get Scarpa to do no more than freshen up the information in his file and make it current, he'd be providing a singular service under our new dynamic probable cause. What sounded like gossip—the stories about who'd been made, who'd been bumped to capo, who'd been knocked down, who was who, and what they were up to—could be invaluable to us.

Scarpa had been closed in 1975 when he quit because he thought he was owed money that a supervisor wouldn't sign off on. I learned that with him it wasn't about the money; it was the disrespect he felt the supervisor had shown him. I planned on showing him respect.

It was a beautiful sunny June day in 1980 when I made that fateful trip to the street Scarpa lived on in an unassuming Bensonhurst neighborhood. I did a sweep past his address to make sure that I had the right house, and to be sure there were no wiseguys close by. From doing my homework, I knew roughly what time he headed off to his Wimpy Boys Athletic Club, where he held court and conducted business. Although never a capo, Scarpa had his own very special status. He later confided in me that he would never agree to be a capo because it would draw too much attention to himself. He remained a soldier under capo Anthony "Scappy" Scarpati, although their relationship was a mere formality. Scarpa always did his own thing.

"Why do I want to put a spotlight on myself," he said.

"You got that right," I said.

"I'm doing very well right where I am. You guys are only interested in the rank of capo and above."

I had to laugh. He had us figured out. We practically threw soldiers and associates back in the water.

It was clear to me from his file that his goal was to draw the Bureau's resources, time, and attention to everybody else around him.

I sat in my standard Bureau-issued car, a beat-up 1975 Plymouth Fury with black tires, and went over in my mind how to approach this celebrated lion. At least I wasn't wearing the Bureau uniform of a coat and tie. I tried to look as much like a local as possible.

I sat parked up the block for about a half hour until Scarpa walked out his front door and got into the big black Lincoln sitting in his driveway. Immediately I pulled up behind him, blocking the driveway.

Scarpa got out with a "who the fuck are you?" look on his face. I'll admit he was a fearsome-looking man and

I could only imagine the feeling of a loan-shark victim who had missed a few payments of vig when confronted by him.

Slowly I got out of my car with my hands casually in front of me to reassure him that I wasn't there to whack him. I had my credentials out.

"I'm an agent," I said immediately. "My name's Lin DeVecchio and I'd like to talk to you about something."

"Talk about what?" boomed this basso profundo like the villain in the opera *Tosca*.

"Not official business. Just need some help."

He didn't say a word but he watched me very carefully, studying me.

"I was close to Tony Villano," I said. "Tony told me to look you up someday if I needed help."

"So why should I help you?" Scarpa's fierce growl was gone and replaced by a tough but smooth demeanor. His voice was very distinctive. When I set my files up on him I labeled them "Smooth Talker." This change in tone was a good sign.

"I'd like to learn more about the ways of the life," I said. "You were a great help to the Bureau in the past and maybe you wouldn't mind helping us out again. I'd owe you."

"Give me a number and I'll think about it."

About two weeks after this initial meeting, I got the call I'd hoped would come. Scarpa said he'd meet me at his home the following morning at ten. "Come alone!"

I was there at the appointed hour and we sat in his living room. He introduced me to his "wife," Linda, and then told her to go to another part of the house. She got us coffee and left us alone.

Linda Schiro had a slim, pert figure and teased brown hair. She was a type of that time and place. She wore a little too much makeup and was provocatively dressed. She was an attractive woman and seemed pleasant. Years later, in a Brooklyn courtroom, she didn't seem pleasant at all.

We sat for at least an hour. I did most of the talking, speaking the language used by the wiseguys, with a lot of four-letter words thrown in. After all, imitation is the sincerest form of flattery. I used to say to the new agent trainees at Quantico—a few of whom were Mormons who'd gone to Brigham Young and Catholics who'd gone to Notre Dame: "Even with a postgraduate degree, my speech has been reduced to gutter language. And if that bothers you, go fuck yourselves!"

During the casual chitchat of our initial conversation, Scarpa identified Junior Persico as the Boss of the Colombo Family, as well as the identity of five other Colombo capos and three buttons. Each name and rank was ammunition for enterprise probable cause. Who was actually the Boss had been a matter of some speculation for us. Boss Joe Colombo was shot in 1971 and remained in a coma for seven years before he finally died, and we didn't know, for sure, who got the Commission's blessing to take over.

Coincidentally, while I was meeting for the first time with Scarpa, Jules Bonavolonta was handling Joe Pistone, who was entering his final year in deep cover with the

Bonanno Family, risking his life as Donnie Brasco. Jim Kossler was busy forming family squads and everybody was really hungry for information.

At the same time I was working a case with Agent Marty Mulholland and the Bureau's northeastern Pennsylvania office against Russell Bufalino. I already mentioned a CI named John Napoli. Napoli helped us get Russell Bufalino. He had taken a $25,000 diamond from one of Bufalino's operatives on Jewelers' Row in Manhattan. Bufalino wanted the money yesterday, money Napoli, of course, didn't have, so Napoli came to me. I offered him one chance to save his life. With that heavy hammer of Russell Bufalino hanging over his head, Napoli agreed to transform from a CI into a CW. We wired Napoli for a sit-down with Bufalino at his restaurant in the theater district, the Vesuvio.

"I want the twenty-five Gs or the diamond or I'll strangle you with my bare hands," Bufalino said, and kicked Napoli in the shins under the table. That threat on tape is extortion, like the Black Hand's "pay or die."

Now we normally wouldn't care about such a small matter, but Bufalino was a powerful Boss and a main suspect of Bob Garrity's in the Hoffa hit. Napoli testified for us at trial. Bufalino, then eighty or so years old, went to jail. When he got out, he used his awesome power to penetrate the U.S. marshals' Witness Protection Program and he found out Napoli's address in California. Bufalino called his old friend in L.A. Jimmy Frattiano and asked him to whack Napoli. Frattiano appears in a famous backstage photo of Frank Sinatra surrounded by

Mafia dignitaries, like then Boss of Bosses Don Carlo Gambino. But Frattiano—soon to be called the Weasel—had gotten into a jackpot in L.A., and he rolled and taped Bufalino. Now they had Bufalino for a conspiracy to murder with his own words. Bufalino went down on that, suffered a stroke in jail, and was released to die at home—which he did in his early nineties.

In 2006 John Napoli resurfaced on the Brooklyn D.A.'s list as a witness against me. He was in jail and figured he could do himself some good by climbing onto the murder case somehow. I never did learn what bullshit this low-life thief was going to say. He was the kind of make-believe wiseguy no one in the Mafia wanted to deal with. He was a treacherous con man, a smooth operator, but a loose cannon. And he had a short attention span. He got sidetracked and was dropped from the witness list in 2007, eight months before my trial. A pretty thirty-seven-year-old investigator with the Brooklyn D.A.'s Office with fifteen years' experience, Maria Biagini, had been assigned to hold Napoli's hand and keep him comfortable while they debriefed him and helped prepare him to testify. This is normal procedure. But Biagini went that extra mile for Napoli and started bending the rules to get him special privileges and to treat him as if he were Joe Valachi. Then one day the prison caught her conspiring with Napoli to smuggle something out of prison. It turned out to be his semen. She'd been charmed by the man and wanted to have his baby. I heard of a made man, but a made baby! Her firing hit the press with a bang after my indictment but before my trial.

The very next day following the news of the Biagini scandal, there was another Brooklyn D.A. scandal reported in the press. Prosecutor Sandra Fernandez was fired for leaking documents about prosecution witnesses to her boyfriend, Douglas Rankin, a criminal defense lawyer.

Law Professor Bennett Gershman was quoted: "These are two serious incidents and occurring at the same time suggests that there may be a problem in supervision and training in that office."

The flak for the D.A., Jerry Schmetterer, said, "These are two bizarre cases. I don't think any conclusion can be drawn . . ."

The very next day following the news of the Fernandez scandal, another D.A. investigator, after hearing about the Biagini affair, got scared and confessed to her recent affair with a witness in her charge. That's three scandals in three days. The two involving sexual affairs came from Vecchione's own rackets bureau. Alexis Sivulich admitted to a romance with her witness during her security detail. While she was watching over him she was all over him. Jerry Schmetterer said that she "came forward, and she's been docked a day's pay because she should have come forward immediately." Now that's what I call supervision aimed to encourage coming forward, but not aimed at discouraging romances with witnesses. Don't they see the conflict of interest? Such romances keep a witness more willing to say whatever will help the D.A.'s Office?

While these scandals don't prove my innocence, they

tell you something about the judgment of the office that was prosecuting me. And they were only the tip of the iceberg.

Back to Scarpa . . . On August 26, 1980, two months after my first meeting with him, he gave me all the information we needed to fill in the Colombo Family organizational chart. At the time we were just learning about RICO from Jim Kossler and about the feasibility of convicting all of the members of a family as a criminal enterprise. And here was the entire Colombo Family laid out for us. I couldn't wait to see Jim Kossler's face. Talk about enterprise theory. Scarpa even put himself in it.

"Someday," I thought, "I want to bring down this family and this informant could help me do it." The organizational chart and the nationwide reach of the Colombo Family became my obsession as the chart continued to change over the years. When I got the Colombo Family to supervise in 1988, as much as I didn't want the enormous workload of two families at once, it wasn't a surprise—I had been training for it for years, thanks to Scarpa.

At that same meeting on August 26, I learned that "Gerry Lang" Langella was now the acting consigliere, taking the place of the fugitive Allie Boy Persico. As consigliere of the Colombo Family, Langella and the consigliere of the Lucchese Family, "Christy Tick" Furnari, met every Monday and Wednesday nights at the 19th Hole Restaurant in Brooklyn. My 209 reads:

"Source advised that there has been a longtime association between the two families with respect to the exchange of information, and Langella is now handling this contact." Hello RICO, how's that?

I shared the information I got from Scarpa with the other family squads. Chris Mattiace ran the Colombo Family squad from 1985 until I took over in '88. He recalls how I shared Scarpa:

"My squad was doing the first RICO case against the Colombo Family hierarchy and we were hungry for probable cause to get permission for Title IIIs. All day it would be, 'Ask Lin.' Lin would call '34'—who years later I learned was Scarpa—and get back to us with the details we needed to plug into our affidavits. Our Colombo Family case against the Boss Junior Persico, his underboss Gerry Lang Langella, capo Little Allie Boy, and eight other capos went to trial on October 15, 1985, on fifty-one RICO counts with hundreds of underlying crimes. The trial ended in June 1986 with complete victory. Frankie 'The Beast' Falanga died before trial or we'd have convicted him, too. Junior got thirty-nine years just before he walked into another court to face the Mafia Commission Case trial.

"The NYPD rewarded my whole squad for bringing down the Colombo hierarchy in our Colombo Family RICO case—we were inducted into the NYPD Legion of Honor. The one important person not on my squad who was inducted along with us was Lin DeVecchio because his '34' gave us most, if not all, of the probable cause in all of the Title IIIs. Conservatively, Greg Scarpa led us to at least 75 to 80 percent of the evidence we developed and used to convict the whole executive branch of the Colombo Family in a trial that lasted seven months."

In six months Scarpa gave me enough to get a Title III on a case in Florida. He gave me insight into one of Jim Kossler's areas of concern, the infiltration of legitimate businesses and unions. There was the Prospero hit. Prospero Funeral Home was a big operation in Brooklyn. The Mafia was bleeding Mr. Prospero pretty well and he got tired of it and refused to pay any more extortion. From my 209: "The source noted that Prospero was well liked by the wiseguys in Brooklyn and was a well-respected businessman, and noted that this hit is an indication of the viciousness of Carmine Persico."

Also during that first six months Scarpa gave me detailed information on the dealings of the Mafia Commission. He told me that Carmine "Junior" Persico was "going to seek a commission meeting soon to ask for new members for the Colombo Family." A month later, I learned that Junior had asked for ten, but got only one new member. The Commission was "concerned that the Colombo Family has taken in too many young and inexperienced individuals and has therefore limited their numbers at this time."

From the day of our first sit-down and for the ensuing twelve years, Scarpa furnished incredibly valuable information that led to countless RICO convictions and life sentences; Title III bugs and taps; solutions of murders and other serious crimes; and the Mafia Commission Case that, along with the individual family hierarchy cases, was a big part of the undoing of the Mafia's power in New York. Seventy-five to 80 percent of what he gave me was singular information, unobtainable anywhere else. Absolutely no other single organized crime source had as much impact on the FBI's efforts toward dismantling organized crime as Greg Scarpa.

Along the way, Scarpa saved a few lives. During that first year he told me that then capo John Gotti was going to whack an innocent union member—a fellow named Tony Califra, who'd gone to the union's executive committee with evidence of racketeering. The executive committee controlled by Gotti "downplayed Tony Califra's allegations . . ." Scarpa said Gotti is "currently deciding what course of action to take." That meant Gotti was going to whack Califra. I gave this information to the Gambino squad. However, before they could do anything with it, they had to consult with me. They needed to go to me first to make sure it was handled in a way that would not compromise my source. I can't reveal how this was done.

Scarpa obtained this union information at the highest level of meetings between the families. Not many would have known. On a lot of my Scarpa 209s the bottom of the page reads:

"THE ABOVE INFORMATION IS EXTREMELY SINGULAR IN NATURE, AND PRIOR TO ANY

ACTION, CONTACT SHOULD BE MADE WITH THE WRITER."

Ten months after I opened Scarpa, his information saved a life in Las Vegas. Scarpa told me of a Las Vegas associate who was heavily into narcotics and it was feared he might talk. I picked up the phone and called Agent Charlie Parsons in Las Vegas, who warned the guy. And the guy rolled over and became a source.

I remember one guy I warned one day in East Harlem, Anthony Benintendi.

"You've got the wrong guy," he said.

"It's pretty good information," I said. "I heard you're not cutting in the right guys on your scores."

"Nah, I don't think so."

"I've got an obligation to tell you."

A month later he was gone. If you've got specific information that a guy is going to be whacked, you've got an ethical obligation to warn him, but no obligation to tell him how you know.

A year after I'd opened Scarpa, Joe Pistone surfaced as Donnie Brasco. On hearing the news, Scarpa advised me that "those dealing directly with him or those having introduced him to other . . . members would be hit by the Bonanno Family." The FBI saved "Lefty Guns" Ruggiero by picking him up before he was hit, but Tony Mirra and capo Sonny Black were not so lucky. Sonny Black had his hands cut off because he'd introduced Joe and let Joe shake hands with Bonanno higher-ups and two Bosses in other families.

As a result of Joe's six years of undercover work, the

Bonanno Family was tossed off the Commission. Before bouncing them, Scarpa told me, the Commission kicked around other ideas: "There is talk it will be broken up and its members spread out among the remaining four NY families," and "an alternate method would be to hit the current leaders of the Bonanno Family, which would effectively destroy that family . . ." Hmm, killing the chiefs sounds like the rationale for the Mafia Commission Case.

This is the thing that makes me most proud about my relationship with Scarpa: When I got an answer from Scarpa that I knew would be useful for another squad and I passed it along, the squad members would then go and get a Title III, and *bango*, they'd listen to the tapes and the wire would corroborate and substantiate Scarpa's credibility every single time. I used to use Scarpa as a check on information my other informants gave me to make sure they were on the level.

The only time he got any help from me was when he was arrested by the Secret Service for buying counterfeit credit cards from a wired cooperating witness. It was a sting. My lawyer Doug Grover's law partner Norman Block was the federal prosecutor. I got Scarpa's approval and my supervisor's approval to go to headquarters for permission to reveal his TE status to Block and for Block and me to go to Judge I. Leo Glasser and tell him privately in the judge's chambers. Which we did. They made the decision from there to give Scarpa probation. We would have extended the same courtesy to the Secret Service if we arrested one of their top sources. During the scandals, I got blasted for this.

I inherited the Colombo Family squad from Chris Mattiace on January 12, 1988, and I kept it ten months. The Genovese squad inherited Colombo from me in October 1988. I got the Colombo Family back a little over a year later in January 1990. Sometime in 1989, before I got the Colombo Family back, an FNG—Fucking New Guy—on the Genovese squad came to me to discuss Billy Cutolo of the Colombo Family and whether Cutolo was still into loan sharking. Billy Cutolo was very big in the Teamsters and other unions.

There were some experienced Mafia-savvy guys on the Genovese squad under supervisor Dave Stone, like Detective Joe Simone of the NYPD, but the agent who sought my help had less than a year doing any Organized Crime work, and what he did do was random: serve a subpoena here; man a wire there. Simone or one of the experienced guys told the young agent that I had an informant on the Colombo Family and told him what information to ask me to try to get for him. This young agent was Chris Favo.

My Scarpa 209 for November 16, 1989, reads: ". . . WILLIAM CUTOLO, COLOMBO Family underboss, has gained considerable power and influence in the family in a short period of time, in part due to his influence in union activities and his skill as a moneymaker for the family. The source said CUTOLO uses his mobile telephone to conduct much of his illegal business, since most wiseguys think that mobile phones are safe from wiretapping techniques. The source identified numerous photos of individuals taken at SECRETS LOUNGE, Brooklyn, New York, and other locations. ADMINIS-TRATIVE: Individuals identified in series of fifty photos have been furnished to case agent."

Here is Chris Favo in his own words on a tape recording he made in 1994 right before my OPR scandal: "Toward the end of 1989 I learned that Lin DeVecchio had an informant with the Colombo Family. I went and talked to Lin and asked him to ask his informant to find out if Cutolo did loan sharking . . . In any case, what Lin's source does—this is Scarpa—he goes to Cutolo at Secrets—talks to him about a loan-shark debt that they have, and then has Billy make a phone call over Billy's mobile phone to this loan-shark victim . . . and that gives us the probable cause to go up on Billy's mobile phone."

Once they are up and running Title IIIs expire in thirty days. The probable cause needs to be refreshed with a new affidavit and the judge needs to approve it. A wire that's producing great results refreshes itself, so to speak.

My Scarpa 209 for December 26, 1989, reads: "WILLIAM CUTOLO finances shylock loans through several loan sharks who meet him at SECRETS LOUNGE . . . These loan sharks make loans to victims for CUTOLO and after making collection of the 'vig' meet CUTOLO at SECRETS to receive their share.

Source added that those victims who do not make their payments are threatened or physically beaten. Source has overheard CUTOLO discuss loan-sharking matters on his mobile telephone."

Actually, Scarpa cajoled Billy Cutolo into taking him for a ride and then using his mobile phone to call a loan-shark victim so that he could tell me about it.

Does anyone think Scarpa didn't enjoy providing me information, didn't take his job seriously?

In January 1990 Favo and two other agents who had been working Colombo for Dave Stone arrived on my doorstep, assigned to my squad. Despite his lack of experience, I was happy to get Favo. He makes a nice impression, is well spoken, hardworking, and eager to serve.

On January 17, 1994, four years after he arrived on my squad, Favo, with two of his "young and inexperienced" followers, went to my boss, the head of Organized Crime, Don North and reported their suspicions that I had been feeding information to Greg Scarpa.

Days to hours before he went to North, Favo had spoken on tape about the help Scarpa and I had given to him regarding Billy Cutolo and his mobile phone. This tape was one of three ninety-minute tapes Favo dictated on his drive to and from work. He dictated them to train an agent named T. J. Harkins—as if Favo were already in charge of my squad. We got our hands on those four and a half hours of tapes dated "1/94" sometime after my first scandal.

One of the revelations on Favo's tapes is that he is the man who started the Colombo Family War.

And he did it through Billy Cutolo.

But that's a story for a later chapter.

Over the years Scarpa and I met in apartments rented by the FBI, hotel rooms in Manhattan, cars in Brooklyn and New Jersey, and on about ten occasions at his home on Eighty-second Street in Brooklyn. Meeting at his home was always risky business and was only done at his request. Naturally, I would have to borrow a surveillance vehicle that did not look like the standard Bureau car, and I always wore my costume of a Brooklyn wiseguy.

Linda Schiro was usually there and she always greeted me warmly, like an old friend. We would exchange pleasantries and small talk and then she would leave before any business was discussed. Never did she sit in on any conversation that I had with Scarpa. Made guys did not discuss family business in front of their wives or *cumares*. If he ever did talk business in front of her, he would never do it in front of me. He and I had strict confidentiality rules for his protection. If he'd gotten careless in front of me, I'd have stopped him.

I imagine that if he told Linda anything, he told her that I helped him out.

"What would you say if we were seen together by some of your associates?" I once asked. We were sitting in the car on a little-traveled street.

"What the fuck could I say other than you were giving me information? If I said anything else, I'd be history."

"At least tell them I'm a DEA agent or NYPD." We both laughed.

I was good with that since I knew what he said was so true.

I liked Greg Scarpa—despite his reputation as a violent criminal and although I certainly didn't approve of his lifestyle or criminal activities. In the fallout from my OPR scandal, a defense lawyer asked me on the stand if I admired Scarpa. I said I admired the way the man was able to conduct himself in such a treacherous environment and survive all the years he had survived without getting killed. That takes a special talent, albeit one warped by any moral, legal, or ethical standards.

Unless you're somebody's son or nephew, you come up a hard path in the Mafia—a dangerously hard path. After going through a criminal apprenticeship wherein you may spend many years involved in day-to-day criminal activity, you then may or may not become eligible to get your button and be formally inducted into a family. If you do "get straightened out," you have protection from that family, but you still have to earn on a daily basis and a piece of your earnings has to be kicked upstairs to your capo. I have known a number of made guys who spent virtually every waking hour devising a scheme to make money to support their own habits and their wives, kids, and *cumares*. Honest work is not an option. Some go so far as to bust open parking meters for quarters. Every day is a new challenge. It's the first day of the rest of your life of days just like the last and a day that could be your last.

I used to visit a poor guy who'd spent his whole life doing the family's bidding and never got his button. He's now deceased from natural causes. Out of respect for his family I'll call him Tootie. Tootie owned record stores that sold albums kids stole from legitimate stores.

"I heard Shorty DeGeorge was doing good," I'd say to Tootie. "You must be proud."

I knew Tootie hated Shorty DeGeorge. This, too, is a fictitious name to protect Tootie's family. Shorty got made quickly and then bumped up to capo. I also knew Shorty was married to Tootie's daughter and was known to hit her. And because Shorty was made, Tootie couldn't do anything about it, not even mention it to Shorty, much less talk to him disrespectfully about it.

"Yeah, he's working on something with Little Vic Orena over there with the Whitestone Bank."

Tootie would seethe every time I mentioned Shorty and he'd give me something useful about what Shorty was up to. I never opened Tootie, but I was able to feast on his anger at not getting made while his piece-of-shit son-in-law was. I really liked Tootie. Everybody did. We'd sit and drink espresso and eat pastry.

The typical wiseguy is always trying to beat you—sometimes literally with a gas pipe. Scarpa was no exception. Everything for him had to be a deal. Every meal in a restaurant was at a reduced price, or on the arm. Every piece of furniture, clothing, cars, you name it, had to be below bargain basement.

I was accused by the Brooklyn D.A. of keeping the entire $66,000 that I was supposed to have paid Scarpa over the course of my twelve years handling him. I always had my share of courage, but even if I was a John Napoli, I wouldn't dream of trying to take a nickel out of Scarpa's pocket. He knew the score. He was more experienced with the informant program than I was. He knew what he was entitled to—at least he knew the value the Bureau had put on it before he was closed in 1975. I did not want to alert him to the notion that his information had become dramatically more valuable under Jim Kossler's business plan. He'd wonder what we were up to. So I continued to ask for amounts consistent with what he had been used to getting—with maybe a little cost-of-living increase.

The first time I paid Scarpa money, I handed him five hundred dollars. Without comment or counting it, he accepted the five Ben Franklins and pulled out a folded wad of his own hundred-dollar bills that was as thick as his file of 209s.

"Maybe you should be paying me instead of me paying you," I said.

"You're in the wrong fucking kind of work."

He then proceeded to give me his usual incredible "may I" probable-cause information on the Colombo Family, the other four families, and the Russell Bufalino Family, which had a major presence in New York.

Scarpa gave me enough once to get a Title III bug inside Russell Bufalino's permanent suite at the Hotel

Consulate in the theater district. Unfortunately, old-school Bufalino was not what you'd call loquacious.

In my OPR scandal, I was questioned about taking gifts from Scarpa. This came up as a result of Favo's fishing for proof to back up his charge of "corruption." I admitted under oath that on three occasions I did, indeed, violate FBI policy and take gifts.

The first was in 1982 when a friend, who lived in another state, asked if I could get a Cabbage Patch doll for her niece. This was when they were popular and very hard to find. I casually mentioned this to Scarpa at one of our rare meetings at his home when I saw one on his couch. Scarpa said Linda had a friend who sold them. I asked her if there was any way I could buy one. I didn't think for a second they were into stolen Cabbage Patch dolls. I didn't hear from Scarpa for several weeks and forgot about the Cabbage Patch doll. I told my friend that I was not able to find one and wished her luck. About two weeks later Scarpa and I met for our usual conversation.

"What's this?" I asked as he handed me a package.

"Open it."

"I'll be damned, where'd you get a Cabbage Patch doll?"

"Linda's friend had one."

I pulled twenty dollars from my pocket and went to hand it to him.

"What the fuck you think you're doing? It's a fucking gift. Keep your money."

He slapped my hand away and gave me an insulted look. He really looked hurt. He wasn't taking it back and would not accept any money. I didn't pursue the matter since I knew to do so would have been a sign of disrespect and a big glitch in our friendship. These guys never forget a slight.

The second occasion involved a bottle of wine at Christmas several years later. At a meeting with Scarpa about a week before Christmas, he got into my car and handed me a bottle of wine as a Christmas gift.

"Here, take this. I got so much damned wine and fruit baskets from my crew that I can't get into my dining room."

"I'm ashamed, I got nothing for you," I said. "Bureau rules."

"Hey, this is no fucking bribe, it's a Christmas gift for a friend."

To refuse this simple gesture again would have been considered an insult, and I was not about to ruin our relationship over a bottle of wine. When I returned to the office I gave it to one of the support employees who had been doing work for my squad.

The last gift involved a dish of lasagna made by Linda Schiro. Scarpa brought it to me saying that Linda had made a large batch and wanted me to have some. At my murder trial she claimed it was eggplant, saying "because that's what I do good." I remember it as lasagna and it was good, damn good. It was the tastiest bribe I ever got. Again, to refuse a gift of food from Linda would have been an insult, not only to Scarpa, but also to her.

So there you have it, a Cabbage Patch doll, a bottle of Christmas wine, and a dish of lasagna. Not much over a period of twelve years. Believe it or not, there are nut-job anti-FBI conspiracy theory books out there and wacko hacks who have used these admissions against me and continue to do so.

Now, I don't want to paint a portrait of Scarpa as a generous guy who was just giving me information out of the kindness of his heart. He was indeed a fearless individual who enjoyed killing.

Here's one example: A bank burglary involves an alarm being bypassed and the bank broken into at night. The safe-deposit boxes are then jimmied open, and jewelry, cash, and other valuables are stolen directly from private citizens. Once a member of Scarpa's crew complained about his son Gregory Jr.'s lackluster performance during a bypass bank burglary and Scarpa responded to the complaint by drilling the man on the spot and having him buried.

Another story involves his daughter with Linda Schiro, Little Linda. Scarpa had a limo take her to school every day. One evening Little Linda confided to Big Linda that the guy who owned the limo, a Puerto Rican not involved in the life, had sexually molested her.

Scarpa got a cane and walked into the limo driver's office limping, as if he were relying on the cane. The driver assumed Scarpa needed a limo because of some injury. Scarpa limped up to the driver and bopped him over the head with the cane, then whipped him with it.

"I told him he was fired. He couldn't drive my daughter to school no more."

What happened after that?

"I went back and killed him. I couldn't live with myself."

CHAPTER SEVENTEEN

THE EULOGY

Even though Scarpa's information was singular right from the start, it was a year before he fully trusted me. Certainly it was around that time that the quality and quantity of his information improved dramatically. But you know, it might not just have been that he trusted me more. It might have been that I was more knowledgeable about what questions to ask as I learned to use Kossler's new business plan.

It was providential that Greg Scarpa arrived for us at the birth of our new business plan and the formulation of the Enterprise Theory of the Investigation of Organized Crime. Over a period of twelve years Greg Scarpa was our secret atom bomb project. What effect did he have on our championship season?

As Jim Kossler put it:

"We couldn't have done it without Scarpa.

"I was the coordinating supervisor of Organized Crime from 1979 to 1989. I had line authority of all eight of the squad supervisors. There were five family supervisors in our heyday—until, as I was leaving, they combined two families under Lin to make room for a Russian gang squad.

"I'd conduct a meeting of squad supervisors every Thursday at 10 a.m. We'd discuss what their squads had accomplished, what came off their wiretaps and bugs. We would find common issues among the squads. We would task handlers of informants to round out the information we were getting on tape. Lin was the boss of bosses there. If we decided to initiate a new investigation, Lin was nearly always the first the other supervisors would go to for the inside scoop on the crew we were about to investigate.

"Of course, as coordinating supervisor, I read Scarpa's 209s. I knew where Lin was getting his information and it was my job to know the dependability, reliability, and quality of it. Scarpa was always right there for us. We kept statistics of every time an informant led to a wire or launched an investigation. To help Lin defend against his murder charges, we tried to get those statistics, but we couldn't get them from the Bureau. However, I don't need statistics. If you're a baseball manager and you don't happen to know your best hitter's precise batting average, you still know who's your best hitter.

"We would not have accomplished those things that we did against organized crime during that decade without Greg Scarpa."

*   *   *

One story Jim Kossler tells puts Scarpa's indispensable role in our championship season into focus:

"We even provided Scarpa's information to our partners in other agencies. Scarpa gave information to Lin that I gave in an affidavit to Ron Goldstock, who headed the New York State Organized Crime Task Force. Scarpa's information led to the bug on Sal Avellino's Jaguar. Using his Jaguar, Sal was the steady driver for Lucchese Boss Ducks Corallo and underboss "Tom Mix" Santoro. Sal had gone to college and had an insatiable desire to learn from his Bosses; he constantly asked questions, wanting to learn as much as possible. By his questions, Sal was operating as an unintentional interrogator at the highest level possible. That bug was unbelievably productive in proving the Mafia Commission Case and other cases. I have a letter on my wall from Ron Goldstock praising the probable-cause affidavit I gave him for the Jaguar. By necessity, Scarpa remained the secret provider of everything I gave Goldstock."

Ironically, Professor Blakey had laid out the path leading to Greg Scarpa's destruction when he instructed us through Jimmy Kossler: "Use what you get on the first wiretap or bug to get another. Then use the evidence from the first two bugs and taps to bug another . . ." When Scarpa helped me out, he was on a suicide mission.

Eventually, Scarpa's information and the Title IIIs it

produced caught up to him. One bit of probable cause led to the next, and in June 1992 my squad was able to bug a car belonging to a Scarpa ally in the Colombo Family War, "Joey Brains" Ambrosino. Brains got his nickname by not being the sharpest knife in the drawer. Upon his arrest, he rolled and that was doomsday for Greg Scarpa. In August 1992 the federal prosecutor in Brooklyn indicted Scarpa for four murders. One of those murders was also one of "my murders," that of Colombo Family old-timer Lorenzo Lampasi. Scarpa and his hit squad committed the murder of Lampasi during the Colombo Family War. And I was charged with supplying Scarpa with Lampasi's home address for the kill. But I'm getting ahead of myself again.

Unbeknownst to me for many years was Scarpa's addiction to aspirin. In the movie *In Cold Blood*, based on Truman Capote's book, you can see murderer Perry Smith, played by Robert Blake, eating aspirin like candy. Scarpa did the same. His alleged reason for taking them was to stave off a heart attack, but I understand he was addicted. Over time the aspirin caused ulcers. This proved to be his undoing.

In 1986 Scarpa underwent emergency surgery for a perforated ulcer. He was given blood donated by his family and criminal associates, the only blood he would trust. One of his crew, Paul Mele, had the HIV virus. Mele was a weight lifter and is thought to have contracted HIV from steroid injections using nonsterile needles. Mele died from AIDS some months after he gave blood to Scarpa. Scarpa became HIV positive and hid this from everyone until he filed a lawsuit against the hospital and it gradually became known. Three days before Scarpa was arrested in the late summer of 1992 for RICO murders committed in the Colombo Family War, he settled his lawsuit against the hospital for $300,000. By that time he was down from 225 pounds to 150 pounds. He insisted the settlement be in cash and he sent a crew member to the bank with a duffel bag to pick it up.

Presumably, Linda Schiro ended up with that money. Linda earned something for her years as Scarpa's mistress and for sticking by him when he learned he was HIV positive.

Among her contributions, Linda personally recruited Larry Mazza into Scarpa's crew. Mazza was a handsome young man who was to prove his worth over the years, especially as a member of Scarpa's elite hit squad during the war. Linda recruited Larry Mazza by first seducing him. The son of a New York fireman, Mazza was an eighteen-year-old delivery boy going to John Jay College. He delivered groceries to Linda Schiro and she got him into bed. Gradually, she and Scarpa seduced the boy deeper and deeper into the life. The trio smoked a lot of pot together. As he learned the rules of the life, Mazza realized what he had done by having an affair with Linda. He had every reason to be concerned that Scarpa would suspect his affair with Linda and kill him for it.

One day Greg Scarpa took him aside.

"I know you're sleeping with Linda," Scarpa said. "It's okay. I'm not going to hurt you. As long as nobody else knows about it. Just the three of us, you hear me. I

wouldn't deny Linda anything. I want Linda to be happy."
From then on, they smoked their pot together on the
plush carpet in front of the fireplace.

At the time of his $300,000 settlement, Scarpa was
gaunt and had one eye. The missing eye had nothing to
do with the AIDS. Because he had AIDS, he was allowed
to remain at home under house arrest, monitored by an
anklet, until his RICO charges came to trial. It was pre-
sumed he'd die at home before his charges were disposed
of. On December 29, 1992, however, Scarpa's son Joey
Schiro came home complaining about two rival drug
dealers in the neighborhood who were encroaching and
showing no respect for the Scarpa name. Greg Scarpa
grabbed his gun and found the two dealers. A gun battle
ensued. Scarpa killed one of them, but had his own eye
shot out. Before he went to the hospital, he returned
home and had a glass of Scotch.

Come on, loosen up, you've got to admire the man.

After getting his wound treated, Scarpa was remanded
to the hospital at Rikers Island prison. He was expected
to die there before trial.

By September 1993 he was still alive and he reached
out to the federal prosecutor Valerie Caproni in order to
become a CW. He agreed to be debriefed in exchange for
permission to die at home. Caproni met with Scarpa, but
ultimately refused to make that deal and debrief him.
Clearly, he was not expected to live long enough to testify, but he certainly could have provided a world of

useful information. After all, I hadn't debriefed him in months, and in the past, even when I did get priceless information from him, it was never all of what he knew. At the very least Caproni could have gotten a whole slew of secret burial sites for homicide victims.

But she had her own reason for dismissing such a deal, and it involved me. I didn't find out what she was up to until after the OPR investigation of me ended in September 1996 and I was able to read her sworn statement. I'll get to that later.

Scarpa, incredibly, lived another nine months after that meeting in Valerie Caproni's office. He pleaded guilty to the murders, was sentenced to ten years, and died of complications from AIDS in a prison hospital in Minnesota in June 1994, five months after Chris Favo uttered his suspicions about me to Don North on January 17, 1994.

Pat Marshall of the Mafia Commission Case fame, now an investigator for a public defender's office, has recollections that can serve as a eulogy for Scarpa:

"I arrived in Organized Crime in 1975. As the FNG, I got spoken to only when one of the old farts with the cigars wanted me to do something. They'd give me reel-to-reel tapes to transcribe. I'd listen and handwrite as much as I could make out, then send it to steno to be typed, and then I'd proof it. It sounds like tedious work, but when you think about what you're listening to and the effort that went into getting it, it's humbling work.

"When I came on, Lin didn't have '34' yet, but everybody knew of Lin's ability to develop quality informants. Getting information from an informant that passes muster for a Title III is not easy. That information has to be of such a high quality that it passes through many levels of approval before you even get to a federal judge. There are layers of supervision in the New York office. Then it needs approval in Washington, at headquarters. Next it goes to the federal prosecutors, then finally to a judge who might say no. The typical information you get from the typical CI is a little nugget that has to be tediously put together with other nuggets from other CIs.

"When Lin started working '34' and passing along his information, it was of the highest level—Title III quality—and it was complete. You'd get full stories with beginnings, middles, and ends. What '34' didn't know he'd go and find out for Lin.

"Except for what Joe Pistone did alone as Donnie Brasco, whatever the rest of us accomplished was a result of a whole New York office effort.

"Whatever recognition or praise I've gotten from the Mafia Commission Case needs to be shared with many others, but chief among them, in a class by himself, is '34.' I'm sure I spoke to '34' on the 'hello' phone, but I didn't know he was Scarpa. The supervisor knows who your informants are, but that's it. I did know that '34' was in the Colombo Family or maybe I figured it out over time. I would go to Lin all the time to get information from '34' about any family.

"I even went to Lin after I left the New York office to

run the L.A. office. Junior Persico was in Lompoc Prison, a couple of hours from L.A. Persico was still running the Colombo Family from there. I called Lin to get probable cause from '34' that would stand up three thousand miles away. Scarpa worked on it, nosed around, and Lin forwarded to me what Scarpa found out. I was able to get permission to bug the two tables in the visiting room that Junior used to plot family business and run the war in Brooklyn. The recordings were very productive and New York used the information to save lives.

"Those who accused Lin DeVecchio of being used by Greg Scarpa are people who have no understanding of what Greg Scarpa did for us at the risk of his own life. They lack this understanding either because they are ignorant, arrogant, blind, evil, or all of the above, and that includes some very FNGs in way over their heads way too soon. A thousand of them aren't worth a hair on the head of '34,' TE Greg Scarpa."

Jim Kossler's comments are another eulogy, this one for the FBI's informant program:

"The Top Echelon Informant Program is dead. The new informant guidelines are so onerous that a handler will never be able to protect the identity of his informant. The handler is required to make it clear to the informant that he can't protect the informant's identity. When you take the word *confidential* out of the equation, you can kiss the program good-bye. You might get a few who would sell you false information that would never come back to bite them. It's an informant program in name only and a disservice to the people the Bureau serves, especially in an age of terrorism."

Valerie Caproni has now worked her way up to being chief counsel for the FBI. She was quoted as accusing the retired agents—who vainly opposed the new guidelines—of "whining."

CHAPTER EIGHTEEN

THE INFORMANT SQUAD

As my lawyer Doug Grover, a former federal prosecutor who worked alongside us fighting the Mafia, said in his opening statement in my murder trial, regarding our championship season cases: "Informants were the fuel that made the engine of all these investigations run." So to load the tank for what was to follow, we needed informants in a hurry.

The informant squad was formed in 1981 and it was manned only by guys who'd demonstrated a knack. Our brass took agents from their other work and put them into a new squad devoted completely to developing informants. I was put on it with some of the best informant developers in the business, including Pat Marshall—who a few years later, with assistance from Charlotte Lang, would do a fantastic job putting together the Mafia Commission Case I supervised. The others included:

Larry Ferreira, Chris Mattiace, John Siracusa, Chuck McCormick, Doug Fencil, Mickey Mott, Bob Tucker, and Pat Collins. Our supervisor had his hands full with these bad boys. He'd be calling it a day as we'd be showing up. We worked wiseguy hours—New York after dark.

Our mission was permission. For Title IIIs.

One of the best ways to develop informants was to meet them on their own turf. I'd often head over to the wiseguys' hangouts and try to introduce myself to the boys.

"Is this business or pleasure?" the guy in charge would ask me.

"Pleasure," I would say.

Then I'd sit down with them at their social club for espresso and cannoli. I don't think espresso is necessarily a healthy drink for some wiseguys. Some have a hair trigger and don't need revving up. But the average wiseguy— if you're there strictly for pleasure, as you lead them to believe—is proud to act like a gentleman and be sociable.

Each one of us on the informant squad developed a lot of confidential informants that way.

Some of the best times we had in the informant squad were on gambling raids. By 1981 we were no longer doing Title IIIs on gambling cases. In fact, we were pretty much out of the gambling business. But we saw gambling raids as a way to meet and greet potential CIs, and getting probable cause for a regular search warrant on a gambling joint from one of our already established CIs was pretty easy. A typical raid was one we did on Cleveland Street not far from the site of the plaque commemorating Lieutenant Joseph Petrosino, who was murdered in Sicily.

The Cleveland Street illegal gambling casino was in an apartment down a short flight of stairs. We showed up for work at midnight. We sat in a truck outside the place and waited for it to fill up. Soon a black Cadillac showed up with Lenny DeMartino, the Gambino soldier whose spot it was, at the wheel. We watched and waited until he got to the front door. Then I backed the truck up closer. When the front door was opened, about a half dozen of us in FBI jackets sprang from the back of the truck and barged through the open door. I had a folding-stock shotgun with a sixteen-inch barrel. Everybody inside tossed their guns and money on the floor.

"Whose gun is this?"

Silence.

"Whose money is this?"

Silence.

Chris Mattiace found money in the old-fashioned overhead toilet box in the water closet. "Whose money is this, please?" Nothing.

"All right, you're all in custody. Get out your identification."

Big Chris had a chain saw like some movie monster. He whacked away at the felt crap tables and blackjack tables. There was some sophisticated gambling equipment in that joint that Chris sawed in half. Chips flying, he went right through them.

We scooped up all the guns and the money—loads of hundred-dollar bills. We took Polaroids of everyone in the room and got all their information. We had a portable copier with us and copied their driver's licenses, credit cards, whatever.

Later, back at the squad, we divvied up these IDs and each agent got a few to try to develop as informants. The gamblers knew it took six months before they'd be indicted and arrested in the federal system, so we had some time. Some of these gamblers were on probation or parole and stood to get thrown back into jail. We'd offer to help them out for them helping us out. While we'd get a lot of bullshit, every once in a while we'd get something hot that not only made the raids worthwhile, but brought a bonus payment to the deserving new CI. We'd get Title III probable cause out of some of them.

We never did arrest any of them. None of them were actually caught gambling. When we got to seeing a few of the same guys at other raids, and they began to realize we weren't serious about arresting them, they had no incentive to become CIs, so toward the end of the days of the informant squad we were doing very few raids.

The thing we missed most about the raids was the food. We never busted in on a joint until we watched the guy with the food arrive and we'd make sure he brought all the food in from his car.

On Cleveland Street, out of respect, we saved Lenny DeMartino for last. Lenny, of course, insisted it was his first time in the club. After we let the gamblers go, we sat down with Lenny and enjoyed pastry from Ferrara's, a famous New York bakery, espresso, the best provolone and Italian cold cuts, meatballs, amazing bread. Chris and I were brought up right. "Nundja waste-a the food-a." It's a sin.

Chris remembers a case that shows the treachery that permeates the Mafia: "I'll never forget that raid we made on Long Island on Vinny Naturo's house. He was a Gambino. We broke his bathroom walls based on the information we had from our CI. We found over a half million in cash that Vinny had accumulated by holding back gambling money from his capo. He had a beautiful house. It was Christmas and Vinny had a fifteen-foot Christmas tree and life-size moving toy soldiers like they have at FAO Schwarz. He made bail, came home, and rather than face his capo and have to explain the half million, he hung himself in his garage. I remember how we started that night, so innocent, in Judge I. Leo Glasser's house. While the judge sat in a back room studying our probable-cause affidavit Mrs. Glasser served us Oreos and milk."

One of our challenges on the informant squad was to get a TE informant from inside the Bonanno Family. That was a tough family to crack. We just couldn't make any of the big guys. Later on I did get a Bonanno capo who helped out for a short period. He was a disillusioned man whose heart gave out about a year after I started working him. But we didn't have to worry.

From wannabes around the Bonanno Family we heard about a new associate with "killer eyes." Joe Pistone surfaced from his years in the Bonanno Family in July 1981. All of a sudden we woke up to discover we had more than cracked the Bonannos. We had our own agent inside every day as one of them. The new guy with "killer eyes" was one of ours.

During those years we all worked together and we all deserve equal credit, except for Joe. He is in a class by himself. The first trial that Joe testified in was the first of the RICO family cases in New York to go to trial. It was the first of a dozen or so that Joe testified in for the New York office. Plus he went all over the country. For that first Bonanno Family RICO trial, Chris and I were temporarily pulled from the informant squad to keep an eye out for Joe during his testimony. A wiseguy in the audience stared at Joe and put his finger to his head and pulled an imaginary trigger. Chris and I had that guy out of that courtroom and into the men's room to inspect the plumbing so fast you'd think it was Clark Kent changing into Superman. Protecting Joe by any means was paramount.

One day during that trial we went out to the food carts in front of the courthouse. In those days there were no credit cards. You'd lay out the cash you were given by the supervisor, but you had to bring back receipts and the change. Joe couldn't go outside to eat with us out of concern that someone might shoot him for real. So we bought a nice Italian sandwich for him from an Umberto's Clam House food cart. We asked for a receipt and it was signed: Matty Ianello Jr. The son of Matty "The Horse" Ianello! Here was the son of one of the most feared and respected men in the history of the American Mafia making a sandwich for the most hated man in the history of the American Mafia. If the Horse's son knew who we were getting that sandwich for, he'd have put some rat poison in it so he could collect the half million that CIs had told us the Commission put out on Joe's head.

On the informant squad we'd occasionally do other "odd jobs." One night we had to serve a subpoena on Chin Gigante, the ex-boxer who, in 1957, failed to kill Boss Frank Costello for Don Vito Genovese. Chin was one of three men we suspected at the time of running the Genovese Family. His strategy to prevent going to trial on a pending Genovese Family RICO indictment was to act as if he had dementia from years in the ring. He'd sit in his social club in a bathrobe with a cabbie's hat on. What a sight that was.

The Chin's crew would congregate outside. His consigliere, Bobby "The Finger" Manna, would come out, touch his chin to signify Gigante, then the Finger would point his finger at whomever the Chin wanted to see and that guy would go in. It would go on all night like that, with the Finger never uttering a word until all their business was done.

It was a hot July night. We pulled up in front of Chin's Triangle Social Club on Sullivan Street in Greenwich Village in our black Plymouth Fury III and parked across the street. The place was like Grand Central Terminal that night—it was packed, and there was a crowd of fellas hanging out outside. As soon as they made us—which took a second once they spotted our agency-issued car—they scrambled inside and closed the door. We got back in our car and turned on the air-conditioning. We knew they had no air-conditioning and no windows. And they all chain-smoked, whether it be cigars or cigarettes.

When we thought it was time to show some mercy, we walked in. The Chin was at the back table. The Finger stepped in front of us and we flashed our credentials and without a word he stepped aside. We headed toward the Chin and it was like the parting of the Red Sea.

Chris recalls: "I got up to his table and I said, 'Mr. Gigante, I have a subpoena for you.' Chin just stared straight ahead as if I wasn't there, with his elbow on the table and his head in his hand—a look that had fooled psychiatrists. I pulled up a chair, bent down and got my face under his nose, and said, 'This is a federal grand jury subpoena.' I tucked the subpoena into his bathrobe. 'You have been served,' I said, and headed out with Lin covering my back. All of a sudden, as I reached the door, I heard Lin at the top of his voice yell at Bobby Manna, 'Don't you ever fucking try to touch an FBI agent again in your life.' Manna froze in his tracks with his pointing finger ready to tap my shoulder. We continued out the door and Manna slammed it shut on us.

"Fuck them, we said. We sat in our air-conditioned car and watched them sweat inside with the door slammed shut for a good long while. They'd open the door to see if we were still there and you'd see the cigar smoke trying to escape. We drove off and they opened the door after us. We just went around the block and pulled up again and they slammed the door shut again.

"We came back again the next few nights, and each time, slam went the door. Again they'd open it to see if we were still there. I think when they couldn't see us it worried them more than when they could. I'm not sure this was informant development, but you've got to have a little fun."

But our job was to develop CIs and that's how we put in most of our time.

When it came to informant development, I believed in just talking to as many people as you could about anything at all—approach them on any pretext, even if you make up a fake reason. If you talk to enough people, sooner or later one of them will talk back. It may be years after you talk to him, but he'll have your name and number and a face to go with it.

As Chris Mattiace puts it: "Informant development is a marathon, not a sprint."

One evening Agent Bobby Levinson asked me if I wanted to get some dinner, but I had just gotten a call from a CI letting me know that Christy Tick Furnari, the Lucchese Family consigliere, had just arrived at the 19th Hole Restaurant—a Lucchese hangout across the street from a Brooklyn golf course. Christy would meet there twice a week with the Colombo Family consigliere, Gerry Lang Langella, and exchange information.

It was a good opportunity to introduce myself to Christy; maybe he could provide some good information. Bobby said he would take the ride with me.

By the time we got there Christy was coming out. So we stood in the doorway and chatted with him. It was pouring down rain, but we were under an awning. A Lucchese made guy, a high-profile soldier named Gaspipe Casso, came hustling toward the door to get in out of the rain. Naturally, to go past Christy he'd have to pay his respects to his consigliere. You don't just try to walk around a consigliere and go inside without kissing his cheek. This was especially true for Gaspipe Casso. A consigliere doesn't have a crew, but he is permitted to keep one soldier as his personal aide-de-camp. Gaspipe Casso was that soldier and he worked directly for and under Christy Tick. These direct connections between Gaspipe, Tick, and Gerry Lang would be important to me later in my OPR scandal.

So Bobby and I did our duty and shifted our position so that Gaspipe couldn't get anywhere near Christy to plant a kiss on him. Bobby was a big guy, six four. Gaspipe didn't want to slight us either because we were with Christy. Meanwhile, he's getting soaked. As he moved, respectfully, we casually moved. Finally, Christy started laughing, and said, "Come on, guys, let the poor guy in." We all laughed.

Christy never reached out to me. I never counted on it, but you take a shot. You never know. Five years after I reached out for Christy, we convicted him in the Mafia Commission Case and he got a hundred years.

Mafia expert Selwyn Raab in his book *Five Families* observed that the Lucchese Family was "more seriously affected than any other" by the job we did in the Mafia Commission Case. Again, thanks to Scarpa.

As the result of our putting away Christy, Gaspipe Casso was made the underboss because of his close relationship with Christy. Gaspipe—way too inexperienced for the job—went on a serial killing spree, suspecting everybody of everything and cleaning house in his family. In January 1993 Gaspipe was arrested on a RICO indictment for this bloodbath.

On Valentine's Day 1994, a month after Favo initiated my first scandal and two weeks before Gaspipe's scheduled RICO trial, Gaspipe offered to become a CW. He confessed to thirty-six murders, and pleaded guilty to several of them on March 1, 1994. He now faced anywhere from zero to four-hundred-plus years. Gaspipe was taken to the Valachi suite in El Paso to be debriefed. If he provided substantial and singular information, he would be given a 5K1, that is, essentially a letter recommending a lenient sentence. Sammy "The Bull" Gravano got five years for nineteen murders thanks to his 5K1 letter.

In his debriefing Gaspipe rolled on the then unknown

but now infamous Mafia Cops—Louis Eppolito and Stephen Caracappa, two Italian NYPD detectives who had provided heads-ups on imminent arrests, the names of informants, and the home addresses of intended murder victims and tons of other inside information to Gaspipe. Gaspipe said they were his "crystal ball." He revealed that he paid them a $4,000 monthly retainer and bonuses for important information like imminent arrests. Over the years they'd gotten over $350,000 from him.

On one occasion in 1986, the Mafia Cops kidnapped a young wannabe and handed him over to Gaspipe so Gaspipe could torture information out of him and kill him. In 1990 the Mafia Cops put their flashers on and pulled over Gambino capo Eddie Lino for a traffic infraction on the Belt Parkway and shot him in the head for Gaspipe.

Another time Gaspipe wanted the address of Nicky Guido, a shooter in a hit attempt on his own life. The Mafia Cop Caracappa used his own ID to access the police computer to find Guido's address. The only problem was that he accessed the wrong Nicky Guido. The address he gave Gaspipe was for a young Nicky Guido who worked for the phone company and who was on the list to join the fire department. The innocent young man was gunned down on Christmas Day while showing his uncle his new car.

Gaspipe gave up everything on the Mafia Cops, but through bad behavior in prison, he lost his CW deal and the investigation against the Mafia Cops went into limbo for a decade. Gaspipe is still in prison for life, trying to get someone interested in his story.

In March 2005 the FBI and the Brooklyn D.A.'s Office finally got another cooperating witness to replace Gaspipe—Gaspipe's bagman—and they arrested the Mafia Cops on a RICO indictment in Las Vegas, where the two had retired to pursue movie careers. The Mafia Cops arrest took place almost exactly a year before my arrest. My murder charges were very similar to theirs, as I allegedly gave Scarpa the address of Lorenzo Lampasi so he could hit him.

Even though an investigator with Hynes's office who would play a vital role against me Tommy Dades, had helped develop the case, the Brooklyn D.A. got kicked off the Mafia Cops case by the U. S. attorney. Dades would not be called as a witness in the trial. D.A. Hynes, always more interested in publicity than in doing his job, had given *60 Minutes* a heads-up on the planned arrests and had tried to persuade the federal prosecutor to make the arrests on a Sunday to accommodate the TV show.

This *60 Minutes* tie-in would also help Tommy Dades and Michael Vecchione. Despite criticism from ethics experts, the two had signed a book and movie deal on the Mafia Cops case.

"Getting kicked off that very high-profile case was very embarrassing for Hynes," recalls my lawyer Mark Bederow. "Lin's case took the heat off Hynes. Even if he lost Lin's case, Hynes would get accolades for at least giving it a shot." Six days after my cold and bright night in the lockup of the Brooklyn D.A.'s Office, cuffed to my chair, the two Mafia Cops were convicted by the feds on all of their RICO counts, including committing eight murders. The murdering cops got multiple life sentences.

And I got lumped in with them in the media. Eight murders! They only got me for four murders.

Wait a minute. What am I thinking? I was framed for five murders. I was indicted for four, but I was sued civilly for one more—a wrongful-death claim brought by the victim's wife seeking monetary damages.

This murder was the original frame, the one hatched by the capo cousins Jo Jo and Chuckie Russo, but rejected by the Brooklyn D.A.

"Nicky Black" Grancio was a capo on the other side of the war against Scarpa. I was accused of conspiring with Scarpa to kill Nicky Black on the afternoon of January 7, 1992, when the war was less than two months old. Nicky Black was the first significant kill by Scarpa's side and he was the only capo killed by either side.

Scarpa and his hit team, including the former grocery boy Larry Mazza, were out scouting in their car. They were armed and hunting for the enemy in enemy territory.

"We're trying to make peace. We gotta stop all this shit," Nicky Black had just told his crew.

Then Larry Mazza spotted him sitting in his high-end SUV. According to the lawsuit against me, Scarpa called me and asked me to pull the police surveillance on Nicky Black so that they could kill him. The lawsuit said I then had Detective Joseph Simone and his partner, Detective Patrick Maggiore—the two NYPD members of the Colombo Family War Joint Task Force who were keeping an eye on Nicky Black—called at 1:30 p.m. to come in for a meeting. At 3:15 p.m., Scarpa surprised Nicky Black.

"This one's from Carmine [Persico]," Scarpa said to the accompaniment of a hail of bullets. At least Scarpa didn't say, "This one's from Lin."

I guess they borrowed that plotline from *The Godfather*. I was Captain McCluskey, who pulled the bodyguards from Don Corleone's hospital bedside so the Don's enemies could move in for the kill.

Coincidentally, and as I'll explain in time, Detective Joseph Simone, a twenty-year veteran and a father of six, was the first fellow law enforcement officer that Chris Favo ever officially accused of corruption—even before me.

The informant squad worked hard and was successful. We made many new contacts and honed our skills. The information we were able to provide—information we got from our CIs—was fed to the appropriate squad and helped further many investigations. The CIs were our heavy artillery in this war, and developing informants and keeping the quality information coming was all-important. This is why we protected our CIs and kept their identities secret. We didn't even identify them to other agents.

Chris Mattiace remembers an incident when an agent made the mistake of trying to find out the name of a CI: "We were on the informant squad and a new agent was working general crime, which would be bank robberies, hijacking, and the like. Lin's informant came up with info on a crime this guy was working, so Lin provided that info to the agent. This agent comes over smoking a cigarette.

" 'Who is your informant?' the agent casually asks.

"There was deadly silence. I thought Lin was going to kill him.

" 'Get the fuck out of here, and you're never getting another piece of information from me again,' Lin said."

"That poor agent probably didn't know what hit him. Maybe he didn't know better. In general crime, your CI is short-lived. He might know where a hijacked load is. In the criminal arena, maybe some agents do exchange names. But in Organized Crime, your informant is for the long haul. And in Organized Crime, what that agent did is a mortal sin.

"As close as we were, Lin never once even hinted to me who '34' was. I never heard of Scarpa until the newspaper leaks. The only thing I fault Lin about is giving Scarpa's name to Favo."

Hey, when that Colombo Family War broke out, I had the majority of my squad working the Grand Finale Case. It was a Bonanno Family social club on Grand Avenue in Maspeth, Queens. Big Joey Massino had about a year left in jail, but he was in communication with his acting Boss, "Good Looking Sal" Vitale and his guys at that club. Next door to the club there was a public library and in front of the library was a pay phone that they used.

According to a June 25, 1991, Scarpa 209 that helped us bug the Grand Avenue club and tap the pay phone in front of the library: "Bonanno Acting Boss SAL VITALE conducts much of the BONANNO Family gambling and loan-sharking business at the club." Scarpa's next 209 reads ". . . most of the BONANNO capos can be found at this location several days each week." Scarpa reassured our Title III judge that at this club in Maspeth: "BONANNO Family business is discussed." On September 19, 1991 Scarpa reported that the club is "a place where the illegal proceeds are counted and distributed." We were getting good stuff on the wire or the judge would not have re-upped it every thirty days.

This case was very labor-intensive: two fresh men every eight hours on shift work monitoring the two wires twenty-four hours a day; several men on surveillance; and men organizing the information we were collecting.

Favo was now my Colombo guy, and while I had Grand Finale to supervise on my Bonanno side, I needed to delegate to him on the Colombo side. In the summer of 1991, with rumors of a war brewing and peace negotiations ongoing, I wanted Favo to understand the reliability of the information that I fed to him. It seemed to me he ought to know about Scarpa so that he knew I could get him singular information if the shooting started.

He was a better choice to coordinate the war information than the rest of the FNGs I had working Colombo. They'd arrived just that spring. Favo was an extremely hard worker. In fact, he worked too hard. He'd work fifteen hours a day seven days a week.

One time he went on a two-week vacation with his wife. I probably forced it on him. He left on a Friday after work and returned to the office on Monday, telling me he had to cut it short. Later that day I got a call from his wife. She was upset with me because they were supposed to have two weeks together and on the fourth day he claimed he got a call from me, something came up, and I needed him back in the office. The poor woman wanted Favo to spend more time at home. I just said I'd urge him to spend more time at home. I did, but to no avail.

I was nearing retirement and I was thinking of grooming Favo to take Scarpa. But Chris Mattiace is right. I'd already sized Favo up as a guy without a knack for handling sources. He could sweep up CWs with Blakey's broom and dustpan, debrief them, and get them into Witness Protection, but that's not a knack.

CHAPTER NINETEEN

OUR CHAMPIONSHIP SEASON

Surely our championship season in the FBI began long before I became an agent and will go on long after I'm gone. But the Organized Crime section in the New York office in the 1980s was like no other before it. We were all making history, seemingly by the minute. Things went so fast that we occasionally missed some of the details, only to learn about them at retirement parties.

The detail none of us missed was that day in July 1981 when Joe Pistone was pulled up from his deep cover after years of being a high-ranking associate in the Bonanno Family, a man who was due to get straightened out at the next ceremony in December. Joe was pulled from undercover against his wishes; he wanted to stay in and get his button because he felt he would then be able to penetrate even deeper and obtain even more information.

Jim Kossler had begun our 1980s run by introducing us to RICO. We knew enough when Joe surfaced to realize instantly that our heroic colleague had already jump-started our RICO business plan. As the Mafia's morale went down when he exposed their secrets, so ours went up. If Joe could do what he did, was there anything that was too hard to do? I don't think so.

The New York office's first family RICO case was the first of the cases that Joe made. It went to trial on July 19, 1982. There were no Bosses or capos among the defendants, but the button men on trial were key figures in the Bonanno Family empire being run by Boss Rusty Rastelli from his prison cell. Two capos had been indicted, but were not available by the time of the trial. Capo Sonny Black—the one who sponsored Joe—got whacked and had his hands cut off for that mortal sin. Capo Big Joey Massino went on the lam. All six feet and 350 pounds of Massino hid out in the Pocono Mountains, Russell Bufalino territory, for two years.

At trial, the jury heard Lefty Guns Ruggiero say to Joe: "Now you're going to get straightened out, Donnie . . ." Then, as an insider on the verge of being made, a witness speaking from personal experience not hearsay, Joe explained to the jury just what it meant to be a made man, a capo, an underboss, and a Boss in a Mafia criminal enterprise and just how the enterprise was all held together by the ruling Commission. Our victory in this case was our first Mafia family RICO win. It was a triumph for all of us. From that day forward we all knew for sure that RICO could be used successfully in labeling a Mafia family a "criminal enterprise."

A year later, in the summer of 1983, I let our ASAC, Frank Storey, talk me into coming off the street—a job I loved—and going into the office as supervisor of the Bonanno Family squad. I agreed on the condition that I could keep my TE informants, including Scarpa, and that I could pick some good agents for my team. Right away I picked Pat Marshall. Pat, a New York Yankee fan from Baltimore, was hardworking, bright, personable, a self-starter, and a team player. More importantly, he was a dynamite developer of CIs. Once I overheard an FNG on the squad ask Pat how come they seemed to give him all the good cases. "What the hell are you talking about?" Pat said. "Nobody gives you a case. You develop your own leads from your own sources and you bring them to Lin and you go from there."

A squad usually has about fifteen men, but for a few weeks it was just the two of us until agents began to arrive from other squads. We started at ground zero because the former Bonanno squad had been handling Joe, his security, his debriefings, his leads, and his cases for the previous two years ever since his surfacing. As a consequence those guys had lost touch with what was happening with the family. First thing I did was assign Pat the job of finding capo Big Joey Massino.

Just weeks after I was put in charge of the Bonanno Family squad, Jim Kossler came to me and said, "We've got a case we want you to supervise. We'll go over it in Rudy's office tomorrow morning."

"Rudy's office," I said. "It must be big."

"It's a dream of a case," Jim said. "I think you'll enjoy it."

Jim Kossler, Jules Bonavolonta, and Rudy Giuliani, then the U.S. attorney for Manhattan, and some other honchos sat me down in Rudy's office and invited me to supervise a case they'd dreamed up, the Mafia Commission Case. This was, indeed, a dream case and I was honored. We would indict the Commission as the "criminal enterprise." But it meant that Pat Marshall would spend all his time on that case and I'd lose his expertise on the Bonanno Family.

"How the fuck are we going to do this?" Pat waved his hand at our absent squad.

I laughed because I knew exactly how. Pat was going to do it. He was one of the best, and if anyone could do it, it was him. I hadn't been a supervisor for long, but I knew that much already. Later I showed mercy and gave him Agent Charlotte Lang to help with the enormous workload.

The case was initiated on September 28, 1983. I gave our new operation the code name Five Star because we were out to get the stars at the top of each of the five families. At the time every squad was working a family RICO case against the hierarchy, except the Bonanno Family squad, because I was just re-forming it.

There were Title IIIs up all over town.

Joe O'Brien of the Gambino squad had one up in Boss of Bosses Paul Castellano's seventeen-room mansion in Todt Hill, Staten Island. It was called the White House because Big Paul designed it to look like the real one. Big Paul had legitimate businesses that included interests in the Key Food and Waldbaum's supermarket chains. This allowed him to show enormous legitimate income. The Gambino Boss did all his family business in that house. Capos came to the White House for meetings.

Big Paul had every conceivable security measure including an eight-foot-tall brick wall, two Dobermans, sensors, floodlights, and video surveillance provided by a security company. What with the live-in domestic help, somebody was home all the time. So Joe O'Brien, Bruce Mouw, and Jim Kallstrom decided to keep it simple. They knocked out his cable-TV service, and posing as a cable-TV repairman, one of Kallstrom's wizards planted bugs.

For the Colombo squad, bugs were installed at table one in the Casa Storta Restaurant in Brooklyn. Junior Persico was in jail, but his right-hand man, Gerry Lang Langella, conducted family business at table one when the restaurant closed. Junior Persico would telephone the Casa Storta from Danbury prison. Thanks to his prisoner's rights, he was able to conduct Colombo Family business and order hits. Later he would run the Colombo Family War from Lompoc Prison in California.

The Genovese squad had bugs installed in Boss "Fat Tony" Salerno's Palma Boys Social Club located in a tenement on 115th Street in East Harlem. In his club Fat Tony conducted both family business and Commission business. While in the basement working on the bugs, one of Kallstrom's guys got bitten on the ankle by a foot-long rat.

Ron Goldstock's New York State Organized Crime Task Force, working with Jim Kossler, had a bug installed in Sal Avellino's Jaguar. The $100,000 Jag was the mobile office and traveling headquarters of the Lucchese Family Boss Ducks Corallo.

In addition, the family squads had telephone wiretaps in all of the above.

"Why do you need our stuff?" a supervisor would occasionally complain to Pat.

"You'll still have your own family cases," Pat would reassure the supervisor, offering the same answer he'd given the supervisor the last time he asked for "stuff." "And you'll still be able to use your tapes."

Luckily Pat was so well liked and respected that he smoothed things over with the tougher eggs. Others like Chris Mattiace, supervising the Colombo Family, gladly made his men and tapes available for the greater good.

Besides these major bugs, there were others and all of them were very labor-intensive. And as Pat and Jim Kossler pointed out, each of these bugs had been green-lighted and been granted permission thanks to a huge contribution from my TE "34."

I don't know whose idea the case was, but I suspect Blakey had it in mind in the design of his plan early on. I know one thing: Manhattan's U.S. Attorney Rudy Giuliani certainly grabbed onto it. He was all over it. We'd go across the street to update him every week at least.

Rudy came out from behind his desk. We'd sit in easy chairs and talk. I found him a very charismatic guy, and he had compassion. He was a very quick study, and made intelligent comments. Plus, he pretty much left us alone to go through the vast quantities of information.

At one point Rudy made a choice not to personally prosecute the Commission in court. He had indicted Stanley Friedman, the boss of the Democratic Party in the Bronx, for taking kickbacks on contracts for parking meters. Rudy applied RICO in this new manner. That is to say, the "criminal enterprise" was a cadre of corrupt politicians. In terms of proof and legal theory, it was a tougher case than the Mafia Commission Case would turn out to be. When it happened that both cases were scheduled at the same time, Rudy opted to try the harder political scandal and turned over the prosecution of the Mafia Commission to Mike Chertoff, who went on to join President George W. Bush's cabinet as director of Homeland Security. However, Rudy continued to guide and champion the Commission Case.

After the Commission Case indictment, Rudy said: "The case should be seen as the apex of the family cases . . . It is an attempt, if we can prove our charges, to dismantle the structure that has been used since the beginning of organized crime in America."

"You can be a royal pain in the ass," I said to the demanding Mike Chertoff more than once.

Chertoff would just laugh. He was an exceptionally brilliant trial attorney and a brilliant organizer of complicated cases. Along with the rest of the Commision Case group, he and I had hundreds and hundreds of discussions and meetings.

Pat and Charlotte, with help from the other squads, went through all the tapes and found a fair amount of evidence of the Commission's existence, its membership, and many of its activities and decisions.

On one tape, Genovese Boss Fat Tony Salerno is heard picking the next Teamsters union president from his perch at the Palma Boys Club on 115th Street. In discussing a troublemaker in Buffalo, Fat Tony is overheard saying: "The Commission wants it straightened out . . . Tell him it's the Commission from New York. Tell him he's dealing with the big boys now." At the Palma Boys, Lucchese Boss Ducks Corallo was heard talking to Fat Tony about made men: "You pick them, and you kill them."

On a tape from a bug planted in his Jaguar, Corallo is heard criticizing the forcibly retired Boss Joe Bananas for spitefully revealing the secrets of the Commission in his 1983 book, *A Man of Honor*, and in a *60 Minutes* promotional interview. Corallo complained that because of the book's revelations and Joe Bananas' appearance on the TV show, the FBI could use RICO and "lock you up under this act over here."

Paul Castellano sitting in his bugged White House was heard to comment about the trouble Joe Bananas had caused with the book and the *60 Minutes* interview: "They're going to make us be one tremendous conspiracy."

After reading Joe Bananas' book, Rudy Giuliani said, "If Bonanno can write about a commission, I can indict it."

The indictment in the case was sealed and set to be opened on Tuesday February 26, 1985, at which time the defendants would be arrested before they could flee.

"My favorite Sicilian, Joe Pistone, was in town on Monday the twenty-fifth to testify in a case," Pat Marshall recalls. "At the end of the day he and I headed out to dinner. On the way to eat we got a call on the radio to return to the office. Jimmy Kossler had gotten a call from our public information agent Joe Valiquette that the media had inside information that Jerry Capeci's newspaper was going to leak the story in the morning before we could make our arrests. We had to scramble together arrest teams and head out to scoop them all up. Within forty-five minutes we had every defendant in custody. I was in the lobby downstairs when Andy Kurins and Joe O'Brien came in with Paul Castellano. Fat Tony Salerno was standing in the lobby. When these two men looked at each other, their facial expressions told the story. They seemed to be saying to each other: 'They got us. It's all over.' They were resigned to defeat."

After the arrests were completed that night, Jim Kossler called Bob Blakey from the office and said: "It's the most exciting moment in my life in the Bureau."

There were two principal underlying crimes.

One was the murder of Bonanno Family Boss Carmine Galante. Galante was gunned down in 1979 with a cigar clenched in his teeth in the backyard dining area of Joe and Mary's Restaurant in Ridgewood on the Brooklyn-Queens border. Murdered along with Galante were Joe of Joe and Mary's, and Joe's insurance agent.

When Galante was a young hit man in 1943, he'd murdered Mussolini's enemy Carlo Tresca on orders of Vito Genovese. During the last twenty years of his life Galante controlled the family's heroin smuggling from Sicily. Evidence that the Commission voted to whack Galante included testimony from a relative by marriage of Junior Persico. His name was Fred DeChristopher. DeChristopher was married to Junior's first cousin. Besides the $50,000 reward, DeChristopher had his own crazy personal reason for cooperating. I didn't learn until a retirement party years later his other motive to turn on his wife's blood.

At the Mafia Commission trial, DeChristopher testified that Junior Persico had reminisced to him about how he got to know Carmine Galante very well when they served time together. Junior Persico said Galante "was a friend of mine and the top man in the Bonanno Family . . . And quite frankly I voted against him getting hurt." There it was, the Commission vote.

On the day Galante was whacked, coincidentally, the NYPD had video surveillance running on the street in front of the Gambino Family Ravenite Social Club. It picked up Bonanno soldier Bruno Indelicato arriving with the outline of what looked like a gun butt under his shirt. Bruno was celebrating and being congratulated for something he had done that was very important—lots of hugging and backslapping. Bruno was also limping.

Pat Marshall suspected that the celebration was for Bruno whacking Galante and that Bruno must have injured his leg during the chaotic hit. Pat decided he needed somehow to obtain a print of Bruno's left hand from the wrist to the pinky tip and to compare it to a print found on the door handle of the abandoned stolen getaway car used in the Galante hit. These were called palm prints and at the time only the FBI took such prints, so there were none on file for Bruno. Pat's solution came after Bruno was arrested with a gun in his possession. Pat got a warrant to search Bruno's body so that a doctor could check for signs of an injury that would have caused him to limp. It was a ruse. All the while the doctor was allegedly looking for signs of an old injury, Bruno, a coke fiend, laughed at them. Pat was really after the palm print. And he got it. *Bango*, it matched.

Coincidentally, in 1981, just before he was pulled, Joe Pistone had been given the contract to find and kill Bruno. Now Pat was killing him in trial with the matching prints.

The other underlying crime in the Mafia Commission trial was the existence of a side deal the Commission had put together for itself called the Concrete Club. Each Boss, except the Bonanno Boss, who'd been booted, participated in a scheme to rig bids on all concrete poured on all the construction jobs in the New York metropolitan area. In addition, the Concrete Club charged a kick-back of 2 percent of the gross on every concrete contract. Bugs in the bagman's car and office produced verbal evidence.

At the trial, Fred DeChristopher quoted Junior Persico as telling him "not a yard of concrete was poured in the City of New York where he and his friends didn't get a piece." DeChristopher said that Persico had told him that "his business was running a crime family."

Other witnesses included cooperating witness Joe Cantalupo, who owned Cantalupo Realty and kept Bensonhurst safe for Italian gangsters. Another was seventy-five-year-old Angelo Lonardo, a former Cleveland underboss who described the nationwide power of the Commission. These CW witnesses did so well that Mike Chertoff decided not to call Jimmy "The Weasel" Frattiano, who had helped us get Russell Bufalino. We had brought Frattiano in and were keeping him in a hotel, but Chertoff wisely knew that the enemy of good is better. By trying to use Frattiano's testimony to bolster his case, he could open the door for vigorous cross-examination by the defense on the murderous exploits of Frattiano.

A nice touch by Chertoff was opening the trial with two New York State troopers who had been at Apalachin in 1957. Here they were thirty years later continuing to expose the Mafia. He had the jurors watch the *60 Minutes* performance by Joe Bananas that Ducks Corallo and Paul Castellano complained about. We wound up using seventy-five recordings out of hundreds that Pat and Charlotte had to go through.

Most significantly the jurors got to see rare photos taken by my investigator on my murder charges Andy Kurins and his partner Joe O'Brien of the Bosses leaving a Mafia Commission meeting in Staten Island. And then the jurors heard Joe Pistone explain the friction in the Bonanno Family at the time Galante was hit, and that Commission approval was needed for such a hit.

In November 1986 Rudy got two RICO victories, the Mafia Commission Case and his own against Stanley Friedman.

Because Big Paul Castellano had been whacked in front of Sparks Steak House nine months before the Commission Case went to trial and his underboss died of cancer, the Gambinos were not in the Commission Case. With the Bonannos off the Commission, that left three families. And all three Bosses were convicted: Fat Tony Salerno of the Genoveses; Ducks Corallo of the Luccheses; and Junior Persico of the Colombos. Judge Richard Owens understood the significance of this trial and gave the Bosses each a hundred years. Also convicted were the Lucchese underboss Tom Mix Santoro and the consigliere Christy Tick Furnari; the Colombo underboss Gerry Lang Langella; and the Concrete Club bagman Ralph Scopo. They also got hundred-year sentences. The remaining defendant, Bruno Indelicato, got forty years.

The day the guilty verdicts on all 151 counts were

announced in court is a day none of us will ever forget. Looking back, I don't know if we were happier for what we did or for how happy we made Jim Kossler and Bob Blakey.

Pretty much right after the Mafia Commission Case we began to see a lot of the word *acting* in our 209s. More and more our CIs were telling us about acting Bosses, underbosses, consiglieres, and capos. My Scarpa 209 of April 4, 1988, reads: "LITTLE VIC ORENA was made official acting Boss . . . of the COLOMBO . . . FAMILY."

Our arrests and convictions created a vacuum at the top of the Mafia hierarchy. These positions needed to be filled and people were getting upped who had little to no experience. My Scarpa 209s talk about the meteoric rise of five-foot four-inch Carmine Sessa, the associate who helped roll Mary Bari into movers' blankets and dump her. He straightened out in 1988. In that same year he was upped to capo.

My Scarpa 209 of October 3, 1989, probably made me laugh because it applied to my Colombo-Bonanno squad, too: "The source said JUNIOR PERSICO seems to think that older, experienced leadership is needed at this time." Sadly, neither Junior nor I could retain the services of a headhunter.

My Scarpa 209 of June 12, 1990, reports: "CAR-MINE SESSA has been made the official consigliere of the COLOMBO Family." Made in 1988 and by 1990, Carmine Sessa, who was shorter than my grandmother, was the family consigliere—the elder statesman, the wise man, the Boss's confidant. It was the same year I got Chris Favo assigned to me.

In my 209 of August 13, 1991, Scarpa observed in connection with another matter that the family couldn't go to the Commission for help or advice to settle a dispute because "there is no formal COMMISSION."

Other agents with valuable sources were getting similar information.

Our business plan was on fire. In less than a year after Governor Mario Cuomo's "baloney" remarks, in which he denied the existence of the Mafia and bellyached that use of the term *Mafia* was an "ugly stereotype," we proved the hell out of it once and for all. As Junior Persico said during the trial: "Without the Mafia, there wouldn't even be no case here . . ."

After the sentencings we all received letters of commendation and cash bonuses from headquarters. I got $1,600 and Scarpa got a few thousand. I don't recall exactly, but it wasn't a lot. Of course, I didn't tell him that it had been his information and his proven reliability over many years that allowed us to win permission for all these bugs.

Clearly, for those who gave us our business plan this was the most important case in the office, the premier case against organized crime because it encompassed all five families and it destroyed their government. It would be two years before the Commission had another meeting and that was strictly to square things between Chin Gigante and John Gotti.

The same way Scarpa never wanted to be a capo, who in their right mind would want to be a Boss after they saw the damage we could do? But obviously there were low-level guys not in their right mind who were too cocky or too stupid to appreciate the danger. Inspired by greed, they were ready to fill the vacuum we created. The indictments in the Mafia Commission Case inspired knucklehead John Gotti to make his move on Castellano at a time when the Commission was feeling the heat and too afraid to meet or to act like a "commission." Before he hit Castellano to make his power grab, Gotti was an obscure hijacker and a degenerate gambler.

The Mafia Commission Case, by and large, was a case that went to school on and borrowed from the hard work done by agents and supervisors on many other major cases in the New York office.

It was RICO trial upon RICO trial.

There was a trial in 1984 in Milwaukee against the Milwaukee Boss and underboss that was based on Joe Pistone's work for the New York Bonanno Family. It was the first RICO conviction of a family Boss, and its roots were in the New York office. That trial alone put an end to any future Mafia family in Milwaukee.

The Colombo Family trial that Chris Mattiace supervised, involving the construction industry and the Concrete Club, ended in victory in May 1986. At sentencing on Friday the thirteenth of June 1986, Junior Persico got thirty-nine years. His son Little Allie Boy got twelve.

Evidence developed by the squads in all the other family investigations and cases, principally that of the Concrete Club, supported many of the allegations in the Mafia Commission Case.

During the two-month-long Mafia Commission trial, we got the exciting news that Laura Brevetti in the federal prosecutor's office in Brooklyn convicted the Bonanno Family Boss, underboss, and future Boss Big Joey Massino in a RICO labor trial involving moving-company union racketeering. Ironically, the FBI, which moved the furniture and equipment of its New York office from Sixty-ninth Street to its new quarters at 26 Federal Plaza, was a crime victim in that case. Boss Rusty Rastelli was now doomed to die in jail, which he did in 1991.

We lost an individual RICO case when Big Joey Massino voluntarily returned from the Pocono Mountains. We tried him on the evidence we'd used in the first Bonanno Family trial. Big Joey and his lawyers knew everything that was coming and were prepared for it all. Mike Chertoff and Pat Marshall had just come off the biggest victory of anyone's career and now Mike tried Massino and Pat testified for the prosecution, but Massino's lawyer, having read the transcript of the prior trial, knew just how to proceed and Big Joey walked. But he walked back to jail, where he was serving ten on Laura Brevetti's RICO labor conviction.

After the not-guilty verdict, Pat Marshall got a letter of consolation from Judge Robert Sweet, who presided over the jury trial. The judge complimented Pat on the job he and Mike did and said the jury just didn't understand RICO.

Our RICO cases kept giving us cause for celebration. There was a Gambino Family trial victory involving murder and the stealing of luxury cars for shipping to Kuwait.

Supervisor Brian Taylor headed a squad that focused on the Genovese Family's domination and control of the Fulton Fish Market, the center of the area's seafood industry. The Mafia charged a premium for every service rendered at the market. Taylor got frustrated trying to build a case because the Mafia didn't need to use any strong-arm tactics. Everyone knew who to pay. Anyone who balked would discover he bought forty pounds of yesterday's fish when he ordered fifty pounds of fresh fish. But without underlying criminal charges like assault or extortion, Taylor was having a tough time making anything stick. He went to Jim Kossler for advice.

"Why don't you try a civil RICO case?" Kossler asked.

"What the hell is that?" Taylor countered.

Soon Taylor was using another Blakey invention to seize back large chunks of American territory from the Mafia enemy. Instead of serving arrest warrants, the modest Vietnam veteran began serving civil lawsuit complaints with the USA as plaintiff and the made men as defendants. I don't think we teased him any more than he deserved for such sissy work. But Taylor had the last laugh when the Mafia was forced out of the market.

When I think of the Pizza Connection Case tried by future FBI Director Louis Freeh and Robert Stewart, it boggles my mind. The verdict in this case brought down the Bonanno Family heroin-smuggling operation carried out by Sicilians. It was called "Pizza Connection" because the Sicilians in the Bonanno Family had set up pizza parlors throughout the country as drop spots for heroin they smuggled into the country in pizza supplies. The operation was created by Joe Bananas in 1957 to avoid the harsh federal drug penalties imposed by the new Boggs-Daniel Act. Bananas brought Sicilians over to handle the work so that his own made men would be spared the harsh sentences if arrested. The Sicilians were expendable and replaceable. Also, the Sicilians were not needed on the street to generate gambling and other income for the family.

The Pizza Connection case against twenty-some-odd defendants went to trial on October 24, 1985, and ended in victory on March 2, 1987—seventeen months after it began. Tommaso Buscetta, who once pointed out that secrecy was more vital to the Mafia's power than violence, was the highest-ranking Sicilian ever to roll. When it was over, Rudy Giuliani said: "No one case can result in a massive destruction of the Mafia; however, the momentum is building."

Meanwhile, in Sicily, from 1986 to 1987, the courageous prosecutor Giovanni Falcone conducted the "Maxi Trial." In it, he convicted 338 members of the Sicilian Mafia. They avenged their convictions in 1992 by killing Falcone, his wife, and three bodyguards with a bomb under a bridge. Two months later they bombed and killed Falcone's protégé and successor, Paolo Borsellino.

We had a badly botched hit for vengeance on federal prosecutor William Aronwald on March 20, 1987. Colombo capo Joel "Joe Waverly" Cacace ordered Frank Smith and the Carini brothers to seek out and kill Aronwald. Frank Smith was a Lucchese Family associate and the Carini brothers were wannabes. That Colombo capo Joe Waverly used a Lucchese Family associate for the hit demonstrates how closely these two families worked together. The shooters found a man they thought was Aronwald and followed him into Young's Chinese Laundry in Queens. They fired into his back, killing him. The man they killed was the prosecutor's father, George Aronwald. Three months later the Carini brothers were killed on Joe Waverly's orders for the offense of doing a sloppy "piece of work."

Reasonably afraid that he was next, Frank Smith appealed to the Lucchese Family, his family of record. The Lucchese Family and the Colombo Family then had two high-level sit-downs in the summer of 1987 to determine Smith's fate. In an appeal like this, it helps the associate if he's a good earner. In the end, the Lucchese Family prevailed and Smith was spared. Smith was an excellent burglar in the Bypass Gang and some of these bypass burglaries were done with Colombo Family Gregory Scarpa Jr.'s crew. So it was win-win for both families.

There was another hit of a federal prosecutor discussed during our championship season.

From a Greg Scarpa 209: "On September 17, 1987, source advised that recent information disclosed that approximately a year ago all five NY . . . families discussed the idea of killing USA RUDY GIULIANI . . . JOHN GOTTI and CARMINE PERSICO were in favor of the hit. The bosses of the LUCCHESE, BONANNO, and GENOVESE Families rejected the idea, despite strong efforts to convince them otherwise by GOTTI and PERSICO."

I believe every word of that and I know Scarpa believed it. A vengeful Junior Persico had nothing more to lose and John Gotti was inexperienced and cocky enough to think he could pull off a stunt like that. And it makes sense that the Commission included the Bonanno Family's Rusty Rastelli in the vote even though he was not on the Commission. The Genovese and Lucchese bosses needed Rusty to break the tie because they knew he had more sense. The source of Scarpa's information probably was Junior Persico's brother Teddy, a capo. Teddy visited Junior every week in prison and talked to Scarpa all the time.

No surprise that Junior wanted to off Rudy; just a year prior he had gotten thirty-nine years in the Colombo Family trial and was then facing another hundred in the Commission trial. The 139 years in sentences were all courtesy of Rudy. As Junior Persico's wife lamented in a letter published in *Newsday*: ". . . just when we thought it was safe to resume our lives again along came RICO and Giuliani." Later we got information from a prison CI that corroborated Junior's plot to kill Rudy.

In 1993, when Joe Pistone's mentor, Lefty Guns Ruggiero, finished his Bonanno Family RICO sentence, we learned from two CIs that Lefty had gone to Big Joey Massino and asked for a hit on Joe. My top Bonanno guy, Jack Stubing, and I paid a visit to Big Joey at his home. He knew better than to let us in because we would have scouted the layout for future bugging locations. We never made it past the door.

"We heard Lefty's been around to see you about Joe Pistone," I said.

I waited, but he didn't say anything, so I went on.

"We just want you to know that if anything happens to Joe, we'll do what we gotta do."

"Nothing is going to happen," Big Joey said. "You can sleep on it."

I learned something from this encounter and I know Jack Stubing did, too. Boss Rusty Rastelli had died in jail in 1991. Big Joey Massino had gotten out of jail in 1992 after serving the sentence he received in Laura Brevetti's RICO labor conviction. Our squad all thought Massino probably was the Boss, but we didn't know for sure. Now we did.

"The man is the Boss," I said. "You can bank on it. He gave Joe an assurance that only a Boss can give."

*   *   *

This glorious period from 1980 to 1990 is the time when we really put a hurt on them. Whatever Eliot Ness and his treasury agent Untouchables did to the Capone gang in Chicago in the 1920s, we—the New Untouchables—did, and plenty more, to the entire Mafia in the 1980s. And what remains of the American Mafia is still feeling the blows we administered.

The Mafia slid straight downhill after that period. The Bureau is still doing pretty good work, but the Mafia never got back the source of power we took away from them—their ability to operate in secrecy. Today everybody comes running in. You make an arrest and everybody rolls over.

Although the Gambino Family's Big Paul Castellano and his underboss Neil Dellacroce died and were not part of the Mafia Commission Case, the work that Andris Kurins, Joe O'Brien, and the rest of the Gambino squad did against them paid off in a 1992 RICO trial when the loose-cannon, power-grabbing Boss John Gotti went away for life because his underboss, Sammy "The Bull" Gravano, rolled over and became a CW.

The Bonanno Family, except for the soldier Bruno Indelicato, was not in the Mafia Commission Case because: (1) Bonanno Boss Rusty Rastelli was already in jail for life; (2) Joe Pistone had wreaked havoc on them; and (3) the Bonanno Family had been booted from the Commission.

For many unfortunate reasons, the Bonanno Family was the only family to maintain a significant presence for about a decade after I was forced off as supervisor in 1994 during my OPR scandal. The Boss Big Joey Massino was regularly referred to in the press as "the Last Don." Then his underboss, best friend, and brother-in-law, Good Looking Sal Vitale, got hammered, rolled and became a CW, and decimated the family.

In 2004 Big Joey Massino met up with RICO again. Pat Marshall returned from his retirement out west to testify. We won the rubber match, best two out of three trials.

Judge Nicholas Garaufis observed during the sentencing of another cooperating witness in the Massino case, Frank Fiordilino: "Cooperating witnesses are essential to achieving justice, and you have done your part."

Fiordilino explained his motives: "I'm totally at peace with my decision to defect. I no longer have to lie, cheat, or pretend anymore. The Mob was and still is a farce that's built on deceit, venom, greed, and destruction. As for loyalty and respect, I never seen it. I could recall hundreds of conversations in which guys would sit around a table . . . bad-mouthing each other. I'm so glad that's behind me."

Fiordilino added something for Lieutenant Giuseppe Petrosino and his heirs, including Rudy Giuliani, Chris Mattiace, Jules Bonavolonta, Joe Pistone, and me: "I apologize as well, especially to anyone of Italian background, by conspiring and utilizing our culture in the same manner [that] the entertainment industry does with its stereotypes . . . Hollywood intensified my love for that life, and in the process blindsided what being Italian meant."

After Massino's RICO conviction by prosecutor Greg Andres, at the hands of, among others, Frank Fiordilino, Good Looking Sal, and better-looking Pat Marshall, Big Joey Massino became the first Boss of a family to roll. Three hundred and fifty pounds can do a lot of rolling.

The secret society was no secret anymore. Nor was it much of a society.

CHAPTER TWENTY

NOT SO QUIET ON THE EASTERN FRONT

Traditionally, the New York office of the FBI chose which of the two New York U.S. Attorneys' Offices—Brooklyn or Manhattan—to bring a case to. In Organized Crime, if we could justify the jurisdictional ties of the case, we all tended to bring our cases "across the street" to the Manhattan U.S. Attorney's Office—the Southern District. Certainly, the major cases of our championship season were Manhattan cases. Later, Rudy Giuliani let Brooklyn handle John Gotti in order to mend fences. In that case, there were Manhattan elements and Brooklyn elements and it could easily have gone to Manhattan. There was always a little undercurrent of neglect felt by the Brooklyn U.S. Attorney's Office—the Eastern District.

The only family RICO loss in our championship season was an early case against John Gotti and the Gambino Family that was tried in the Eastern District.

This was a case the FBI pulled out of and refused to participate in because the Brooklyn federal prosecutors, Diane Giacalone and John Gleeson, despite personal pleas by Jim Kossler and his boss, Tom Sheer, to Giacalone and Gleeson's boss, exposed the identity of one CI and planned on exposing a second.

Somehow the prosecutors learned that one of their Gambino associate defendants, a half Italian and half Mohawk Indian named Willie Boy Johnson, had been a CI for about a decade. The two put deadly pressure on Willie Boy to become a CW by threatening to expose his CI status. Willie Boy refused, fearing Gotti. You have to wonder how Willie Boy could be expected to trust federal prosecutors who threatened to breach the federal government's promise to him that his CI status was confidential.

They added pressure by threatening to expose Willie Boy in open court and he pleaded with them not to. They repeated their threats, continued to offer the Witness Protection Program, and still Willie Boy refused.

Giacalone stood up in open court and exposed Willie Boy as a "rat." Johnson scowled, denying the accusation while trying to look fiercely loyal to Gotti, his childhood friend.

Failing with Willie Boy, Giacalone and Gleeson then planned on exposing CI Billy Batista, a hijacker and bookie in Gotti's crew. Feeling the prosecutors' pressure, Batista vanished, leaving a note for FBI Supervisor Pat Colgan: "Thanks for everything, Pat. I'm out of here."

Giacalone and Gleeson lost their trial. A few months

later, Willie Boy lost his life, gunned down on his way to his construction job. I don't know what happened to Giacalone, nor do I care. Gleeson, who was second chair to Giacalone, went on to become a well-respected federal judge.

Five years later, when Sammy "The Bull" Gravano rolled, he confirmed that it was Giacalone's actions that got Willie Boy killed.

Treatment of CIs like that by federal prosecutors is why we uniformly and steadfastly refused to reveal CIs' identities. Some prosecutors were tempted to be what Professor Blakey called them—"scalp collectors." They were shortsighted, only trying to win their case. It's the kind of thinking that caused federal prosecutors to ignore and ridicule RICO throughout the 1970s. It took the FBI in the persons of Jim Kossler and Jules Bonavolonta to think long term and to turn RICO into what it became in our hands during the 1980s.

Giacalone did another shortsighted thing before trial when the prosecution filed a motion to revoke Gotti's bail despite pleas from Ron Goldstock, the head of the New York State Organized Crime Task Force. Goldstock, of the Sal Avellino Jaguar bug, had a bug up and running in John Gotti's office. It had been up for four months, but by law would have to be taken down if Gotti went to jail. Giacalone refused to drop their motion to send Gotti to jail and the bug had to come down. Sending Gotti to jail pending trial and thereby losing that bug cost us a great deal at a crucial time and over the long haul. And there was absolutely no prosecutorial reason to remand Gotti to jail. The move was just a headline grabber.

This Gotti case in 1986 was the only sour note in our whole season, but the FBI was not involved in the case, except in the instance when our Gambino supervisor, Bruce Mouw, warned the federal prosecutor in Brooklyn that the FBI had CIs that had reported an effort by Gotti's people to get to a juror. It turned out to be corroborated information when Sammy the Bull rolled in 1992 and ratted out the juror involved. Nevertheless, that was one juror. All twelve voted not guilty.

The Eastern District's jurisdiction included Queens, Long Island, and Staten Island, but the bulk of its Mafia cases came from the streets of Brooklyn. As the 1980s came to a close, there were three other matters in the Eastern District that would later come back to haunt me. Two of these were murders I got indicted for.

The way Mario Parlagreco got in with the crew was that his father bought a half interest in a deli for Mario to work in, legit. His father had a partner in the deli who also had a son. This son gets out of jail and he comes to work in the deli, too. Only he thinks all he has to do all day is smoke pot, put his hand in the till for money, and let Mario take care of the business. Mario's father goes to his partner and says *either you buy me out or I buy you out. The partner took over the deli then welshed on the $50,000 purchase price.*

It happened that the deli was two doors down from Greg Scarpa's club, the Wimpy Boys Athletic Club. Mario had seen wiseguys and associates come and go at the club and he'd gotten friendly with those who came into the deli. Mario hated to see his parents' life savings go down the drain. Who can blame him? So he went into the Wimpy Boys Club looking for help.

Greg Scarpa had a sit-down with Mario's father's partner and got all the money Mario's parents were entitled to. Scarpa announced to eighteen-year-old Mario that he's now with the crew that hangs out at the Wimpy Boys. At first it was harmless enough. Mario would run personal errands for Scarpa. Slowly he became more involved in their activities. He enjoyed the life. He really liked this leisure class of well-dressed young Italian men. Soon he was doing cocaine with them . . . and murders.

One murder that Mario was party to was that of Joe Brewster. Mario knew Joe Brewster from the Wimpy Boys. Joe Brewster's real name was Joseph DeDomenico, but Mario had no reason to know that. Mario did know that Joe Brewster, Gregory Jr., and Carmine Sessa were bosom buddies. Joe Brewster was a made man and he had been sponsored to get his button by the best man at his wedding, Greg Scarpa the father. Joe Brewster was the godfather of Gregory Jr.'s daughter.

By the summer of 1987, Gregory Scarpa Jr. was also a made man and was in charge of a crew of bank burglars that would bypass burglar alarms, break into banks at

*night, and invade safe-deposit boxes. Joe Brewster did a lot
of these bypass bank burglaries with Sal Fusco and Frank
Smith, the Lucchese Family associate who botched the hit on
federal prosecutor William Aronwald. Brewster also did
these bypass burglaries with Gregory Jr.'s crew.*

*In the summer of 1987, around the time of the high-level
sit-downs between the Lucchese Family and the Colombo
Family over the fate of Frank Smith, Gregory Scarpa Jr.
came up to Mario Parlagreco outside the Wimpy Boys and
said to him and some of the other Wimpy Boys' associates:
"Keep an eye on Brewster. He's been makin' himself scarce.
We want to see if he's flashing a lot of money. And swag,
too. Keep an eye out if he's got rings and shit from safe-
deposit boxes." Associate Kevin Granato reported back that
he heard Brewster was doing bypass-bank-burglary scores
with Lucchese Family associate Frank Smith and Sal Fusco
that Brewster did not report about to Gregory Jr.*

*One day at the Wimpy Boys, Joe Brewster brought in
some diamond earrings for his godchild, Gregory Scarpa
Jr.'s daughter. That got everybody's attention. Did Brewster get these earrings from a safe-deposit box during a bank
burglary he did on this own? Gregory Jr. didn't want earrings for his daughter; he wanted to know what Joe Brewster was up to. The alarm guy that Brewster used to bypass
the alarms was their guy and it was they who'd brought Joe
Brewster into the line of bypass burglary. That was more or
less Gregory Jr.'s justification.*

*Two years before this happened, Greg Scarpa told Lin
DeVecchio, who wrote up a 209, that Joe Brewster was doing
bypass bank burglaries and he identified Brewster's part-*

*ners as Frank Smith and Sal Fusco. For sure, Greg Scarpa
was pissed and made sure he got a share. Now here Brewster
was, two years later, still doing bypass burglaries with the
same two guys, but this time not reporting his scores and no
longer sharing.*

*Gregory Scarpa Jr.'s capo was Anthony "Scappy" Scar-
pati. Scappy was in jail in the South. Mario Parlagreco
would later testify as a CW that on two occasions he accompanied Gregory Scarpa Jr. to visit Scappy. The first trip
was to seek approval to kill Joe Brewster. Gregory Scarpa Jr.
gave Scappy two reasons for the kill. The first reason was
that Brewster had refused a "piece of work" that had been
assigned to him by Greg Scarpa. Refusing to kill is sufficient grounds to be killed. The second reason was that Brewster was dating a born-again Christian from Manhattan
and had "found God." That he was dating a born-again
was true. Gregory Jr. also tossed in a reference to Brewster's
cocaine use, but then they all did that.*

*On the second visit to Scappy in jail, Gregory Scarpa Jr.
was given permission by Junior Persico by way of Scappy to
kill Brewster. Junior Persico said, "If he found God, it is
time for him to join God."*

*Mario knew the real reason Brewster was being killed,
but he had to keep his mouth shut until seven years later
when he testified against "The Cousins," Jo Jo and Chuckie
Russo, in their RICO involving a Colombo Family War
murder. In that testimony Mario said that Joe Brewster
was killed "because Greg Jr. found out that he was doing
scores behind his back."*

Now this gets a little complicated because Scappy was

*Brewster's capo, too, not just Gregory Jr. and Greg the fa-
ther's capo. Joe Brewster was a made man, a soldier. He
didn't have to split a score with either of the Scarpas, who
were only soldiers, too. Ordinarily Brewster is obliged to
split upstairs, with Scappy, not sideways with the Scarpas,
who somehow feel entitled. So, no way Gregory Scarpa Jr.
can tell his real reason to their capo Scappy. It would com-
plicate matters.*

*Four years later, future CW Billy Meli, an associate and
accomplice in the Joe Brewster murder, ended up in the
same jail as Scappy. One day they talked about the Joe
Brewster hit and Scappy said he never believed the reasons
Gregory Jr. gave for wanting permission to kill Brewster,
and that Brewster's failure to split burglary scores made
more sense. Future CW Carmine Sessa would later say that
he was so incensed by the Brewster murder that as soon as he
became a made man and could go out on his own, he broke
off his ties with Greg Scarpa. People liked Joe Brewster.*

*Without saying why, on September 17, 1987, Gregory Jr.
told Mario Parlagreco to be outside his personal garage in
Bensonhurst at 7 p.m. At that time and place a white Cutlass drove up to Mario's garage. Gregory Jr. got out of the
passenger seat and told Mario that Joe Brewster was in the
backseat, dead. Mario looked inside and could see Joe Brewster slumped sideways. Joe "Sap" Saponaro drove the car
into the garage. He cleaned the fingerprints and drove
back out.*

*Future CW Billy Meli was driving a crash car. If a pa-
trol car came along and got nosy, he was to crash into it so
the Cutlass could go on its way. Gregory Jr. and Mario got*

into the crash car and followed the white Cutlass being driven by Joe Sap. Associate Kevin Granato drove another crash car in front leading the way. When they got to Seventy-second Street near Twentieth Avenue, Joe Sap parked the Cutlass, left the motor running, and got into the first crash car.

Billy Meli stopped his crash car near a sewer so Gregory Jr. could dump the gun after wiping off his prints.

The men rendezvoused at Romano's Restaurant.

Joe Sap complained loudly that his ears were killing him. Joe Brewster had been told that there was going to be a meeting of all made members of the Colombo Family. Brewster met Gregory Jr. at a restaurant and waited to be picked up. When they saw Joe Sap pull up in a white Cutlass, they left the restaurant and got in the car. Joe Sap was in the driver's seat. Gregory Jr. got in the front passenger seat. Joe Brewster got in the rear behind Gregory Jr. As the Cutlass pulled away from the curb Gregory Jr. reached under the seat and found the .38 that Billy Meli and Joe Sap had planted. It was like that scene in Dog Day After-noon. *Gregory Jr. turned toward Joe Brewster and shot him in the face and chest.*

Joe Sap said the windows were all up and the gun was right near his ear and he couldn't hear anything at Romano's. Joe Sap was not too happy.

Joe Sap used his ears as an excuse about the keys.

See, Joe Sap had stolen the Cutlass about two weeks prior for use in the murder. He had hot-wired the car. Now there's no way Joe Brewster gets in a car that doesn't have keys in the ignition. Right away he's going to know that he's

My father, Roy DeVecchio, and me, 1942.
My father served as captain in the financial branch
of the army during World War II.
Courtesy of Lin DeVecchio

My kid brother, Jay (age 5), my mother, Lois Lindley
DeVecchio, and me (age 17) standing on a dock in Yokohama
in 1957 around the time I left Japan for college.
Courtesy of Lin DeVecchio

My credentials photo for new agent training, 1966.
Courtesy of Lin DeVecchio

An Organized Crime squad, early 1970s.
I'm in the back row, second from the right.
Courtesy of Lin DeVecchio

A SWAT team that was sent to Wounded Knee, South Dakota,
during the AIM siege, 1973. I'm on the far right.
Courtesy of Lin DeVecchio

Me as a firearms instructor, early 1970s.
Courtesy of Lin DeVecchio

Me as a brick agent taking a break at the office
in the late 1970s.
Courtesy of Lin DeVecchio

Commission Case (1985–1986) Award Presentation
Left to right: Pat Marshall, Charlotte Lang, me,
Joe Pistone, Jim Kossler.
Courtesy of Lin DeVecchio

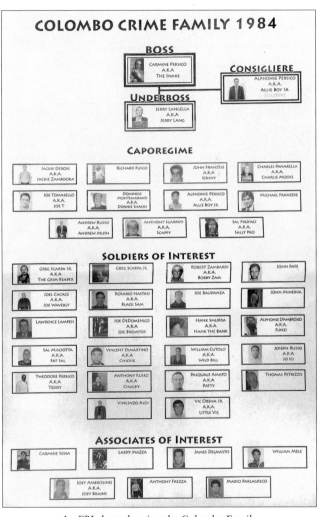

COLOMBO CRIME FAMILY 1984

BOSS
CARMINE PERSICO
A.K.A
THE SNAKE

CONSIGLIERE
ALPHONSE PERSICO
A.K.A.
ALLIE BOY SR.
FUGITIVE

UNDERBOSS
JERRY LANGELLA
A.K.A
JERRY LANG

CAPOREGIME

JACKIE DEROSS A.K.A. JACKIE ZAMBOOKA	RICHARD FUSCO	JOHN FRANZESE A.K.A SONNY	CHARLES PANARELLA A.K.A. CHARLIE MOOSE
JOE TOMASELLO A.K.A. JOE T	DOMINICK MONTEMARANO A.K.A. DONNIE SHACKS	ALPHONSE PERSICO A.K.A. ALLIE BOY JR.	MICHAEL FRANZESE
ANDREW RUSSO A.K.A. ANDREW MUSH	ANTHONY SCARPATI A.K.A. SCAPPY	SAL PROFACI A.K.A. SALLY PRO	

SOLDIERS OF INTEREST

GREG SCARPA SR. A.K.A THE GRIM REAPER	GREG SCARPA JR.	ROBERT ZAMBARDI A.K.A. BOBBY ZAM	JOHN PATE
JOEL CACACE A.K.A. JOE WAVERLY	ROSARIO NASTASI A.K.A. BLACK SAM	JOE BAUDANZA	JOHN MINERVA
LAWRENCE LAMPESI	JOE DEDOMENICO A.K.A. JOE BREWSTER	HANK SMURRA A.K.A HANK THE BANK	ALPHONSE D'AMBROSIO A.K.A. FUNZI
SAL MISCIOTTA A.K.A. FAT SAL	VINCENT DIMARTINO A.K.A. CHICKIE	WILLIAM CUTOLO A.K.A. WILD BILL	JOSEPH RUSSO A.K.A JO JO
THEODORE PERSICO A.K.A. TEDDY	ANTHONY RUSSO A.K.A. CHUCKY	PASQUALE AMATO A.K.A. PATTY	THOMAS PETRIZZO
	VINCENZO ALOI	VIC ORENA SR. A.K.A. LITTLE VIC	

ASSOCIATES OF INTEREST

CARMINE SESSA	LARRY MAZZA	JAMES DELMASTO	WILLIAM MELE
JOEY AMBROSINO A.K.A. JOEY BRAINS	ANTHONY FREZZA	MARIO PARLAGRECO	

An FBI chart showing the Colombo Family
that includes many of the key players in my trial.
Gregory P. Mango, Polaris

Gregory Scarpa Sr. and Linda
Schiro, New Year's Day 1991,
ten months before the outbreak
of the Colombo Family War.
Polaris

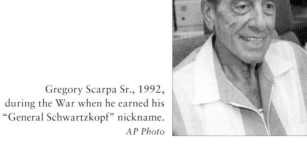

Gregory Scarpa Sr., 1992,
during the War when he earned his
"General Schwartzkopf" nickname.
AP Photo

Alone with my thoughts as my trial got underway,
October 15, 2007.
Jesse Ward, AP Photo

The DA's lead prosecutor, Michael Vecchione,
speaking to the media after the charges were dismissed
on November 1, 2007.
Paul Martinka, Polaris

Me and Carolyn leaving court after the charges
against me were dismissed, November 1, 2007.
Louis Lanzano, AP Photo

going to get whacked if he gets into a car that's obviously stolen. So Joe Sap jammed Kevin Granato's keys into the ignition, making the car look legit.

Sitting at Romano's, Billy Meli mentions the keys. Joe Sap had left Kevin Granato's own personal car keys in the stolen Cutlass with the dead body in the backseat. Billy Meli and another associate, Joe Savarese, ran out of Romano's and drove to the Cutlass. Luckily, Joe Brewster's body had not been spotted in the backseat. Billy Meli got Kevin Granato's keys and saw Brewster dead, which was helpful later on because he could testify that he had actually seen the body.

Back at Romano's, the associates Billy Meli, Mario Parlagreco, Joe Savarese, and Kevin Granato were sworn to secrecy. They could not claim this murder among their own cohorts at Wimpy Boys. No associate is allowed to participate in or observe the murder of a made man. Here four mere associates were participants in this murder conspiracy. This is a bad breach of Mafia rules and no way Gregory Jr. wanted that to come back to haunt him after he murdered his daughter's godfather.

Like Mary Bari, Joe Brewster was a victim of my allegedly leaking information to Scarpa. The second matter that occurred in the Eastern District in the late 1980s that came back to haunt me did not involve a murder.

On the exact day of the hit on Joe Brewster, September 17, 1987, another agent's CI revealed in a 209 that Colombo capo Benny Aloi and Colombo house counsel

Stanley Meyer got word that an indictment was coming down on some members and associates in the Colombo Family "at the federal and state level."

There is no way I would ever have remembered the details of this incident had my lawyer not provided me with the records. Included in the records was the 209 referred to above that blamed Colombo house counsel for the leak of imminent arrests and not me.

No doubt Stanley Meyer got his information about the incident from a clerk in the Eastern District. In my opinion, most of our leaks came from the Eastern District and I said that loudly and often over the years, and I was not the only agent to say so. There was something about Brooklyn that seemed to crave attention like a spoiled child.

In the summer of 1987, federal prosecutor Valerie Caproni, with two years under her belt in the Eastern District, had a joint Drug Enforcement Administration and NYPD Major Case Squad investigation against Gregory Jr. and his nine-man crew of associates, including Mario Parlagreco, Billy Meli, and Kevin Granato. It was a RICO case that included the murder of crew member Albert Noccia and a marijuana- and cocaine-dealing conspiracy that itself included the shaking down of rival dealers. Gregory Jr. viewed Staten Island Community College as his turf. Dealers who roamed his turf were required to pay him $1,000 a day. Two such dealers who protested the unfairness of this were severely beaten.

Valerie Caproni and the DEA/NYPD did a nice job putting the case together as a RICO case—the way we were doing them in the Southern District. Although during the trial in April 1988, they were unable to prove the murder, they were able to prove the rest of it and each defendant got a stiff sentence. It was while serving their sentences that Billy Meli and Mario Parlagreco rolled in 1994 during the tail end of the avalanche of Colombo Family War rollovers.

The ten defendants were indicted on November 2, 1987. All were arrested, except Gregory Jr., who went on the lam and became a fugitive. All DEA fugitives become the jurisdiction of the FBI and are referred to the FBI fugitive squad.

With trial looming in April 1988, Valerie Caproni desperately wanted Gregory Jr. caught. She correctly viewed Gregory Jr. as the principal defendant in the case, as he was the only made man and it was his crew, his criminal enterprise. She did not want to go to trial without him. And she did not want him sitting on the sidelines, going to school on her case and being well prepared when he returned after trial to be tried alone, the way Big Joey Massino had.

As it turned out, the DEA referral to open a fugitive case on Gregory Jr. had been made to headquarters in Washington, D.C., but no referral had been passed on to our New York fugitive squad. It had fallen through the cracks of the FBI and the DEA. Impatient with the FBI, Caproni referred the FBI's fugitive case to the U.S. Marshals' Office. When that was discovered, it ruffled feathers at the highest levels of the FBI. That was no way to conduct business. Our relationship with the Eastern

District was once again troubled. An investigation was launched into why it had been done. For example, why had not the U.S. attorney called the head of the New York office of the FBI if she had a complaint?

Caproni's complaints were twofold:

First, she had heard a rumor that Gregory Jr.'s father was a CI for the FBI. As was our policy, especially in view of what had just happened to Willie Boy Johnson, the Bureau denied this. Prior to the indictment in November 1987, Caproni had invited a Colombo Family agent to attend a meeting to see if he could provide any insights and to see if his squad was interested in joining the case. The supervisor of the squad was Chris Mattiace.

As Chris recalled: "At that time we were only interested in capos and above. Our whole effort in every squad was focused on bringing down the hierarchy of each family. Here was a case with a single soldier and a bunch of associates. And what were they involved in? Shaking down kids who sold pot and coke to other kids! We had absolutely no interest in such a case. Greg Scarpa himself was not big enough for our interests at the time, much less his son and the Dead End Kids. And it was a DEA/NYPD case and their agents and cops were handling it. I didn't know that Scarpa was a source for anyone, much less Lin. Lin didn't get my Colombo squad until Gregory Jr. was already more than two months gone."

Anxious to find Gregory Jr. after Caproni turned the case over to the marshals, our supervisors—who knew of Scarpa's TE status—asked me to inform our fugitive squad agent Charlie Gianturco of Scarpa's TE status and asked me to try to get information from Scarpa. I did so, knowing that the brass now wanted to beat the U.S. marshals to Gregory Jr. We thought it best that Charlie be the heavy in this, and for the first and only time I arranged for Scarpa to meet with another agent. Charlie made it plain to Scarpa that until Gregory Jr. was apprehended, Scarpa's life was going to be miserable. There would be cops everywhere he went. His collections on his loan-shark "book" and gambling businesses would suffer. Charlie explained the consequences of violating the statute against harboring a fugitive. Scarpa said he understood, but there was nothing he could do. Scarpa said that Gregory Jr. would likely turn himself in after the trial and sentencing of the others.

This was not an unexpected response from Greg Scarpa the father when you consider that he killed a bypass burglar for bad-mouthing Gregory Jr., killed a limo driver for molesting Little Linda, and killed a drug dealer and got his own left eye shot out when the drug dealer disrespected his son Joey Schiro.

Second, Caproni said she had heard a rumor that the FBI had Gregory Jr., in her words, "under wraps." She heard we were holding him and refusing to turn him over. She said she heard our motive for holding him was that we planned on using him as a witness in congressional hearings.

Here's a line from the FBI's investigation into Caproni's referral of her FBI fugitive case to the U.S. marshals: "She described her conversation with [Charlie] Gianturco as 'bizarre.'" It was bizarre, but this was only because of what was coming out of Valerie Caproni's mouth.

Caproni "suggested that a Title III be placed on the telephone of Scarpa Sr. and a surveillance instituted." That would require a minimum of eleven agents around the clock every day. But besides this, as any lawyer should know, there was no "may I" information, no probable cause that would have justified a judge authorizing a Title III here. She had given the legally deficient grounds that Easter was coming up and that Senior was the father of Junior. Plus, there could never be grounds to use a Title III to find a recent fugitive since there are many other available means of finding one besides wiretapping. "As a result of the aforementioned responses, she said everything led her to be suspicious that the FBI indeed had Scarpa and would not produce him for her trial," Gianturco wrote.

Charlie Gianturco opined in his report that he found Caproni's comments to him "personally degrading and exceptionally unprofessional."

By this time I had the Colombo Family for about a month. Jules Bonavolonta and I met with Caproni and assured her that the FBI did not have possession of Gregory Jr. On the way back to our office I said to Jules, "I'll double-check my house in New Jersey when I get home tonight, maybe he's under the bed."

Finally, Caproni accepted the fact that we didn't have Gregory Jr. "under wraps." James M. Fox, the assistant director in charge of the New York office, put it succinctly in his report: "This matter was further exacerbated by Assistant United States Attorney VALERIE CAPRONI, Eastern District, New York. AUSA CAPRONI had put herself into practically a 'siege mentality' by her false belief that the FBI had SCARPA 'under wraps,' to use in what she mistakenly believed were upcoming congressional hearings."

In 1988, Gregory Jr. was caught and Valerie Caproni took him to trial. He was convicted and he got his twenty years like Mario Parlagreco. Chalk up another one for RICO.

A year later, Caproni ventured into an urban development job where she stayed three years, only to return and shortly become an integral part of Team Favo in October 1992.

Together in January 1994 they would revive this DEA/NYPD incident, and make an allegation that during the summer of 1987 I had tipped Greg Scarpa off that his son Gregory Jr. and his crew were about to be indicted.

That I handled Scarpa looked suspicious and that was enough for Valerie Caproni to join Favo against me, as if she could justify her "bizarre" and embarrassing behavior in 1987 at my expense in 1994.

The third incident in the Eastern District in the 1980s that came back to haunt me was another murder.

As the decade of the 1980s wore down, an old Chrysler six-door stretch limo with tinted side windows and no muffler noisily cruised down Fifteenth Avenue in Bensonhurst. It was Halloween 1989. The night was clear. Like the moon, the limo was white. The limo belonged to twenty-year-old Ray Aviles and he was driving. The car was loaded with Thirteenth Avenue Boys Patrick Porco, Joey Schiro, Messy Marvin, Luccho, Petey, and Binja. The Thirteenth Avenue Boys were full of trick-or-treat mischief. They spotted some Fifteenth Avenue Boys on a corner and jumped out and started an egg-throwing fight. Then some Fifteenth Avenue adults came out of the corner bar and got into it with the Thirteenth Avenue Boys. Fists started flying.

"Do you know who the fuck I am?" seventeen-year-old Joey Schiro yelled at one of the larger adults, a really big guy named Bundy.

"Fuck you and your father," Bundy said. "Get the fuck back to Thirteenth Avenue."

"I called the cops," the bartender came out and warned everybody. "Yez better clear the corner."

The Thirteenth Avenue Boys got in the limo, and one at a time, Ray dropped them off.

By the time they got to Joey's father's house, there was just eighteen-year-old Patrick Porco, Ray Aviles, and Joey Schiro. Ray was Joey's bodyguard and Patrick was Joey's best friend. The three of them supported themselves by charging local dope dealers a weekly street tax to peddle dope outdoors on Thirteenth Avenue. Once a week Ray would drive Patrick and Joey to make their collections. Ray was dark-skinned, big, and muscular. He always said, "I'm not tough, but I was blessed with strength."

"We got into it with the Fifteenth Avenue Boys," Joey

said to his father, Greg Scarpa. "Then some older guys came out the bar and got into our business."

"You tell them who you are?" Greg asked his son. The kitchen smelled of recent marijuana use.

"The world knows who he is," Ray said.

"I told this fucking Bundy, 'You know who I am,'" Joey said, "and he tells me fuck me and fuck my father."

"I'll handle this," Scarpa said to his son, and went into another part of the house.

Greg Scarpa returned with a black .25, which he gave to Patrick, and a steel 9mm, which he gave to his son Joey. The three boys left, loaded, and returned to the limo to head for Fifteenth Avenue.

"Look, there's Craig," Joey said. "Let's get that Craig. He just got out the marines. Craig got a medal for being a good shot, marksman, some shit."

"He ain't gonna want to spray no corners," Patrick said.

Patrick was a nice-looking boy, about five six and 165 pounds.

"I give him a hundred dollars, he'll come. Here, Ray, here's a hundred. You give it to Craig. Tell him it's to spray corners. It's for shootin' Bundy. If we don't see Bundy, he can shoot whoever the fuck he wants."

Joey, who was round and overweight, prided himself on being called the "Killing Machine." Joey handed Ray a hundred-dollar bill and they pulled up to the corner where Craig was standing with a couple of guys. Craig was tall with tattoos, a pointy nose, and a receding hairline. Nobody knew his last name. Ray called Craig over to the driver's window.

"We need to go spray corners," Ray said. "Some mother-fuckers. We need a good shooter. Give you a hundred dollars to shoot a motherfucker on Fifteenth Avenue."

"I'm in," Craig said, held out his hand for the money, and got into the limo.

"Maybe we should get a shotty," Joey said.

"I know who's got one," Ray said, and drove to another kid's house. Ray went in and came out with a loaded shot-gun wrapped in a newspaper.

Ray started driving over to Fifteenth.

"Look over there by the church." Joey spotted two of the Fifteenth Avenue egg throwers.

"Joey," Patrick said. "That's the kid you hate."

These boys were not drug dealers and they didn't shake down drug dealers. They were good kids. One of the boys was Dominic Masseria. He stood on the steps of Our Lady of Guadalupe with his back to the door so nobody could come up behind him. He was expecting eggs.

Ray made a sharp loud U-turn over a curb, heading for the two boys.

Patrick Porco's pretty blond sister with high cheekbones, twenty-year-old Lori, used to go out with Ray Aviles. Lori lived with her sister and her husband and their two kids. Inside the house, Lori heard the loud engine with no muf-fler and the screeching U-turn and knew it was Ray. She opened a window and stuck her head out to get a better look. She saw the limo head in the direction of Our Lady of

Guadalupe. Lori heard one and then another shotgun blast. She was full of fear for her brother Patrick. Then she saw the limo zoom back past her and speed away. Lori couldn't see if Patrick was in the back because of the tinted glass. She definitely saw Ray driving because his window wasn't tinted.

Lori looked back at the church and saw seventeen-year-old Dominic Masseria sprawled on the steps. He was dead.

"Call the cops," she screamed at her older sister. Lori ran down to the church. Lori's brother Mike came down to the church and the two of them drove to Ray's house to look for Patrick. They found Ray's white limo in front. Ray was still in it with Craig when they rolled up. All the windows were down to get the smell of gunpowder out of it. Ray had already dropped off Patrick and Joey to be with their alibi witnesses after they dumped the gun down a sewer.

"You killed an innocent kid," Lori screamed at Ray, who just sat there silently. "You killed an innocent kid." She was shaking, but she was relieved that Patrick was not in the limo. "Where's my brother?"

"I don't know what you're talkin' about, Lori," Ray said.

"Patrick's a good kid. Patrick never did anything wrong till you brought him around to that Joey."

"C'mon, Lori," Ray protested. "I never even seen Patrick tonight."

"Yo," Mike Porco said. "You guys fucked up."

"C'mon, Mike," Lori said. "I'm telling the cops what I saw."

Lori and Mike headed toward the church, which was now a crime scene crawling with cops and detectives.

"I know her," Ray said to Craig, "She's got a big mouth. She'll go tell the cops. There's no talkin' to her."

"That's fucked," Craig said. "I'm gettin' the fuck out of Brooklyn."

"I got no place to go," Ray said. It was sinking in.

"Better torch this fuckin' limo," Craig said.

"Yeah."

"Holdin' anything?"

"Glove compartment," Ray said.

Craig fished in the glove compartment, pulled out a bag of marijuana, and got out of the car.

"Later," Ray said.

"Semper Fi," Craig said, and disappeared.

Greg Scarpa sent Joey and Patrick to his son Frank's farm in New Jersey. They hated it there and came back to Brooklyn in two weeks. Ray abandoned and torched his limo.

Ray told his mother the truth about what happened, including the part about Lori. Her heart was broken and Ray knew it. "You've got to turn yourself in," she said to her son. Less than a week after the murder on the church steps, Ray found homes for his dogs and turned himself in. He was held on $300,000 bail.

"That lawyer you got is going to fuck you in the ass," Detective Bill Powell of the Sixty-second Precinct told Ray Aviles, reaching across the small table and putting a hand on Ray's shoulder. "He works for Greg Scarpa. He don't work for you. I bet you're even paying for him."

"I thought Scarpa was going to pay for him," Ray said. "My mother had to borrow fifteen grand so far to pay the guy. I seen him three times. He wants five grand every time he shows up."

"What I'm saying. Scarpa ain't paying."

"Every time I call over there to Joey to tell him what's up on my case, he already knows from my lawyer that my mother's paying for and he's reporting everything to Scarpa, who tells it to Joey."

"You got problems with these people, Ray. Very scary people. Very scary problems."

"I don't even want to get released on bail." Ray bowed his head and slumped forward in his chair. "I'm afraid I hit the street and I'm dead."

"Get rid of this guy, Ray. We'll get you another lawyer. Won't cost your mother a dime. You cooperate and we'll give you manslaughter for acting in concert. You'll do three years in Sing Sing till everything cools down. Learn to play the drums up there. Scarpa will be dead from AIDS by the time you get out. Give me an idea what you can give us before we give that to you. Just between you and me. Off the record. Just give me the names to start. Let me see if they match what I know so I can tell if you're on the level or what."

"Craig done the shooting. I don't know his last name. He looks like Ichabod Crane. Me, Joey, and Patrick Porco were in the limo."

"Where's the shotty."

"I can take you to it. It's in a sewer."

"Good."

"*I talk to Patrick Porco on the phone every day. He's a weak link. He's planning on turning himself in. I feel, anyway. For acting in concert.*"

Detective Powell knew he'd need Patrick to prove a case against Craig or Joey because of the "uncorroborated accomplice rule." Unlike other states, New York law says you can't convict a man on the testimony of his accomplice unless you have corroboration. In this case, that would be Patrick Porco. Detective Powell at the precinct house and Detective Joe Lombardo at the Brooklyn D.A.'s Office each met separately at their offices with Patrick one time, but Patrick wouldn't cooperate against his best friend Joey.

During Memorial Day weekend, Patrick went for a drive at night with Joey and Joey's cousin Johnny "Loads" Sinagra. Whoever was driving, the other one turned around to face Patrick. Patrick saw the gun and stretched out his hands to fend off the bullets. The first bullet went through his left hand and into his teeth. Another bullet grazed his right wrist before lodging in his brain. After the shooting stopped they pulled over on a deserted street near the Belt Parkway. They tried to get Patrick out of the backseat, but his leg got tangled up in the seat belt. Finally, they were able to dump him in the street in a fetal position, a pack of Marlboros near his outstretched hand.

Later on, when talking to their pals, Joey Schiro and his cousin John each took credit as the actual shooter.

* * *

Lori Porco got the horrible news from her sister Debbie that Patrick had been murdered. She went straight to Romano's Restaurant, where Joey Schiro was having dinner with his crew.

Lori walked straight up to Joey and yelled in his face, "You killed my brother."

Joey remained silent.

Joey didn't go to Patrick's funeral, but Linda Schiro did. Greg Scarpa made her go. Linda hugged Patrick's mother and cried. Linda said she felt toward Patrick as if he were her own son.

Five years later Joey would be shot and killed in a dispute with a rival drug dealer. The detective who would later gain fame and a book deal on the Mafia Cops case, Tommy Dades, investigated Joey's murder and arrested and convicted Vincent Rizzuto. In the decade that followed, Tommy Dades maintained a close personal relationship with the grateful Linda Schiro, her divorced daughter Little Linda, and Linda's small children, all of whom lived together.

At Vincent Rizzuto's sentencing, all hell broke loose. The Joey Schiro contingent gave passionate victim impact testimony about what a wonderful son, brother, husband, and father Joey had been and what a lowlife Rizzuto was. Rizzuto wondered aloud how much Joey cared about the families of his victims. Rizzuto's mother said about Linda Schiro, "She's such an actress. She should get an Academy Award. Look at those tears."

* * *

After her son's murder, Linda Schiro had to be institu-
tionalized twice in a mental hospital and she became addicted to prescription medication. Like Mary Bari and
Joe Brewster before him, Patrick Porco was a victim of
my allegedly leaking information to Scarpa.

CHAPTER TWENTY-ONE

THE NEW UNTOUCHABLES

I may have shared plenty of information that I got from Scarpa and my other good sources during my career, but I also got plenty from other agents who had the knack.

I'd like to introduce two more pretty talented informant developers from our championship season, Andy Kurins and Kenny Brown. These are men who were involved in their own cases at the time, men with whom I had no special friendship or social relationship. They are a representative sample of the quality of the New Untouchables who whirled around us in the 1980s.

Andris "Andy" Kurins was a street agent for the Gambino squad. He's now retired and a private eye. As a result of his relationship with my lead attorney, Doug Grover, stemming back to their Mafia fighting days in the 1980s as federal prosecutor and agent, Andy did the investigating for my defense team. Andy was born in

Latvia, and coauthored, with retired Agent Joe O'Brien, *Boss of Bosses*, the biography of Gambino Boss Paul Castellano.

Here, in his own words, is his take on informants:

"When I came on board in 1980, the Gambino squad had just been formed under Bruce Mouw. And let me tell you, we had nothing. We didn't even have a current photo of Boss Paul Castellano. None of the Organized Crime files or records were kept in a way that signified family activity. It had all been about individuals. I came over from the spy side—the Russians. Now we were setting up as if the Gambino Family was a foreign country, which it really was. Only we weren't sure who was a citizen and who wasn't.

"If you don't have confidential informants, you might as well close up shop.

"When I left the Bureau to write my book, I turned over five dynamite informants to agents I knew I could trust to treat them right. The agent who develops the informant usually takes the best care of him. Not many people in this world will risk their lives to talk to you. You have to appreciate that, and from time to time you have to show that appreciation. You have to protect the informant and serve justice at the same time.

"Often I was careful not to spell out everything clearly in a 209, and careful what agent or supervisor I sent a 209 to. When I read Scarpa's 209s after Lin got indicted,

I couldn't believe how truly good Scarpa was. I saw stuff I wish Lin had disseminated to me—but it was singular and might have exposed Scarpa and gotten him killed.

"We all knew that Lin had the crown jewel of Top Echelon informants. So if we needed to know a particular thing our informants didn't happen to know, we'd ask him to find out for us, informally. He'd come back with an answer every time.

"Another source I relied on because I was so new to Organized Crime was Kenny McCabe, a retired investigator for the Brooklyn D.A. who was working for the Manhattan federal prosecutors. Kenny was the kind of guy who on his own time would go to Mafia weddings and funerals and secretly take photos and jot down license plates. He saw who got the respect, the deference paid—who got the kiss on the cheek. He not only knew who was who, he knew the names of their wives and kids. If I got information from one of my informants, I'd go up to his office and he'd fill in the blanks for me.

"I helped develop a Top Echelon informant in the Gambino Family whose information literally helped the FBI take down the Dapper Don, John Gotti.

"We knew the Gambino capos met with Gotti at the Ravenite Social Club on Mulberry Street in Little Italy. With the help of my informant, we had bugs planted in the club. But there was so much noise inside that we couldn't make out the words. We noticed, however, that every once in a while the sound of Gotti's voice would go missing. I went back to my informant with the problem.

" 'I checked it out,' my informant reported back to me. 'Gotti sometimes goes out a rear door and talks privately in the hallway.'

" 'Nice work,' I said.

"So we bugged the hallway. The conversations in the hallway were clearer, but they would end abruptly. Again, I went back to my informant.

" 'Here's the thing,' he told me. 'They got this old lady upstairs on the third floor. Apartment 10. She used to be married to a Gambino old-timer, but the guy died. Gotti makes her leave the building, then he walks upstairs and he uses her apartment to meet with the capos. If you see her leave the building and he's still in there, you can bet he's upstairs.'

"Now we were cooking.

"A bug needs to be hot-wired into an electrical source, so Jim Kallstrom's wizards broke in and planted a bug in the old lady's stereo. We sat in a nearby perch at our recording equipment and listened in awe while Gotti had sit-downs with his capos.

"Perhaps the last major piece of evidence gathered in our heyday in the 1980s was heard by us on December 12, 1989. Transmitted from our new peaceful third-floor bug, we distinctly heard John Gotti talk about three men he had ordered killed. Gotti bragged that one man was killed 'because he refused to come in when I called. He didn't do nothing else wrong.'

"We had already noted a pattern. Gotti would bad-mouth whichever capo he wasn't meeting with. On this December 12, 1989, tape, Gotti crucified his underboss and longtime friend Sammy 'The Bull' Gravano behind his back. Later this would prove to be Gotti's undoing."

"I left the FBI before the start of the Gotti trial, but I was there for the arrests. Bruce Mouw had an arrest team staked out at the Ravenite for Gotti's arrival for a 7 p.m. meeting of the capos. I was uptown behind Macy's on Thirty-fourth Street waiting to bust Tommy Gambino. The arrests were to be coordinated. I was to do nothing until Bruce beeped me that Gotti had arrived. If I busted Tommy Gambino prematurely, Gotti and Gravano and the rest would get the word at once and likely go on the lam.

"Around 5:30, there goes Tommy Gambino walking down Thirty-fifth in a jungle of pedestrian and vehicular Christmas traffic. He was moving swiftly away from us. I backed up against traffic after him and told the agent I was with to 'get him or we'll lose him.' I meant follow him—tail him. But my cohort jumps out, chases him down, and arrests him in the middle of Broadway with a million horns honking. We get Tommy in the car and I know I'm in a world of trouble. I need to sit on him for an hour and a half.

"Tommy Gambino ran Consolidated Trucking. Not a garment manufactured in the Garment District went anywhere unless it went in one of his trucks. Otherwise, Tommy was a gentleman. He had royal blood in his veins. He was the son of the deceased Boss of Bosses Carlo Gambino. He was the nephew of murdered Boss of

Bosses Paul Castellano. Tommy's wife was the daughter of a Mafia founding father, 'Three-Fingers Brown' Lucchese.

"Tommy's driver was sitting in a limo waiting to take Tommy home. But I couldn't let Tommy tell his driver he'd been arrested. I made believe I went out and told the driver myself. I stalled and stalled with Tommy. When Tommy got too impatient I drove him out to our Queens office to make believe I was processing him. All the while I denied him the right to call his lawyer by incompetently stumbling around: 'Yeah, Tommy, in a minute. Just let me find the papers I need so you can make bail. You want to make bail, don't you?' Finally Bruce beeped me. I put Tommy back in the car and drove him to Manhattan so he could join the Gambino Family RICO party and get booked for real. I waited a few days before I told that story to Bruce.

"After Gotti and Gravano were arrested on a RICO with eleven murders, they were taken to court for their bail hearing. To show the judge how murderous the defendants were and why they should be denied release on bail, the federal prosecutor John Gleeson played that December 12 tape.

"Gotti and Gravano sat and listened with their lawyers. Gravano could hear for himself that Gotti was a backstabbing treacherous Boss. Gravano got back to his cell and reached out to Staten Island office agents Frank Spero and Matty Tricorico to test the waters of cooperation. Why them? Because over the years these agents behaved like two class-act agents. The Bull knew from interacting with them that they were gentlemen. They were human. They were professional. He felt comfortable around them. He knew that he could trust them with his life.

"Not only did Gotti go down in his RICO trial in 1992, thanks to the tape that turned Gravano, but also what was left of the Gambino Family withered away. Today the Gambino squad is solving decades-old murders with the help of CWs. As recently as February 3, 2009, Gambino hit man turned CW Peter 'Bud' (for marijuana) Zucarro testified about the time he learned his Boss John Gotti had died of cancer in federal prison: 'I didn't feel anything. By then, I thought he ruined it. The way he was so flamboyant . . . It was supposed to be a secret society and now everything was overexposed . . .'

"My informant on the Ravenite bug continued to work—even after I retired in 1991—and ended up getting hundreds of thousands in FBI money. He probably got a hundred thousand alone for Ravenite. You ask the Bureau for the moon and you give your informant whatever gets approved. But he wasn't in it for the money.

"Before he dreamed of seeing ten cents, he expressed to me—as a friend—the disillusionment Zucarro expressed in court twenty years later. My Ravenite source was not someone we had a hammer on. He saw that this life wasn't what he believed it to be going in. He saw the dishonesty among these 'men of honor.' This was not a life he wanted to be associated with. But you can't get out of it. The only way out was to die or help put it out of business. My secret in dealing with him was to keep encouraging him about the overall progress we were making in getting the Gambino Family.

"When I helped Lin out for his murder trial, I was amazed at how little money Lin ever gave to Scarpa for all the monumental work Scarpa did for Lin—about $66,000 over a twelve-year period.

"I guess Lin was a bit tight with a dollar.

"It amused me that Lin was accused by Linda Schiro of pocketing that money instead of giving it to Scarpa. If Lin wanted to take money, he could have easily doubled his requests."

"Maybe the thing I'm most proud of was the afternoon my partner Joe O'Brien and I spent in the dark in the back of an old truck in Staten Island with cardboard propped up against the windows and against the front seats so no light got in and so no one could see us from the outside. An informant of Joe's told us the Commission was having a meeting at a house in Staten Island and gave us the address. With cameras in hand we went quickly to stake it out.

"Can you imagine how big that was for us that we had information about the location of a Commission meeting? This was singular information that very few people ever possessed. At that time Colombo Boss Junior Persico was in jail and the Bonanno Family had been kicked off the Commission because they let Joe Pistone infiltrate them. We were praying to photograph the three remaining Bosses who, along with Junior Persico's designated representative, now wielded all the power.

"The first person we saw come out was Tommy Bilotti, Paul Castellano's right-hand man—a capo who would be killed with Paul in front of Sparks Steak House. Tommy gave the area a few sweeps. He drove around and around to make sure there was no law enforcement.

"From inside our truck we watched Tommy Bilotti put his nose up against one of our windows and try to see what was inside. He looked satisfied that it was loaded with cardboard. We watched him go into the house and we hoped he wasn't telling them to stay inside until after dark because he'd spotted us or our cameras.

"Meanwhile, we'd been cramped in the back of the truck for three or four hours, and it was getting darker by the minute. Would we have enough light to take usable pictures?

"But little by little and one after the other, all three Bosses and Junior's designated representative, plus their entourages, began to appear in the doorway and leave that house: Paul Castellano—Boss of the Gambino; Fat Tony Salerno—Boss of the Genovese; Tony Ducks Corallo—Boss of the Lucchese; and Gerry Lang Langella—underboss and Junior Persico's spokesman for the Colombo. Even their bagman in the Concrete Club was there.

"Joe O'Brien and I got the only photos ever taken of a Commission meeting. They are historic. And their use in Lin's Mafia Commission Case was especially gratifying.

"Let me just add one more thing: Without Greg Scarpa, there would have been no Mafia Commission Case, and where would we all be now?"

Agent Kenny Brown, a southern gentleman, was another man with a knack, a Colombo Family specialist par excellence. He knew them all personally, including James Caan's "dear friend" Jo Jo Russo and Chuckie Russo, the cousins who we would later find out had framed me for murder and plotted to kill me.

As a result of all the destabilization of the Mafia in the 1980s, the brass added the Colombo Family to my Bonanno Family squad from January 1988 to October 1988 and then again permanently in January 1990. Kenny Brown went wherever the Colombo Family went. Whenever he was with me, Kenny was my Colombo Family go-to guy. Kenny and I didn't always see eye to eye, but there's nothing wrong with that.

Kenny Brown worked with Chris Favo in 1989 for about a year before they both came to me, and he uses some pretty strong language when he talks about Favo that I've had to tone down for this book. So, I'd better fill in some blanks on Favo ahead of time.

Favo entered training at Quantico the same month we initiated the Mafia Commission Case, September 1983. Favo jumped around a lot for a young agent. He worked in Minneapolis in the spy side as a First Office Agent for a couple of years. Next he got transferred to New York to work terror cases under Kenny Maxwell for a couple of years. I learned much later as we were writing this book that Favo complained a lot to Kenny that he wasn't getting any of the high-profile cases that he felt he deserved. Favo wanted to move on. Kenny Maxwell responded by having him transferred.

Favo spent 1989 on the Genovese squad under Dave Stone. Dave temporarily had the Colombo Family for that year before it came back to me. He assigned Favo to a joint task force that was set up with the NYPD to investigate the major Colombo loan shark, Billy Cutolo. Favo and Dave Stone were close; they worked out together and jogged together. Although Favo has a nerdy look and is five eight and about 150 pounds, he was always in terrific physical condition. Dave Stone, who recently retired after a distinguished career, was a monster ice hockey player on the FBI's A-team.

Then, in January 1990, I got Favo, Kenny Brown, and one other agent for what was now permanently the Colombo side of my two-family squad. My feeling was that any friend of Dave Stone's was a friend of mine. By that summer, Kenny Brown went upstairs as informant coordinator of the New York office. If I had to do it over again, I'd have rewarded Kenny Brown somehow. Maybe he'd have stayed with me longer and not gone upstairs. I lost all my Colombo experience when I lost Kenny. The workload of two families in one squad was pushing me, and I probably pushed my men in turn. But Kenny was still extremely valuable as informant coordinator. Here, in his own words, is his take on everything that went down during our heyday:

"I didn't care for Chris Favo at all and I don't mind saying it. He was not the kind of agent we had in the 1980s when we went after the Commission and each one of the families in their own cases. We worked together as a team. We shared information. We encouraged each other. Nobody was a glory hound. But Favo was a one-way guy 100 percent. It was all about him and nobody else.

"When I became informant coordinator, I had two really good informants that I took with me from Lin's Colombo Family squad. I ended up giving one of them to Favo because he was now the senior Colombo guy. I took Favo to meet my informant and it was a disaster. Favo had no warmth, no people skills, and no flexibility. He took down everything the guy said, including the obvious bullshit. He ended up doing a four-page 209. Usually, 209s are a single relevant paragraph. Otherwise they're useless. I've seen a lot of agents and I never saw anything like that. Favo was just not suitable for that kind of work.

"Later this same informant—who was truly tremendous for me over the years—got in the jackpot for a murder that he had no choice but to do because a Boss ordered him to do it. You get whacked for failing to do a 'piece of work,' and someone else still murders the victim. Favo gave the informant no slack and jammed him with life. Meanwhile the Boss, who had become a CW and admitted to a dozen murders, only got five years or so. My old informant even pleaded guilty, but got no break for all he'd done for us over the years. I still feel bad about that.

"What's worse is that Favo gave me the very strong feeling that he believed that I knew my informant had done that murder all along. He never accused me outright, but I can spot an attitude of suspicion a mile away. The way he looked at me when he talked to me about it, the pregnant pauses, like he was trying to get me to fill in the blanks and admit the informant told me he murdered the guy and I failed to report what he told me.

"My God, the informant never told me he'd murdered anyone. But—gasp—we knew these informants of ours all did murders as part of their job description. CWs told you who they murdered because they were required to, but not CIs.

"Listen, if you're talking to your informant and he admits he killed so-and-so, what can you possibly do about it anyway? You report it and he'll deny he said it. He'll bring in eight guys he was playing cards with on the night of the hit. You have no case and that's the end of your informant. If a handler is crazy enough to wear a Nagra recorder when he's talking to his informant and the informant clearly admits to an old murder on tape and you give the tape to some silly federal prosecutor and your informant is arrested for murder, you just single-handedly ended the use of informants by the FBI, possibly forever. That story gets in the paper and all of a sudden the 'hello' phone stops ringing all over the country.

"Favo buddied up to some federal prosecutors in Brooklyn under Valerie Caproni. They loved him.

"I know from my own experience, Valerie Caproni had her hand in that first OPR scandal they put Lin into. Caproni called me during the OPR investigation. She was hoping to get some dirt on Lin. She was trying to make something out of a dispute I had with him over closing Scarpa as an informant during the Colombo Family War. She was way off base and way out of line. Fishing for nothing. And what was Valerie Caproni doing in the first place taking it upon herself to nose around in the investigation? She was acting like a vigilante on the phone with me. They had OPR investigators up from headquarters doing the interviewing. I guess she was bird-dogging, clutching at straws, trying to lead them to something, to anything.

"When you're the target of an OPR investigation, it's supposed to be confidential, in order to protect you in case you're cleared, like Lin was. But the OPR on Lin was a rumor that flew around. Favo blabbed to everybody about it. It hit the papers within months. None of Lin's friends—which was just about everybody from top to bottom except Favo and his cohorts—wanted it out there.

"I watched Favo lead around these two or three new young agents on the Colombo side like he was a guru. I can't blame the young guys for going along with him. To these FNGs he was an old-timer like Kenny McCabe.

"I'll tell you who else had no use for Favo—with a

passion. Our boss, Don North! And this was before Favo reported Lin to Don in January 1994. This was while I was still there, and I transferred out of New York in 1992.

"I lost a good friend when Don North died. As close as we were, he never did tell me why he couldn't stand Favo.

"The holier-than-thou agent like Favo, a Notre Dame grad, is very handicapped in this kind of work. You cannot go around seeing everything in black and white with the Mafia. Maybe in terrorism or white collar, but not in our world. You had to deal with people as people and you had to have a little bit of flexibility and sometimes navigate in a gray area.

"I know that before he came to Organized Crime, where he didn't belong, Favo was on Kenny Maxwell's squad working terror cases and Kenny had some kind of problem with him and dumped him, but I don't know what it was."

"Don North, who, by the way, was the most knowledgeable man I ever met, did close Scarpa in 1992 during the war when I thought he should have been closed. That informant of mine—the one that later got life—told me Scarpa was doing murders in the Colombo Family War on behalf of the Junior Persico faction against the Little Vic Orena faction. As informant coordinator, just before I left New York, I felt strongly that Scarpa should be closed. Don didn't want to close Scarpa. And Lin certainly didn't want to close him. I got into a pissing contest with Lin about it even though I love Lin. Finally Don had to close Scarpa. About a month later, Lin got approval to open him back up again. They had to go over my level of authority to do that. I didn't sign off on it.

"But it was strictly a tactical policy issue that reasonable men can disagree about, and Lin and I never took it personally.

"Then later I read that Lin was accused by the Brooklyn D.A. prosecutor of reopening Scarpa because Lin was getting cash every week from Scarpa. Come on. That's laughable for a million reasons. But first, a rogue agent doesn't need to have a man opened as his informant if he wants to feed him information and get paid. In fact, he's better off—if he's rogue—doing all his business over safe phones. A beeper signal from either one of you sends you both to safe, prearranged pay phones at a prearranged hour. Then you'd get your cash sent to a post office box. To begin with, as hectic as life was for all of us, Lin didn't have time to be running off to Bensonhurst every week. I guess it wasn't funny to Lin, but I can't do anything but laugh at something that stupid.

"We all liked and respected Lin because he was always straightforward. He was a good guy. Nobody ever had any doubt about the integrity of Lin DeVecchio. I enjoyed working for him. He let me do my own thing with the Colombos because his specialty was basically the Bonanno Family.

"I was with the Colombos forever. I started under Damon Taylor, who started the Colombo squad. Damon was a little eccentric, but he was uncanny. He knew what was going to happen three moves ahead of anybody else. Then Chris Mattiace had the family. Chris was something else, a real pleasure. Chris was a tough boy from Hell's Kitchen in Manhattan, where the Westies came from. The whole time I was on the Colombo squad we were a team. We all worked our asses off all the time.

"Other than the fact that Lin had Scarpa as a Top Echelon, he let me carry the ball a lot on the Colombos. 'You got the Colombos,' Lin said. 'Just do it. I'll feed you info from "34."' If it was the other way around and Lin was feeding info to Scarpa, he would have been looking over my shoulder once in a while. But I'd come to Lin only after I'd put something together. And even then he wouldn't go through the details. He'd just hear what I wanted to do, give me some advice to maybe make it better, and then let me do it. Lin treated his agents with respect."

"I know Jo Jo Russo and his cousin Chuckie started off the frame of Lin for murder, but they weren't bad to deal with one-on-one. I was the case agent on Jo Jo. 'The Cousins' had a social club together down the street from Two Toms steak house in Bensonhurst. We'd harass them by going to Two Toms for dinner where they hung out.

"We had two types of surveillance: one where we

wanted them to see us; and one where we didn't want them to see us. When I wanted my presence known, I'd walk into a coffee shop and go to Jo Jo's table.

"'Slow down tonight, Jo Jo. We've been following you all day and you're wearing us out.'

"'Go home and get some rest.' He'd laugh. 'I'll call you if I need you.'

"The Cousins were similar in appearance. Dark hair, good-looking, five foot nine, 185. We probably mixed them up from time to time, but Chuckie's hair was shorter. They were both fairly intelligent—on the order of Billy Cutolo or Junior Persico's son, Little Allie Boy.

"Andrew 'The Fat Man' Russo was Jo Jo's father. Andy wasn't fat at all. I don't know why they called him that. Andy was Junior Persico's cousin. We had a Colombo Family RICO trial, a seven-month trial. It ended in 1986 just before the Commission Case went to trial that year. James Caan was a regular in the audience. He came to the Commission trial, too. I remember when Johnny Minerva got killed coming out of a donut shop in Massapequa, Long Island, during the Colombo Family War. I know the Cousins shot Minerva for Uncle Junior Persico, but when I was Jo Jo's case agent, he and Johnny Minerva were buddies. Jo Jo owned a florist shop. We put a Title III in the shop and this older guy, Johnny Minerva, would come around to hang out with Jo Jo. Minerva was strictly a Long Island guy and Little Vic Orena owned Long Island. As an act of self-preservation, maybe Johnny Minerva stayed cozy with Orena's side when the shooting broke out. These guys used to kill with each other; now they were killing each other.

"Jo Jo wasn't in our Colombo Family RICO because he was still a soldier then. This was like five years before the war. On that RICO we had thirteen of the Colombo hierarchy. The indictment was under seal, but before we could make the arrests, Jerry Capeci broke the story. We could only find eleven of the thirteen because after they read the *Daily News*, Junior Persico and Donnie Shacks went on the lam.

"Junior Persico went on the FBI's top-ten-most-wanted list and I was the co–case agent on that with Michelle Millane. Junior Persico was hiding out at Andy the Fat Man's sister's house. She was married to a real fat man, Fred DeChristopher, who was five eight and 250 pounds. Boy could that fat Freddie cook like crazy.

"Here's the biggest reason Fred DeChristopher turned against Junior Persico.

"Jo Jo Russo ran the gambling on a cruise ship. Just before Junior Persico came to stay at Freddie's house, Freddie went on the cruise ship to gamble. Freddie had a shipboard romance with a honey named Patricia. After the cruise, he began having an affair with her. Here comes Junior Persico living in the house full-time, bringing people over, and getting 302 statements from the cooperating witnesses. Junior got these 302s from the lawyers for the other defendants who'd been arrested. Junior would go over the 302s with Freddie. Not that this bothered Freddie; what bothered Freddie was that he was cooped up and couldn't get free to see his lovely Patricia.

"Years earlier Freddie had been a confidential informant. So he called FBI headquarters and tracked down his old handler, Jim Nelson, who now ran the L.A. office. That call to Jim says a lot about the relationship between a good developer of informants and his sources. Before Lin brought Scarpa back into the fold, Jim Nelson had Scarpa for a while.

" 'I got a top-ten fugitive living in my house,' Freddie said to Jim. 'You want him? I need something in return.'

"Jim Nelson flew to New York overnight. They made contact and made a deal.

" 'Look,' Freddie said. 'I'll give you what you want, but you gotta bring my girlfriend, Patricia, wherever you put me.'

"We arrested Junior Persico and Donnie Shacks that very Friday at Freddie's house. *Time* magazine had a photo of Michelle Millane and me escorting Persico into the federal building.

" 'Mr. Persico,' Michelle asked, 'why do people call you "The Snake"?'

"He just looked at her with those cold eyes for about a minute.

" 'Little lady, nobody calls me the Snake to my face.'

"Freddie did a great job on the witness stand for two weeks of cross-examination by thirteen defense attorneys in the Colombo Family RICO. We housed him on Governors Island in the harbor. He never did go into Witness Protection. The marshals, who administer it, have a rule that once you're in the program, the FBI can no longer have contact with you. Freddie wanted to keep that connection with us. He ended up divorced from Junior's cousin and in California somewhere. Maybe with Patricia.

"Junior Persico's in California, too. Lompoc Prison.

"When I retired in 1997 I sent an FBI top-ten wanted poster of Junior Persico to him at Lompoc and asked him to autograph it. I got it back and he inscribed it: 'To Ken Brown, Good luck in the real world.'"

CHAPTER TWENTY-TWO

THE UNREAL WORLD

It seems Kenny Brown's instincts about Favo were right on the money.

Although Kenny Brown will be learning about this for the first time when he reads these pages, here's what Chris Favo said about him on four and a half hours of training tapes Favo made for Agent T. J. Harkins days to hours before Favo ignited my first scandal by going to Don North on January 17, 1994:

"Brown . . . Brown used to be the Colombo guy before he voluntarily left the squad to become the [informant] coordinator . . . One of our problems with him is that when he left he didn't turn over any of his informants to us. When he left he kept his hand in the family . . . In addition, he had 'New York' as one of his informants and now when . . . uh . . . he was very protective of 'New York,' and when we had indications that 'New York' was involved in things, Brown would naturally deny it and we were concerned that he was passing information to 'New York.' "

That would be a very serious federal crime. By first covering for "New York" and then "passing information to 'New York' " Brown would be a member of the RICO criminal enterprise and would be criminally responsible for what that enterprise did.

This was a blatant attempt to plant in the brain of a fellow agent a suspicious thought about the New York FBI office's former informant coordinator. According to Favo, he and others in the know suspected Kenny Brown, the top Colombo guy, a fellow agent then in our South Carolina office, of "passing information" to the Mafia in the person of his informant code-named "New York" while he was the informant coordinator. And Favo did not utter a word indicating that his suspicion was unfounded. The suspicion is still on the table as part of these training tapes; fortunately, these tapes were handed off to T. J. Harkins, who kept them, and passed them into our hands.

Favo used similar language about thirty days prior in reference to Detective Joe Simone, who, because of Favo's accusations, was arrested for "passing information" to the Mafia. Favo again used similar language days to hours later when he expressed concern to Don North that I was "passing information" to the Mafia.

Sadly, Detective Joe Simone was arrested on December 8, 1993, the day he'd planned to put in his retirement papers after twenty years of service to the NYPD, and it cost him his pension.

Favo first brought his suspicions about Joe Simone to me some six months earlier. As was my duty, I reported it to Don North. Don North, Valerie Caproni, and I had a meeting with Favo and an agent from our public corruption squad. That squad investigated other agencies of government. For FBI corruption we had the OPR unit to investigate FBI agents. Favo told us that a CW named Big Sal Miciotta had implicated Simone in passing information to a guy who passed it to Sal. Big Sal was still on the street and offered to wear a wire in order to trap Simone. I advised Favo to give Simone a red herring—untrue information that Favo would make up—to see if the bogus information came back to Big Sal. This is known as an integrity test. I didn't know Favo already knew about this technique, and had used it on me. I'd get an earful about this from Dave Stone much later down the road.

Favo was working with the federal prosecutors in Brooklyn under Valerie Caproni in order to make the case against Simone. He cultivated the often-neglected federal prosecutors of the Eastern District in Brooklyn and they appreciated the attention he gave them. It was all right with me. Before my Favo scandal, I always had a great relationship with the prosecutors in the Eastern District. The lawyer I chose to represent me in the OPR case and in my murder case, Doug Grover, was an Eastern District federal prosecutor I'd seen in action and admired.

A week or so before Joe Simone's scheduled arrest, Dave Stone, a well-respected supervisor, paid me a visit. I knew Dave, the ice hockey player, had been Favo's first supervisor in Organized Crime and he always spoke well of Favo.

"No way Joe Simone is corrupt," Dave said. "I just heard about it. No way Joe is a dirty cop."

"Favo says he's got a good case," I said.

"Favo sees everything in black and white. And he's too zealous. He believes it, but that doesn't make it true."

"He's got the backing of the Eastern District on it," I said.

"Lin." Dave sighed. "Joe Simone was one of my best detectives. I worked with him even before I became a supervisor. I've worked with Joe for ten years. I know him personally. I tell you, Joe's life is dedicated to putting these people away."

"Favo said he's got him on tape with Big Sal Miciotta."

"Joe may not be the smartest guy in the world, Lin, but he's not dirty. To get information he might have given some out. Maybe to develop Miciotta. Joe lives on Staten Island near some of these people. He cultivates them. He has for years."

"I don't know the details," I said. "Favo worked the case with our public corruption squad and the Eastern District."

"The public corruption squad doesn't know dick about Organized Crime. You know as well as I do . . . anybody works an informant is always on the edge of being accused. You ask questions, and in the question you're giving up information. They turn around and go back and tell everybody they've got an agent telling them such and such. They all brag they've got a law enforcement source. You know that's true."

"I really don't think Simone was trying to develop Miciotta as a source."

"We lent you Joe Simone in the first place. At least let me arrest him. It'll be easier on him."

"It'll be rough on you."

"I'm thinking of poor Joe. I'll take him in my car. No cuffs."

"It's your arrest, Dave. I'll send Favo out on the other arrests Big Sal gave us."

"Favo worked with Joe on my squad for a year," Dave added. "Joe Simone helped teach him a lot. They should have let him surrender himself."

"It's in the Eastern District's hands. The best I can do is let you arrest him."

"You've always been such a nice guy, Lin, I appreciate it. But I'll be testifying for Joe."

At his arrest, when he was told that three-hundred-pound Big Sal Miciotta was prepared to testify against him for corruption, Joe Simone said: "You are going to believe that fat shit over a cop?"

Favo would also testify against Detective Joe Simone at the latter's trial in October 1994. I have the transcript of his testimony.

At the time of Simone's trial, Favo's OPR investigation of me was in its ninth month. It would take two more years before it was concluded. The OPR investigation effectively put me "on the shelf"—out of the business of fighting the Mafia.

Unfortunately, at the time of Detective Simone's trial, no one yet had Harkins's tapes of Favo demonstrating his penchant for making accusations of corruption. When he accused me I was just one of three he'd accused in one month.

Was Favo a zealot, as Stone told me, a true believer living in an unreal world? Or was there a method to his madness, rooted in ruthless ambition? Like the loose cannon Vito Genovese, was Favo a power grabber?

"Favo was arrogant," recalls Pat Marshall. "I stayed away from him. And he certainly didn't fuck with me."

But wait a minute. I left something out. On the tape Favo provided a solid source for his concern about Kenny Brown: "We were concerned," he said, "that he was passing information to 'New York.' [Carmine] Sessa makes an accusation in that regard during the war."

Oh, so it's a real cause for concern, one with a basis in the real world. The CW Carmine Sessa, the former consigliere of the Colombo Family, made "an accusation in that regard." So there was evidence to support the concern. Just as there was in Big Sal Miciotta's tape recording of Joe Simone.

Or was there? Did Carmine Sessa ever say or imply that Ken Brown was "passing information" to him or to anyone in the Mafia? An "accusation in that regard" needs to be reported to the brass at once, not to a fellow agent on a so-called training tape. And had either Sessa or Favo made such an accusation, an OPR would have been opened against Kenny Brown at once. But of course, none ever was.

A dozen years later the Brooklyn D.A.'s Office listed both Carmine Sessa and Larry Mazza as witnesses against me in my trial for "passing information" to Scarpa so he would commit murders. Was there "an accusation in that regard" that was coming down the pike against me from either Sessa or Mazza or both? I'd have to wait for the trial to find out.

CHAPTER TWENTY-THREE

GIVE PEACE A CHANCE

The CW of CWs, Sammy "The Bull" Gravano, revealed that during a sit-down between John Gotti and Chin Gigante, Gotti, like a proud papa, told Chin that he'd just straightened out his son John Gotti Jr. Chin sadly looked at Gotti and said, "I'm sorry to hear that."

The sensible made men of the Mafia wanted to give their sons a better life than theirs had been. More *Moonstruck*; less *Godfather*. The particularly volatile ones like Gotti, Greg Scarpa, and Junior Persico, on the other hand, encouraged their sons to enter "the life" they had lived.

The Colombo Family War, which broke out on November 18, 1991, was a war over just one thing. And that was Little Allie Boy Persico. It was a war of succession to the royal throne of the House of Colombo.

When he was facing his 139-year stretch, good manners, if not Mafia tradition, dictated that Junior Persico abdicate as Boss. Had there been a fully functioning Commission at the time, it would have taught Junior some manners. Without a Commission to stop him, he became obsessed with biding his time in jail as the official Boss until Little Allie Boy could ascend to the position.

At his 1986 sentencing in the Colombo Family RICO case, Junior did not beg for mercy for himself. Instead, he begged the judge to go easy on his boy. While the father got thirty-nine years, his thirty-year-old pride and joy got twelve. If the young capo Little Allie Boy kept his nose clean in jail, he'd be released in May 1993, at which time he'd don the crown and take over the family as official Boss.

Toward that end, Junior Persico appointed, first, a three-man board, and when that didn't prove efficient, an acting Boss to administer the family and keep the throne warm for Little Allie Boy.

"Little Allie Boy had everything going for him," recalled Kenny Brown. "He was tall, dark, and handsome. He was smart and personable. He even considered going to law school. Instead, he dropped out of St. John's University, got made, and became the youngest capo around. I only dealt with him once when I went into a social club looking for his uncle Allie Boy, who was on the lam. When I went in, Frank Sparaco—who was trying to look good to the Boss's son—started hurling insults at me, telling me to get the fuck out. Little Allie Boy told Sparaco to be quiet. 'He's got a job to do,' Little Allie

Boy said. Then he took me all through the club so I could see for myself that his uncle wasn't there."

Speaking of Sparaco, he took a big step to advance his career while Little Allie Boy was in prison. My Scarpa 209 for February 21, 1992, reads: "The recent hit on MICHAEL DIVINE, the owner of HEDGES, for going out with LITTLE ALLIE BOY PERSICO'S wife was done by FRANK SPARACO and several of his associates. The source noted that SPARACO is in trouble with the PERSICO faction in view of the bad timing involved in hitting DIVINE, and that no authorization was given for the hit."

The timing was "bad" in that the war was under way and hitting a civilian was bound to bring even more heat. Sparaco carried out this unsolicited hit in order to curry favor with Little Allie Boy. This kind of hit was something we always worried would be taken out on Joe Pistone— some eager beaver cowboy trying to please. I passed this hot tip on Divine along to NYPD homicide, and we did not spin our wheels investigating it as an example of a wartime casualty.

At the time Divine paid the price for unauthorized dating in the first degree, Little Allie Boy had a little over a year to go on his twelve years.

In 1988, after some fits and starts, Junior decided to anoint as acting Boss a short, stocky, loyal, and obscure soldier who was then serving as an acting capo and taking care of Little Allie Boy's crew. This five-foot six-inch, two-hundred-pound man was Little Vic Orena.

From all indications, Orena, dripping in jewelry and

swathed in finely tailored suits, was the perfect choice. He was a successful loan shark, bookmaker, construction mogul, and waste-hauling tycoon. He was not a volatile hair trigger like some.

However, Little Vic turned out to be a big surprise. As obsessed as Junior was at installing his heir apparent as Boss, Orena became equally obsessed with making his acting Boss job permanent. You have to consider, Little Vic had two straightened-out sons in the family business. Orena had a little bit of Little League father in him, too.

Orena did all the things an Italian Renaissance duke, schooled by Machiavelli, might have done. He curried favor with John Gotti by putting a whack on a Gotti enemy. He straightened out men loyal to him. He appointed capos loyal to him. He reduced the rank of other capos and blamed Junior for the demotions. And he smiled a lot and bowed and scraped to Junior's relatives.

With Little Allie Boy due to have a coming-out party in two years, Orena decided to make his move in 1991. He ordered the family consigliere, Carmine Sessa, to poll the capos to see if they wanted Junior to continue as Boss in light of the reliably reported attempts of Junior to debate Rudy Giuliani from his jail cell on *60 Minutes*. So much for *omertà*!

A "siege mentality" was setting in. Cautious that such political polling could get him killed, Sessa reported Orena's order to Junior's brother, capo Teddy Persico. The predictable communiqué from Junior was "off with Orena's head"—and in order to prove his loyalty, Carmine Sessa was handed the executioner's ax.

Our first peek at this crack in the Colombo Family foundation came on July 8, 1991. Scarpa's 209: "CARMINE SESSA and MICHAEL SESSA, BOBBY ZAMBARDI, and HANK SMURRA plotted to kill acting Boss VIC ORENA. The source said ORENA saw the individuals involved outside his residence, which stopped the intended hit. The source said this attempt on ORENA has divided the COLOMBO Family into two factions . . ."

Scarpa went on to accurately list the men in each faction. He listed himself on the minority Persico side. Including associates, the Orena faction would be able to count on a hundred men, while the Persico faction could count only on thirty.

Scarpa's 209 continued with hope for everlasting peace: "The source said this dispute will be settled soon, with the assistance of another family who will act as a mediator and ensure protection of all parties."

I gave this report to Favo. I explained that Orena knew that these three or four Colombo buttons had no reason to be out his way on Long Island. They spotted each other—it turned out—at a stoplight in Orena territory on June 20. Since Sessa's car contained the spotters, not the shooters, Sessa's people weren't armed. Nothing actually happened. But this fluke encounter more than piqued Orena's suspicions, and it should pique ours, I added.

While we had at least a moral duty to warn intended murder victims, to do so here would only inflame matters, and it was reasonable to assume that Orena was in possession of all the warning he needed. Because this nonincident was potentially explosive, I made sure to check in with Scarpa more frequently.

Three days later Scarpa had nothing new on Orena vs. Persico, just the usual singular Crimestoppers tip: "MICHAEL SESSA was the one who shot and killed the owner of an auto body shop across from the produce stand owned by SESSA on Staten Island." Of course, I passed this hot tip about Carmine Sessa's brother on to NYPD homicide.

Then on August 13, 1991, Scarpa reported on Orena vs. Persico for the second time: "ORENA is trying to assume full control of the COLOMBO Family by having CARMINE PERSICO relieved of his position as Boss. This has caused a major division within the family . . . The source noted, however, that according to tradition, there are only three ways to change a family Boss: by death (PERSICO is in prison); by the Boss voluntarily stepping down (not likely in PERSICO's case); and by a vote of the Commission to relieve the Boss.

"The source said the third option is not feasible at this time since most of the New York family Bosses are currently in jail and there is no formal COMMISSION . . ."

There was no more formal Commission thanks to our work.

I told Favo that the war dance might lead to war paint if either side stirred the pot.

Scarpa told me on August 20, 1991: "Word from COLOMBO Boss CARMINE PERSICO is that VIC ORENA is being removed as acting Boss . . . CARMINE SESSA, and capos CHUCKIE RUSSO and JO JO

RUSSO, will begin advising ORENA's people immediately of this decision. The source said reaction to this is unknown at this time, but some problems could arise from those loyal to ORENA."

After stirring the pot by dethroning Orena, Persico anointed Joseph "Joe T" Tomasello as acting Boss. Joe T was a partner in a school-bus company with one of my alleged murder victims, Lorenzo Lampasi. My future co-framer capo, Jo Jo Russo, was anointed acting underboss, and a future witness against me, Carmine Sessa, was retained as the consigliere.

On August 31, 1991, Scarpa speculated about which knights of the Orena Round Table might be targeted first if war broke out. "The logical move," he said, "would be to take out Vic Orena and Benny and Vinny Aloi . . ."

Around this time we learned that Junior Persico had been placed under punitive detention in prison. He had temporarily lost certain visitation privileges and had thereby lost an important means of communicating with his faction. His female lawyer was seen on a prison video monitor performing oral sex on him. She followed this attorney-client-privileged performance with a love letter. Naturally, we had the tape sent to us for our files in the interest of thoroughness. We'd have been remiss if we hadn't. We got a lot of laughs out of this one. As an attorney, she had been able to visit Junior pretty much at will and was not restricted to visitors' days and hours. Now she was banned from seeing him for any reason.

* * *

Things seemed quiet for over a month, then Scarpa reported "that a meeting was held on October 6, 1991, between the PERSICO and ORENA factions to resolve the dispute." But the peace talks ended in a stalemate.

On October 23, 1991, the "source said the mediators sent in by the other families were not able to resolve the COLOMBO dispute and have stopped meeting with the respective sides. However, none of the families want to see a shooting war break out." Of course not—it's very bad for business. It interrupts collections from victims on the loan-shark "book" and gamblers. It interrupts doing scores. And it brings heat.

On November 4, 1991, Scarpa told me something that would someday be relevant to my understanding of the unfortunate things that later happened to me, but at the time it was just one of those things: "The recent hit on JACK LEALE was done by the ORENA faction of the COLOMBO Family, although the PERSICO side was as anxious to have LEALE hit. The source said LEALE made the fatal mistake of relying on too many nonmade individuals to dispose of TOMMY OCERA's body, which was subsequently found by the FBI . . ."

Tommy Ocera had been a collector for Orena's loan-shark "book" on Long Island before he disappeared in 1989. Because Ocera reported to Orena, it was more than safe to assume that Orena ordered, or at the very least sanctioned, the hit. Our Long Island office was investigating Orena. And they seemed to be doing pretty good work on Orena, who lived and worked on Long Island.

The hit on Jack Leale appeared to be an Orena screwup. It was punishment for being sloppy in the first degree.

As to the Orena vs. Persico matter, on the same day Scarpa reported on the late Jack Leale, he stated that "the PERSICO faction is growing impatient with the current division in the COLOMBO Family, and said despite the apparent inaction on either side, something would break soon. The source noted that JOEY SCOPO and possibly BILLY CUTOLO would be likely victims on the ORENA side, and that CARMINE SESSA and GREG SCARPA SR. would be the ORENA's side pick to be hit."

This is where matters stood on November 4. Chris Favo's training tape picks up the action from there. Al D'Arco, whom Favo mentions, was in the Lucchese Family. In 1991, D'Arco, a Korean War veteran, had become a CW in order to avoid being a victim in the bloodbath of serial killings that Gaspipe Casso was orchestrating with the secret help of his "crystal ball," the corrupt Mafia Cops.

According to Favo:

"After D'Arco came on board, he told the interviewing agent that one of his problems, and the problems of many mobsters, is that they might . . . they would probably talk to the FBI, but they didn't know any agents. If they had—and if the agents at least went out and met the mobsters, you know, when the mobsters became vulnerable, they would contact the agent. It was, uh . . . because of this [that] Don North told us to all go out and talk to people. It was kind of meet-your-local-agent plan. And uh . . . Ray and me and Robert, Randy Biddle, Jeff Tomlinson, we all were then assigned people to go out and say hello to. I took Cutolo. And uh . . . in early November '91 we went around saying hello to all the mobsters."

This was a brilliant idea of Don North's for three reasons. One, because if a shooting war broke out, it would be important for potential CWs seeking to avoid being killed in the war to have an agent they could call. Two, because it would alert all sides that we were aware of hostilities and were keeping an eye on them. Three, because it was always my policy to send my agents out to talk to wiseguys. It was what I taught in my informant development classes. It was about time that Favo headed out the door and dived right in.

But Favo knew better. He continued: "We had actually advised against this to North. It fell on deaf ears. Our problem was that since there was a war on, we couldn't just go and say hello to these people."

There was no war on yet. And yes, you *could* just say hello to "these people." That's what you were being ordered to do.

Favo explained: "We would have to say that there was death threats against them 'cause at this point there were death threats against everybody in the family."

No, you wouldn't have to say there were "death threats" because there weren't any "death threats" against anybody in the family, except for Carmine Sessa's June 20 plan to kill Orena. Scarpa speculated that it was logical that Joey Scopo and "possibly" Billy Cutolo, on the Orena side, and he himself and Carmine Sessa, on the Persico side, would be the first to be targeted. Earlier, without mentioning Scopo or Cutolo, Scarpa said: "The logical move would be to take out Vic Orena and Benny and Vinny Aloi." But that's all we had, logic and speculation. We had no information that anyone was threatening to hit anyone. Our information was that at this time there had been an uneasy truce in effect for five months.

Favo continued: "In any case—I think that—we go see Cutolo on November 13. I think it was me and Mike Jenkins that went to see him the first time."

What Favo could have said when he visited Billy Cutolo, for example, is that: "We know there is division and we don't want to see things get out of hand. You're an important person in the Orena faction and you could logically be among the first to be targeted." Of course, someone like Billy Cutolo already knew that. So saying it wouldn't stir the pot.

Favo explained why he thought it would be the wrong thing to tell anyone especially at a time when there were "death threats against them": "And, uh, we were afraid that this would kind of destabilize whatever truce they had at the time."

So, following his interpretation of North's orders, Favo went to talk to Billy Cutolo on November 13, 1991, five days before Cutolo's crew fired the first shots of the war.

According to Favo:

"So when we went and talked to him and told him

there was a death threat against him, he kind of looked a little panicked—who was after him and so forth. He had a lot of questions along those lines. He said that he would be fine and, you know, we extended an offer for him to cooperate or protection, whatever he needed.

"Of course, then Greg Scarpa gets shot five days later on the eighteenth of November.

"I was always concerned about this, and that you probably heard me say it before because . . . I felt that our stirring Cutolo up had something to do with stirring the war up."

But, of course, it was Don North's fault to begin with.

Favo was "concerned" again, like he was "concerned" that Kenny Brown was corrupt. On this one, though, he was right to be concerned. It was cause and effect. Cause: ". . . we . . . told him there was a death threat against him . . ." Again, there wasn't any such death threat. Effect: ". . . he kind of looked a little panicked—who was after him and so forth. He had a lot of questions along those lines." In his panic, Cutolo predictably wanted to know who was going to come after him. Of course he had "a lot of questions." He wanted details about this "death threat against him." Who can blame him? Cutolo's reaction demonstrates why we didn't pay a visit to Little Vic Orena after Sessa and his carload of spotters were spotted in Orena-ville.

Favo's self-condemnation was an endearing trait and he used it well. However, he immediately put a spin on this topic for the agent he was training: "Now, none of the cooperating witnesses that have come forward have said that."

Of course, the CWs hadn't come forward and said Cutolo was stirred up or panicked by inside information from the FBI. How could any CW on either side possibly know about Cutolo's reaction? Cutolo wouldn't talk about that visit with anyone but Orena and his inner circle. Cutolo would only act. He'd act to get off the first shot against Scarpa, who, he now knew in his gut, was planning to get him.

Favo explained: "They [the CWs] all attributed the war to an argument between Greg Scarpa and John Rosatti after which Rosatti went, excuse me, Scarpa went and beat a guy in Rosatti's car sales place for pinching Scarpa's niece. And then Rosatti then goes to the Café on N and complains to Vic Orena about it."

I never heard that one. I guess it's possible that a CW said that, but this explanation is laughable at best—that a shooting war would start over the beating of a non-made man for the pinching of a made man's niece.

Favo and the agent who accompanied him were eyewitnesses to Cutolo's reaction to the warning about a "death threat against him." And Favo recorded his eyewitness account and we have the tape.

I interpret all this as Favo's trying a clumsy power play on Billy Cutolo. Because he had no knack for talking to people as people, he tried to scare Cutolo into becoming a CW the way Al D'Arco had become one for the Lucchese Family. What a prize that would have been for a man too good for Kenny Maxwell's terrorism squad! Whether my analysis is right or not, the way Favo handled Cutolo was unethical and unconscionable. We have no right to use our power to provoke anyone.

Not knowing any of the above at the time, when the shooting war started I appointed Chris Favo as the Colombo Family War case agent and I trusted him with the information that "34" was Greg Scarpa.

Scarpa called me immediately after the attempt on his life and I met with him at once: "On November 18, 1991, source advised that an attempt to hit GREG SCARPA was made on November 18, 1991, by members of the ORENA faction of the COLOMBO Family. Source said there were several shooters and SCARPA's daughter was almost shot in the attempt. The source did not know which crew attempted the hit but noted that this would start the shooting war between the two factions."

Of course Scarpa knew "which crew attempted the hit," but he'd settle that score personally. You didn't mess with his children—ever.

Scarpa was livid. A white truck sitting sideways had blocked his street, while shooters in ski masks came running out of a van and went after his car. They fired shotguns at him. Scarpa evaded the shooters by driving onto the sidewalk and past the blocking white truck. A Mercedes pulling out behind Scarpa's car took the blasts meant for Scarpa. Little Linda Schiro was driving the Mercedes, and her two-year-old son was a passenger. Luckily, no pellets hit Little Linda or her son, but they strafed her car.

Scarpa was furious that they had fired on and hit a car occupied by his daughter and grandson. Remembering what he'd done to the limo driver who molested Little Linda on her way to school, I said to him: "I know you very well. I know what you are going to do. I just have to tell you, if you get caught you'll get prosecuted like anyone else." Scarpa just laughed. He had AIDS; what could anyone do to him.

Billy Cutolo had the jump on the Persicos. Billy's crew gunned down Hank "The Bank" Smurra in front of a donut shop on November 24, 1991.

On November 25, 1991, Scarpa observed "that the principals of both sides are very cautious, and the lesser players, who are easier to find, are becoming the targets of retaliation." That's "the life" in a nutshell.

And these "lesser players, who are easier to find" would become our new CWs.

On Thanksgiving Day 1991, five months after I'd told Favo that "34" was Scarpa, an article appeared in the *New York Post*. It revealed that Greg Scarpa was believed to be an FBI informant. I feared that Scarpa might now dry up as a source. Looking back, now sadder but wiser, I wonder if maybe somebody wanted that to happen and attempted to dry up Scarpa with a public accusation.

I also had to consider that the effect of publicly branding him an informant might only be to make Scarpa kill more ferociously in a quest to disprove the allegation. Perhaps it did. But I think the original botched attack on his daughter and grandson was all the motivation he needed.

CWs revealed that on the day the article was printed, there was a plan to hit Billy Cutolo. Greg Scarpa was going to dress as a Hasidic Jew so that he could get close enough to Cutolo on the street to kill him. The article aborted that plan. Scarpa's co-conspirators casually withdrew from contact with Scarpa until the *Post* printed a retraction a few days later.

I hate to view this war in personal terms, but I ended up getting one of my murder charges out of it, so I'd like to explain that as an administrator, I had way too much on my plate by then to deal with the additional burden of a Mafia war, what with both the Bonanno Family Title IIIs and the normal Colombo Family matters and all of it squeezed into my supervisory responsibility in a single squad. Meanwhile, I was still half a street agent. I still had my TE informants and all the work that this entailed.

Under the first President Bush, drugs had gotten the spotlight and the brass had invaded my squad. By the time the Colombo war broke out, the brass had taken many of my experienced agents and put them in drugs. I lost my Colombo Family expert Kenny Brown when they made him informant coordinator. They restocked me with agents for the Colombo side with little to no experience. I couldn't imagine trading Kenny Brown with all his Colombo Family experience for Chris Favo as my go-to guy, much less for the brand-new agents that followed Favo. And I do mean "followed" Favo in both senses of that word. They were FOAs—First Office Agents—and Favo, with a year or so experience, was the old-timer. They were FNGs—Fucking New Guys. To the brand-new guys with no experience at all, Favo could pass himself off as an old-timer. I kept begging to have one of the families taken from me or to get some experienced guys on the squad. Chris Mattiace and I fought hard against the brass to try to prevent the blending of the Colombo Family into another squad and manning it with guys with no Organized Crime background. We argued that fighting the Mafia was unlike any other crime fighting. The Mafia had its own way of thinking, speaking, and acting. You could have twenty years experience in general crime and be out of your element on an Organized Crime squad.

But we were told we had done such a good job on the Mafia in the 1980s that other gangs like the Russians, Chinese, and Vietnamese were filling the vacuum and they needed squads for these other ethnic gangs.

None of us foresaw that as a result of the century-length prison terms in the Mafia Commission Case and the Colombo Family hierarchy RICO convictions, the Colombo Family would spin out of control and deteriorate into gang warfare. None of us foresaw the enormous strain that daily warfare would put on the workload of fourteen agents handling two families. Imagine working a major shooting war with inexperienced agents at the same time as you're working major cases on another family.

There hadn't been a shooting war within any family since the Gallo brothers' uprising in 1961—in the same family. But that uprising hadn't been the FBI's problem. It was the NYPD's. The FBI had no history of dealing with a Mafia war. We had no Mafia war protocol to follow.

Despite all I've been through because of that first scandal, a part of me feels that I am partly to blame; I simply didn't have time to supervise Favo correctly, to notice what Favo was really like, his strengths and weaknesses, much less keep a tight handle on all he was doing out there—much less have a clue that he thought I was dirty and that every time I asked him a question he thought I was fishing for information to report to Greg Scarpa.

Meanwhile, the bodies started rolling in.

CHAPTER TWENTY-FOUR

THE COLOMBO FAMILY WAR TIMES TWO

Rat-a-tat-tat.

That's the sound of a Mafia family shooting itself in the foot, the hand, the heart, and the head.

Brooklyn federal prosecutor George Stamboulidis summed up the results of the carnage: "The war helped us destroy the family from within. Instead of pulling together in the face of government investigations, they were worrying about saving their lives and that gave them incentives to become cooperating witnesses."

The rat-a-tat-tat would produce the "rat"—a word I still hate to use.

My accuser, Brooklyn District Attorney Charles "Joe" Hynes, put it another way when the war was about a year old: "I have no problem letting these folks blow each other away. I think it's good for us ultimately."

As Favo testified in one of Little Vic Orena's hearings on appeal: "[DeVecchio] said . . . that he wanted to be the first supervisor to dismantle an organized crime family, and that was true. He said that many times."

Indeed, I had. That was my dream and everyone knew it. And now, thanks to the impact of our championship season on the Mafia, it looked as if the dismantling of an entire family was going to happen to the Colombo Family on my watch. Still, it was my sworn duty to prevent violence and stop the war if I could, and I took that duty very seriously.

When war broke out I borrowed Dave Stone's NYPD detectives under Lieutenant Billy Shannon. These included Joe Simone and his partner, Patrick Maggiore. We formed a joint task force under my supervision. I put Favo in charge of taking Scarpa's war tips and gathering all the other CI war tips. Favo's job was to identify hit teams, autos, social clubs, safe houses, shooters' home addresses, and intended victims, and get the names of those who were on parole and were forbidden from associating with organized crime figures. Favo was to convey that information to the NYPD detectives in the field. The detectives were to look for a pretext to stop a car— for, say, an improper lane change without signaling.

All these Colombo warriors had guns and could be arrested for carrying them—or for tossing the gun out a window, as some did. Many of these guys were convicted felons, which added a more serious crime to the gun possession charge.

It was a great idea, but within a few days something seemed to be going wrong with our tactic of stopping the cars of the wiseguys. We couldn't seem to find any guns on them. Scarpa's hit squad was stopped and no guns were found. Then Scarpa reported to me that the hit squads had tuned into the NYPD radio frequency and were using police scanners to avoid the patrols. If there was a patrol in the area, they would pull over and off-load their guns. Scarpa confessed that he had done this very thing minutes before his hit squad had been stopped. Immediately, I had the NYPD switch to an undetectable FBI-coded frequency and we were back in the business of protecting citizens from stray bullets— these people were not the best shots in the world, and on several occasions they traded gunfire from moving vehicles.

Many of these gun arrests we made wouldn't stick because of court rulings of the 1960s that forbade frisking for a gun or drugs on "mere suspicion." But at least we were getting guns off the street—over a hundred. And the rules against "pretextual stops"—that is, stopping a suspect on a pretext and searching him in a way that fit into one of the exceptions to the new rules— didn't require that we give the guns back. Although, logically, if the new rules said we didn't have the right to take the gun in the first place, how in the world did we have the right to keep it?

When we'd obtained enough probable cause from Scarpa and the other informants, we'd get a search warrant for a safe house where the principal players tended to hide themselves and their weapons until it was time to go out and draw blood.

The detectives provided surveillance on Scarpa's house off and on until April 15, 1992, when the NYPD ran out of overtime money to finance their contribution to the strike force. Which reminds me: Given the surveillance on Scarpa's house, how did I get over there two or three times a week to meet with him and give him information for cash, as Linda Schiro was to claim? Another conundrum . . .

There was an episode of *NYPD Blue* about a joint NYPD-FBI investigation of a kidnapping. Dennis Franz played the NYPD detective Andy Sipowicz. The script depicted a lot of friction between the two agencies. Sipowicz pointed out that the FBI was trying to take all the credit. He said, "They're pretty good with their elbows." I never found such friction in Organized Crime. Just the opposite. We had camaraderie. We'd all been seasoned on the same streets of New York, had all learned to concentrate on our common enemy, and we were all too busy to rush to a microphone and brag about our exploits, unless ordered to cooperate with the media.

The ideal tactic for our joint task force was to climb

the legal hurdles and get permission to plant a bug in a hit team's car. Kenny Steiger, the outstanding case agent on the Orena case, working out of the Melville, Long Island, office, had excellent informants, as did Joe Fanning, an agent on Kenny's squad. They managed to get a bug up in an Orena hit squad car belonging to Chubby Audino. Kenny Steiger's squad got that Title III up and running a little over two months after the war began.

"What took you so long?" I joked with him.

The Chubby Audino tapes from that bug were used to convict Little Vic Orena of RICO murder conspiracy for the wartime murders that were committed by the Orena faction. I testifed as an expert witness on the Mafia and the Colombo Family War in that trial.

Seven months after the war began, my squad finally did get a bug up on a Persico hit team car. The car belonged to Joey Brains Ambrosino, who carried a machine gun. Rat-a-tat-tat, indeed. As I said before, Joey Brains got his nickname because he wasn't the sharpest knife in the drawer. It turned out to be a very productive bug and it helped end the war.

Meanwhile: rat-a-tat-tat.

December 3, 1991: The Persico faction struck back and had their first kill. It was not exactly a trophy kill. The victim was seventy-eight-year-old Gaetano Amato. He was a Genovese made man who was then "on the shelf," that is, semiretired. Gaetano made the error in judgment of hanging out in front of a social club belonging to my civil lawsuit murder victim Nicky Black Grancio. Drive-by shooters under Greg Scarpa were looking for Nicky Black and were aiming for another Colombo button when they shot and killed Gaetano by mistake. Since the old guy was no longer a Genovese Family moneymaker, his Boss, Chin Gigante, took the hit in stride. Chin generously blamed Gaetano for getting himself killed and paid for the funeral.

December 5, 1991: Two days later the Orena hit squad that attacked Scarpa and killed Hank the Bank went on patrol and whacked an extremely low-level Persico cohort named Black Sam Nastasi and his female companion inside a social club.

On that same day Scarpa told me: "TEDDY PERSICO and CHUCKIE RUSSO have visited CARMINE PERSICO in prison in Lompoc . . . and have discussed . . . the individuals who should be killed on the ORENA side . . . TEDDY . . . is planning to visit CARMINE at Lompoc in the near future to keep him apprised of the ongoing dispute."

This 209, along with other information from Scarpa, gave Pat Marshall the "may I" he needed to bug the Lompoc visitors' tables.

Rat-a-tat-tat.

December 6, 1991: Greg Scarpa and his young drive-by hit team of Larry Mazza and James Delmasto spotted Orena low-level loan-shark collector Vincent Fusaro on a ladder. Fusaro didn't see Scarpa and his young killers because he was busy hanging Christmas lights for his wife and children. Fusaro never knew what hit him. The Fusaro home went undecorated that Christmas season.

December 8, 1991: Orena hitters went to a bagel shop looking for Persico loyalist Frank Guerra, who owned Wanna Bagel. Instead they found an eighteen-year-old boy working behind the counter—Matteo Speranza. They killed the boy in cold blood.

On December 11, 1991, in view of the killing of Matteo Speranza, I thought that I ought to pay Scarpa a rare home visit in order to get a full dump from him, with lots of time for questions and answers. To make it look like an official FBI visit in case anyone saw me go into his house, I took along an FNG, a follower of Favo, a partner of Favo, and, like Favo, a man without a knack, Ray Andjich.

I had no clue of this at the time, but this visit would come back to haunt. I was just trying to get my job done. I parked Ray Andjich in the living room in front of the TV and sat down in the kitchen with Scarpa. Bewildering all who heard it, Andjich would later come to my murder trial and testify against me for parking him in front of the TV.

In the privacy of his kitchen, Scarpa identified Billy Cutolo's crew as the shooters of Hank the Bank and Black Sam, as well as the team that had attemped to murder him. The Cutolo hit crew consisted of Chickie DeMartino, Frankie Notch, and Nigger Dom. We knew them well.

Scarpa said that the hit on Gaetano Amato was "an

accidental shooting by the PERSICO faction," the hit on Vincent Fusaro while he was hanging Christmas lights had been "done by the PERSICO faction," and "the killing of SPERANZA who worked at the bagel shop was not done by the PERSICO faction."

He gave me some reason to be hopeful when he said, "There is to be a sit-down next week between the two factions in an attempt to resolve the dispute." However, if it couldn't be settled amicably, "there would be more hits. The source noted that law enforcement pressure may slow down the active shooting, but it would resume in short order unless some of the major players are killed or indicted as a result of current federal investigations."

On December 30, 1991, Scarpa told me that "an arrest of VIC ORENA would temporarily halt the shooting war." Kenny Steiger was on the job on Long Island in Orena-ville.

Recently, Favo's first Organized Crime supervisor Dave Stone had told me that toward the end of 1991 and the beginning of 1992, but certainly before I would close Scarpa as an informant on March 3, 1992, Favo came to him to talk privately about me. Favo said that he suspected that I was giving FBI information to Scarpa. He said he'd put a phony and fictitious 302 in my in-box to see if the fake information came back to him from an informant, and it did. This is another example of what I called an integrity test. Supervisors had to read and sign off on all 302s created in their squad. When pressed on this point because I'd never heard of this fake 302, Dave Stone said to me: "Favo might have said that he *planned* on doing that, but I'm pretty sure he said that he'd *already done* it." If Favo did run an integrity test on me, he never mentioned it in any of his OPR interviews, or his grand jury or trial testimony against me.

At this meeting Dave Stone assumed that Favo had encountered one of those situations where an informant gleans information from the questions an agent asks him. Dave Stone assured his friend Favo that there was no way that I was corrupt. He warned Favo that he was not permitted to undertake an internal investigation on his own initiative. The FBI and the Department of Justice have an Integrity Section and an independent Office of Professional Responsibility—the OPR—that investigates allegations against an agent.

There's more than one reason for that rigid rule. But in the case of Favo and me, the one that sticks out in my mind involves the many conflicts of interest inherent to the relationship between a supervisor and his agent. It was to Favo's personal advantage in many ways to claim I was corrupt. If I went down, he'd go up. That inherent personal advantage might cloud his thinking about the things he saw and heard.

For example, let's say Favo had an ambition to be assigned to high-profile major cases and to be credited and rewarded within the Bureau for solving those cases, something he expressed to Kenny Maxwell when he asked to be transferred out of Maxwell's terror squad. If he promoted the idea that I was corrupt, then he'd get to justify keeping information from me and to work the major cases as if his supervisor didn't exist. Then no one could accuse him of "being pretty good with his elbows."

If I was kept in the dark about the facts or progress of a major case, there was no way I could reassign the case to a more experienced agent and have him develop and follow leads while Favo was his subordinate. For example, if I wasn't kept in the dark, I would have sent Favo to Melville, Long Island, to work on the Little Vic Orena case; there, Kenny Steiger was case agent and Favo would have been working under him.

Another example of a personal conflict concerns his going to Dave Stone instead of going up the chain of command to Don North, who had the authority to make the decision about a referral to the OPR. The conflict of interest here is that by going to Stone, Favo might be motivated by personal interest, namely the wish to create a reasonable explanation for himself if he were ever caught concealing information and decisions from me. With Stone, he made a record for himself that I couldn't be trusted with information. This may sound like a stretch, but when someone with a conflict of interest takes action in spite of the conflict, he's liable to finding adverse inferences being drawn from those of his actions that end up benefiting him personally. In short, by going to Stone, Favo was covering his ass.

Favo told Dave Stone that he was thinking of going to the Eastern District federal prosecutors in Brooklyn for help and advice in dealing with me. Stone warned him that the only place he was permitted to go with such an accusation was to the head of Organized Crime in New York, Don North. Stone reiterated that there was no way that I was corrupt and told Favo that I'd been an extremely well-respected agent and supervisor for over two decades in Organized Crime. He said that I'd done an outstanding job against the Mafia. Following this conversation, Favo never returned to confide in Dave Stone again.

To say I had no idea that Favo thought anyone was corrupt, least of all me, is an understatement. I viewed Favo as a hard worker, an aggressive and eager member of my squad, and I gave him some outstanding ratings despite his shortcomings in informant development.

The notion that Favo had an informant that he could use in an integrity test of anyone is ludicrous. Favo is still in the FBI. I wouldn't be surprised if to this day he has never developed an informant. Certainly, he didn't truly develop a single one during the four years he was under my supervision. He often spoke about CWs as if they were informants. Sure he may have shown up with an arrest warrant in hand and some wannabe agreed to testify in exchange for leniency. But really developing someone, forming a relationship, cultivating a source? No, I don't think so.

Here's some amusing expert testimony Favo offered during the trial of Detective Joe Simone in the latter's bribery and corruption case on October 18, 1994. Let's see if we know more about the difference between a CW and a CI than Favo pretends to know:

The Court: Now, approximately how many informants have you developed in your career?

Favo: Approximately twenty.

The Court: And what is the nature of the relationship between an informant and an agent?

Favo: The agent gathers the information, and the informant is usually paid for the information provided. Or some receive no compensation and others receive different sorts of compensation. There are people waiting trial or other . . . sometimes they make an agreement along those lines.

The Court: Your voice is dropping.

I'll bet Favo was looking down at his shoes, too. Meanwhile, as 1992 began, my squad had a mountain of work to do just on the Colombo side alone. But without knowing it, I was involved in two Colombo Family Wars: the real one in the street that I knew about, and the clandestine war Favo was waging against me behind my back.

It was time to roll up my sleeves and get busy on the war I did know about.

CHAPTER TWENTY-FIVE

"WE'RE GOING TO WIN THIS THING"

Rat-a-tat-tat.

January 7, 1992: Scarpa's drive-by hit team sought out and slaughtered Nicky Black Grancio, who was sitting in his Range Rover. Nicky Black is the one who had told his crew: "We're trying to make peace. We gotta stop all this shit." That was just before he found himself deep in "all this shit" when he heard Scarpa's basso profundo voice tell him: "This one's from Carmine."

Speaking to me the next day, Scarpa pinned this murder on the Persico hit squad of Richie Fusco. Later on, I got accused of being "duped" by Scarpa over this one.

In my heart, as Scarpa's handler, of course I knew he was doing hits. Scarpa had a natural coyness, but sometimes he would try to act like he wasn't being coy. If I were playing poker with him, I'd pull out all the stops when I saw that effort not to be coy. I wasn't playing games with him. I was simply receiving my judicially required "may I" information that sooner or later would lead to bugs and taps and to CWs that eventually would lead back to Scarpa, perhaps as the last man to tumble in the downfall of the Colombo Family. And I believe this complicated man knew that.

The Orena faction knew that Scarpa was the Persicos' best killing machine. That's why Billy Cutolo suspected Scarpa of making Favo's fictitious "death threats against him" and why he made Scarpa their first target. Get Scarpa and you've materially weakened the Persico side. This wasn't rocket science.

In early February 1992, my boss, Don North, pressured me into closing Scarpa as an informant because another CI was telling his handler that Scarpa was doing hits in the war. The CI reported that Scarpa engineered a hit to take place in jail on an inmate. I argued with North. "Is closing Scarpa going to prevent the man from doing hits? How much longer are we going to have him? He's wasting away from AIDS. Right now he's a source we can rely on." We'd certainly need him if we got far enough along to apply for a car bug like Kenny Steiger and Joe Fanning had at the time on Chubby Audino's car in the Orena case.

Working against me was our informant coordinator, "Downtown" Kenny Brown. He had the informant with the jailhouse hit information, a CI who told him Scarpa was out scouting and killing. The Persico faction had started calling Scarpa "General Schwarzkopf" because of his killing prowess. I had some rough words with Kenny about closing Scarpa. I said: "This is bad timing. Look at the help he gave us on the police scanners and changing our radio frequency."

But Kenny and Don were adamant that I close Scarpa. This meant that I could not reach out and call Scarpa if we needed something. I could not pay Scarpa, not even out of my own pocket. I'd have to tell him he was closed. He could voluntarily call me if he wanted and I could listen to whatever he had to tell me, but I could no longer actively work him. I told Don and Kenny that I was going to ask for a review to reopen him.

On February 22, 1992, investigators from the Brooklyn D.A.'s Office arrested Persico associate Carmine Imbriale on drug charges while he was on his way to hit Orena underboss Patty Amato. Imbriale was a member of Carmine Sessa's Persico hit team and he had had more than enough of "all this shit." His one and only way out was to tell D.A. investigator George Terra that he wanted to become a CW. Terra wanted to keep Imbriale on the street, wearing a wire. But to stay on the street Imbriale would have to come up with $6,000 each and every week. It was the weekly vig on a considerable amount of money Imbriale owed the loan sharks. The D.A. didn't have money for that.

We, however, did have the money, and we also had the federal Witness Protection Program to offer Imbriale.

Terra reached out to us and I agreed to get Imbriale a federal stimulus package to include his weekly vig and said that we'd work Imbriale on the street. As long as he was paying his money, those who might judge him on the street had a conflict of interest. They'd be more likely to cast aside any suspicion they might form about a man who was just arrested if that man continued to feed them money. Blinded by the color green, many of Imbriale's associates continued to talk to him and his little friend the Nagra recorder.

On March 2, 1992, Favo prepared to wire Imbriale and send him back into the fray to spy on and record his Persico best friends and blood brothers. Imbriale and his body mike would remain on the street gathering evidence until July 10, 1992. You've got to admire a guy like Imbriale for his balls. Sometimes, when these guys change sides, they actually get caught up in their new cause.

But I wasn't caught up in the cause.

Favo later testified on more than one occasion that anything Imbriale told Favo about Scarpa, Favo purposefully concealed from me, including the full extent of Scarpa's participation in a murder conspiracy meeting at a Red Lobster in New Jersey. At the meeting, Carmine Sessa berated the others in attendance about how Scarpa was the only one doing any killing.

At the Red Lobster, Scarpa confessed to Imbriale that he'd shot Orena warrior Joe Waverly—the capo who ordered the botched hit on federal prosecutor William Aronwald. He bragged that he almost blew Joe Waverly's guts out. Waverly survived, but what Scarpa admitted was murder conspiracy, a RICO crime. Imbriale's word alone was probably not enough to arrest Scarpa, but had I known about the attempted murder, I would have mobilized my entire squad and the other supervisors at our Thursday meetings to get corroboration from the next CW we debriefed.

Meanwhile, the only mention of Waverly in Favo's deceptive 302 report of his debriefing of Imbriale was that Scarpa offered a toast to celebrate Waverly's being shot—by whomever—and said: "Another one for the good guys." Making a toast is not even remotely an admission of conspiracy to murder. And Favo, a law school graduate, knew this when he wrote the report. It seems that Favo was purposely not putting the full extent of Scarpa's involvement in the 302 that I would see. He was withholding significant information from me, his supervisor. If that isn't insubordination, I don't know what is.

The minute Favo stopped telling me things, he should have reported me to Don North, rather than waiting two years, during which time he abused the freedom I gave all my agents.

On March 3, 1992, as Imbriale was about to put on his wire, I closed Scarpa. Without giving him any details, I told him that if he had a contract out on a guy in jail, he'd better call it off. He denied this, but I knew that if he did in fact put the contract out, he would now call it off.

Although I could no longer contact Scarpa, on March 6, 1992, he called the "hello" phone and told me that "there was a contract to hit Greg SCARPA put out by Patty AMATO in view of the recent hits on ORENA faction members."

Well, there it was. It could be read no other way by

anyone experienced with the Mafia, with how they think and how they speak. Scarpa had been doing "the recent hits" on Orena faction members, and because of that, the Orena underboss Patty Amato put a contract out on him. And Scarpa was volunteering this information to me because of the relationship I had with him, a friendship that survived his closing.

Rat-a-tat-tat.

March 25, 1992: Guns blazing, acting underboss Jo Jo Russo, his cousin Chuckie, and pal Joe "Monte" Monteleone ambushed two men in front of a pastry shop in Massapequa, Long Island. The Cousins opened fire on Johnny Minerva, their old playmate from the florist-shop days, and another Orena associate, Mike "The Plumber" Imbergamo. For the two murders, the Cousins would later get life imprisonment and the motivation to frame me to aid their appeals. They would draw the inspiration to do this from Favo's OPR investigation of me.

Although I could no longer contact Scarpa, six days later, on March 31, for old times' sake, Scarpa called and reported to me that "the hit on John Minerva was handled by Jo Jo and Chuckie . . ."

On March 31, 1992, the same day Scarpa reported on the Cousins, our NYPD task force detectives spotted him tossing a gun from his car. They lost him, but retrieved the gun. As the war case agent, Favo was in charge of all information on the war. As Colombo coordinator, he was in charge of all information on the family.

The NYPD reported this incident to Favo as soon as it happened and Favo told our NYPD detectives not to make an arrest on Scarpa until he told them to. He also told them to keep this information to themselves.

Next Favo went to the Brooklyn D.A., whose office would prosecute the state gun charge. In the 1995 RICO trial of Little Vic Orena's straightened-out sons and others, Favo admitted that he lied to the Brooklyn D.A.'s Office to keep them from arresting and prosecuting Scarpa on the gun charges. He admitted that he told the Brooklyn D.A. that an informant would be burned if they proceeded to arrest Scarpa now. He told the D.A.'s Office we needed some time to elapse in order to protect the source of our information. Naturally, believing there truly was a source who might be in danger from a prompt arrest, the Brooklyn D.A. agreed that protecting the source's life was paramount to protecting whatever unknown person Scarpa might kill while on the loose. Favo said he would tell them when an arrest could be made. In his testimony he called this lie a "ruse." He did not report to me any of his manipulative nonsense with the NYPD and the Brooklyn D.A. And he admitted this in his testimony as well.

Favo told me the cops—both of whom knew Scarpa by sight—had not actually seen him tossing the gun, leading me and Eastern District federal prosecutor George Stamboulidis to believe, as Stamboulidis put it, that "the state had a weak case." With one gun tossed from a car with three men in it and no one seen tossing it, it would be considered an unprovable case.

Favo fed me manure and kept me in the dark.

The next day, April Fools' Day 1992, Little Vic Orena was arrested, along with his two straightened-out sons. The three were arrested by Orena Case Agent Kenny Steiger of the Melville, Long Island, office on a RICO indictment for Colombo Family War murders, for the prewar murder of Orena's crew member Tommy Ocera and for crimes like extortion, loan sharking, and money laundering.

Kenny Steiger's men made the arrest of Orena at his girlfriend's Valley Stream, Long Island, house. Steiger and his men found a loaded shotgun in each of three closets. There was a loaded pistol-grip shotgun in an upstairs closet. In other places there were: a bulletproof vest; tons of ammo; illegally obtained telephone records and reverse phone books to get names and addresses from phone numbers; and $55,000 in cash.

In a crawl space under the deck, Agent Steve Grimaldi found a black plastic garbage bag. Inside the bag were six fully loaded handguns and loads of ammo.

After Orena was convicted and sentenced to three RICO life sentences plus seventy-five years, he got Gregory Scarpa Jr. to testify at his appeal hearing. Scarpa *fils* testified that Scarpa *père*—now deceased—and I planted the garbage bag o' guns under Orena's deck. Actually, Gregory Jr. said his father had them planted, but I gave

Scarpa the address of Orena's girlfriend so he could do this. Gregory Jr. said that his father killed Tommy Ocera and that Scarpa and I framed Orena for it. Gregory Jr. also said that I did a bank robbery with him. He said that I told his father that Joe Brewster DeDomenico "was getting nosy about my father's business and may have known that my father was an informant. After my father killed Brewster, he reported the killing to DeVecchio, who protected him by attributing the murder to another crew." Judge Jack B. Weinstein found this testimony to be as "spurious" as it sounds. Come to think of it, this was the first time the Mafia tried to frame me. But I didn't count it as one. I might be the only agent ever to be framed twice—once by each of two different Mafia groups. Make that more than twice. I forgot about the "Scarpa Defense," in which Scarpa and I were supposedly "comrades in arms" in 1995 in Orena's straightened-out sons' trial, and about Billy Cutolo's trial, and about the Cousins' appeal hearing, but these little frames came later.

Here's how Kenny Steiger recalled the Orena arrest:

"When we arrived at Orena's girlfriend's house, there were construction workers there building the interior. Orena had control of the construction company that was remodeling the Nassau County Jail. Orena had pulled off the workers to build the girlfriend's brand-new house while the county was paying them to be working on the jail. Orena also had them using material meant for the jail.

"We couldn't find Orena at first and the construction workers dummied up. Eventually, we made our way down [to] the basement and there was Little Vic Orena hiding with his two sons, also in the life. The basement was a beautiful self-contained living quarters, finished with wood paneling. Orena had velvet curtains on the windows to prevent anyone peeking in . . . As long as I live, I'll never forget walking down those stairs."

Kenny Steiger went way back with the Colombo Family. He was with Ken Brown when Fred DeChristopher reported for duty as a CW in order to get free from his own house—more specifically, his wife—and from Junior Persico's grip so he could be with the lovely Patricia, his mistress. Kenny Steiger recalled:

"Another reason besides the $50,000 reward and his desire to be with Patricia that made Freddie call his former handler Jim Nelson in L.A. to turn Junior in is that Freddie was stealing from Junior's stash upstairs in the house. Junior had a considerable sum of cash that he planned on using to finance his escape to Europe. Freddie was stealing from the stash a little at a time, and ended up with quite a chunk hidden in another part of the house. Freddie knew that the moment Junior decided to flee the country and went to his stash, it was bye bye Freddie. Downtown Kenny Brown and I hid Freddie in a motel that first Sunday he'd left his house. We got a case of beer and Chinese food, and had a blast. You'd get fired today for that."

I viewed the Little Vic Orena case as a Melville, Long Island, case of Kenny Steiger's with some help pro-

vided by Favo. As will be seen, I now know better. Favo
helped himself to other agents' information and hoarded
it the way Freddie helped himself to Junior's cash and
hoarded it.

During the two years and nine months of the OPR
investigation—from January 1994 until September 1996—
I had no idea what CWs and other people were saying
about me in their sworn interviews. They were forbidden
to discuss even the existence of an OPR. At some point
thereafter we gained access to all 239 pages of OPR reports. Before we got the documents I knew nothing about
how Favo had kept me in the dark.

I was astounded by how much one person observed
about Favo. I was very gratified after reading the interview of the squad's longtime secretary, Bernadette Mac-
Millan. No matter who might be the supervisor, she
went with the squad.

I never discussed anything about the OPR with her
before or after her interview. Six months after the OPR
was opened, investigators interviewed Bernadette under
oath, and like a tape recorder, she poured out her observations from her perch in the squad where she sat all day
every day. Bernadette told the OPR:

"I believe SA [Special Agent] Favo to be a rather
strange individual who has been extremely protective of
the information that he has learned during the course of
the Colombo Family War. I believe he wanted for himself a lot of the glory from the success in the Colombo
Family investigations.

"SA Favo wanted the United States Attorney's Office

in the Eastern District to depend on him as the principal source of information regarding the Colombo Family and War."

Bernadette added: "His reluctance in giving information to others has been noticed by other squad members and task force members who have complained that they did not receive all the information they needed to from SA Favo, on a timely basis."

I might add, hopefully in all modesty, that Bernadette had nothing but nice things to say about me and my integrity.

Anyway, as Scarpa predicted, Kenny Steiger's arrest of Orena was devastating to the Orena faction. How could they complain that Junior was ruling from a jailhouse throne when their own choice for ruler had just joined Junior as a member of the cast of *Jailhouse Rock*?

On April 6, 1992, Scarpa, still closed, called the "hello" phone to voluntarily tell me that Orena heavyweight John Staluppi and two others "have made it known that they are looking to come over to the PERSICO side in view of VIC ORENA's arrest."

On April 14, 1992, my closed TE Scarpa called the "hello" phone to tell me that "word has come out from Junior . . . to keep hitting members loyal to ORENA in an effort to force ORENA's people to come over to the PERSICO side."

On April 22, 1992, I won the right to reopen Scarpa. Not knowing anything that our fully cooperating witness Carmine Imbriale—who was prepared to testify—had said about Scarpa's war crimes (because Favo had deliberately omitted that information from his 302s) and not knowing about the strength of the eyewitness accounts of Scarpa's tossing of the gun from his car and his pending arrest for this, I reopened Scarpa at once. I had gotten so much pressure to close him in the first place (from my good friends Don North and Kenny Brown) that had I been kept in the loop by Favo as FBI regulations require, I would have reported to them at once about what Imbriale was prepared to testify to about Scarpa's murder conspiracies. While I may not have liked it, Don and Kenny would have slammed Scarpa closed forever as a source. And I would have supported that decision.

As well, I would have told them about the pending gun arrest. No, let me take that back. There would not have been any pending gun arrest. Scarpa would already have been arrested and taken off the street had I known about it. There was no chance of having the arrest tossed out on a 1960s-style search-and-seizure technicality because the NYPD never searched Scarpa on a "pretextual stop." They merely observed him litter the street with a gun. They saw that it was Scarpa—whom they knew—and they retrieved the gun. Open-and-shut case. Further, there was no one for Scarpa to suspect of informing on him because he knew he was the one who tossed the gun out of the car when he was surprised by a police car.

With Scarpa off the street, this war would have been settled. Even if he were granted bail because of his health, a home anklet monitor would have neutralized him as the raging force he was in the war. He might have been able to stray from home long enough to get in a gun battle with teenagers and get his eye shot out. But with an anklet monitoring his movement, his days of roaming the streets searching for enemies to kill would be over. In fact, if Scarpa were on home confinement while the war was raging at its peak, the NYPD would have been haunting his house.

More importantly, from a supervisory point of view, had I been informed about Scarpa's confession to Imbriale that he gut-shot Waverly and that the gun charge was legitimate, I would have added the two pieces of evidence together. At that point I would have scheduled a meeting with the federal prosecutor to see if the circumstances of the gun possession—that is, cruising in a car with a gun during a war near the time of the Waverly shooting—was sufficient corroboration of Imbriale to arrest Scarpa for murder conspiracy in shooting Waverly. It might not have been sufficient to corroborate the word of a killer like Imbriale, but that was for a federal prosecutor to decide. And getting it to the federal prosecutor is what an FBI supervisor is for.

Because Scarpa had tipped me off, he no longer had access to our police radio frequency to warn him of NYPD presence in the area so he could get out of the area and off-load his gun. That's why he was surprised by the NYPD car advancing toward him, and then had to toss the weapon.

* * *

The man who started the war—by stirring up Billy Cutolo—may have extended the war by keeping the intended victim of Billy Cutolo on the street on a day when, at least for the gun charge, Scarpa could have been taken off the street. They could have arrested Scarpa the day after they saw him toss the gun.

That day was April Fools' Day, the same day that Kenny Steiger arrested Vic Orena and his two trusted lieutenants, his straightened-out sons. Arresting Scarpa, the Persico faction's one-man army, on the same day as Orena, in a well-publicized coordinated arrest, would have been a major step toward ending the gunfire on the streets of Brooklyn that had already claimed the life of an eighteen-year-old innocent bystander and wounded other innocents.

Meanwhile, as things stood, I was set up to look pretty foolish to headquarters for convincing them to reopen Scarpa. I'm not one who cares much about how I look, but no one wants to embarrass the Bureau. We've got enough enemies. Just go to the movies.

During the grand jury hearings that led to my being indicted for murder, Favo testified that I lied on my March 1992 Teletype request to reopen Scarpa. I didn't. My Teletype was accurate. But Favo claimed it wasn't. This, however, didn't stop him for one second from coming to my desk for information and to make great use of Scarpa's information as he continued to build "his" major cases.

Favo is on record in an appeal hearing of Little Vic Orena:

Q: *Did Agent DeVecchio provide you information from Greg Scarpa during the war that was of use to the Colombo squad?*

A: *Yes.*

Rat-a-tat-tat.

May 22, 1992: Senior citizen Lorenzo Lampasi left for work every weekday morning at four—a time when most wiseguys were just heading home for the night. Lorenzo was an unlikely made man, one with a humble job at a school-bus company near his Brooklyn apartment. Lorenzo co-owned the bus company with acting Boss "Joe T." Tomasello, the street Boss of the Persico faction. Lorenzo's street name was Larry Lamps.

A blue station wagon in which Larry Mazza, James Delmasto, and Greg Scarpa were sitting patiently had its engine running. It was parked on the street near the fenced-in and gated parking lot of Lorenzo Lampasi's apartment building. The three in the vehicle watched and waited. After about twenty minutes they heard a car door open and shut from the other side of the fence. An engine started and lights went on. A black Cadillac pulled up to the gate and stopped. The driver got out and walked to the gate. Six Italian eyes inside the station wagon were fixed on the older Italian man in the light blue jacket, dark slacks, and loafers who was plain to see in his own headlights as he swung open the gate. The men inside the station wagon knew that now wasn't the time, not according to their plan.

The older man got back in his Cadillac and drove it through the open gate. The Cadillac stopped on the street side of the gate. Lorenzo Lampasi got out of his Cadillac, left it running, and walked to the gate, reaching out to close it. The blue station wagon pulled closer in order for the hit men to get a cleaner shot. Greg Scarpa fired his rifle into Lorenzo's back, dropping him. All three killers jumped out of the station wagon and rushed over to the victim, who was still alive, trying to say something. "What did I do?" he implored. But no one had time to catch any more of his words. By Mafia tradition, all three killers were required to shoot and they opened fire on Lorenzo, finishing him off. Larry Lamps' lights went out.

The book writers of the Brooklyn D.A.'s Office—and there are many who saw me as a golden opportunity for fame and fortune—indicted me for setting up this murder by giving Scarpa the daily routine and home address of Lorenzo Lampasi, something I supposedly did with full knowledge of the fact that Scarpa planned on using the address to find and kill his Orena enemy. I'd heard the name Lampasi, but really knew nothing about him, except that he was an old-timer. I certainly didn't know his address or his daily routine.

Throughout all of this—from the moment Favo caused an OPR to be opened on me to this very day—I wonder along with Lampasi, "What did I do?"

I got indicted for it, but by sitting on the gun arrest of Scarpa and leading me to believe it was not a provable case on the facts, Favo is the one who kept Scarpa on the street and caused this death of Lorenzo Lampasi.

I got indicted for it, but by giving me a misleading 302 of what Imbriale said about Scarpa gut-shooting Waverly, Favo is the one who caused this death of Lorenzo Lampasi.

At 9 a.m. Favo walked into my office to give me my morning briefing. My door was always open. It was a small office and the desks of my squad were right in front of me, facing me in an open bullpen, so that anyone could call in to me to show me something or ask me a question. And anyone could hear anything I said as long as I didn't say it sotto voce. The "hello" phone had its own desk in the middle of the squad. If I got a call from Scarpa or one of my other TEs on this phone, whoever answered it could just call out for me. At the time Favo walked into my office that morning, there were half a dozen agents in easy hearing distance of my voice.

Favo told me that two members of the Orena faction had been shot and one, Lorenzo Lampasi, had died.

"We're going to win this thing," I said, slapping my desk.

"We're the FBI," Favo said. "We're not on either side."

"That's what I meant," I said, not thinking any further explanation was necessary. To me, if the war had reached an old-timer on the shelf like Lampasi, no one was safe. And if no one was safe, that would lead to more and more CWs lining up in the hallway outside our squad. I knew Favo had a lot to learn, and not knowing all that he was doing behind my back, I didn't take his comment personally.

While I didn't recall a lot of the little details Favo stored up in the dungeon of his brain—some of which, as petty and harmless as they are, I don't believe ever happened—I did recall the incident I just recounted because of his strange demeanor when he reacted to my comment. He looked weirder than he sounded.

That was May 22, 1992. I had no reason to consider that incident again until January 17, 1994 . . . and then for the rest of my life.

On June 3, 1992, the cooperating witness with the wire, Carmine Imbriale, borrowed the hit squad car of Joey Brains Ambrosino. Imbriale said he needed to borrow it to go to a funeral. We had a bug put in and Imbriale returned the car to Joey Brains. We also tapped Joey Brains' phone. Where did we get the "may I" to invade Joey Brains' car with a listening device and tap his telephone in order to try to keep him from roaming the streets with a machine gun?

Let's let Favo explain. This is his testimony before Judge Weinstein in Little Vic Orena's appeal hearing:

Q: *There is a discussion of Title III in Joseph Ambrosino's car and telephone. Do you see that?*

A: *Yes.*

———————

Q: *Did Agent DeVecchio know about those two Title IIIs?*

A: *Yes.*

———————

Q: *Did he assist in preparing the information that went into the affidavit in support of the Title IIIs?*

A: *Yes.*

———————

Q: *Did he provide information from Gregory Scarpa that went into that affidavit?*

A: *Yes.*

———————

Q: *Was this authorized and approved by Agent DeVecchio to go up on both of these wires?*

A: *Yes, it was.*

———————

Q: Now the targets, what side of the family did you believe
   they were part of, what side of the dispute?

A: The Persico faction.

_____

Q: What date was the arrest made?

A: The tenth [June 10, 1992].

_____

Q: Did Agent DeVecchio agree with this?

A: Yes.

_____

Q: Did he particpate in the arrest on June 10?

A: Yes.

And then, the clincher:

Q: Was there evidence on these wires that implicated Greg
   Scarpa?

A: Yes.

And that is not a surprise and should not be a surprise. How could the same man who testified as Favo did here honestly believe I was protecting Scarpa?

The Ambrosino car bug was only up for six days, from June 4 to June 10, 1992, but it turned out to contain an enormous amount of evidence against the whole lot of the Persico side, including Carmine Sessa, James Delmasto, Larry Mazza, and Greg Scarpa.

On the morning of the tenth, I was out alone in my car as part of the surveillance team tailing Joey Brains Ambrosino's wired hit squad car. These were killers, and while other agents could listen to their conversations from our monitor room, those of us on surveillance, who couldn't hear them talk, nevertheless needed to be close enough to them to act if we saw them spot a victim or if we got a radio call saying that they were jumping off to make a hit.

We were on Staten Island and lost them. I happened to pick them up. I followed them into a housing development. I tried to reach the rest of the surveillance team to tell them we had turned off the main road. But we were in a dead spot where my police radio didn't work. I watched the Ambrosino car drive into a cul-de-sac. I pulled over, tried my radio again, but couldn't reach any of the other surveillance cars. My mobile phone also didn't get reception. This was before cell phones. Joey Brains and I had lost the rest of my surveillance team.

I stayed in my car with one eye on them. Then it occurred to me that I was Italian and I looked Italian. The killers had no idea who I was. But if they thought I was a spotter for the Orena faction, it would be all over for me. There had already been a couple of incidents of these guys trading gunfire from their cars. If they turned around and came at me, they'd be coming loaded, I thought. And Joey Brains has a machine gun. This was a "pucker situation," time for discretion. I put my car in reverse and backed out of the development.

The men monitoring the wire learned that the shooters in Ambrosino's car were planning to spend the next two days in a safe house in New Jersey, then return to hit Billy Cutolo and Joey Amato. If we let them get to safe houses, they wouldn't be driving the car and we wouldn't be listening to them reveal their next move. So that night we moved in and arrested Ambrosino and another with him. It took Joey Brains less than one day to join the growing crew of CWs. The Witness Protection Program of Professor G. Robert Blakey was the broom and dustpan for CWs, just as he'd envisioned it.

Some desk-slapping cheerleader I turned out to be for the Persico side. I'm out risking my life to protect the Orena side from a Persico hit squad with a machine gun. And everything I did was known to Favo as I did it. Not much of what he did, especially regarding Scarpa, was known to me.

Joey Ambrosino corroborated his own car tapes and provided corroboration for Imbriale. More importantly, Ambrosino was a fount of additional singular information. On June 11, 1992, the FBI had more than enough to arrest Scarpa for the murder of Nicky Black Grancio, the gut shooting of Joe Waverly, and for other war crimes and murder conspiracies. But Favo told me nothing that Joey Ambrosino said about Scarpa. In fact, he lied to me, minimizing Ambrosino's information regarding Scarpa. I was on his ass for not giving me paperwork. "Where are your 302s? Get them done. I don't care how busy you are." When Favo gave me information, he gave me carefully worded misinformation.

On July 2, 1992, we arrested Carmine's brother, capo Michael Sessa, based on Ambrosino and his tapes.

Also in July 1992, based on Ambrosino and his tapes, Favo and his followers went to New Jersey to arrest Persico faction capo Johnny Pate. I learned about this when the supervisor of our New Jersey office called my boss to raise hell about my agents making an arrest in his jurisdiction without my calling him. Can you imagine how embarrassing that was to have to admit to Don North that I didn't know about the arrest? It was my job to sign off on it, approve the arrest, and call the New Jersey supervisor to let him know that I had men in suits and ties carrying guns in his area, but I couldn't do my job because I knew nothing about what Favo was doing.

When Favo and his crew arrived at the squad, I gave him hell for failing to notify me of his plans. Although I only knew the tip of the iceberg of his misdeeds, I had caught him doing this in the past. I told Favo and his followers that they were never to make an arrest without asking me first. That's not a rule I made up. As much leeway as I always gave my men, from Pat Marshall on down, the FBI and I always required that I sign off on everything of any importance that an agent wanted to do before he did it. If they wanted a Title III or a search warrant of any kind or an arrest warrant, or to present a case to the federal prosecutor or to go to another agency for assistance, or to go to another jurisdiction to work any part of a case, they had to get my approval. Here, they were making an arrest I hadn't approved in a jurisdiction I hadn't approved.

Later I learned that Favo, like Iago in *Othello*, used my angry outburst to create a further wedge between me and the FNGs—his followers on Team Favo.

At least I was getting information from somebody. On July 9, 1992, Scarpa told me: "[CARMINE] SESSA has decided to remain in hiding . . . SESSA apparently believes that if apprehended, he would not get out on bail, and would most likely be convicted on current federal charges of conspiracy to murder."

On July 13, 1992, Scarpa told me that "a truce was called between the ORENA and PERSICO factions in view of the ongoing problems associated with a shooting war and the pressure being applied by law enforcement."

Effectively, we now knew from "34" that the war was over. That was big news and it was trustworthy news.

Here is an example of what Damon Taylor, his former handler, said about Scarpa: "He was the crown jewel, for all his faults. I would give credibility to anything he said."

From subsequently arrested CWs like Carmine Sessa, when we finally got him, we learned that the hit on Lorenzo Lampasi had not been a war crime. It was about a private grudge. Scarpa and Lampasi had a dispute over how much money an associate of Lampasi's owed Scarpa on a loan-shark debt. In the envelope with the money that he sent over as payment in full for the debt, Lampasi included an imprudent note. It said that he could not have a sit-down with Scarpa to arbitrate the amount of the loan because there was talk that Scarpa was an informant. This would be the wrong approach with Scarpa at any time, but it was particularly inopportune at a time when he was noticeably losing weight as his AIDS continued to ravage his body and when his "General Schwarzkopf" behavior was making him appear to be eager to take everyone down with him.

As Favo had reported to me, another man was wounded on the day of the Lampasi hit. That man turned out to be the man who owed Scarpa the loan-shark debt in the first place. May 22, 1992, was double grudge day for Scarpa.

By killing Lorenzo Lampasi, he sent a message to Sessa, and through Sessa to others, that they were never to debate the issue of whether Scarpa was a "rat."

In his debriefing by Team Favo, CW Carmine Sessa said that Lorenzo Lampasi, as someone who was "on the shelf," was not on any Orena hit squad. He said that Lampasi worked under the Persico faction acting Boss every day. Sessa said that Scarpa showed him the note that Lampasi sent over accusing Scarpa of being a rat. Sessa revealed that Scarpa instructed him (Sessa) to show the note to acting Boss Joe T Tomasello and to get the latter's permission to whack Lampasi. Joe T gave permission for the hit, but cautioned Sessa that he didn't want Lampasi whacked at work because he had a niece that worked in the same place. He gave Lampasi's home address and work schedule to Sessa. Sessa said that he gave all of this information to Scarpa.

So according to 302s in Favo's possession, I'd be innocent of that murder unless Sessa later altered his story somehow. Maybe Sessa, in questioning by the Brooklyn D.A.'s Office, added that at the same time as he gave Scarpa the address, Scarpa told him that I had already provided Lorenzo Lampasi's address and work schedule. I'd have to wait to hear Sessa at my trial.

There was another sort of war-related hit, one that occurred on October 23, 1993, fifteen months after the truce Scarpa told me about.

Although some people consider it a war hit, it wasn't a hit that would provoke any reprisals, and it didn't. By the time the hit took place, both sides were back tending to their business interests and Little Vic Orena was a nonfactor serving three life sentences plus seventy-five years.

What happened is that on October 20, 1993, the owner of Wanna Bagel, Frank Guerra, got exquisite personal revenge for the killing of eighteen-year-old Matteo Speranza by sending an eighteen-year-old hit boy to kill Joey Scopo—the son of the Concrete Club's bagman, Ralph Scopo, who was then doing his hundred years thanks to the Mafia Commission Case. It seems that Joey Scopo was behind the hit at Wanna Bagel, and no one on either side thought that the hit on Matteo Speranza made Joey Scopo look like anything but a *stunod*.

Frank Guerra's wannabe eighteen-year-old hit boy had a tattoo across his back, written in Italian, that said "Death Before Dishonor." The wannabe ended up getting several life sentences for killing Joey Scopo, his own two accomplices, and a rival drug dealer.

There was one more sort of war-related hit and that was the 1999 disappearance of Billy Cutolo. After the truce was agreed to, Junior Persico, in order to give the appearance to the Colombo Family that everybody was now living happily ever after, decreed that Billy Cutolo would be the underboss to the new Boss, Little Allie Boy. The Persicos bided their time, let Billy think all was forgiven, and then took him out in 1999, seven years later. In 2007 Little Allie Boy succumbed to a severe case of RICO for this murder—thanks to eight CWs, who were by then a dime a dozen—and thanks to Billy Cutolo's son, who went around wearing a wire. Little Allie Boy is now doing life for the Cutolo hit. Like father, like son. Such is life in "the life."

They found Billy Cutolo's body in a Mafia burial site along with the remains of his bulldog, Alexo.

All in all, from the first shot in November 1991 to the truce in July 1992, there were twelve hits, including the bystanders Gaetano Amato and Matteo Speranza and the noncombatant Lorenzo Lampasi. There were many more wounded, including civilians. Yes, this is "the life."

CHAPTER TWENTY-SIX

THE SPOILS OF WAR

Scarpa gave us the communiqué from behind the lines that the war was over, and now we had a lot of grunt work ahead of us. We needed to survey the battlefield and bring home the spoils of war. There were CWs to debrief. There were a slew of trials to help prepare for and defendants to present for indictment and for more trials. We had arrests to make and fugitives to find. We had a lot of evidence to sort and sift through.

It was clear to me that we would be going over the bridge and across the East River to the Eastern District on these cases, as nearly all of the Colombo Family War murders took place in Brooklyn. The Eastern District also covered Long Island, Staten Island, and Queens, heavy Colombo Family territories. Orena himself was almost purely Long Island. We had no excuse to take the war cases across the street into our more convenient office of choice, the Southern District in Manhattan.

To avoid arrest and certain conviction and to make more work for us, five-foot four-inch consigliere Carmine Sessa, and former seduced grocery delivery boy Larry Mazza and his buddy James Delmasto, went on the lam.

In August 1992, Favo came to me to ask for Scarpa's help in locating these fugitives. I asked Scarpa for information, but he refused because Delmasto and Mazza made collections on his loan-shark "book" and he was too sick with AIDS to make them himself; he needed them on the street. He could simply have told me he didn't know where the men were, but he leveled with me. I reported this to Favo and he stored it in his brain to use later in order to justify his insubordination. As long as I was in a corrupt and "unhealthy relationship" with Scarpa, he was in the right to elbow me out of his way.

The following is Favo's testimony in 1997, five years later. It was given during Little Vic Orena's appeal hearing and relates to Favo's request of me in the summer of 1992—two years before he reported me—that I get information from Scarpa to help locate the fugitives Larry Mazza and James Delmasto:

Q: *Well, at that time, Agent DeVecchio told you that he couldn't provide the information, right?*

A: *He told me that he had asked Scarpa and Scarpa wouldn't give them up.*

———

Q: *He wouldn't give them up because Delmasto and Mazza were out, according to Scarpa, collecting loan-shark payments for Scarpa; correct?*

A: *Right.*

———

Q: *In other words, that he was doing his criminal bidding; correct?*

A: *Yes.*

———

Q: *And you thought that was pretty bizarre that an FBI agent—I think you said in one of your reports—that an FBI agent such as DeVecchio would tolerate an answer like that from an informant: "I am not giving you the information because they are collecting my loan-shark money." Right?*

A: *I didn't think it should be tolerated.*

In a later hearing, Favo said that I should have "forced" Scarpa to help us locate the fugitives. Maybe Chris Mattiace and I should have escorted Scarpa into the men's room for a little head-in-the-toilet-bowl persuasion.

Ironically, Favo testified that when we put Imbriale on the street, he continued to do his loan sharking, but he was not authorized to commit any other crime besides gambling. So didn't Favo tolerate Imbriale making a windfall profit? We paid his loan-shark vig of $6,000 a week on the big money he borrowed from the big boys to lend out to littler boys. While he was out there he was collecting from his customers, but was now keeping all the money, not slicing $6,000 off the top to kick upstairs. Imbriale was out there about twenty weeks. That's $120,000 extra in a federal stimulus package that went into his pocket, along with his normal profit. And I'm sure Imbriale didn't report this extra income on his tax returns. I guess Favo "tolerated" that crime, too.

I have to watch myself here and not get too wrapped up in the details of Favo's treachery. I believe these accusations that I "tolerated" Scarpa, that I passed information to Scarpa, that I protected Scarpa and his crew from arrest, and that I lied to reopen Scarpa were all part of Favo's games. He'd like the focus to be on the accusations and my detailed defense against them. The worst that Favo comes out of that debate is as overzealous, perhaps a little paranoid, perhaps in over his head. But in order for the truth to come out, we needed to focus on the bigger picture.

The Colombo Family War case was a once-in-a-career opportunity for an agent at that time and place. This was not a case Favo would likely ever see again. Joe Pistone's groundbreaking Bonanno Family RICO, the earthshaking Mafia Commission Case, the Pizza Connection Case, and the family hierarchy RICO cases—such cases were a thing of the past. If working major cases was your ambition, this was as big as it was ever going to get during the declining years of the Mafia.

Trusting him and having no one else for the job, I had put Favo in a powerful position. In June 1991, six months prior to the start of the war that landed Favo the high-profile major case as Colombo Family War case agent, I had already made him the coordinator of the Colombo Family side of my squad.

As part of his job description, Favo was the recipient of all the knowledge that passed through the FBI relevant to the Colombo Family. He got the call when an agent in another squad had anything to share with our squad regarding the Colombo Family—like a CW to hand over for debriefing. Favo was privy to every matter concerning the Colombo Family in every FBI office in the universe. Knowledge is power. As recently as this past year, I chatted with Kenny Steiger, the Orena case agent from Melville, Long Island, and heard again what the squad secretary, Bernadette MacMillan, had observed—that Favo kept the cream of this knowledge for himself and did not pass it on where it belonged.

At some point during my two scandals, my attorney Doug Grover was given the complete set of 302s of Carmine Sessa. I learned a lot from them. I thought back to the training tapes Favo recorded and how he spoke about Kenny Brown's unhealthy relationship with his informant: "We were concerned that he was passing information to 'New York.' Sessa makes an accusation in that regard during the war." Finally, I had the 302s to read, and guess what? Turns out Sessa didn't make any such accusation. I'm convinced that Favo made up the accusation of Kenny Brown and attributed it to Sessa.

The more I investigeted, the more I learned that I was not the only one Favo had kept in the dark, lied to, and made false accusations about.

Along with many others I had no idea what Favo was really doing. I had no idea what he really thought about me when he thanked me for asking Scarpa for help on the fugitives. I had no idea what kind of person Favo really was.

And as always, my squad of fourteen agents and I had a thing or two to do on the Bonanno Family Grand Finale RICO case and on the many Colombo Family War cases and trials, which, in sum, were about to toll the final bell of the Colombo Family.

By the time Favo reported me to North, on January 17, 1994, we had used RICO to convict thirty-seven men in the Colombo Family War and had forty others under RICO indictments for murder and conspiracy to murder.

On August 16, 1992, in a voice made less profundo by AIDS, Scarpa told me that "the truce was still in effect . . . ORENA has been effectively bypassed in any attempts to give orders, and most of the COLOMBO Family believe he will be convicted on the federal murder."

On the morning of August 31, 1992, Favo finally told me about the pending gun charge on Scarpa. However, I had just learned about it on my own. Only I didn't know the details of Favo's role in suppressing the arrest for five months. Because of Favo's deception, I still assumed it was an unprovable charge. Scarpa called to tell me he was surrendering himself on a state gun charge brought by the Brooklyn D.A. He said that his lawyer would surrender him at 11 a.m. and that it was agreed with the prosecutor that because of his health he would be released on bail so that he could keep his afternoon AIDS treatment appointment. I told Favo what Scarpa had told me, not aware that Favo knew those details.

It was clear to me at the time that Favo, at the least, had to have known that there was sufficient eyewitness identification by the NYPD to justify an arrest of Scarpa on the gun case. It was detectives on our joint task force that had made the case. And they reported to Favo, the war case agent. This was the first inkling I had that anything pertinent regarding Scarpa had been withheld from me. I thought it was insubordination, but it was not particularly troubling to me since it was a state, not a federal, gun charge. And from time to time things slipped through the cracks, as busy as we all were, especially Favo.

Favo left my office and returned to tell me he had just gone over to the Eastern District to pick up a federal RICO murder warrant against Scarpa. This stunned me. This is a warrant that my squad and the Eastern District would have prepared well in advance. Favo should have obtained approval from me to present the case to the federal prosecutor. Then, after going over the evidence, the federal prosecutor would have to approve the arrest and get approval from his superior. I suspected I had been left out because Scarpa was my informant, but that was no reason to leave me out. I had no personal interest that conflicted with an arrest of Scarpa on a RICO murder. While I had a relationship and a friendship with Scarpa, I knew the day would come when he'd have to go. And I had told him this back when the war had started.

Favo told me that he planned on surprising Scarpa with the federal indictment at the state courthouse when he surrendered himself on the gun possession charge. Now I was appalled. Favo had held the gun arrest in abeyance, I thought, while he built his federal RICO case, then he coordinated it all, including this eleventh-hour report to me.

The federal RICO arrest would result in Scarpa not being allowed to post bail and his being carted off. Favo had planned all along to double-cross Scarpa and his attorney. This is not the way any defendant should be treated, much less one we were using right up until the moment we double-crossed him. I would have had no problem arresting Scarpa at his home and then opposing bail for him. But this grandstanding manipulation, the purpose of which was to make fools out of Scarpa and his lawyer, was repulsive. I let Favo have it, then I picked up the phone and tried to reach Scarpa, but he had already left for state court.

Favo rushed out to make his arrest.

I headed straight to Don North to report Favo. I was furious with Favo and the Eastern District federal prosecutor who'd played his game with him. How can you fail to tell a supervisor you're planning to make an arrest? Don North should have called them all to the carpet. But because Favo had the Eastern District on his side, North told me to chalk it up to youthful exuberance on the part of Favo. After all, everybody knew how hard he worked. North was satisfied that I had handled the situation with Favo at my level of authority, and if it happened again, we'd deal with it more expeditiously.

I was resigned to this reaction. I knew the hold that the U.S. Attorney's Office in Brooklyn had on our office through the guilt card. They resented our bringing most of our big cases to the Manhattan U.S. attorney on any pretext we could concoct. "Creative jurisdiction" on our part to justify taking a case to Manhattan might include a Brooklyn wiseguy making phone calls from Brooklyn to Manhattan. So every time the Eastern District guys bellyached about something besides that issue, our supervisors bent over backward to placate them.

This was the first of the weak responses I got from the Bureau about Favo—who was now the golden boy of the Eastern District federal prosecutors, whom he seduced with the adroitness of a Casanova.

The rule requiring a supervisor to sign off before an agent presents a case to a prosecutor for indictment is a rigid one. It has to be rigid so the supervisor can plan the most effective use of his most limited resource—his man-power. You can't have all fourteen of your men going across the street on their own and presenting a case to a federal prosecutor. You have to plan these things out—right down to determining who you have left to monitor the office phone. You have to prioritize—which arrest is more important right now of the two you are consider-ing, and which one can wait a bit. You have to secure the resources you need. You have to figure out how much help you can get from the NYPD or from another squad or from headquarters or another FBI office. Once an agent walks into that prosecutor's office to present a case for arrest or indictment, you stand a chance of losing that man for months.

However, I figured with Scarpa dying of AIDS, this would be a case that would not take much, if any, time from Favo's other duties. I figured Favo's immature power play would not do much practical harm to the administration of my squad.

Scarpa was released on bail on the state charge, but was arrested immediately on his way out of the court-house and taken by Team Favo first to his AIDS doctor for treatment and then to a federal magistrate for commitment.

Scarpa's lawyer was outraged. He explained the double-crossing tactic to the federal magistrate. He produced evidence from the AIDS doctor that Scarpa had only two to six months to live. He explained to the magistrate how he and Scarpa had been duped into believing Scarpa had a deal to be released. The magistrate obviously caught on to the fact that the two courts had been used as a tool by the FBI. The dramatic courthouse arrest might have made a terrific headline, but no federal judge would stand for such a thing. You don't want to live in a country where a judge would. As a result of Favo's tactic, Scarpa was released on reasonable bail and went home with an anklet monitor.

Favo and his federal prosecutors—some of whom had clocked less time in law enforcement than Favo—were outraged at Scarpa's unheard-of release on bail on RICO murder charges, and they should have been. However, it was a release they had unknowingly orchestrated by their own duplicity.

Many years later Favo ignorantly claimed that I had used my influence on the federal magistrate to help Scarpa go home that day. First, no federal judge or magistrate would allow a stray FBI agent to act on his own in any capacity. We are not members of the bar. Whatever we do in court is done with and through a federal prosecutor, even getting search warrants that we might prepare ourselves. Second, in order to go to bat for an informant, we'd need the prior approvals of Don North, the U.S. attorney, and the FBI headquarters informant unit.

Knowing the system as I do, I am convinced that Scarpa went home that day with an anklet because Favo pissed off the magistrate by his headline-grabbing manipulation. I believe if Favo had followed procedure, gone through me on his way to the Eastern District in June—when he clearly had the evidence to arrest Scarpa—we would have gotten an arrest warrant on Scarpa at the same time and with the same evidence we used to get the arrest warrants on the likes of Pate, both Sessas, Mazza, and Delmasto.

I hate to put it this way, but in getting an indictment against Scarpa, we did not need a bulletproof ironclad case. We did not need a slam dunk. Scarpa would be dead before he ever came to trial.

Because of his need for AIDS treatment, Scarpa could not have fled. We'd have arrested him in June on RICO murder charges. There would have been no juvenile courthouse trickery and he would have been denied bail. We would have been in the driver's seat then. Do we allow him to be in a prison hospital of his choice in return for information on the whereabouts of Mazza and Delmasto? If he had offered any reliable information, information that panned out, we would have helped him be in a prison hospital closer to Brooklyn so that Linda Schiro could visit him.

Not to forget, had Favo arrested Scarpa at home or on the street in June the right way, through channels, on RICO murder and murder conspiracy—without immature trickery that would piss a magistrate off—he would have been locked up in a prison hospital in June and would not have been in a position to kill that marijuana dealer in December, and he would not have had his left eye shot out.

CHAPTER TWENTY-SEVEN

DOWNHILL IN THE DARK

The war was over, Scarpa was dying, and I figured whatever bug was up Favo's ass was now a nonissue. Of course, I still knew only a small fraction of what he'd done and said and thought about me—not to mention what he had in mind to do for me later.

In October 1992 Valerie Caproni returned to the Eastern District afer a three-year stint in urban development. She was now put in charge of the prosecution of all our Colombo Family War cases. By June 1993 she had become the head of organized crime cases in the Eastern District.

Although technically a part of the Department of Justice, the FBI has always maintained its independence from the federal prosecutors. We were to them as the NYPD was to any District Atttorney's Office. As the local D.A. had, the federal prosecutors had their own investigators, but we weren't them. Of course, on cases we brought to them, we helped out while maintaining our independence, just as the NYPD did with the D.A.'s offices they dealt with. It was a system of checks and balances.

Favo wasted no time in "grooming" Valerie Caproni, but I figured that couldn't hurt the squad. She became his new best friend. If he couldn't develop an informant, at least he could develop federal prosecutors. I didn't know Favo was using the Eastern District as a giant battery to plug into as a power source.

On November 2, 1992, the first of our squad's trials began. It was a RICO against Carmine Sessa's brother, capo Michael Sessa, who Scarpa told me had murdered the owner of an auto body shop across the street from brother Michael's produce market in Staten Island. I testifed in the trial in the Eastern District as a Mafia expert. I was proud of the fact that of all the supervisors we had, both the Brooklyn and Manhattan federal prosecutors viewed me as the go-to expert in RICO trials. When I retired I threw out a big pile of my testimony transcripts. I testified as an expert in a good twenty-five RICO trials. I testified in many more trials as the case agent in charge of the investigation.

Favo testified in order to authenticate the wires that Carmine Imbriale wore and the bug operating in Joey Brains Ambrosino's car.

Our testimony was a good one-two punch.

Brother Michael was convicted, a good sign for all our upcoming trials. It looked as if my often-expressed dream of presiding over the methodical dismantling of a Mafia family on my watch was coming true.

Around this time, Don North authorized Gambino supervisor Bruce Mouw and me to give interviews to Jerry Capeci for a book Capeci was writing about the Mafia. It got back to me that Favo thought Don North should have assigned this to him. Later Favo accused me of leaking stories to Capeci—without a pinpoint of evidence, of course. Accusing me of leaking to Capeci was very clever because such leaks were a royal pain in the ass to the FBI.

Needless to say, that accusation about my possibly leaking information to the writer was as "spurious" as the accusation made by Gregory Jr.—inspired by the OPR ordeal I had endured and by Orena's offer to finance his appeals—that I helped plant guns under Little Vic Orena's deck. Come to think of it, if Greg Scarpa, the father, knew where Orena was hiding, he would have planted *Orena* under Orena's deck.

In the end, and fifteen years down the road, in 2007, my downhill path would put me in a courtroom with Jerry Capeci in the most unexpected of ways and a ray of light would relieve the darkness.

"Lin," Linda Schiro said. "Greg really needs to see you about something. He's in bad shape. He was hoping you'd stop by the house. It would mean a lot to him."

So, on November 17, 1992, I visited Scarpa at home. He was housebound and was being monitored by an anklet. He was in better shape than I thought he'd be. At that point he still had two eyes. As a cover, I took two agents from Team Favo with me and parked them in front of the TV in the living room.

Scarpa told me he'd summoned me because there had been a "serious discussion . . . to kill Joey AMBROSINO's mother in retaliation for his cooperation with the government. The source said Greg SCARPA put a stop to the plan . . . The source said Frank SPARACO was a major push behind the plan to kill AMBROSINO's mother."

This kind of thing has to be carefully analyzed. Was Scarpa telling me this as a way to send a threat through me to Ambrosino that if he didn't stop cooperating and recant his statements thus far, his mother would be hit? Or was it a warning to get the mother into Witness Protection along with her son? Or was it something that was already under control?

I sized it up as truthful and something that Scarpa had already handled.

This was the same Frank Sparaco who had been rude and crude to Kenny Brown when Downtown Kenny went to Little Allie Boy's social club to look for Uncle Allie Boy. Frank Sparaco is also the one who killed Michael Divine for dating Little Allie Boy's wife. And Scarpa was handing me a plot that never got hatched. Even though Scarpa was dying of AIDS, there's no way a punk like Sparaco would buck Scarpa on this or on anything else.

Scarpa added that the "PERSICOs now feel that the

ORENA faction will come over to their side, since
Vic ORENA is on trial . . ."

As to Carmine Sessa, still a fugitive, Scarpa said that
Sessa "has not talked directly to any members of the
PERSICO faction, especially since the conviction of his
brother MICHAEL SESSA."

This was a hopeful sign. Sessa was too afraid of getting whacked to fraternize with the old crowd. If we
could get our hands on him, he'd likely roll. Because he
was still collecting a lot of money on his loan-shark
"book" with the help of his relatives, he probably would
not come in on his own.

A month later, in December 1992, I testified as an
expert in the RICO trial of Little Vic Orena. Favo testified on the gathering of much of the evidence. Orena was
convicted on all counts. This was when Orena landed his
Boss-sized three life sentences plus seventy-five years.

By the way, by the time of my indictment in 2006,
and with all his appeals exhausted, Orena had become a
lay minister of the Catholic Church in prison. I hope he's
on the level.

December 29, 1992, by the way, was the day when
that home confinement alarm went off, signaling that
Scarpa had strayed from his home without permission
only to get into a gun battle and have his left eye shot
out.

Also in December, capo Johnny Pate and about nine
others entered guilty pleas or were found guilty on wartime murder conspiracy RICO cases.

A month later, in January 1993, the Orena faction underboss Patty Amato was convicted and landed his underboss-sized three life sentences plus sixty years.

Around that same time, the loose-cannon serial killer of the Lucchese Family, underboss Gaspipe Casso, a fugitive, was caught.

Jerry Capeci, in his book *The Complete Idiot's Guide to the Mafia*, explained the effect the Mafia Commisson Case had on the Lucchese Family: "The conviction[s] . . . brought chaos to that family." He added that replacement Boss Vic Amuso and underboss Gaspipe Casso "began a family killing frenzy that left dozens of mobsters and associates dead." Capeci figured that Vic and Gaspipe were "totally out of their league when it came to the subtleties of running such an operation."

What's interesting to me, in view of what I myself have endured, is that every time these new Lucchese Bosses suspected a family member of not being trustworthy and whacked him, they inherited his illegal business, whether it was a loan-shark "book" of customers or a thriving gambling book or whatever. So, while acting out their seemingly paranoid thoughts, they personally benefited from the hits. Even hit men have conflicts of interest.

Gaspipe, not Amuso, was the ringleader. And we now know that Gaspipe had his "crystal ball." He controlled the two Mafia Cops, the NYPD detectives who gave him hot tips for $4,000 a month, with bonuses for extra work.

I thought a lot about the tie between the Colombo Family and the Lucchese Family.

The two had a long history of working together and exchanging information. Before the Mafia Commission Case took them off the street for a century apiece, the consiglieres Christy Tick Furnari and Gerry Lang Langella met twice weekly at the 19th Hole to exchange information.

No earlier than March 1994, two months after Favo reported me to North, Gaspipe gave up the Mafia Cops to his debriefers at the Valachi Suite in El Paso. When Jerry Capeci broke the Mafia Cops' story, did any of my accusers stop to consider that in view of the close relationship between the Lucchese Family and the Colombo Family, Scarpa's law enforcement information, if he truly got any, could have come down the pipeline from Gaspipe? Gaspipe was getting extremely singular information from the Mafia Cops.

In April 1993, on Palm Sunday, Colombo Family consigliere Carmine Sessa was caught outside St. Patrick's Cathedral in Manhattan. He fainted and had to be rushed to the hospital. The next day the roly-poly Sessa rolled over and agreed to testify against a ton of people. Team Favo debriefed him several times. On the first three of these occasions, I sat in. After all, this was a consigliere talking and I was the premier developer of sources in the Bureau. Team Favo appeared annoyed by my presence. Much later Favo accused me of sitting in so I could gather information to use for corrupt purposes. Would I send the information to a prison hospital so one-eyed Scarpa could escape and return to Brooklyn to whack somebody? Or did I have another wiseguy I was now too cozy with? Or was it simply that Team Favo wanted to talk privately to Sessa about me?

At any rate, in the fourth debriefing, a debriefing I didn't attend, according to Team Favo they asked Sessa questions about me, including whether he thought it strange that I'd sat in on the prior debriefings. Yes, come to think of it, Sessa thought that was strange.

In May 1993 the Orena faction capo Big Sal Miciotta walked in the door, perhaps prompted by the publicity surrounding Sessa's arrival as a CW, and rolled. Under questioning by Favo about a possible law enforcement source, his favorite topic, Big Sal claimed that Detective Joe Simone told things to a neighborhood friend named Phil, who was the nephew of wiseguy Chips DeConstanzo. Chips would then tell these things to Big Sal. Big Sal agreed to go back out on the street wearing a concealed tape recorder. Was Big Sal on the level about Joe Simone or did he see Simone as an easy bus to hitch a ride on and head into the Witness Protection Program with his secret stash of cash? Well, Big Sal's tape recording would clear this little matter up.

I suspect that anytime Favo asked any of these CWs about a law enforcement source, he was hoping to get me. And poor Joe Simone got the bull's-eye that was intended for me on his back.

In May 1993, under a plea agreement, Scarpa pleaded guilty before Judge Jack B. Weinstein and admitted, among other things, to committing three murders, including that of Nicky Black Grancio.

The dismantling of the Mafia continued apace. With

our new cooperating witnesses we were already lining up several RICO cases—the spoils of war—to go to trial in early 1994. One of those trials concerned the Cousins, who were accused of whacking Johnny Minerva and Mike the Plumber. I expected to testify as an expert in that trial and in the others. I thought I might retire when they were over and observe the Colombo Family in ruins from the nice office that would come with my private-sector job. But first, of course, I'd travel.

Around this time I made some personnel shifts in my squad. Favo came into my office and complained about them. This was okay. In the FBI, if you're ordered to do something, you do it. But an agent does have the right to voice his opinion. And if his opinion is persuasive, a supervisor is free to change his mind. But Favo didn't press me hard. He left my office and everything seemed okay.

About a week later I was called into the office of the New York boss to whom Don North reported. He explained that the changes I'd made had impacted the work that the Eastern District was doing. Favo had gone to Valerie Caproni, now head of the Brooklyn federal prosecutor's Organized Crime section, and complained to her. She went to the Brooklyn U.S. attorney and he went to the head of the New York FBI office. And now I was being told to undo my personnel shifts back the way Favo wanted them.

I had the right to protest and I did. How dare Favo go outside the chain of command to an agency without my approval in a matter that concerned internal FBI affairs! If the Eastern District needed more manpower they had their own investigators to call on and they had an office in Washington with a budget that could authorize their hiring more of them. Retired NYPD detectives coveted these federal jobs. But in the end I was no match for the power of the U.S. attorney of the Eastern District.

In the summer of 1993, with Don North's approval, I was interviewed by the BBC in my office for a series they were doing on the Mafia in New York. It got back to me from more than one of my squad members that Favo thought he should have done the interview. Favo had worked Organized Crime for four years, while I had worked it for twenty-six years. Who would you consider the better person for the interview?

On August 27, 1993, I got a call from Scarpa, who was in a prison hospital. He sounded weak. He was not doing well. He probably wanted me to visit him, but I was just too busy to make such a trip. This was to be my last 209 contact with him. In it, he gave me a lot of stale information about Billy Cutolo's loan-shark "book," and he gave me a list of who was doing hits for Billy "during the height of the COLOMBO war." Clearly, Greg Scarpa was well out of the loop by this point. I thanked him as if all that he said was helpful. He had nothing left. He ended with a whimper.

We were already building our RICO murder case against Billy Cutolo and his crew. They were all going to go down. Or so I thought.

A month later, on September 29, 1993, I was summoned to a meeting at Valerie Caproni's office. At the meeting were Greg Scarpa and his attorney, an agent named Jim Brennan, Caproni herself, and one or two prosecutors on her staff. I think Favo was there, too, but I don't recall for sure. I was surprised to hear that Scarpa had offered to become a CW. In exchange he wanted to get a sentence that would allow him to die at home. He was emaciated. His skin was gray and he wore an eye patch. We all listened to the pitch made by Scarpa's lawyer. I couldn't imagine that Scarpa would live long enough to be of much help as a witness, but I was sympathetic to the idea that he certainly could provide a lot of useful information, including maybe a burial site or the likely location of a fugitive.

I remember saying good-bye to him. I remember wondering what Agent Jim Brennan was doing there. He was with the Lucchese squad and had been for years. Oh well, agents who happened to be in the office would sometimes get pressed into duty by prosecutors. I remember that Scarpa, his lawyer, Brennan, and Caproni stayed behind when the rest of us left. It would take nearly three years before I would learn what transpired after I left.

Unbeknownst to me, in November 1993, Favo told one of my new agents, Robert Neuendorf, that he was planning on going to Don North because CWs were telling him that Scarpa had a law enforcement source, and as Neuendorf put it in a sworn statement, "the implication [was that] the law enforcement source was Supervisor DeVecchio."

To protect the reputations of the innocent, the very existence of an OPR is supposed to be a secret. Only those who were interviewed and supervisors would know about it, and they were required to keep it to themselves. OPR interviews are sworn statements made under oath, like grand jury testimony, and the information they contain is supposed to be sacrosanct. It says so right on the form the witnesses sign. Here was Favo leaking the substance of the allegation and spreading the rumors two months before he even initiated the OPR.

On December 8, 1993, indictments came down against the Orena faction shooters of eighteen-year-old Matteo Speranza. In the indictment they were also charged with seriously wounding another innocent bystander. While they were chasing two Persico faction members, one of their stray bullets struck the head of a sixteen-year-old boy on a park bench in Bensonhurst.

Also on December 8, 1993, Detective Joe Simone was arrested on bribery and corruption charges on the day he'd expected to put in his retirement papers. In the NYPD you can't get your pension if there are pending criminal charges or departmental administrative charges against you—like an OPR, for instance. Your retirement is put on hold until you are cleared. If you are not cleared, you lose your pension.

In the FBI, you can be charged with murder and have a dozen open OPR investigations going on against you and you can retire anytime you are eligible to do so; if you are not cleared of all the criminal and OPR charges against you, the Bureau still cannot deprive you of your pension.

On December 10, 1993, Greg Scarpa appeared before Judge Jack B. Weinstein for sentencing. He got ten years. Had he been given a stiffer sentence, he would not have been allowed to stay in a prison hospital. Scarpa said to the judge: "I tried to help, Your Honor." More than he ever knew.

Around the same time that Detective Joe Simone was arrested and Scarpa sentenced, the former grocery delivery boy and fugitive Larry Mazza, who had been caught about a year earlier, began cooperating. Favo debriefed him.

The dismantling of the Colombo Family on my watch was becoming a very real possibility. I was honored to have been in the right place at the right time. I'd get lots of credit that I knew belonged to J. Edgar Hoover for creating the informant program in the first place; to Professor G. Robert Blakey for creating Title III, RICO, and the Witness Protection Program; to Rudy Giuliani, Mike Chertoff, Joe Pistone, Pat Marshall, and Charlotte Lang of the Mafia Commission Case; to Chris Mattiace and his squad on the Colombo Family hierarchy case; and to our leader, a man who was in a class by himself, Jim Kossler, and the rest of our team during our championship season.

In early January 1994, Favo "debriefed himself" on the four and a half hours of tapes which he made for T. J. Harkins.

In one tape he talked to T.J. about a CI named Otto Heidel, who had been a member of a bypass-bank-burglary crew with the Lucchese Family called the Bypass Gang because they were very adept at bypassing alarms. At times Heidel had worn a wire on his body at his handler's request. On October 8, 1987, while changing a tire, Heidel was whacked. This was three weeks to the day after bypass burglar Joe Brewster was killed by Gregory Scarpa Jr. for concealing bypass burglary scores he'd done. It was less than a month before Gregory Scarpa Jr. and his crew would be indicted in Valerie Caproni's DEA/NYPD case.

In 2006, during the Mafia Cops trial, the world would watch witnesses describe how the Mafia Cops gave Otto Heidel up to Gaspipe as a government informant. The Mafia Cops went so far as to provide proof to Gaspipe of Heidel's status as a "rat." They gave Gaspipe a cassette tape obtained from the wire that Heidel had worn.

But at the time that Favo made the tape for T.J. in January 1994, no one had ever heard of Gaspipe's Mafia Cops. Gaspipe would not begin cooperating until at least two months following Favo's recordings.

Favo recounted the October 8, 1987, killing of Heidel, a killing that happened when T.J. might still have been in high school. Why would Favo be telling him about a seven-year-old hit on the Lucchese Family, a family that, while closely allied to the Colombos, was a family we didn't handle?

Favo stated that Supervisor Pat Colgan, Heidel's handler, felt that Heidel's girlfriend had given him up as an informant. Favo, sounding rather cocky, as if he had insider information, said: "The story Pat Colgan told me" was that the girlfriend leaked to the Lucchese Family that Heidel was informing to the FBI.

Favo then went on to refer again to Al D'Arco, the Lucchese CW whose advice that the FBI should make personal contact with wiseguys had inspired Don North to order what Favo earlier on the tape derided as a "meet-your-local-agent plan."

Favo explained to T.J. that D'Arco reported in his debriefing as a CW that there was an FBI leak. This FBI leaker told Gaspipe that Otto Heidel was an informant and should be killed. In a creepy, conspiratorial tone Favo counseled T.J. that this was something to "keep in the back of our minds . . . whoever that was . . . or is."

I might be getting touchy here, but I'm thinking that "whoever that was . . . or is" would be me. I think Favo believed that I leaked the information about Heidel's cooperation to Scarpa, Scarpa passed the information down the pipeline to Gaspipe, and together Scarpa and I—as Al D'Arco's FBI leak—got Heidel killed. After all, it was common knowledge that the Colombo and Lucchese Families were extremely close and the lines of communication were wide open. There were Colombo members from Gregory Jr.'s crew on the Lucchese Bypass Gang. In the summer of 1987 the Colombo Family and the Lucchese Family had two high-level sit-downs to discuss the fate of Frank Smith—a Bypass Gang burglar, a burglary partner of Joe Brewster, and a Lucchese associate—who had done sloppy work on the Aronwald hit for Colombo capo Joe Waverly.

A few months later "whoever that was . . . or is" would turn out to be not an FBI agent, but the Mafia Cops. Gaspipe likely told Al D'Arco that his "crystal ball" was an FBI agent in order to protect the confidentiality of his paid CIs in the Detective Division of the NYPD.

Before anyone anywhere was to learn about the existence of the Mafia Cops—later in 1994—irreparable damage to me would already be done on January 17, 1994.

CHAPTER TWENTY-EIGHT

1994

The first time I heard that anyone in my life suspected me of breaking the law I was in my office and I got a phone call to go to Bill Doran's office. Bill was Don North's boss, and looked and sounded like everybody's uncle. Later Bill was a staunch supporter who traveled from North Carolina to attend my trial. When I got to his office, Don was already there. I sat down.

They both looked glum and serious. Don spoke first.

"There's been allegations made that you've given information to Greg Scarpa."

"That's horseshit," I said. "Whoever said that is a fucking liar."

"Lin," Bill Doran said, "we've got no choice but to look into it."

"I know where this is going to go," I said. "If an OPR is opened on this, it'll take two years."

None of us could ever figure out why, but we all knew that OPRs took two years.

"We may have no choice," Bill said.

"I don't want to be hanging under a cloud for two years," I said. "I'll call Scarpa now. You can listen to us. You can tape us."

"That may be a good idea," Don interjected. "If we call him right now, no one can claim you got to him beforehand."

"Okay," I said. "Let's get at this right now. Head it off before it becomes an OPR."

"We have to run it by headquarters, of course," Bill said.

"Bill's right," Don said.

"There's a better way," Bill said. "Let's see if they can send up a couple of guys from Organized Crime to talk to Scarpa. When they find out quickly from Scarpa that it's a crock, we can close it before it gets to an OPR."

"We know it's a crock, Lin," Don said. "Organized Crime men will know what it's like when you ask a question and inadvertently give information."

"I didn't even do that. I know what the fuck I'm doing when I ask a question," I said. "I hope." I paused, then asked, "Favo?"

North wasn't allowed to tell me, but he smiled.

"Of course you know," he said, "you're not to attempt to contact Scarpa in any way. That goes for Linda Schiro, too."

"Of course not," I said. "That would defeat the purpose of what I'm trying to accomplish. Scarpa gets a cold call."

The next day Don North called me into his office.

"Valerie Caproni called me," he said. "She made a complaint about you, too. She said you passed information to Scarpa back in 1987 during a DEA/NYPD case she was handling against Gregory Scarpa Jr.'s crew."

"What the hell," I said. "She's a lunatic. Back then she accused us of harboring Gregory Jr. so we could use him to testify at a congressional hearing."

"I remember," Don said. "Jim Fox said she had a 'siege mentality.'"

I was sure some CW from the war was filling Favo's head with a load of horseshit and he didn't have the skills to know he was being taken for a ride. I figured he got Valerie Caproni worked up and she was happy to go along for the ride—to try to redeem herself for the fool she made of herself in that 1987 DEA/NYPD matter when she accused us of having Gregory Jr. "under wraps." I felt toward this nameless CW who was lying about me the way Joe Simone felt about Big Sal Miciotta at the time of his arrest: "You are going to believe that fat shit over a cop?" the detective asked.

"Whoever the CW is who's now telling them crap about that old case of Caproni's is full of shit," I said to North. "Let's hurry up and talk to Scarpa and put this to rest."

"We can't talk to Scarpa just yet," Don said. "Caproni bitched to headquarters that we were whitewashing this thing and they're going to send up two men from OPR instead of the two from Organized Crime. It's in the Integrity Section now."

"Son of a bitch," I said. "Son of a bitch. Son of a bitch!"

"I know how you feel," North said.

"Well," I said, "let's get the two men from OPR out to see Scarpa while he's still alive. Or they should just call him. They can call him from their desks in Washington."

North nodded.

Two weeks later Don North told me that Valerie Caproni talked OPR into holding their investigation in abeyance. She had nine Colombo Family War trials coming up and she didn't want to create 302s about agent corruption that she'd have to turn over to the defense. She didn't want the OPR investigators talking to any CWs until after the first trial, which would start in April and was expected to last six weeks. Ironically, the accused in that trial were the Cousins, for the piece of work they'd done on Johnny Minerva.

I held a squad meeting and lambasted as a "fucking moron" any idiot stupid enough to give any credence to a CW who made a charge that I passed information to an informant I was handling. As I was talking the four members of Team Favo looked down at their shoes. To a man, the ten members of my Bonanno Family crew rallied around me. They looked at Favo and his three minions and made comments like "Who the fuck in their right mind would think something like that?"

After news of this meeting reached the ears of the brass, I was yanked from my squad and transferred to the drug side as coordinator of all the drug squads. I have to say that even though I was disgusted at how the Bureau was letting Caproni prolong my OPR, I did enjoy the new job. And I was in charge of a million dollars in discretionary funds. Some security risk the Bureau thought I was!

I knew the people who knew me didn't take this allegation seriously, but still, when one CW makes an allegation, it leads to another CW picking up on the investigator's questions and trying to please. Soon there's a little network of CWs in possession of what they consider to be valuable information—information that could later help them win sentence reductions. I wondered how much damage Team Favo's heavy-handed questioning had already done if Caproni had put a halt to all questioning of CWs about a "corrupt agent." If Team Favo had questioned a number of CWs about a dirty FBI source of Scarpa's, there's no way she could keep that subject out of all these trials. One of the CWs would blurt it out. Once it was out, the defense would smear the entire prosecution with it. Why should a juror trust any part of the case beyond a reasonable doubt if the case's supervisor is crooked?

The Eastern District and Favo won the Cousins trial. Jo Jo, Chuckie, and their accomplice, Joe Monte, got life for doing the work on Johnny Minerva and Mike the Plumber. I had not been invited to testify as an expert witness.

Finally the OPR investigation could begin.

"Lin . . ." It was Don North. "I've got some bad news. Scarpa died in a prison hospital in Minnesota."

"Tell me OPR has talked to him. Tell me that, Don."

"I can't, Lin. They didn't get to him. He's gone."

"I'm gone, too," I said, and hung up the phone.

I flew from my desk on the drug side to Favo's desk to beat the snot out of him. I got there to find that he had taken the day off. North had alerted some of my old Bonanno men to be ready for me. They calmed me down and made me realize that hitting a subordinate meant immediate dismissal and that I didn't want to go out that way.

Scarpa's obituaries in the New York papers stated that he had been my informant, but thankfully didn't mention the OPR against me.

Little Allie Boy went to trial later that summer on four RICO counts of murder stemming from the war. His attorney tried to ask an agent questions about Scarpa's informant status. The agent hesitated. The prosecutor picked up the agent's cue and objected that the topic was irrelevant to the charges. The questions were kept out of the case. But it was a foreshadowing of a later defense strategy that would be used when the Colombo Family War cases came to trial.

The key witness for the prosecution against Little

Allie Boy was CW Johnny Pate, who had visited him in jail for instructions on whom to kill during the war. Pate had to go to Little Allie Boy for guidance because Junior Persico had lost his visitor's privileges after that blow job his lawyer had given him. According to the prosecutors, Johnny Pate was too shrewd for the Eastern District to handle. Pate's subtly subversive testimony, they claimed, turned out to be helpful to the defense and blew the case for the prosecution. At any rate, found not guilty on all counts, Little Allie Boy was on his way to ascending to the throne. The dismantling of the Colombo Family took its first hit in the Eastern District that summer of 1994.

I tried to concentrate on my new drug job and not be impatient with an OPR process that normally took two years, but would now take at least two and a half years because Valerie Caproni had put her hand up like a traffic cop and held it in abeyance. I tried to be normal, but the stress was taking a toll on me and on those around me. I'd remarried in 1991, to a fellow agent. Our marriage fell apart during this period. She transferred to Washington, D.C., and we divorced.

I spent the next two and a half years in a state of bewilderment.

My fellow supervisor Ray Kerr, whose Russian squad was right next to mine when I supervised Favo, said only the other day: "I worry about what this has done to your health, Lin, what effect this will have down the road."

On October 13, 1994, the New York *Daily News* delivered the one blow I feared. The tabloid reported that unnamed sources had revealed that I was under investigation by the OPR for passing FBI classified information to Greg Scarpa during the Colombo Family War. The rumor had finally reached the press that DeVecchio "may have given Scarpa the addresses of rivals he wanted killed in exchange for his cooperation." Naturally, the Bureau would not confirm that report.

When, further down the road, Doug Grover got his hands on the OPR reports, I read that T. J. Harkins, a stand-up agent, revealed to the OPR that in February 1994 Favo, in violation of Bureau rules, told him he had reported me to Don North for passing information to Scarpa. During the Little Allie Boy trial in July 1994, Favo casually told Agent Kevin O'Rourke that I was the subject of an OPR investigation. Around that same time he told Agent Maryann Goldman that he suspected me of leaking information on the Colombo Family War investigation. That's three of a total of fifteen agents who happened to be interviewed by the OPR, in addition to the three FNGs on Team Favo who knew. We already knew Favo had improperly told Caproni, who went on to tell her prosecutors. Favo may not have leaked the OPR directly to the press, but he was at least the Johnny Appleseed who spread the seeds for the media to discover.

The day after the unconfirmed report in the *Daily News*, Favo was on the witness stand in the trial of Detective Joe Simone. Under questioning by defense counsel, Favo blithely authenticated the news report about me without pausing for the federal prosecutor to object that it was an irrelevant topic and should not be publicly corroborated:

> **Q:** *Am I not correct, Mr. DeVecchio is the subject of an inquiry that he was leaking information to the Colombo Family?*

> **A:** *That is correct.*

The remainder of Favo's and Big Sal Miciotta's testimony in the trial was disgraceful. Big Sal testified that he had his tape recorder on while he and Chips DeConstanzo were waiting for Detective Simone to show up at the house of Simone's friend Phil. The detective visited the house regularly because both men were football coaches for the team Simone's teenage son played on. DeConstanzo and Phil were relatives. With the tape running, Big Sal said to DeConstanzo that when Simone showed up, he was going to offer him a bribe. Chips responded on tape: "The guy's not asking for anything. He don't want no money." Big Sal then turned the tape recorder off and never turned it on again. The young Team Caproni prosecutor allowed Big Sal to take the stand and testify under oath that even though it was not tape-recorded, Big Sal offered the cop a bribe and Simone accepted it.

This is gross incompetence on Favo's part. If Big Sal gave Favo a useless tape and Favo, nevertheless, persisted in believing the "fat shit over a cop," it was his duty to send that fat shit back to friend Phil's a couple of weeks later with some more money for Detective Simone and with a body wire that Big Sal could not turn off or on. Since Simone had allegedly accepted one bribe, he'd surely be eager for another. Favo's failure to follow protocol, and to arrest and prosecute in spite of this, was unconscionable.

On cross-examination Favo admitted that he ignored information that while Big Sal was a CW, he may have perpetrated insurance fraud by claiming that valuables were stolen from his Atlantic City hotel room. Favo explained that he had no interest in looking into the incident because Big Sal was the "victim."

Worse, Team Favo failed to write 302s of their debriefings of Big Sal. Who knows what song and dance Big Sal gave Team Favo to convince them that he was their man of the hour. Their failure here is neglect of duty. By denying the defense attorney an account of Miciotta's words, words he would need in order to cross-examine him, Team Favo perpetrated a gross injustice.

And worse than that, Valerie Caproni's Eastern District staff failed to tell Joe Simone's lawyer that a few weeks before the trial an unidentified FBI agent had looked in Big Sal's gym bag and pulled out a gun.

Shortly after this trial, Big Sal was dropped as a CW.

The jury not only promptly found Detective Joe Simone not guilty, but ten of them, despite the cold November rain, swarmed him after the trial to express their sorrow that he had to suffer such an ordeal. They felt that government officials had participated in a frame of Joe Simone.

Sadly, Detective Simone was bounced from the NYPD without a pension, and this was done by brass that had no idea what it means to investigate the Mafia. Simone had freely admitted that Chips knew he wouldn't take money because they had already tried and he had refused. During a visit at his fellow coach's house, someone pushed an envelope toward him that he assumed contained money. Simone didn't touch the envelope and walked out. The brass faulted him for not reporting the possible bribe attempt at once. Detective Simone, as Dave Stone, his boss for years, can attest, was dedicated to fighting the Mafia. But sometimes you have to fight the Mafia with a little honey and not vinegar. If you get the reputation of a straight arrow who reports the slightest infraction, you will never develop the sources of information that fighting the Mafia requires. The need for sources was especially high during the years when Detective Joseph Simone was a part of our championship season.

The injustice done to Detective Simone is underscored by the Mafia Cops, both of whom retired before their convictions for eight murders, including CI and Bypass Gang burglar Otto Heidel in 1987. Retired NYPD Detective Lou Eppolito receives $46,752 a year for life—life in prison, that is. Retired NYPD Detective Steve Caracappa receives $63,756 a year till the day he, too, dies in jail. All of it is tax-free and none of it can ever be the subject of a lien, not even on the fines they received as part of their sentences.

When I got arrested Detective Simone was quoted in the New York *Daily News*: "I feel bad for him because

I was accused of being a rogue cop also and I know what he's going through. But if it comes out that all of this happened because of him, I would hold grudges against him."

In November 1994 the Colombo Family War RICO indictment against Billy Cutolo and his crew went to trial. The defense attorneys tried to explore the now publicly known allegation that I had leaked information to Scarpa, but the judge wouldn't allow it. However, unlike Little Allie Boy's judge, Cutolo's judge did allow the defense to argue that Scarpa was an informant for the FBI who fomented the war for his own gain. Billy Cutolo and his crew claimed self-defense against Scarpa, as, essentially, a government operative. All were acquitted. The defense the lawyers used came to be known as the Scarpa Defense.

The dismantling of the Colombo Family was being dismantled. All of Favo's cunning deceptions were allowing the Colombo Family to regroup.

The next important RICO case went to trial in May 1995. The defendants were the two straightened-out sons of Little Vic Orena and five others. This judge went the extra step and ruled that the defense could introduce evidence that I was under an OPR investigation for giving information to Scarpa during the war. He ordered the prosecution to turn over any documents the government possessed regarding allegations of my corruption. Without knowing any of the facts and hearing from two sets of lawyers on both sides who were against me, Brooklyn Federal Judge Edward Korman based his decision to order the release of documents on the grounds that I had "certainly crossed the line by a fairly wide mark."

The OPR was still ongoing—barely at the halfway point—and no one but the OPR was in possession of any facts or lack of facts against me. OPR would never release reports to anyone who was entitled to them until all witnesses had been questioned. They didn't want one future witness to learn what another had already said. They especially didn't want me to know what witnesses had said for or against me before they interviewed me, and this would not occur for a year. Although this rule of secrecy had not stopped Favo and Caproni from admittedly comparing notes.

Following the judge's order to turn over documentation of the investigation of my wrongdoing, Caproni returned to her famous "siege mentality." She had her prosecutor Ellen Corcella prepare a letter that would satisfy the judge's requirement of disclosure and would take the place of OPR reports that were not yet ready for disclosure. The contents of this letter would go to the jury.

As she sat down with Corcella to prepare the letter, Caproni had a King Kong of a personal conflict of interest. She had already accused me of leaking the planned November 1987 DEA/NYPD arrest of Gregory Jr. to Greg Scarpa Sr. In this letter she was both the accuser and the evaluator of whether I had done anything wrong. Having lost the Simone and Cutolo trials, she was motivated for it to appear that whatever setbacks had occurred and would later occur were the fault not of Favo's and her false accusations, but of my corruption.

Neither Doug Grover nor I had any input into the drafting of the letter. I was portrayed in it as being as guilty as sin. In his newspaper column the next morning Jerry Capeci called the letter a "stunning concession." Capeci's lead told it all: "A top FBI crime buster fell into cahoots with a key mobster and fed him confidential federal information at the height of the bloody Colombo crime family wars, a U.S. prosecutor admitted yesterday as seven gangsters went to trial on murder conspiracy charges."

In the lead to his article in the *New York Times*, Selwyn Raab astutely predicted dire consequences from Caproni and Corcella's two-page letter: "In an unusual twist that could damage the government's campaign against the Colombo crime family, Federal prosecutors in Brooklyn said yesterday that an FBI agent had for years disclosed confidential information to a high-ranking member of the Mafia group."

What the hell! I didn't do any such thing. But I was talking with a pillow strapped to my mouth and facing a windstorm.

In their opening statements, the defense called me a "rogue agent." The defense explained: "The idea that this was a war with two sides is nonsense. This war was sparked and fueled, believe it or not, by a special agent of the FBI." Orena's straightened-out sons and fellow warriors "did nothing more than try to protect themselves" from that "crazed killer" Scarpa and his co-conspirator Lin DeVecchio.

Corcella told the jury they shouldn't dwell on Lin De-Vecchio's corruption. My criminal acts didn't matter in considering the defendants' criminal acts. Referring to me, she said: "He'll get his day in court."

As the last witness on the last day of trial, Favo got to imitate me, saying: "We're going to win this thing." I wasn't there, but I heard he really milked it. Jerry Capeci was in the courtroom and reported that Favo "had a pained look similar to one most people have when they talk about going to the dentist." Favo was good. But why did he take nearly two years to report me? the defense lawyers wanted to know. He answered that I was "well respected." He explained: "If I said this to somebody, they would take it about as well as I would take it if somebody came up to me and said my wife was unfaithful. They would not believe it, they would never believe it." But they might have believed him if he had any proof. You know, proof—the evidence that establishes that an accusation is true? Even the not-so-bright Joey Brains Ambrosino knew this. In his debriefing he said that Scarpa's deceased brother Sal had schooled him in the way of the wiseguy and had told him, "If you couldn't *prove* that somebody was a 'rat,' you shouldn't be making statements about the person you suspect." Maybe Favo should have taken lessons on ethical behavior from Joey Brains.

All defendants were found not guilty on all the counts of the indictment.

"They all believe there was a cover-up," one of the defense lawyers observed to the press. "And many jurors wondered how come DeVecchio wasn't indicted."

One juror told the press: "Something like this really knocks the credibility of the FBI. If the FBI's like this, society's really in trouble." Another said: "You're always brought up to believe in your government and the American way. If you can't believe in the government, what can you believe in?"

All the articles ended with one sentence: "DeVecchio denies any wrongdoing."

Technically, I hadn't denied anything yet since I hadn't been confronted with any detailed charges by the OPR. And I was still waiting to hear whether the OPR was going to recommend criminal charges against me. I knew the OPR investigators were monitoring all this vicious talk about me. I hoped that it wouldn't influence their decision.

With the help of a slew of incoming CWs, on July 5, 1995, Gregory Scarpa Jr. was indicted under RICO for his role in his father's and his own "criminal enterprise." He had yet to leave jail on the 1988 DEA/NYPD charges. In 1998 Gregory Jr.—despite relying on articles about my scandal and blaming his father and me when he testified—would be convicted of enough charges that he, like his father, would be condemned to die in jail. I testified against him—under immunity, of course. While in jail, he would attempt to peddle information on terrorists in return for a sentence reduction. Federal prosecutor Patrick Fitzgerald, who prosecuted vice presidential aide Scooter Libby, saw through Junior's scam, but wacko journalists still write about it as a government cover-up of some kind.

CHAPTER TWENTY-NINE

FAVO'S BUSINESS PLAN

In September 1995, with a year to go on the OPR investigation, Jerry Capeci took inventory in a feature story headlined "Call Them Untouchable—Colombos Rebuild . . ." He wrote that the Colombo Family was "capitalizing on legal problems triggered by a rogue FBI agent. Call them the untouchables." That stung for more than one reason.

Capeci predicted that the Colombos would be out there with a vengeance to reclaim their power on the streets. He wrote, "Prosecutors hoped to stamp out that possibility forever with 61 indictments in 1992 and 1993. At that point the feds seemed unstoppable. But last year, the tide suddenly shifted. Top FBI agent R. Lindley De-Vecchio was accused of leaking investigative secrets to a Mob informant. In four consecutive Colombo trials, jury doubts about the rogue agent's actions resulted in acquittals." In truth, sixteen of sixty-one indictments ended in acquittals and many of the remaining cases ended with lenient plea bargains to reduced sentences.

I can come up with no single word to describe the mixture of emotions that swelled through me as I read that article. I'd go from being demoralized over what was happening to all my squad's cases to wanting to strangle Favo over what was being done to me. Essentially, my life's work was going down the drain. And in the public's eye, it was all portrayed as being my fault. It was my corruption that caused us to lose or compromise case after case. Who would ever talk again about the work I did on the Mafia Commission Case or in bringing down Russell Bufalino? Lurking beneath all this was the embarrassing question of whether I'd done enough as a supervisor to prevent all this from happening. I can't articulate exactly what I was feeling, but *torment* and *turmoil* are the only words that spring to mind.

Those defendants who were convicted before my OPR was leaked now jumped on the bandwagon. Little Vic Orena filed a motion for a new trial before Judge Jack B. Weinstein claiming he should have had the right to blame the war on me. Orena also accused me of helping to plant guns under his deck. If his newfound religious faith is as strong as he claims, he ought to write me a letter of apology.

The Cousins filed a motion for a new trial before Judge Charles P. Sifton, again claiming that they should have had the right to blame me for the murders of Johnny Minerva and Mike the Plumber. The torment and turmoil continued—now at the appellate level.

In May 1996 the OPR finally interviewed me. It was now my turn to take the pillow off my face, open my mouth, and let it all out. Somebody was at long last listening to me. And listening not in order to twist my words, but to record them accurately. I confessed to receiving the Cabbage Patch doll, the lasagna, and the bottle of wine. I was asked about my comment "We're going to win this thing." I said, "What I meant was that the fighting inside the Colombo Family was going to help us—the FBI—win the war against the Colombos by providing us with tons of defectors and intelligence. I had made my comment out loud in front of half a dozen men who all understood what I meant except for Favo, who was personally motivated to put his political spin on it. I am proud that I established an excellent rapport with Scarpa, but I always remembered that he was a wiseguy and I was an FBI agent." I responded to all the rest of the suspicions—not charges—leveled at me. It was cathartic, at least for a day or two.

In June 1996 Favo was transferred to South Bend, Indiana. In the world of the FBI that was a huge comedown. The New York office was the plum assignment if you wanted action, and action is why an agent joins the Bureau. South Bend, the home of Notre Dame, Favo's alma mater, was a snoozer of an assignment. He'd been put where he could do no harm. That was really cathartic for me—until the next barrage of incoming fire.

On September 4, 1996, Doug Grover got a letter from OPR clearing me. Strangely, it was an anticlimax.

It took a long while before I could bring myself to read the OPR interviews.

I immediately retired, effective October 1996. I could now go out and try to find a job, any job, knowing I was no longer a candidate for the plum job I'd have been a shoo-in for had I not been soiled and grimy from this public scandal.

I didn't know when I retired that the mud would keep on being slung at me. On the second day of my murder trial, October 16, 2007, a headline about me in the *New York Post* read: "Dirt Bag Is Grime of the Century."

In December 1996, a long article about me appeared in the *New Yorker* magazine. For its lack of understanding of organized crime and informants, it might as well have been written by Favo and Caproni. And Caproni got the last word. It was a fond farewell to Favo: "The fact that he's no longer working organized crime cases in New York is to me just a horrible fallout of this whole thing . . . It's been a very difficult situation as it always is for a whistle-blower." I focused on Jim Kossler's quote: "If I'd been there, I would have cut Favo's nuts off."

In February 1997, four months after my retirement, the trial judge Charles P. Sifton threw out the Cousins' RICO murder convictions. He granted them a new trial because my corruption had not been made known to them when they went to trial. Brooklyn Federal Judge Sifton said: "Scarpa emerges as sinister and violent and at the same time manipulative and deceptive with everyone, including DeVecchio . . . DeVecchio emerges as arrogant, stupid, or easily manipulated but, at the same time, caught up in the complex and difficult task of trying to make the best use of Scarpa's information to bring the war to a close."

You looked down at me from your bench, Judge Sifton. You judged me and found me "arrogant, stupid, or easily manipulated." Yet once again this was a case in which I had no representation. I was not a party to this case. My reputation didn't get a hearing, much less a fair hearing. Judge Sifton, try saying "Mr. DeVecchio" the next time you use my name in a decision in case my grandsons go to law school and have to read it.

But here's where Judge Sifton's ignorance of the Mafia became dangerous. He pointed out that he was not throwing the charges out completely; he was only giving the Cousins a new trial. The reason he was not throwing the charges out completely was that I had not, as far as he could tell, crossed over the line into a "level of uncivilized and indecent behavior." Whatever that means!

The Cousins had a pretty good idea what that "level" might be and set about framing me for some "uncivilized and indecent behavior" so that next time Judge Sifton would throw their charges out completely. They sought to demonstrate that I'd gone from passing helpful information to Scarpa to actually participating in a murder with him. The case they used for their frame was the Nicky Black murder. They had a report put together that claimed that Scarpa, Mazza, and Delmasto spotted Nicky Black in his Range Rover and wanted to kill him, but they were afraid they'd be caught in the act by NYPD surveillance on Nicky Black. According to the report Mazza told one of the Cousins' investigators that Scarpa, in front of Mazza and Delmasto, called me and told me to pull the surveillance from the scene. The Cousins' team said that because Mazza refused to sign off on this report, the investigator who "took" the statement prepared his own affidavit and signed it himself. This tale was comparable in its credibility to the one about Big Sal turning off his tape recorder.

A minor defect in this frame was that in his debriefing—although Favo pressed him like crazy for evidence that I'd been leaking information—Mazza made it clear that the Scarpa hit squad accidentally happened upon Nicky Black and killed him at once without any phone calls for help from me or anyone else.

This frame was based on a known and reported unhappy coincidence: A couple of hours before the Scarpa hit squad spotted Nicky Black and killed him, Favo had pulled the surveillance team of Joe Simone and Patrick Maggiore. Yes, the surveillance was pulled that day—hours before Scarpa's crew ever came across Nicky Black—but it was Favo who'd done the pulling.

A month after Judge Sifton found me "arrogant, stupid, or easily manipulated," both Favo and I were called as defense witnesses in Little Vic Orena's hearing on appeal in the Eastern District. Not trusting Caproni even a little bit, I wouldn't testify without an agreement that whatever I said could never be used against me.

For some strange reason, the Orena defense lawyers

grilled me a lot about my reopening of Scarpa on April 22, 1992, as if that had any significance at all to Orena, who was arrested on April 1, three weeks earlier. I testified that the decision to reopen Scarpa was made "by me in consultation with my superiors," and that I didn't lie when I reopened him.

Valerie Caproni's notorious siege mentality was in full swing. By her remarks you would have thought that I was the defendant in this trial. She told the judge that DeVecchio, on the witness stand, "came close to admitting . . . that he misled" the brass in his reopening of Scarpa as an informant. She told the judge that it was "horrible to watch Mr. DeVecchio sit up there and make up his answers as he went along." She said there was "a strong circumstantial case that DeVecchio leaked information to Scarpa." She did add, however, that my alleged corruption was "not relevant" to Orena's "guilt or innocence."

Boy, was I ever right not to take the stand without immunity for my testimony. Valerie Caproni had no access to the OPR interviews. Yet, as an officer of the court, she told a federal judge that there was a "strong circumstantial case" that I was guilty of felonies.

Understandably, with Caproni's comments on record, Judge Weinstein took some shots at me. Using words like *may well have*, *arguably*, and *there is suspicion that*, the judge cast doubt on my reputation and my accomplishments. Again, I had no representation in this appeal hearing. I was the piñata in the middle of the fiesta. The Team Caproni prosecutors were against me. Favo was against me. The defendants and their attorneys were

against me. Talk about a "level of uncivilized and indecent behavior"!

There turned out to be, however, one civilized person
at the piñata party, the venerable senior Judge Jack B.
Weinstein, the author of the go-to volumes on federal evidence called, *Weinstein's Evidence.*

Although he took shots at me, in the end, Judge Weinstein upheld Orena's conviction. As to Favo's pained testimony about my infamous comment, the judge wrote:
"In retrospect when DeVecchio declared 'We're going to
win this thing,' he meant only that law enforcers would
successfully prosecute and destroy on behalf of the FBI
and the Department of Justice all elements of a major
portion of New York's Mafia. His prediction proved
largely correct."

The judge also wrote: "Allowing accumulations of
vague suspicions supported by conveniently arranged
evidence to give rise to misleadingly dark conclusions of
deep, dark governmental conspiracies is a not uncommon
process in today's lay world. It does not suffice in court."

Based on the vast experience he'd accumulated since
Lyndon Johnson appointed him, and not based on any
of the arguments he'd heard from Valerie Caproni, the
judge wrote: "The starting point . . . is examination of
the DeVecchio-Scarpa relationship in the context of law
enforcement practice. Associations between investigatory
agencies and their informants are often necessarily char-
acterized by fraternism. Information trading on a 'friend-
to-friend' basis is an important, and at times vital, means
for these agencies to insure a productive flow of reliable

information . . . As a practical matter, an informer must have some incentive to take on the risk inherent in assuming this role. Investigative agencies utilizing informants routinely tolerate and sanction some continuing criminal activity . . . Even the courts are deeply enmeshed and partners in the complex civil-criminal justice enterprise. They recognize and enforce the deals and promises that help induce and protect the criminal informers."

Judge Weinstein found that I had not "conspired on the side of the Persico faction" and that I had not "stirred up the war."

Judge Sifton's decision granting the Cousins a new trial was overturned and the Cousins' RICO murder convictions were reinstated.

Our dynamo of a co-counsel on my murder charges, Mark Bederow, recalls: "I tape-recorded an interview with a Brooklyn thief, an Italian wannabe, who was in jail in Rikers Island. He'd read about Lin in the *New York Post*. He had what he thought was information the D.A. ought to know. He reached out and was brought in for an interview. He told them that when he was previously in jail, he was housed with the Cousins, Jo Jo and Chuckie Russo. The Cousins offered him $40,000 to kill Lin when he got out. He accepted the contract. He was released from jail, and he told a friend about the contract. The friend was a Bonanno Family button who told him that if he killed Lin, the Colombo Family would in turn kill him. So he withdrew from the contract. The Brooklyn D.A.'s Office, shamefully, had no interest in this witness's information or in investigating it. Instead, they promptly sent him back to Rikers. Unfortunately, we couldn't use him as a witness. The only connection between the Cousins and Lin was their attempt to frame Lin for pulling the surveillance on Nicky Black. The Brooklyn D.A. had cleverly chosen not to indict Lin for the Nicky Black murder. The man joked with me that he had solid information, but it was for the wrong side of the case."

That was another reason I didn't want to be committed to Rikers in lieu of bail at my arraignment on the murder charges. It's a lot easier to get murdered in jail than it is at my home in Sarasota. Unlike Judge Sifton, I understand men like the Cousins. When they kill someone in a Mafia hit, it casts a shadow on the victim. He looks dirty. That very thing happened to young Nicky Guido, who was killed by mistake on Christmas Day while showing his new car to his uncle. Neighbors inevitably wondered what he'd been mixed up in to have been killed in such a way.

To say I was disgusted every time I looked at the stack of OPR statements is an understatement. Gradually, I forced myself to read them. I started with Favo. When Favo with two of his minions in tow, reported me on January 17, 1994, Don North ordered them to put their charges in writing. What was the evidence on which Favo based his suspicion that I'd passed information to Scarpa?

Favo responded with an eight-page single-spaced report dated February 6, 1994. It was the first of four OPR
statements he was to give.

I was further sickened to see that the first page was
devoted to Favo puffing up his role in the Colombo
Family War cases, bragging to the OPR interviewers.
When I got to the bottom of the page, I read that he
"believed DeVecchio was leaking information to both
Scarpa and Jerry Capeci."

A belief is not even an allegation, much less a fact.
There was no evidence presented against me on page
one, but I had seven more to go. The only relevant fact
Favo stated on that page was against himself: "Initially
all information received . . . was relayed to Supervisor
DeVecchio. However, over the length of the war, I began
to withhold information . . ." This amounts to a confession of insubordination.

I read page two twice just to make sure I wasn't missing anything. But Favo didn't make an accusation against
me on that page. Again, though, he admitted that he hid
things from me. This time, to my horror, it was Colombo
Family War information the Brooklyn D.A. investigators
were finding out on wires they had up: "I told him that
they were doing nothing or were telling me very little of
what they were doing . . . In reality Detective Terra kept
me informed of their wires and I provided them with
assistance whenever needed."

On page three there was finally something resembl-
ing an allegation. Favo described his version of an overheard conversation that may or may not have occurred

two years earlier. He said that when George Terra, a Brooklyn D.A. investigator, called to tell us they had arrested Carmine Imbriale and offered him to us to wire and keep on the street, I was interrupted by a phone call. I told Favo the call was from Scarpa. Standing next to me, according to Favo, he heard me say, "I don't know what he's saying about you. We haven't even talked to him yet. The Brooklyn D.A. has him."

Favo told the OPR investigators that by this conversation I informed Scarpa that Imbriale was cooperating.

This reported conversation supposedly took place four years earlier and I honestly couldn't remember having the conversation much less the details of that call when I was finally confronted with this in my OPR interview. If it did happen, I'm sure it didn't happen in those words. And if the OPR investigators had been experienced Organized Crime investigators, what they would have made of Favo's comments, if anything at all, is that when Scarpa called me he already knew Imbriale was in custody. I was just learning about Imbriale's arrest myself when Scarpa called. So that means Scarpa had a law enforcement source who told him Carmine Imbriale was under arrest and might be talking about him. If the conversation did happen, Scarpa was calling me to see what I could add to what he already knew—or suspected. An Organized Crime investigator would understand that this is the game we played with our informants—the appearance of one hand washing the other. I taught agents at Quantico how to maintain that appearance.

Then Favo went on to claim that the next day he "told

DeVecchio that [he] believed [DeVecchio] disclosed Imbriale's cooperation with law enforcement to Scarpa the day before." This is a blatant lie. Informant development was my field; it was what I taught. And the protection of a source's identity was the first thing I taught. Had an agent of mine ever brought something like that to my attention I'd never forget it.

More importantly, without hesitating, I sent Imbriale out on the street with a wire for four months and he made twenty-four recordings. No one in his right mind would do that to a witness whose cooperation was even mildly suspected by the Mafia, much less carelessly admitted to by an FBI supervisor. If Favo had so much as hinted that I had carelessly disclosed "Imbriale's cooperation with law enforcement," I would never have allowed Imbriale back on the street—with or without a wire. And if I did, Favo should have called me out on such a dangerously irresponsible decision. If I did what Favo accused me of, he should have reported me to North at once, before Imbriale hit the street.

I believe Favo anticipated that I would point out that Imbriale had no problems on the street, so he brazenly claimed that he "suggested that DeVecchio call Scarpa and warn him that he had been overheard on a wire advocating Imbriale's murder and therefore if anything happened to Imbriale, Scarpa would immediately be arrested." In a TV show, that plot device might pass for credible, but there's no way it could be believed in the real world of the Mafia. Such a call would have told Scarpa that someone he spoke to about Imbriale was cooperating with the FBI, was himself a "rat" wearing a wire.

Favo went on: "Approximately a half hour later I observed DeVecchio talking on the confidential telephone. After completing the conversation, DeVecchio told me he had spoken to Scarpa and that Scarpa understood that he had a problem if anything happened to Imbriale." This is impossible. Forget Favo's grandiosity in suggesting that I took orders and instruction from him. In a twenty-four-hour period from Imbriale's arrest to my fugazy telephone call warning him, Greg Scarpa would have known exactly where he had been and exactly what he said to whom. He'd first check for bugs in his car and would find none. He would know that it wasn't a bug he should be looking for, but a "rat" wearing a bug. Then he would kill whomever he'd bad-mouthed Imbriale to: "When in doubt have no doubt."

These blatant fantasies of Favo's are the kind of lies that Organized Crime investigators sent from headquarters would have caught on to immediately, which is why Bill Doran and Don North wanted Favo's charges—assuming he had any—to go to Organized Crime and not to OPR. It wouldn't have taken Organized Crime investigators more than a few days to dispose of this drivel.

On page four of his OPR report, Favo accused me of asking him to obtain addresses for two phone numbers two years earlier. Favo said I then told him "the numbers were for one of Scarpa's loan-shark vicitms." If I were helping Scarpa find a delinquent loan-shark victim,

I would be guilty of RICO enterprise activity. Why would I give Favo a criminal reason to get me the addresses? Why would I give him any reason? Why wouldn't I just look up the numbers myself?

At any rate, in subsequent testimony on cross-examination by a Mafia defense lawyer, Favo swore under oath that I actually had said that the addresses were for "Scarpa's business," not for his "loan-shark victims." He explained away the words *loan-shark victims* that he had used in his OPR statement: "The use of that term was my opinion. The term that he used was *business*."

When, in 1994, Favo gave his sworn OPR statement, he'd used language that made it very clear he was accusing me of a very serious federal crime. Later, in court, when he backpedaled, changing his statement, it was probably an attempt to save his RICO case. Both sworn versions can't be true. The truth is that neither version is true.

Favo changed his tune again when he testified under oath during my 2006 trial for murder. He said that I said "these are business numbers or customer numbers." The choice of the word *customer* gets it back into the range of "loan-shark victims."

By page five I wondered if any CW at any time had ever used my name in vain or whether it all came from Favo's head. Page five of the OPR contains no accusation, but is devoted to justifying Favo's lying to me about Scarpa's gun charge. Favo did this by slandering NYPD Sergeant Brogan, making Brogan out to be either a cop who didn't know how to express that he had a simple gun case without sounding "confusing" or who improperly swore out an arrest warrant when he really didn't have a case.

Favo stated: "On March 31, 1992, Sergeant Brogan and Detective Jon Willoughby surveilled Scarpa and observed him drop a gun out of his car. Because there were no backup NYPD units, Brogan and Willoughby retrieved the gun and did not arrest Scarpa. Brogan called me and asked a series of confusing questions which indicated that he did not see who threw the gun or know Scarpa by description."

This was a task force case and Favo was the case agent. Favo admitted on this page that he put Brogan's "confusing" and baseless gun charge on a back burner. He said he accomplished this by lying to Lieutenant Bill Shannon about the need to hold off on the arrest in order to enable a nonexistent informant to continue to work the Scarpa crew.

My eyes widened when I read: "I stated this in a manner to indicate our source was probably Mazza or Delmasto. Lieutenant Shannon agreed to stop pursuing Scarpa." Favo is damn lucky Joe Simone wasn't really corrupt or this blatant lie to Lieutenant Shannon would have gotten both Mazza and Delmasto killed.

At this point in my reading, I confess, I was enraged but I knew I had to stay calm to make sense of all of this.

I read this page over and over again. Even though he was using the format of an OPR accusation against me to explain his insubordination, nothing Favo said on this page about any of his dealings with Brogan and Shannon made any sense, even if I were a rogue agent.

Finally, going outside the task force—outside Favo's chain of command—"Brogan went to [the Brooklyn D.A.] for an arrest warrant and got permission . . ." for an indictment. I imagine Brogan was exasperated with Favo. He must have been bewildered over Favo's exercise of control in stalling the Scarpa gun charge in the system.

This hard-to-follow explanation of the history of how a gun charge was temporarily suppressed had to cause the OPR investigators to wonder what the hell I was being accused of.

Favo tacked on a few lines about his "impression" of my slapping my desk and saying "We're going to win this thing." He wrote: "My impression was that when Supervisor DeVecchio said 'we' he meant the Persico faction." And? And? Is that cheering for the Persico faction in the first degree or the second degree?

As I read, this testimony seemed to be more Favo's admission of insubordination and not an allegation against me. I could imagine Don North hearing all of this and calling Favo's bluff, telling him to put it in writing for Organized Crime investigators to read.

Favo was stuck. He could freely spread lies about me to his followers, to the Eastern District, to the NYPD, or to his wife. But pinned to an OPR, he had to be very careful what he said. Lying, making up tales about me under oath, would be felonies if he got caught.

Inadvertently, Don North's demand that Favo put his complaints in writing sparked a full-blown OPR when Caproni called the very next day to report me herself.

Her 1987 DEA/NYPD allegation was not an "impression." It was a hard allegation of serious felonies.

I knew in my heart by page five that Favo had to have panicked after his meeting with North. I suspect he didn't expect the reaction he got. He expected to just drown me in suspicion. But Don North was Organized Crime through and through. I bet he could tell at once that Favo's suspicions were nonsense. Favo had no hard allegation of his own and he knew it from North's reaction. So after he left North, Favo needed help from the Eastern District. Caproni provided it. Caproni—who later in the *New Yorker* called Favo "an excellent agent . . . an extremely hard worker" and "very bright"—called Don North and resurrected her old stale incident, but with a new twist. No more allegations of congressional hearings. Now it was all about my corruption.

On page six of the OPR, Favo confessed that in July Lieutenant Bill Shannon, clearly tired of the stalling on Scarpa's gun charge, told Favo that the NYPD planned to indict Scarpa for the gun.

Favo testified: "The following day I approached Shannon in his office and asked him not to tell me anything else about their plans for Scarpa until the night before they were going to arrest him. I was then comfortable telling DeVecchio that the NYPD was not telling me about their weapons possession case." I couldn't believe he so easily admitted to insubordination.

On page seven Favo finally returned to discussing me. He swore that he was suspicious that I had given confi-

dential information to Jerry Capeci. To support his suspicion he said that "several times" after I got a call from
Capeci, I went out into the squad and asked a question
and got an answer to it. The next day the answer appeared in Capeci's column. This made me laugh because
Capeci had asked me questions that made me curious
and I did go out into the squad and ask for answers—
immediately after I hung up with Capeci. But I never
called Capeci back. Why would I? Prosecutors in the
Eastern District were my suspects for media leaks over
many years, not just the few years Favo had to observe
the phenomenon. I suspected they leaked hoping to be
repaid by generous ink in future articles, ink that would
further their careers.

Favo then claimed that when we arrested Carmine
Sessa at St. Patrick's Cathedral on Palm Sunday, I told
Favo "immediately after Sessa was handcuffed" that I
"had to give Capeci a call so he could send a photographer over." It's possible I said these words as a joke. But
there's no way I could call Capeci and expect to make
everyone hang around with Sessa in custody until a photographer showed up. Sessa did faint upon arrest, but
whether he fainted or not, our goal was to leave the
crowded Fifth Avenue scene as quickly as possible. Agents
who were there were interviewed by the OPR and confirmed my version. I'm sure that if I called Capeci and
wanted to stall until his photographer made it to the
scene, I would have fainted myself.

Bernadette MacMillan told the OPR: "I have never
met Jerry Capeci, reporter for the *Daily News*. I have

received about a dozen phone calls from Capeci, who was looking for Supervisor DeVecchio or Agent Chris Favo . . . more often than not, Supervisor DeVecchio would instruct me to refer calls from Capeci to the media office rather than putting the call through to him."

I read the last page of the OPR hunting for a sign that a CW such as Sessa or Mazza had said I fed information to Scarpa. Instead, I found Favo saying that he was suspicious that I might let the BBC copy classified photos from old cases for their TV program about the Mafia, so he hid them where I couldn't find them. Favo really did do that, although I didn't know he'd done it intentionally until I read his OPR. He locked the photos away, took the key with him, and took the next day off. His action prevented me from getting approval from Don North to give the BBC copies of certain of the photos. This story that constituted the final page of Favo's statement corroborated what I'd heard about the resentment he'd felt over the BBC's decision to interview me and not him.

With all my anger I found myself laughing out loud like a lunatic. This was really funny.

And that was it. Factually, Favo's report about me was all about the many important things he kept from me, or in the case of the photos, locked away from me.

On April 4, 1994, Favo gave another OPR statement, and when I read that statement I finally found out the truth of what he'd been up to on that fateful day of January 17, 1994, when he went into Don North's office. Favo revealed: "We were not interested in getting Supervisor

DeVecchio in trouble." You could have fooled me. "We only wanted to see if he could be transferred to another squad and replaced by another supervisor so we would be able to continue our investigations and prosecutions in the Colombo Family War matters, without concern that he might disclose information regarding certain of our cases."

My jaw dropped. Favo wasn't reporting me for any crimes at all. He merely wanted me transferred!

A month or so prior, Favo had enlisted the support of the Eastern District D.A.'s Office in preventing me from making some personnel changes. Emboldened by his victory in this effort, he believed he could get away with making the mother of all personnel changes. I bet he thought he could walk in with the Eastern District behind him and a handful of vague suspicions and Don North would cave.

When I reread that sentence in his second OPR statement that all he wanted was for me to "be transferred to another squad" I was livid.

All this while I'd blamed some unknown CW for my misery. There was no CW accusing me of anything. It had been Favo all along.

On calm reflection, which took me a few days to achieve, I saw that Favo's first OPR statement was nothing but an eight-page shabby defense of his insubordination in withholding information from me. In that first statement, ordered by Don North, he put the major instances of withholding down on record and tied it all up in knots of vague suspicion about me.

Also, Favo knew full well that his "impressions" and "opinions" could never form the basis of a perjury charge against him.

With the war jury trials about to start when he walked into North's office, trials in which I would be an active particpant and an expert witness, all his insubordinate hoarding of information would come to light. I would say, why didn't I know this, why didn't I know that, what's going on here? It would then be Favo on the hot seat, on formal charges for insubordination, lying to a superior and lying to outside agencies like the NYPD and the Brooklyn D.A.

Favo lied to me and withheld vital information from me and then sought my transfer and requested I be replaced. Why? What was his motivation? I could only imagine that he hoped the new supervisor wouldn't know the first thing about the Colombo Family or the war so that Favo himself could be the man in charge, the man who brought down the Colombo Family. My *impression* is that every time Favo heard me say that I wanted to be the first supervisor to bring down an entire family, his eyes turned green with envy. I believe he hoarded information so that by necessity he'd become the Eastern District's source for all things Colombo and for any information about the war. In possession of all the facts, he'd become their go-to guy and all the glory would be his.

Favo's business plan was a three-ball combination pool shot with me the last ball to fall in the pocket. Accusing me of being fishy in the first degree gave Favo legal justification for his lies and deceit in keeping evidence and decisions from me. Accusing me of being fishy fed into Valerie Caproni's 1987 DEA/NYPD "siege mentality" lingering suspicions. Accusing me of being fishy was designed to give me a one-way ticket off my own squad.

While Favo was careful to add no facts or allegations against me in his second OPR statement, he closed by giving the OPR investigators a list of twenty-two people he thought might possibly have evidence against me. The list was sprinkled with words like *may have seen*, *may know*, *may have been*, *should be able*, *possibly knows*, and *should know*. Favo added: "I believe it would also be beneficial to interview U.S. Federal Judge Jack Weinstein . . . U.S. Federal Judge I. Leo Glasser . . . Magistrate Caden . . . it is possible that Supervisor DeVecchio might have contacted the judges prior to sentencing."

I'm ashamed that the FBI followed Favo's wishes, went on a fishing expedition, and interviewed everyone on the list, including the federal judges—further staining my reputation with each question.

Of course, because I was in the dark, I had no witness list to submit. All Doug Grover could do was to keep repeating, when asked in the press, that the OPR was "ridiculous and pure nonsense."

In July 1995, after the case of the straightened-out sons of Orena had been lost and a year and a half after Favo had walked into Don North's office in hopes of getting me booted off my squad, Favo gave two new statements on the same day. Lots of suspicion, lots of impression and belief, no facts, no allegations, except maybe against the OPR investigators. In the second statement he gave that day he said: "I did not intend, in my previous statement, to suggest that there was any impropriety on the part of the special agents conducting the OPR investigation." I'll bet they breathed a healthy sigh of relief.

CHAPTER THIRTY

CAPRONI'S BUSINESS PLAN

In the end there was only one hard allegation that did not involve Favo's "impressions" or his opinion about the meaning of words I may or may not have spoken to him. That hard allegation was Valerie Caproni's. It was alleged that I had given Greg Scarpa Sr. a list of the members of Gregory Jr.'s crew, including Gregory Jr. himself, who were about to be indicted in November 1987 on a DEA/ NYPD Major Case Squad investigation involving Staten Island Community College drug activity.

In her initial OPR statement, Caproni swore that at her request an agent with the Colombo Family squad attended a DEA/NYPD meeting on that drug case in the summer of 1987. Her OPR states: "Caproni complained that neither the Eastern District, DEA, nor the NYPD received any positive information back from the N.Y. FBI's Colombo squad regarding Scarpa's crew." I believe this. It made sense. Caproni's drug case was minuscule compared with those we were handling in 1987. Nevertheless, Caproni believed the Colombo squad's lack of interest was suspicious and an example of the control I exercised.

Caproni stated that at the drug-case meeting she told those assembled that a Gregory Jr. crew member, Cosmo Catanzano, was a weak link and she felt he might cooperate.

She told the OPR investigators that now, seven years later, she learned from a Wartime CW that Greg Scarpa Sr. and Gregory Jr. had stated in 1987 that Cosmo Catanzano was a weak link and should be killed. The CW, on orders from Gregory Jr., dug a grave for Cosmo, but everyone was arrested before Cosmo could be whacked. Caproni viewed this as cause and effect. The agent who attended the meeting heard her say that Cosmo was a weak link. That agent told me, and then I told Greg Scarpa. When interviewed seven years later, though, the agent had no recollection of any discussion about a weak link. He did remember talking to me, wasn't sure when, but it was not about a weak link. I'm sure I talked to the agent, but it would have been in connection with Gregory Jr.'s flight to avoid prosecution, which was the only issue on the table after I became supervisor of the squad.

Caproni had determined that Cosmo might be a weak link, but it's not unlikely that Greg Scarpa came to the same conclusion. Cosmo was brand-new to the crew and had a prior drug arrest that might cause him to be facing a very tough sentence. (It turns out that everyone misjudged Cosmo. He did his time and kept his mouth shut.)

Further regarding the summer 1987 meeting: "Caproni advised that she believed the supervisor of the Colombo squad at that time was Lindley DeVecchio and that DeVecchio would have been made aware of the DEA/ NYPD investigation by the agent attending the meeting." The OPR investigators added in parentheses: "It is noted that Supervisor Christopher Mattiace was the supervisor of the Colombo squad at that time and DeVecchio was supervisor of the Bonanno squad."

It was nice to see that the OPR investigators noticed that I didn't get the squad until two months after Gregory Jr. went on the lam. I have no memory of doing so, but I'm sure I would have sought out the agent who had attended the drug-case meeting once I took over the squad in January 1988 and had to deal with the issue of finding Gregory Jr. before the April trial date and before the U.S. marshals found him.

Reading Valerie Caproni's OPR interviews wasn't easy for me. Because of my newly diagnosed high blood pressure, I had to take lots of breaks. I just couldn't read all her statements in one sitting. I thought I'd relax by occasionally reading some of the obviously less relevant OPR interviews.

I wondered when I saw his OPR statement why Supervisor John Coleman had been interviewed. I'd known John for twenty-five years, but had never worked with him. John was the supervisor of the Joint Bank Robbery

Task Force. Whenever you see the words *"joint squad,"* you can assume, as was the case here, that the squad is composed of both FBI agents and NYPD detectives.

As I read the following from John Coleman, something clicked:

"During the course of my supervision of the bank robbery investigations within the New York Division, there did come a time, as I recall, that we investigated a group known as the 'Bypass Gang.' This group was composed of members who did bank burglaries by bypassing the alarm systems of those institutions . . . I recall that Supervisor Pat Colgan had an interest in this group as well . . . I also recall that there was some concern about informational leaks regarding this investigation . . ."

I reflected back on one of the tapes Favo made for T.J. It was the tape about the hit on Bypass Gang member Otto Heidel on October 8, 1987, three weeks after Gregory Jr.'s hit on bypass burglar Joe Brewster and four weeks before Gregory Jr. went on the lam.

No doubt, I thought, the OPR interviewed John Coleman because of Favo's suspicion, as he stated on the T.J. tapes, that Otto Heidel was given up by an FBI agent "whoever that was . . . or is." Namely, me.

Coleman continued: "My recollection includes the fact that members of the Scarpa crew were involved with this gang." This last line really got my attention, and I kept rereading it.

That casual observation gnawed at me. Then I began to put it all together. Joe Brewster didn't just get whacked for not splitting his scores with Gregory Jr. Joe

Brewster, as a soldier, owed a split to his capo, Anthony Scappy Scarpati, not to the Scarpas. Joe Brewster got whacked merely for doing the scores that he did with Frank Smith and the Lucchese Family Bypass Gang, scores that Gregory Jr. felt entitled to do because the Scarpa crew had originated that moneymaking partnership. The Scarpa crew had introduced Joe Brewster to it and now Joe Brewster had made himself a partner—a secret partner. Joe Brewster's scores would have been Gregory Jr.'s had the latter not been kept in the dark about them. So Joe Brewster got caught using his elbows. Now that piece of work on Joe Brewster finally made sense to me.

And suspicion fell on Joe Brewster for making secret bypass burglary scores in the summer of 1987, the same time as the Lucchese and Colombo Family were having sit-downs over the fate of Joe Brewster's Bypass Gang partner Frank Smith. No doubt, I reasoned, the information that Joe Brewster was doing bypass burglaries with Frank Smith was gleaned from those sit-downs. The Lucchese Family would have pointed that fact out as evidence of why it was mutually beneficial for both families to keep Frank Smith alive.

"You can bet on that," I heard myself say out loud. No wonder, I thought, that Gregory Jr. filled Scappy's head with all that crap about Brewster becoming a born-again Christian.

At some point right in this time frame, the Mafia Cops injected a piece into the Bypass Gang mix, I remembered. That piece was that Otto Heidel was a government informant, and they backed up their allegation by providing Gaspipe with actual tape recordings.

Could the Mafia Cops have also passed along information that other members of the Bypass Gang, namely, Gregory Jr. and his Colombo Family crew, were about to be indicted in a joint DEA/NYPD Major Case Squad investigation? Of course, I thought. How could the Mafia Cops not have passed that piece of information along? That was their job. Tip-offs of imminent arrests is high on the list of what they got $4,000 a month for. The Mafia Cops had total access to the NYPD Major Case Squad's activities.

This is not to say that Gaspipe himself would have passed the information to Greg Scarpa Sr. But it could have come down the pipeline from the Lucchese Family. Someone in the mix could have passed it to Scarpa, if only to be owed a favor someday, I figured.

This time I returned more eagerly to where I left off on Valerie Caproni's OPR statement and I read further.

On page four of her single-spaced report, Caproni—who had kept my OPR in abeyance while Greg Scarpa died of AIDS before he could be interviewed—spoke about that September 28, 1993, meeting in her office in which Scarpa offered to cooperate so that he could be allowed to die at home: "Caproni advised that during the fall of 1993, the attorney for Scarpa Sr. approached the Eastern District and proffered his client's cooperation in return for being released from prison."

Of course he wanted to die at home, I thought. By the time he died, he weighed fifty-six pounds.

Caproni went on: "The debriefing of Scarpa Sr. was attended by Supervisor DeVecchio, Agent Favo, and Agent Jim Brennan (the agent responsible for the . . . [Lucchese] Family law enforcement leak investigation) . . ."

So that's what Brennan was doing there, I thought. But it still puzzled me.

Caproni continued: "After debriefing Scarpa Sr. with respect to his role in the Colombo War investigation, the other interviewees, with the exception of Brennan, departed."

I remembered that. We all left and they stayed behind.

And then she got to it—I could feel my heart racing as I read each word: "Caproni advised that she and Agent Brennan interviewed Scarpa Sr. concerning his alleged law enforcement contact, and Scarpa denied having any such contact, and said he received his law enforcement information from . . . Gaspipe Casso."

Bango, there it was! My shoulders felt like a great weight had been lifted from them.

Caproni ended with: "Scarpa denied having ever received any investigative information from Supervisor DeVecchio."

I did some long slow breathing to calm down. Then I put Caproni's OPR interview down, went to my garage, got out my motorcycle, and went for a long hard ride.

* * *

This private interview of Scarpa that was kept secret from me took place many months before Gaspipe rolled and began telling the Lucchese squad, including Jim Brennan, about the Mafia Cops' existence and their being on a monthly retainer for information about things like imminent arrests and their role in the murder of Otto Heidel.

Jim Brennan told me that during Gaspipe's debriefing in the Valachi Suite in El Paso, Gaspipe denied that he gave information to Scarpa, but that doesn't change what Scarpa said.

I could put it together more clearly and with more certainty now that I knew that Scarpa said his law enforcement information came from Gaspipe Casso.

I began to reassemble the facts in my mind. The leaked information Caproni focused on during her interview of Scarpa was information about an imminent arrest of Gregory Jr.'s crew. Supervisor John Coleman stated in his OPR interview that Gregory Jr.'s crew members were Colombo members of the Lucchese Family Bypass Gang. The Mafia Cops would have easy access to information on this DEA/NYPD investigation and of these imminent arrests by the DEA, and more importantly by the NYPD Major Case Squad. The imminent arrest of Gregory Jr. and his crew would have been passed on to Gaspipe by the Mafia Cops at roughly the same time as they passed on the information that Otto Heidel was an informant. Information on imminent arrests of members of the Bypass Gang, I reasoned, would be extremely important information for Gaspipe to receive from his Mafia Cops and to pass down the pipeline for action. To protect his Lucchese Family Bypass Gang, already damaged by Heidel, Gaspipe would need to be sure that Greg Scarpa Sr. had weeded out any weak-link members of Gregory Jr.'s crew prior to the mass arrests. That's why Gregory Jr. had a grave dug for Cosmo Catanzano. Gaspipe would have put the Colombo Family imminent arrest information in the pipeline during that summer of negotiations between the two families over the fate of the Bypass Gang burglar Frank Smith. And whoever personally passed the information to Scarpa would have credited Gaspipe.

Or Gaspipe personally gave it to Scarpa, as Scarpa said he did. When he was asked at the Valachi Suite, maybe Gaspipe simply didn't want to rat on Scarpa or on Gregory Jr. and so denied personally giving information to Scarpa. Sammy "The Bull" Gravano did this very thing when he lied and denied involvement of John Gotti's son, John Gotti Jr. in any murders.

Besides all that, in our judicial system, it wouldn't ever be my job to prove it was Gaspipe who gave Scarpa the law enforcement information that enabled Gregory Jr. to go on the lam from his DEA/NYPD drug case in 1987. It was Caproni's job to prove it was me. And she had to know, as did Favo, that there was not a single CW who implicated me in any way during that entire episode; if any one of them had implicated me, you can be sure that quotes from their 302 debriefings would have been plastered all over Favo and Caproni's OPR interviews.

Scarpa told Caproni to her face that it was Gaspipe, and yet she went ahead and helped lynch me.

And all the while I was kept in the dark. I watched her add her own charge against me to the OPR—aiding Gregory Jr.'s flight—the exact charge she already knew had been denied by Scarpa. I watched Caproni hold my OPR investigation in abeyance. I waited in vain for the OPR investigators to interview Scarpa, and I watched him die before they could. I watched Caproni and Ellen Corcella convict me with a letter in court on the Orena sons' trial. I watched Caproni tell Judge Weinstein during the Little Vic Orena appeal hearing that there was "a strong circumstantial case" against me for passing law enforcement information to Scarpa. And yet every step of the way, she knew I had been cleared by Scarpa.

Even when the OPR cleared me, Caproni gave a statement on the record to Jerry Capeci. She said that the OPR had not "exonerated DeVecchio." The OPR simply decided that "they don't have proof beyond a reasonable doubt." The chief of the Organized Crime Division of the Eastern District of New York said this to Jerry Capeci in September 1996, knowing what Scarpa had said to her in September 1993.

I didn't know it as I continued to read these OPR interviews, but the worst of what Favo caused to happen to me with the help of Valerie Caproni was yet to come.

Doug Grover and Mark Bederow would have Jim Brennan waiting in the wings to testify at my murder trial if the Brooklyn D.A. brought up the DEA/NYPD leak as further evidence of my "unhealthy relationship" with Scarpa. Jim Brennan would have testified that the scope and direction of every one of Caproni's questions of Scarpa was intended to expose me as Scarpa's source of law enforcement information. Brennan would also have testified that Scarpa was adamant that he'd gotten no information from me or from any of his FBI handlers, living or dead.

Unquestionably, Valerie Caproni had invited Jim Brennan to her office that day for one purpose. She expected Jim to watch her break open his leak case. She expected to deliver proof to the Lucchese Family leak investigator that the Lucchese Family leak dripped down the pipeline from Greg Scarpa and the Colombo Family, courtesy of the corrupt Lin DeVecchio.

Greg Scarpa, in the first phase of his meeting to plead for mercy that day, had just confessed many murders and near murders to Caproni. He was in her office with a mind-set to tell her the truth. I wonder: If he had lied, if, instead of telling her the truth, he threw me under the bus and told her what she obviously hoped to hear, would she have granted his wish to die at home?

I am dead certain Scarpa knew exactly what she wanted from him and that it would help him to tell her what she wanted to hear, but he wouldn't lie about his friend Lin DeVecchio. And I never thought he would.

Reading what he said to her was one of my proudest moments.

Gradually, however, the anger boiled over in me. Favo had nothing on me all along. Caproni did have something. But what she had would have *cleared* me.

CHAPTER THIRTY-ONE

PRETRIAL JUSTICE

"Honey," Carolyn called out, "you got a message to call Doug Grover. He said to watch *The Sopranos*. It's the last episode tonight."

In the TV program's final year, the character of FBI Agent Dwight Harris had gone native. He relished sitting with Tony Soprano and eating Italian hero sandwiches at Tony's hangout, Satriale's Pork Store. Tony was supposed to be supplying Agent Harris with information on Muslim terrorists. Instead, the FBI agent was helping Tony in his internal war with rival Boss Phil Leotardo. Agent Harris had supplied Tony with the location of Phil Leotardo's hideout. Uh-oh!

In the final episode, the balding agent is shown sitting at a table watching TV and hearing that Phil Leotardo had been murdered, the victim of a Mafia hit.

We watch his eyes widen. Harris excitedly slaps the table with glee, saying, "We're going to win this thing."

Thank you, David Chase. As popular as the show was, my "guilt" was now immortalized for my grandsons.

Fifteen years earlier Favo had laid the minefield and the mines were still exploding.

After my retirement in 1996, the anger had subsided and I was able to put this thing in the back of my mind. I had a lot to be grateful for. I had a wonderful wife and family. I'd developed a private investigating business. I never got the quality of work I'd have gotten had this never happened to me and the bad publicity had cost me hundreds of thousands of dollars in potential income. Nevertheless, the anger was gone or buried deep.

But with my second scandal, it was more than daily anger. It was daily fury. And I had to keep it in check if I was going to make rational decisions.

The day after the offensive *Sopranos* episode aired, my codefendant in the Patrick Porco murder, Johnny Loads Sinagra, had his murder charge dismissed by Judge Gustin Reichbach. Sinagra's lawyer, Joe Giaramita, convinced the judge at a Singer speedy trial hearing, accusing the D.A. of unnecessary delay in making an arrest. Giaramita proved that there had been sixteen years of unnecessary delay in bringing Sinagra's murder charge. The Brooklyn D.A. had Sinagra's name as the shooter in 1990 and failed to investigate the lead. Unnecessary delay didn't apply to me because the D.A. didn't have my name until 2005, when Linda Schiro gave it to them and they indicted me a year later. But the fairness of the judge's decision reinforced our decision to go nonjury and to let him decide my guilt or innocence.

We also liked his language. He quoted *Alice in Wonderland* to describe an Assistant D.A.'s testimony at the Singer hearing: "When I use a word, it means just what I choose it to mean, neither more nor less."

When we elected to be tried without a jury, Judge Reichbach asked me to reconsider and disclosed a possible conflict of interest. He had a domestic counterintelligence FBI file, the kind of file I researched in my first job as a clerk with the FBI. In 1968 he'd led a Students for a Democratic Society (SDS) revolt at Columbia University and had been ratted on by a CI working for the FBI from within the SDS. In court, he recited the informant's words to me from memory: "Subject is one of the most dangerous people known in the SDS . . . Subject is an extremely powerful speaker and has a strong charismatic appeal . . ."

" 'Subject,' that's me," the judge said, beaming. "I've always appreciated, indeed proudly cherished, that characterization, even though it was not meant by the FBI to be flattering."

The judge set an example in disclosing conflicts of interest; I only wish that everyone connected to the tribulations I had endured, from the time I uttered the words

"We're going to win this thing" to the day, fifteen years later, when my murder trial began, had shown the same integrity.

Doug spoke for me and for our team the next day in the *Daily News*: "I give [Judge Reichbach] all the credit in the world for disclosing it at this time. It just tells me this is a fair judge."

In his twenty-seven-page opinion dismissing Sinagra's case, the judge ripped into the D.A.'s office from top to bottom for a "failure of both oversight and direction."

One of Doug's comments at my arraignment that was critical of the Brooklyn D.A.'s office was quoted in newspaper articles about the Sinagra dismissal: "They don't make these kinds of cases and they don't know how people act in these kinds of cases, and they don't know how to deal with witnesses in these cases."

That's true, but in my case, decisions were made that would be improper in any kind of investigation, Organized Crime or not. And there were, without doubt, improper motivations involved in the Brooklyn D.A.'s decision to bring murder charges against me.

First, there was the Favo scandal. The Brooklyn D.A. did not sit down with my OPR file and analyze it. But their prosecutors knew every bit of gossip, smear, opinion, or impression that you could learn from secondhand sources and blatant hearsay. The D.A. had called Favo to testify before the grand jury that indicted me and would call him again at trial. As he'd done from day one, all he did was rehash impressions and opinions without proof.

I'm convinced that this murder indictment was merely

a logical extension of Favo's original widespread smear against me, which was motivated by a desire for personal gain. Only this time the information I supposedly passed along to Scarpa had to do with murder.

Second is the fact that Vecchione and D.A. Investigator Tommy Dades had gotten a six-figure book deal on a related case. It was to their personal advantage to join the lynch mob against me.

Dades and Vecchione had worked together in 2005 in the murder case of the Mafia Cops. The Mafia Cops conspired to murder for the Mafia. What I supposedly did for the Colombo Family they did for the Lucchese Family. Tommy Dades did a professional job helping to break the Mafia Cops case. He pursued and developed a star witness, the mother of one of the Mafia Cops' murder victims. He brought her to Vecchione. Together, they worked with the feds to bring a RICO case in the Eastern District.

As partners, Vecchione and Dades signed a $300,000 book deal.

Early on, the book was entitled *Skels: The Inside Story of the Mafia Cops Case*. *Skels* is an NYPD term for bad guy, short for *skeletons*. The publisher's promotional pitch boasted that this was the "full inside story of the investigation of their crimes, as told by Vecchione—who led the investigation—and Dades—whose work broke the case." There was a $600,000 movie deal with Warner Bros. in the mix. The publisher promised "never-before-released documents and information." One has to wonder why such documents belonging to the taxpayers of Brooklyn were to be used exclusively by these two insiders.

Skels was scheduled for release in January 2007. Can you imagine the tremendous free publicity Vecchione and Dades would have gotten by bringing me to trial at any time during that year? A corrupt FBI agent who supplied information to the Mafia to commit murders would be extremely high profile at any time! But with a book about their investigation and prosecution of two NYPD detectives who did the exact same thing in the stores, this investigator and this prosecutor and their *Skels* would be in the daily headlines for many months before my trial began and after my trial ended—regardless of the verdict.

Allowing either of them to participate in any way in my case was, in my opinion, unethical.

To begin with, their Mafia Cops book deal concerned a case that was still open, and this irregularity was noted in the press well before there was any thought to indict me. Legal ethics expert Professor Monroe Freedman was quoted as saying: "It's really egregious judgment, because it's the kind of thing every prosecutor should know. It clearly puts the prosecutor's personal interest in self-promotion and making money ahead of his obligations as a public official."

Nevertheless, D.A. Hynes approved the book deal. After all, he himself did the exact same thing with another open case. Hynes had a book in the pipeline for 2007, a fictionalized account of a cold case that was still open in his office, a 1992 murder case in which corrupt cops were strongly suspected of being the perpetrators, but were never arrested. His novel was promoted as being based on fact. It was called *Triple Homicide*, and it was scheduled for release days before my trial began in October 2007. Hynes was at a book signing in Bethesda, Maryland, promoting his novel—about corrupt cops who were murderers—and as a result, he missed the second day of my trial—about an allegedly corrupt agent who murdered.

Unfortunately for Dades and Vecchione, a legal technicality caused their book contract to stall. There was talk that they might have to return their advance. Meanwhile, other Mafia Cops books—including one by Pulitzer Prize winner Jimmy Breslin—were beating theirs to the marketplace.

Ultimately, the Brooklyn D.A.'s Office was thrown off the Mafia Cops federal RICO case for unethical press leaks, the kind they employed to their advantage against me. The last straw was, of course, their attempt to convince the federal prosecutor to coordinate the Mafia Cops' arrest with the *60 Minutes* segment about the case. Leaks from discussions with the *60 Minutes* people already could have foiled the arrest.

"If the takedown came on a Sunday," retired Mafia Cops investigator Bill Oldham recalled in his book *The Brotherhoods*, "we were told, the television show *60 Minutes* would run footage from the press conference on that night's broadcast. The publicity that the U.S. Attorney's Office and the Brooklyn D.A. would receive would be enormous. If things went wrong we couldn't have dug ourselves a hole deep enough to hide in. The stupidity of the notion was stunning."

The banishment from the Mafia Cops case was complete. Dades would not even be called to testify in the case he himself had helped break.

Wouldn't my case make a terrific book for Dades and Vecchione? Win or lose the trial against me, and the book writers in the D.A.'s office would still win. What an advance such a sequel to their Mafia Cops book would bring! Or what a substitute it would make if their book got canceled!

Dades is the man who broke the murder case against me. To me that says it all about conflicts of interest. In pretrial proceedings and from material turned over to us by the D.A., we learned a lot about how I came to be indicted. As he did with the Mafia Cops, Dades developed and brought in a star witness against me to the D.A.'s office. However, unlike the Mafia Cops witness, this one was clearly lying. And it should have been clear that she was lying.

With their Grancio file on me gathering dust on a shelf, Dades brought in Greg Scarpa's common-law wife, Linda Schiro, to save the day. Simply put, without Schiro's stories about me, there would have been no murder case.

Dades and Schiro and Schiro's divorced daughter, Little Linda, had been close for a decade, since Dades handled the case against Joey Schiro's murderer. In her trial testimony against me, Schiro was to say, "I love

Tommy Dades." Dades's relationship with her and her family clearly screams "conflict of interest" to me.

Dades's relationship with the Schiro women could easily cloud his judgment. It seems to have done so on at least one occasion. During a pretrial investigation into my grand jury leaks, Dades admitted that he had leaked information to a *New York Post* reporter and photographer who had snapped a candid photo of thirty-seven-year-old Little Linda outside the home she and her four children shared with Linda Schiro. Little Linda was irate and didn't want the photo used. Dades, in order to help her, negotiated with the *Post* reporter. He gave the reporter information on a subject he had testified to earlier in the day at the grand jury, namely, that Johnny Loads Sinagra and not Joey Schiro was the shooter of Patrick Porco. Dades gave the reporter other Schiro family photos and agreed to give the *Post* an exclusive interview of Little Linda. In exchange, the *Post* agreed not to use their candid photo of Little Linda. Violating the secrecy of the grand jury when he fingered John Sinagra as Porco's shooter is a potential crime.

Dades and Schiro had a lot in common. Like Dades, Schiro was a wannabe author, even more wannabe than Dades. Her pitch was a book called *Mafia Mistress*. As a result of the reams of publicity she got from my 1994 Favo scandal, no fewer than five established authors interviewed her for a book deal. Proposals had been written and circulated, but she never got a publisher.

With each try at publishing over the years, Schiro enlarged her own role—and mine as well—in Greg Scarpa's murderous doings. By the time Dades delivered her to the Brooklyn D.A., she had a story that planted her at the right hand of the seat of Mafia power in Bensonhurst. Linda Schiro morphed into an eyewitness to my acceptance of bribe money, and to my four powwows with Greg Scarpa in which we discussed whom to kill and why, and how to locate one of the victims.

Ultimately, Dades struck out on three pitches and would not testify in my case when it came to trial almost two years later.

Strike one: A few months after my March 30, 2006, arraignment, Dades and a neighbor got into an altercation and the neighbor died. The man's ribs were broken and he bled to death. The medical examiner ruled it a homicide. There was an allegation that the man had been stomped. Although not present when it happened, Vecchione drove over the Verrazano Bridge to Staten Island and testified for the defense before a Staten Island grand jury and Dades was cleared of the homicide. Vecchione then refused to give a statement to the NYPD Internal Affairs Bureau, which was investigating Dades independently from the Staten Island grand jury. Vecchione said: "I don't report to you guys and I don't have to talk to you."

As an aside, Vecchione never once offered my lawyers to present any evidence at the grand jury on my behalf. Furthermore, his assistant entirely avoided discussing certain topics with the CWs they questioned at the grand jury. Those topics would have convinced the grand jurors of my innocence. For example, Carmine Sessa was not asked a single question about his procuring Lampasi's address and work schedule for Scarpa.

Strike two: During the Singer speedy pretrial hearing of my codefendant, Johnny Sinagra—the man accused of actually shooting eighteen-year-old Patrick Porco on my orders—Dades admitted filing a false affidavit. He claimed he hadn't read it before swearing to the truth of it. It was a simple affidavit, which would have taken a minute to read. The prosecutor who wrote it testified that he'd gotten the information he put into it from Dades himself. Initially, the judge had relied on the false affidavit to deny the defendant's motion to dismiss. When the defendant's lawyer, Joe Giaramita, uncovered the truth, the judge rescinded his prior ruling and ordered a hearing. After the hearing, the judge blasted Dades and ended up dismissing all charges against the alleged triggerman.

Strike three: During the Singer hearing that led to the alleged triggerman's victory over Vecchione, Dades, and Hynes, the defense lawyer in the case, Joe Giaramita, asked Dades a surprise question. His client, the alleged triggerman, was married to Linda Schiro's niece. Based on information he'd gotten from Schiro's niece, Giaramita asked Dades if he'd had an affair with Linda Schiro's thirty-seven-year-old daughter, Little Linda. The judge disallowed the question. A flustered Dades exploded out of the courtroom, almost slugged a photographer in the lobby, and promptly resigned in disgrace from the D.A.'s office.

Whether Dades had an affair with Little Linda or not

doesn't matter. What matters is the conflict of interest his closeness with Schiro's family presents for both investigator and witness. The witness is eager to give the investigator whatever she thinks will help him, and help his career, while seizing at the same time the opportunity a friendly investigator is giving her to help herself. The investigator is eager to accept from any friend, especially an intimate one, whatever he thinks will help her, while at the same helping himself. It's Ethics 101.

By coming up with four murders that resembled those committed by the Mafia Cops, Dades had truly rescued the D.A.'s dormant file against me from a state of oblivion.

The original file against me, which had been delivered to the D.A.'s doorstep on January 29, 2005, was about a different murder—a fifth murder, if you will. It was the drive-by murder of capo Nicky Black Grancio, an Orena enemy of Greg Scarpa during the Colombo Family War of 1991 to 1992. It was the only murder I was accused of from January 29, 2005, until Dades spoke with Linda Schiro about ten months later.

The file against me for the Grancio murder had been put together by an ally of the Russo cousins. She'd brought her file to Massachusetts Congressman William Delahunt, who was then investigating a Boston case involving accusations that an FBI agent fed intelligence to a gangster. She hoped to spark a congressional hearing about my corrupt relationship with Greg Scarpa using

the Nicky Black Grancio drive-by murder. Because of my
Favo scandal, Delahunt believed I was corrupt, but he
was busy with the other case of alleged FBI corruption. He therefore picked up the phone and referred the
Grancio/DeVecchio murder file to his friend and fellow
Democrat, the Brooklyn D.A. Charles "Joe" Hynes. I
was the supervisor of the Colombo Family War case that
led to the convictions of the Cousins, Jo Jo and Chuckie
Russo. Judge Charles P. Sifton's judicial opinion on their
appeal had been issued during the height of the publicity surrounding my 1994 scandal. It was that one sentence in the opinion about my conduct not having risen
to the "level of uncivilized and indecent conduct" that
led the Russo cousins to believe that if they could prove
a Colombo Family War murder case against me, they
would win their appeal and be released. The Brooklyn
D.A. sat on the Grancio/DeVecchio murder file for ten
months, perhaps because statements made by the actual
drive-by shooter, Larry Mazza, easily proved my innocence. Ironically, the Grancio/DeVecchio "investigation"
implicated Favo in the murder conspiracy. When Dades
came in like the cavalry with Linda Schiro in tow, bran-
dishing these brand-new four murders against me, the
D.A. abandoned the Grancio murder and embraced Linda
Schiro's stories.

The Russo cousins didn't need the Grancio drive-by.
I'm sure they would be satisfied to see me framed and
convicted of any one of Dades and Schiro's four brand-
new allegations.

However, for their appeal to succeed, it would be better to have a Colombo Family War murder to pin on me. Grancio fit perfectly, but the Brooklyn D.A. wouldn't bite. And only one of the four murders that Linda Schiro accused me of had occurred during the war. It was the "We're going to win this thing" murder of the old-timer Lorenzo Lampasi. So to be on the safe side, the Russos' ally helped on a civil lawsuit against Favo and me for the wrongful death of Grancio. For an appeal on government misconduct, having two rogue agents to blame is better than having one. Having Favo sued along with me for pulling the police surveillance on Grancio made that one bearable, even laughable.

In accordance with court procedure, we were supplied with prior statements made by Linda Schiro and other witnesses before Schiro told the four stories to Dades. They made for some strange reading. I'm so conditioned now to be defensive that I need to point out a few examples. In order to entice one author to work on a book with her, she told him that I had been a lookout on a million-dollar bank bypass burglary in Queens; that I got a detective drunk, tape-recorded him, and used the tape to get him to drop hijacking charges against Gregory Jr.; and that my predecessor, Tony Villano, did not die of heart failure: Scarpa murdered him—at the request of the FBI! And on and on.

One book Schiro *was* going to be involved in was a biography of Gregory Jr. The book's author wrote to Schiro: "I have recently written to Greg [Jr.] telling him that I expect him to walk out of prison one day soon, and that you and I will be waiting outside the prison gates to embrace him and laugh and cry with him and take him out to a good steak dinner . . . I also believe that this story will have a tremendous publicity, which, as you know, presells books. I also believe that there is potential for a movie sale."

If this is getting confusing, you can imagine how my wife, Carolyn, and I felt each day when we reviewed a fresh supply of discovery material supplied by the D.A. I couldn't do much outside the house because of my anklet monitor, so we stayed in a lot and talked about the case.

"So," Carolyn said one day. "If these two turkeys get Gregory Jr. out of jail, they will sell a lot of books."

"Don't get any ideas," I said, "about putting me in jail so you could sell a lot of books, 'Mrs. Mafia Agent.'"

Another day, my lawyer Mark Bederow called to chat.

"Has the D.A. done any investigation at all?" I asked him. "They've got some pretty good investigators over there. Ken McCabe used to be with that office."

"Except for Dades developing Linda Schiro," Mark said, "the D.A. did no independent investigation at all. And I mean from the time Delahunt sent the Grancio file to them in January 2005."

"They've got some damn good investigators over there," I repeated. "Too bad they never used them."

Another day Doug Grover called.

"Carolyn can't get over Linda Schiro," I said.

"Have you noticed the pattern of her lies," Doug said.

"I think so," I said. "She goes from the first OPR interview, where she has nothing bad to say about me, to gradually building a case against me."

"You know she became a CI after her OPR interview. She was hoping for some steady money. But she never got it from the FBI. The D.A. pays her twenty-two hundred a month."

"Yeah, we saw that. Is that when you think she started making up stuff?"

"Yes, but it really was precipitated by her going to see the Boss of the family, Little Allie Boy, in an effort to inherit Scarpa's loan-shark 'book' in 1994. To get Scarpa's 'book'—worth hundreds of thousands, I might add . . ."

"At least," I said.

"And then, when she failed at that, she went after the other kind of book. I can't wait to cross-examine her."

Carolyn spotted a 302 from Schiro in 2000 when she was trying to earn money as a CI. Schiro reported to her FBI handler that Orena was going to pay for Gregory Jr.'s attorney and finance his appeal if Gregory Jr. blamed me for planting the guns that Kenny Steiger's crew found under Orena's deck; blamed me for tipping off Scarpa Sr. about informants; and blamed me for framing Orena for the Tommy Ocera murder. Schiro turned out to be a pretty good CI. Lo and behold, two years later Gregory Jr. signed an affidavit containing all the above allegations against me. Gregory Jr. would go on to testify about these things at Orena's appeal hearing before Judge Weinstein—who blasted him.

The fact that Vecchione even listed Gregory Jr. as a witness against me is an unforgivable sin when his own star witness had previously exposed Gregory Jr. as Orena's paid perjurer.

One of the several pretrial hearings my lawyers and I had to face dealt with the immunized testimony I had given in the past; members of the D.A.'s office had read this testimony, and they were making use of it despite the rule against using immunized testimony. Two prosecutors were booted off the case for violating the rule.

At the tail end of this hearing, Vecchione sent in an assistant D.A. to mop up some of the minor details. It was Joe Petrosino, the grandnephew of Lieutenant Joe Petrosino. Assistant D.A. Petrosino has a son named Joe who's on the NYPD. I took this as a good omen.

We knew that in 1998 Linda Schiro had signed on as a witness for Gregory Jr. in his RICO trial, but when the judge warned her about perjury, she bailed. We knew that around the time of that trial, Jerry Capeci and his writing partner, the award-winning journalist for the *Village Voice*, Tom Robbins, interviewed her. We also knew that these two respected journalists would not simply write down whatever Schiro said without questioning her. We were confident that if we could obtain the authors' notes, we'd have yet another prior inconsistent statement from Tommy Dades's star witness.

We sent Capeci a subpoena for any notes or tapes he might have of their interviews. His lawyer filed a motion to quash our subpoena under New York State's press shield law, which protects sources as if they were CIs. You'd think the Brooklyn D.A. would be interested in joining us to take a peek at what Schiro said to the two journalists. Instead, Vecchione came to our hearing and sat in the back of the courtroom.

Our subpoena was quashed.

As for the judgment of Vecchione as the prosecutor and the chief of the Rackets Bureau, a mere ten days before my indictment the *New York Times* printed an article about one of his cases. The writer began by quoting from an article that had appeared in *Newsday* "detailing Vecchione's romantic ties to his assistants."

In the *Newsday* article, Vecchione admitted that he had traveled to Puerto Rico with an assistant named Stacey Frascogna, but claimed the trip was strictly D.A. office business, involving a subpoena for a witness in a murder case named Adrian Diaz. Vecchione said that he did have an affair with his assistant D.A. Stacey Frascogna, but insisted that it began after they'd returned from sunny, tropical Puerto Rico.

The *Times* article revealed that during the trial of the murder case referred to above, two witnesses lied about a significant issue. Both Adrian Diaz and another witness, Edwin Oliva, claimed during cross-examination that they'd gotten no special favors or deals in return for their testimony. In his closing argument, Vecchione called the very notion of his offering deals in return for testimony "laughable" and "absurd." According to the *Times* article, however, newly discovered evidence revealed that he had given both witnesses deals and he knew it when they testified to the contrary.

This was the second time a newspaper article had accused Vecchione of concealing a leniency deal in exchange for a witness's testimony in a murder case. The first incident was reported in 2003 and was covered by the New York tabloids. According to the *Post*: "A robber who spent the past decade behind bars got five years knocked off his sentence after accusing a Brooklyn prosecutor of hiding key evidence." According to the *Daily News*: "The lookout in a deadly 1991 liquor store heist is getting out of prison five years early, allowing a well-connected prosecutor to avoid a potentially embarrassing appeal."

So Vecchione was exposed in the press during my pretrial period for an affair with his underlings; for recent and past cover-ups about leniency deals for cooperating witnesses; and for mismanaging the investigators in his Rackets Bureau, two of whom had sordid affairs with witnesses in their charge: Alexis Sivulich, who got docked a day's pay, and Maria Biagini, the semen smuggler.

Before my trial, at a hearing in August, Vecchione told the judge that he had no deal or understanding with Gregory Jr. for his cooperation should he be called as a witness for the prosecution. However, in Gregory Jr.'s biography, the author wrote that "Vecchione promised that if Gregory told the truth, he would write a letter to [Gregory Jr.'s attorney] to present to the court outlining the help Gregory had given the prosecution." On the jacket Vecchione called the book "[an] accurate account."

Before the first day of my trial, October 15, 2007, justice had been done to Tommy Dades. Justice had been done to Hynes and Vecchione when Sinagra's case was dismissed and the judge delivered his scathing opinion. Dades and Vecchione's book on the Mafia Cops had been postponed because of a legal technicality and wouldn't be published until 2009, so the daily headlines of my murder trial wouldn't give them millions of dollars' worth of free publicity.

Less than a month before my trial, Jo Jo Russo died in prison of cancer.

With my trial coming up, my team and I were not out to get anyone. All we looked forward to was justice. If we were successful, it would mean that Linda Schiro got what she deserved, but this would be an inevitable consequence; it was not our purpose. I looked forward to finally getting my side of these two scandals out in the world and paid attention to.

To coin a phrase, I was confident that "we were going to win this thing." But you never know, do you?

CHAPTER THIRTY-TWO

THE REVENGE OF THE MAFIA

". . . we are going to make the cop the bad guy, we are going to paint this guy as the dirtiest fucking cop in the world."

These were the last words on my mind when I went to bed, but in the morning, as I showered, I was able to silence them.

Carolyn and I left our rented apartment in Brooklyn Heights to begin our seven-block walk to the federal courthouse in downtown Brooklyn for the first day of trial. The Heights is a quaint historic section adjacent to downtown and the court district. Winston Churchill's American mother, Jennie Jerome, was born down the street from our building. One block to our rear as we began our walk was the promenade, a walkway overlooking the East River with a dynamite view of the New York skyline and the Brooklyn Bridge. As the song said, it was autumn in New York.

We used the trip to New York for my trial as an opportunity to visit family members. We visited Carolyn's family in New Jersey for Yom Kippur and then went to visit my daughter and her family in Philadelphia. On our stroll to the courthouse, Carolyn and I talked about these visits and our plans to tour Italy once I got my passport back.

In the street and on the sidewalk outside the tall courthouse building, the punishing cameras couldn't get enough of me. One head shot became the front page of the *New York Post* the next day under the banner headline "Agent of Death."

A long snaking line of humanity greeted us inside the state court building's vast lobby. In the crowd were jurors from all walks of life, and defendants and their families waiting to be screened. We got on that line while I watched my colleagues from our championship season bypass the screening process with a flash of their credentials. When it was my turn to walk through the metal detector, I knew my anklet would set off the alarm. While Carolyn breezed through I had to be wanded by hand. This would become a morning ritual from October 15 to November 1, 2007.

If Chuckie Russo, Vic Orena, and Gregory Jr. could see me now, they'd be smirking, I thought. That I used Scarpa to betray their secret society was an outrage that cried out for vengeance. In their eyes, Scarpa deserved to die of AIDS and I deserved the fate of Lieutenant Petrosino, three bullets to the head. At the very least, in their eyes, I deserved to spend the rest of my life in jail, whether the sentence ultimately helped their appeals or not.

While being wanded that first time, I was a step away from my "New Untouchable" brothers and our supervisors, Jim Kossler and Bill Doran. They stood and waited with Carolyn and my attorneys as the wand found my anklet. My chest swelled just looking at them standing tall, as they had stood at my arraignment. I was encouraged at this moment, believing that this Mafia attempt to get revenge—orchestrated by the Russos, Orena, Gregory Jr., and their agent of lies, Linda Schiro—was about to get a thorough exposure in a fair trial the way we exposed the hell out of the secret society in our RICO trials in our championship season with Jim Kossler's Business Plan.

Once more it was us against them. We even had our former federal prosecutor Doug Grover on our side. Although not with us in the 1980s, Doug's co-counsel, Mark Bederow, was so much like one of us that he wore an American-flag lapel pin. Our third attorney was Ginnine Fried. As I had been Scarpa's handler, Ginnine was my handler. She sat next to me throughout the trial. We shared observations.

Vecchione sat at the prosecutors' table. He worked for the state, but as he sat there waiting to prosecute me, it was as if he was also representing the Russos, Orena, Gregory Jr., and Linda Schiro.

From what we already knew about their case and Linda's history of inconsistent statements, Vecchione didn't have enough evidence to get a Title III approved, much less to convict me beyond a reasonable doubt.

Still . . .

Vecchione might have more arrows in his quiver than we knew about. While he wasn't allowed to spring a surprise witness on us, the witnesses we knew about could have some surprises of their own.

The first order of business was a motion Doug and Mark filed to introduce new evidence. Over the weekend they had received two 302 reports from Vecchione, and if it became necessary, we wanted Judge Gustin Reichbach to consider the information they contained.

The first 302 recounted conversations between an incarcerated CI and the Cousins. The conversations occurred in 1997. Judge Sifton had just overturned the Cousins' convictions. Team Caproni in the Eastern District had appealed Sifton's decision, which kept the Cousins in jail. Pending the appeal, Caproni offered the Cousins a plea bargain. She'd drop the government's appeal if they agreed to a ten-year sentence, three years of which they had already served. The Cousins made the wrong choice. That first 302 said:

1. The Russos told source, fuck the ten years, we are going to make the cop the bad guy, we are going to paint this

guy as the dirtiest fucking cop in the world. We have the money and people to do it.

2. The Russos' plan was to say that the FBI agent started the Colombo War by telling Greg Scarpa who to kill. The Russos were going to say they were only defending themselves against individuals the FBI agent was sending against them.

3. Chuckie Russo told source, in summary, with the old man (GREG SCARPA) dead, we are going to win our appeal, we are going to make the cop (DEVECCHIO) the bad guy and say he (DEVECCHIO) told him (SCARPA) to do it.

4. The Russos had a private investigator and a female attorney named [redacted] to get messages back and forth from the [prison] to the family so everyone could get their story straight.

The second 302 was from a different informant. This source spoke to Jo Jo Russo in early 1994, months prior to the public leak about my being corrupt. At this point all they wanted to do to me was kill me for revenge, not frame me: "Russo told [informant] that 'he wanted DEVECCHIO out of the way because of the stuff he did with SCARPA, and he was hurting a lot of people.' [Informant] believed PERSICO wanted DEVECCHIO killed for all the prosecutions that resulted from SCARPA's cooperation, and DEVECCHIO was doing a lot of damage to the COLOMBO CRIME FAMILY."

The night before trial, Doug and Mark showed us these two newly provided 302s.

"In other words," I said, "by his decision Judge Sifton actually saved my life."

"Huh?" Carolyn said.

"There was no need to kill me anymore, just frame me a little better than Favo and Caproni had done."

Doug laughed. "Even though Jo Jo is gone," he said, referring to Jo Jo's death in prison, "don't forget Chuckie's got a pending motion. All these Mafia guys in jail still believe strongly that they need to convict you on at least one murder."

"In Sifton's opinion," Mark said, "he used the words 'highly reprehensible trading of information.' But that was well short of a conviction. It was just an accusation."

"I love these fucking accusations in cases where I'm not heard," I said. "Even in British schools they taught me that accusation without representation is tyranny. At some point this shit's going to start getting on my fucking nerves."

Carolyn smacked her forehead. "Oh, brother." At that point we called it a night.

The next morning, in court, Vecchione said the new 302s had "no import on the case." Judge Reichbach took our request under advisement. The judge allowed a representative camera crew to film the opening statements and share the footage with the other networks.

The opening statements would be the only televised part of the trial, thank God.

The first row of seats and the entire jury box were crammed with news reporters. Among those in the jury box were three of Linda Schiro's former would-be book writers, including Jerry Capeci, who was covering the trial for the *New York Sun* and for his great Web site, www.ganglandnews.com, and Tom Robbins, covering the trial for the *Village Voice*. Capeci and Robbins often collaborated on writing projects and would be heard from in my trial. All the writers' and reporters' notebooks were poised to jot down juicy quotes from the opening statements.

Sitting there in my anklet, looking at all the reporters, I felt like a common thief in a town square in colonial times with my head, hands, and feet in the holes of a wooden pillory. My punishment was public scorn and ridicule.

It seemed to me that many things the Team Vecchione prosecutor said in his opening were designed less for the judge's ears and more to set the reporters' pens in motion.

"Brewster suspected that Greg Sr. was an informant, and said so." I'd never heard this. Anyone familiar with the rules of the secret society would know that the moment Brewster accused Scarpa of informing, he became a walking dead man. Brewster didn't need my help in dying.

"Detective Al Lombardo, from the Brooklyn D.A.'s office, warned Patrick [Porco] that the Scarpas were not as loyal to him as he was to them. Al Lombardo warned Patrick that the Scarpas would kill him. Patrick was eighteen and scoffed . . ." Patrick Porco, likewise, was a walking dead man. Al Lombardo knew it and warned him. Porco, too, didn't need my help in dying.

"Mary Bari was a woman who knew Colombo Family secrets. Linda was there in 1984 in the room when De-Vecchio told Scarpa that Mary Bari was a weak link, a big liability to Big Allie Boy; she had to go."

Speaking of the killing of Lorenzo Lampasi, the prosecutor recited Carmine Sessa's account up to a point. He paraphrased the imprudent note Lampasi had enclosed with cash to pay off a loan-shark debt: "You can take it or leave it, and I don't want to have anything to do with you because you are a rat. I know you are an informant."

I looked at Doug and Mark, wondering what the hell was going on. The prosecutor was speaking as if he were representing the defense. I leaned forward to hear Vecchione say that Carmine Sessa showed the note to acting Boss Joe T, who gave approval to kill Lampasi, but ordered Scarpa to do the job at Lampasi's home and gave Sessa the address.

Now the judge was told: "Larry Mazza, himself, is going to come here in this courtroom . . . and he will tell you . . . he knew what time to be there in Brooklyn in front of Lampasi's garage, because they got that information from the man sitting at the table." That would be me, the guy in the pillory. And this would be bad news we hadn't known about. There was nothing in any Mazza 302 about my supplying the time—four in the morning—when Lampasi left his garage for work. Unfortunately, Mazza could simply explain that the FBI agent who debriefed him—that would be Favo—hadn't asked him who supplied Lorenzo's work schedule.

Although I wasn't charged with them, the particulars of certain other crimes were admissible if they proved my corrupt "unhealthy relationship" with Scarpa.

The prosecutor turned to the "hello" phone conversation Favo claimed I had with Scarpa after learning that Carmine Imbriale had been arrested. I was confident. We were given one of Favo's OPR statements in which he told his former supervisor Dave Stone that he thought my comment was "inadvertent." In his grand jury testimony Favo said:

> **Favo:** *I can only hear DeVecchio's side of the call. But he said, in sum and substance, the district attorney's office has him and so forth. They were statements to that effect.*

> **The Court:** *Give us all the statements.*

> **Favo:** *I'm drawing a blank.*

While the prosecutor shamelessly helped him with leading questions in the grand jury room—where no member of the defense is permitted—Favo finally got some version out. He said: "In essence Lin had just disclosed that Carmine Imbriale was possibly talking to the

Brooklyn District Attorney's Office. It opened that possibility."

Since you can't convict on possibilities, Team Vecchione tightened up my words and turned a possibility into a fact: "Chris Favo overheard the defendant on the phone saying, 'I know the D.A. has him, and *he is talking*, but I am not sure what he is saying about you.' Favo was stunned . . ."

I wondered, was Favo going to come to court and give this new exaggerated version of his own fairy tale or was all this just being said for tomorrow's paper? On cross-examination, we could easily impeach Favo about his ridiculous claim to the OPR that he told me to call Scarpa and say we'd heard him the day before on a wire plotting to kill Imbriale.

The Team Vecchione prosecutor expressed another vague Favo incident as if it were a fact. He said: "While Chris Favo was looking for Vic Orena, he came up with an address for Vic's girlfriend. Now, it turns out this address was wrong, but when Favo got the address, he gave it to his boss, Lin DeVecchio. Now Larry Mazza . . . told the FBI . . . they went looking for Vic Orena at the same wrong address that Chris Favo gave to Lin DeVecchio . . . the exact same wrong address." Expressed that way, with a specific wrong address given to me by Favo—like an integrity test—I'd be suspicious of that Lin DeVecchio myself.

But that's not the way Favo had expressed his flight of imagination at my OPR. When interviewed, I told the

OPR flat out: "That conversation could not have occurred." Favo's story then was that I asked him for Orena's girlfriend's address. Favo couldn't remember the address, so he described the house to me as a two-story structure with white sideboard on a corner. He said the house was either on 101st Street or the house number was 101.

I told OPR: "If I—no, if any supervisor in the FBI asked for an address from Favo, we would never tolerate that answer. If you ask a subordinate for an address, he goes back to his daily notes and gets the address. You don't accept a description of a house. You don't accept a vague recollection of a nonaddress. If Favo didn't have an address for me in his notes, I'd have told him to get it from the Orena case agent, Kenny Steiger, in Melville, Long Island." The OPR investigators understood that concept at once.

Favo had brought this invention to the OPR when he was desperate to come up with some justification for having reported me to North in January. I wonder if Mazza's debriefing earlier, in the spring of 1994, inspired him. Mazza recalled the Scarpa hit squad going to the wrong address of Orena's girlfriend. Mazza said the wrong address was supplied to the hit squad by a source Scarpa called his "girlfriend." Scarpa told Mazza his "girlfriend" was in the Orena camp. Did Favo take that setup from Mazza's debriefing and make me the "girlfriend"?

But how would Favo now express that incident in my trial? Would it be an "exact same wrong address," as the prosecutor expressed it, or would it be a nonaddress, as Favo expressed it to the OPR?

On the same day Favo had given the OPR investigators that anecdote, he gave them an even more impeachable tale: "At some point in 1993 . . . I encountered DeVecchio in the walkway near the C-10 rotor [filing cabinets]. He was happy and I asked why. He said he had been to closed files and examined a file from an old OPR investigation, which concerned him. I asked why he was the target of an OPR and he responded it was some time ago and that he put the file where it would not be found."

OPR files are kept at OPR, that is, at headquarters in Washington. They are secret. They are not kept in common filing in the New York office, where anyone could view them. Team Vecchione must have known this and bypassed that one.

I focused on every word when I heard: "Vinny Rizzuto pumped bullets into Joey Schiro's head and ended his life . . . Tommy Dades took the case and brought Vinny Rizzuto and his accomplices to justice. While Tommy Dades was solving the case, [Joey Schiro's] entire family, Little Linda, too, developed a very close bond [with him] and it still exists today."

"In the fall of 2005," the prosecutor said, "the office started to look into the DeVecchio-Scarpa relationship."

I whispered to Ginnine: "They'd had the Grancio file since January 29, 2005—ten months it sat there."

"And," the prosecutor continued, "being he [Dades] still had such a good relationship with Linda Schiro, he approved her and asked her if she'd finally reveal the things she knew about what I have just described this morning."

Before I could say anything to Ginnine, lead counsel Doug got up and tore Team Vecchione apart.

Doug focused most of his opening on Linda Schiro. He methodically compared her accusations to the news accounts that provided her the material for each new draft of her script. He wove in the timing of her attempt to get Scarpa's loan-shark "book" and how that influenced her decision to go negative on me. He wove in as much as we knew about the book proposals, such as her claim that Tony Villano didn't die of a heart attack, but that Scarpa killed him for the FBI. Doug pointed out that Schiro told one potential author that murder victim Dominick Masseria was a member of "a rival gang . . . involved in drugs." Doug added, "I don't think the D.A. believes that."

In fact, the D.A. did not believe it. Schiro had described the youth her son had gunned down on Halloween—whose only weapon had been eggs while Joey Schiro's weapon was a shotgun—as a "piece-of-shit kid."

Doug struck several blows at once: "Her family became close with the detective that solved the homicide of her son. Ten years with Detective Dades, 1995 through 2005 . . . for ten years she never said a word about these four homicides to Detective Dades."

Using her own words from 302s, Doug laid out Schiro's pursuit of informant money from the FBI while the Mafia was offering her money to frame me.

"The Mob is all over this," Doug said. "And she's telling the FBI she doesn't want to be a part of it. A part of this obstruction [to frame DeVecchio.] But what she is not getting from the FBI, which is what she's looking for, is money."

Doug told the judge that Schiro reported to the FBI as recently as 2004 in a 302 that the person who ultimately sent the Grancio/DeVecchio file to Congressman Delahunt "wants her to testify on behalf of the Mob . . . You will hear she told the FBI that they want her—the Mob wants her to testify about FBI corruption. [This person who was persuading her to testify] . . . was working with Orena. . . she is told that there's plenty of money in it for her if she does this."

I whispered to Ginnine: "Vecchione is looking at the same 302s we are."

Next, Doug addressed three huge "ifs."

As to Carmine Sessa: "If he tells the same sworn testimony that he has testified to under oath in the past on a number of occasions, he will exculpate Lin DeVecchio."

As to Larry Mazza: "If Larry Mazza tells the truth, he will tell you that all he knew was that Greg Scarpa had two sources of information. One was . . . described repeatedly as a made member of the Orena faction." Doug explained that the other one "was someone that he believed was a law enforcement source. He had no idea who the law enforcement source was. He didn't then, and if he does now, fifteen years later, let's see it."

Let's see "it" because we had Jim Brennan waiting to testify that Scarpa told Caproni that "it" was Gaspipe Casso.

As to Gregory Jr., the "if" was whether the Brooklyn D.A. would stoop to call him at all. Doug said: "His MO is to take the information he has gotten from lawyers and newspapers and document production and [then] tailor his testimony."

As to Linda Schiro: "No human being . . . deserves to be sitting here as a result of the stories this woman is making up."

I looked behind me when Doug was finished and saw nothing but confidence and encouragement on Carolyn's face in the third row.

CHAPTER THIRTY-THREE

THE PEOPLE V. LIN DEVECCHIO

"Detective Dades is like a brother to me. I talk to him every day," the first witness said.

He was a muscle-bound Italian from Brooklyn and an NYPD expert on organized crime, a substitute for the disgraced Tommy Dades. Before resigning, Dades prepared a large chart of hit squads who had participated in the war. The chart listed Lorenzo Lampasi as a member of Billy Cutolo's squad. This expert contradicted Dades. He correctly stated that Lorenzo Lampasi was "a shelved member" of the Colombo Family.

Vecchione next called three of the four members of Team Favo.

The first was Ray Andjich, a tall dark-haired young agent who'd been Favo's partner. He had not reported me to Don North. He was flown up from the Miami office at taxpayer expense. He was called to testify so he could say that I'd taken him to visit Scarpa at home during the war. At Scarpa's house, I deposited him on the couch in front of the TV while I met with Scarpa in the kitchen. There was no door to the kitchen and he'd been able to hear the words *murder* and *hit*. An FNG at this time, Andjich had been in Organized Crime for ten months. Being left out of the kitchen had "shocked" him and made him suspicious of me. Likely, it was during this visit that Scarpa told me of the discussions to "murder" Joey Brains Ambrosino's mother.

It would have been crazy for me to meet Scarpa in a car. An Orena hit team could have shot us both. And I'd brought Andjich as window dressing. During the war, the NYPD regularly staked out Scarpa's house. I didn't want them to see me going in alone because it could be a tip-off to the fact that Scarpa was my informant. During the trial, Team Vecchione was also using Andjich as window dressing, and Judge Reichbach plainly saw through their little game. He asked if Andjich's suspicion "was based on something concrete." It wasn't. And so the judge said: "I would observe, for the record, that the witness was unable to really give a concrete response." On cross-examination, Andjich admitted that he didn't even know what a Top Echelon informant was.

Second was Jeffrey Tomlinson, an agent assigned to me after the nine-month clerkship he did following graduation from the Academy. He was now a supervisor in the Philly office. Tomlinson had lost his hair over the years. As an FNG, he had accompanied Favo to Don

North as window dressing. From his testimony, it became clear that Favo had kept Tomlinson in the dark back then, too. Tomlinson testified that Scarpa had been closed as an informant because, according to Carmine Imbriale in his first debriefing, Scarpa admitted that he'd gut-shot Joe Waverly. Tomlinson didn't know that Favo had kept the Joe Waverly gut-shooting information from me. He didn't know that Scarpa was closed because a Kenny Brown informant revealed that Scarpa ordered a jailhouse hit on Orena's bagman, Frankie the Bug.

As Tomlinson testified, it dawned on me that he was so hoodwinked by Favo that he still believed that I knew all along that Imbriale had given up Scarpa for the Waverly shooting. No wonder he thought I was improperly protecting Scarpa. Boy, that Favo was good.

In explaining to the judge why he helped Favo keep Scarpa's pending arrest a secret from me, he testified: "Greg Scarpa was a longtime informant. Lin was his handling agent. There was an assumption on my part that should [the pending arrest] be made known to [DeVecchio], there was a possibility that Mr. DeVecchio could have tipped off Mr. Scarpa."

Tomlinson admitted that he had no knowledge of any information I had ever leaked to Scarpa. Luckily, he was present when I made my "hello" phone comments to Scarpa about Imbriale. His version of what I'd said was realistic: "I don't know. I haven't seen any reports yet." Although I don't remember it, I could easily have said that to Scarpa.

Last but not least came Favo. I hadn't seen him since his transfer to South Bend in June 1996. His hair had grayed a bit, but otherwise he looked unchanged.

However, during his testimony I thought I saw something new. He didn't seem to be too sure of himself. It looked to me like in his heart of hearts he knew the charges against me were horseshit. He never thought that his effort to cast me as a corrupt agent in order to elbow me off my squad would evolve into a series of murders.

We'd received word before trial that Valerie Caproni had called the D.A. to say that she believed there was nothing to these charges.

Favo testified accurately that Scarpa was closed because of the jailhouse contract on Orena bagman Frankie the Bug. When Vecchione asked if that information had come from one of Kenny Brown's informants, Favo giggled and refused to answer. Two of Caproni's FBI lawyers conferred with Favo and determined that he could answer. Vecchione repeated the question. Favo hesitated, giggled again, turned to the judge, and said, "Your Honor, I prefer not to answer." His arrogance in overruling his own attorneys was astounding. The judge cleared the courtroom and ordered him to answer.

Favo testified that he'd given me a nonaddress description of Orena's girlfriend's house and not the "exact same wrong address." He said: "I gave him a description of the house . . . a white two-story house, wood-paneled house, that was on a corner, and that I could not remember the street corner it was on, but I believe it had something to do with 101st Street or 101 might have been the address."

Unsatisfied with that answer, Vecchione tried again. "At the time that you were asked about the address, what, if anything, did you provide to Mr. DeVecchio?"

Favo replied, "A description of the house and that I had recalled it having something to do with the number 101. Either the street or the house number . . . I don't know that I gave anybody enough information to figure—I know I didn't give them the exact address."

As grateful as I was that his answer was at least consistent with his earlier testimony (during the OPR scandal), it annoyed me to hear him suggest that I could have asked for an address and then have settled for a horseshit description like the one he made. As harmless as it was in the context of a murder trial, it was still all made up.

Favo's version of the "hello" phone incident was as vague and impressionistic as it had been when he first gave it to the OPR. The fast tracking of phone numbers was in the trial version done for "Scarpa's business." It was not done to find "loan-shark victims." But it was still horseshit.

Favo was stuck with his nutty story that: "I told [De-Vecchio] that I thought he should contact Scarpa and say to Scarpa that he had been overheard on a wire the day before advocating the murder of Imbriale . . ." As I said, that would have been a death sentence for whoever Scarpa was with ". . . the day before advocating the murder of Imbriale . . ."

Favo dramatically presented his version of my infamous prediction: "we're going to win this thing." Like a pony with one trick, Favo testified that his impression of that remark was that I favored the Persico side in the war.

Judge Reichbach interrupted and asked Favo if during the war, agents discussed among themselves whether they favored a particular side. Favo admitted there had been such "discussions." The judge asked Favo if he had ever expressed an opinion about which side he'd like to win. Ginnine Fried kept me from falling out of my chair when Favo answered: "I would say Persico's side winning helps us most."

My New Untouchables in the audience just shook their heads in disgust. Had Favo forgotten that we're the FBI, we're not on any side?

Larry Mazza was next. He looked clean and sober, in his forties, handsome. He was now a personal trainer at a gym in Florida.

Was Mazza going to say, as Team Vecchione promised in their opening statement, that I had told Scarpa the time Lorenzo Lampasi left for work every morning? While Team Vecchione had built up some suspense to keep the reporters' pens moving during their opening statement, Mazza testified just as he had done many times before. He said that the information about when Lorenzo left for work came from inside Lampasi's office.

What about the story of my pulling of surveillance on Nicky Black Grancio? Mazza repeated his prior testimony that he'd spotted Grancio sitting in his Range Rover and immediately pulled up alongside and shot him.

What about Scarpa learning from me that Imbriale

was "talking"? Mazza had no information that Scarpa had been tipped off by anyone. Mazza said: "Scarpa said he's arrested; he's a rat; we have to kill him. Imbriale spent a long time with the law, and he's been cooperating since the eighties." So, Mazza is the one who would have been killed if I had followed Favo's instructions to tell Scarpa we had him on a wire threatening to kill Imbriale.

The supervisor inside me was working overtime. I blamed Favo for keeping Imbriale in custody too long. Such a thing raises suspicions in the street.

On cross, Doug pointed out that in reporting what Mazza said to him in a 302, Favo wrote only the first part, but not the second part, the part about Scarpa's suspicion being aroused by the length of time Imbriale spent in custody. Had Favo written that part in the 302, it would have contradicted the "hello" phone story that I tipped off Scarpa.

Nor did Favo record in the 302 that it was the consigliere, Sessa, who overruled Scarpa and saved Imbriale's life, not Favo with his implausible ploy. Mazza testified that as to killing Imbriale: "Sessa said no. That was the end of that."

Again, Vecchione's own witness contradicted his case.

Interestingly, Mazza said that Linda Schiro had counseled him to become a CW and the two had talked about doing a "book-type thing." Mazza had written thirteen pages in prison and was visited by Jerry Capeci when Capeci was trying to do a book with Linda Schiro.

Mazza testified that once he'd overheard Scarpa talk to a "Lin" on the phone and believed it was Scarpa's law enforcement source. But he offered no evidence for this belief, nor was anything incriminating said in the conversation. Furthermore, on cross, Doug confronted Mazza with a prison tape recording of a conversation Mazza had with his father a dozen years earlier. The OPR had just taken a statement from Mazza about me. Mazza told his father that he had no idea who Scarpa's law enforcement source was, and that he wished he did know because it could help reduce his sentence. Mazza admitted that the first time he ever mentioned a personal belief that a "Lin" was Scarpa's source was at my grand jury in 2006. Over time, the little bits that he absorbed had crystallized into a belief. Our rules of evidence, of course, require facts. Beliefs are okay for news stories. Vecchione was playing to the reporters.

Mazza did not incriminate me in any crime, much less in murder. Mazza turned out not to be a "big surprise."

Vecchione shifted direction to the Patrick Porco murder. Ray Aviles took the stand and admitted that he drove the noisy white Chrysler limo and participated in the murder of seventeen-year-old Dominick Masseria. On cross-examination, Mark Bederow sought to reinforce Aviles's memory of those events he had just testified to. "Good morning, Mr. Aviles," he began. "My name is Mark Bederow . . . Sir, is it fair to say that you remember the evening of Halloween 1989 very well in your mind?"

"Pretty well."

"And isn't it a fact that you remember that evening pretty well because on that evening you did the most despicable thing you've ever done in your life?"

"Yeah," Aviles replied. "I fucked your mother."

Very firmly, Mark took control of the witness, who quickly dropped his tough-guy attitude. "Mr. Aviles, what's your answer?"

"Yes, I remember very well . . . That I did a very bad thing."

Mark then got a dynamite surprise from Ray Aviles. It was none other than Patrick Porco himself who admitted to the Scarpas that he'd been talking to the cops about the Masseria Halloween massacre.

> **Q:** *Just so we are all clear, sir. Patrick Porco told you that he had told Joey that he, Patrick, had spoken to the police about the Masseria case?*
>
> **A:** *Yes.*
>
> ———
>
> **Q:** *How many times did he tell you that?*
>
> **A:** *I don't recall, maybe two or three times that we had talked.*

Interestingly, Aviles admitted that he had met with Linda Schiro's first potential book author, the one who wrote a proposal in late 1996. He stated that the author had talked about a $2 million advance for Linda, a woman Ray Aviles said he hated. Aviles stated that Linda's son

Joey told him that his father had a source in the Brooklyn D.A.'s Office. Hearing this, I turned and smiled at Carolyn.

The next witness, Patrick's thirty-eight-year-old sister, Lori, sadly blamed herself for Patrick's murder. She felt her brother was "murdered after I pushed him to talk." She shouldn't have been so hard on herself, however, as the next witness made clear.

Detective Alphonse Lombardo, an investigator with the Brooklyn D.A., testified that he warned Patrick that he'd be killed whether he cooperated or not. Detective Lombardo admitted on cross-examination that when he warned Patrick that he was doomed, he truly believed it. It wasn't a ploy to get Patrick to cooperate.

An assistant D.A., Jeffrey Leavitt, testified that he knew that Patrick was in a dangerous position. Patrick was needed in court in order to corroborate Aviles who was an accomplice. This is because of New York's law that requires corroboration of an accomplice's testimony for a conviction to stand.

Slowly, day by day, the press coverage began to swing favorably in my direction. I didn't want to get too cocky, but so far there was not a drop of corroboration for Linda Schiro's anticipated testimony. During a break, Carolyn overheard a surly Vecchione say to a reporter, "Are you watching the same trial we're watching? Haven't we had one good day?"

Five-foot four-inch Carmine Sessa took the stand on October 25, 2007, the fiftieth anniversary of the hit in the barber chair on Albert Anastasia.

Sessa told the full and truthful story about Lorenzo Lampasi. Joe T gave Sessa Lampasi's home address on a piece of paper. Sessa gave that paper to Scarpa with the instruction not to kill Lampasi at work. Sessa corroborated Mazza, not Linda Schiro.

During Mark's cross, Sessa ripped into Dades's hit squad chart. Dades had listed three men who had in fact spent the war in jail as being on Scarpa's hit squad during the war.

Sessa testified that Lampasi was not an active member of any faction during the war. Dades's listing of Lampasi on Cutolo's hit squad had given credibility to Favo's worn-out story that Lampasi was with the Orena faction when I said, "We're going to win this thing." Now Sessa's testimony revealed the absurdity of that argument. Vecchione's own witnesses were exposing Vecchione. As to the motive for killing Mary Bari, Sessa said: "There was concern Mary Bari might be dating a police officer . . . or became inflamed [sic] with a police officer." On cross by Mark, Sessa admitted that the order to kill Bari came from Junior Persico: "The order came from the top."

As to Joe Brewster, Sessa recalled that Scarpa was pissed that Brewster was doing bypass burglaries on his own. Sessa revealed that he warned Brewster that Scarpa was pissed and that Brewster was in danger. Sessa didn't think Brewster "took it as seriously as I did."

Listening to Sessa, I almost had to wonder what I was doing there. "Hey, what about me?" I felt like asking. But I knew that with Linda Schiro up next, it was going to be all about me. Everything was riding on her. Vecchione had been building up her testimony for months.

Two weeks before the start of my trial, Vecchione filed a motion to remove Doug as my lawyer. He claimed that in 1994 Doug intimidated Linda Schiro into not revealing all she knew about me to the OPR. The witness against Doug was John Baran. He was a heroin addict who'd been housed with Scarpa in the Rikers Island AIDS wing. After Scarpa's death, Schiro and Baran married for a while. Apparently, Baran had good taste in clothes; he got busted in October 1994 while trying to steal a coat from a Ralph Lauren store.

Mark recalled: "Not only is Doug's reputation as a perfect gentleman legendary, but Baran made the mistake of claiming that he and Doug had gone drinking together when Doug threatened Schiro. Everyone knows that Doug is famous for not drinking."

The judge denied the motion, calling it a "tit for tat" on Vecchione's part, meaning an effort on the prosecutor's part to make up for pretrial victories Doug and Mark had won against him. But the attempt to frame Doug demonstrated just how low Vecchione was willing to stoop in order to get a conviction. It also hinted at how intense the final week of testimony from Vecchione's star witness would be. The best was saved for last.

CHAPTER THIRTY-FOUR

MY TWO SURPRISE WITNESSES

On Sunday, October 28, 2007, the New York *Daily News* headline was "Mobster's Fickle Girlfriend Has History of Changing Her Tale." According to the lead to the article: "When former mob moll Linda Schiro takes the stand in the trial of a disgraced FBI agent, she could be the best witness for the prosecution—or the defense."

The article made me feel good, but at the same time it disgusted me that Vecchione was actually using such a loose cannon of a liar as Linda Schiro against me.

The article traced the star witness's changing stories from 1994 when she said she "knew enough about 'the life' in the Colombo Family not to ask questions."

On the first day of the third week of trial, Linda Schiro entered the courtroom wearing a dark pantsuit and a green sweater. Her brown hair was stylishly cut, just above the shoulder. Over the years she'd kept her petite figure. At one time she'd been Miss Staten Island. She flashed a smile at the judge and waved her slender arms, like a magician pulling a rabbit out of a hat, when she spoke. The seventeen-year-old girl who'd asked Greg Scarpa to dance at the Flamingo Lounge was now sixty-two.

The night they met, she testified, he impressed her by pushing the bartender's head into a toilet bowl. Greg Scarpa was "thirty-five or so" when they fell in love. He was already married and would never divorce. As their love grew, they discussed having children, but Linda wouldn't agree to be an unwed mother out of regard for her father's feelings.

"I wanted children. Greg was married. So I married Charlie," she told the judge, "to have Greg's kids."

Charlie Schiro, a local Jewish insurance man, had no idea his daughter, Little Linda, and his son, Joey, were not his children. Poor Charlie nurtured them, fed them, clothed them, and gave them a house. That is, until Linda and Greg decided to live together with their children and without Charlie.

"Tell the court why you are testifying," Vecchione asked Linda.

"I'm testifying," she said, "because a good dear friend of mine, Tommy Dades, called and approached me and asked if he could come over and talk to me about Lin DeVecchio and Greg Scarpa."

And so she testified: "[DeVecchio] says, we have a problem with this Mary Bari. She was looking to rat out

Allie. Allie was on the lam . . . He said, you know, you have to take care of this. She's going to be a problem." She said I had a smirk on my face when I supposedly uttered these words. She claimed that I conspired to kill Mary Bari in her presence in her kitchen.

Linda went on: "After [Lin] said [Greg] was right about [Joe Brewster] drinking, doing drugs, and the burglaries, [Lin] says, you know, we got to take care of this guy before he starts talking." Again she said I had a smirk on my face as I spoke and that I made the talking sign with my thumb and fingers.

When she gave her first statement to the D.A., after Dades brought her in, Linda made the mistake of placing the Brewster conspiracy between Scarpa and me in a house that she'd moved out of eighteen months before Brewster's murder. Stuck with this time line, she explained away the eighteen months by testifying that during this time Scarpa "didn't want to kill him. He wanted to try to smarten him up. He loved Joe Brewster."

She'd also made the mistake of repeating what she knew Gregory Jr. had claimed at the time in order to justify the hit and so she had to weave that into her tale at the trial: "And [Greg] had asked Joe Brewster to do a murder. And when Joe Brewster refused, because of his new religious beliefs, that's when Greg saw that he couldn't change him—you know." By now everyone in the courtroom knew that refusing to do a "piece of work" meant instant death.

She said Scarpa took a call from me at a pay phone,

and then "he got into the car. And he says, 'This fuck'—can I say that? 'This fuck kid. I cannot believe that he is going to fucking rat on Joey.' And I said, 'What are you talking about?' He says, 'Patrick. Lin just told me that he is fucking ratting Joey out.' And I said, 'Patrick . . . Patrick would never do that.' He said, 'Listen to what I am telling you. He is ratting him out.' " They got home and confronted Joey: "So, Joey went nuts. He said, 'Dad, what are you, nuts?' . . . So, Greg says, 'Listen to me.' And he banged his hand really hard on the table. 'Where this came from, Joey, it is a high up.' "

I was baffled as I listened to this surreal account, and wondered how in God's name would I ever even know of the existence of Patrick Porco and the Halloween egg-throwing murder of Dominick Masseria? The judge must have been just as baffled when he interrupted Vecchione to ask Schiro: "But, what I am asking is, did he tell you—either did he, or didn't—where—how the defendant knew this information about Patrick?"

I guessed that the judge had been paying attention when Ray Aviles testified that Patrick told Joey Schiro he'd talked to the cops. Or he'd paid attention when Detective Lombardo testified that Patrick was going to be killed whether he cooperated or not.

Linda next testified about the Lampasi hit: "[Greg] said I need you to find out exactly where he lives and his, you know, what time he leaves in the morning." Schiro testified that I returned with the requested information about Lorenzo Lampasi and a little something extra:

"When Lin walked in, he had this smirk on his face . . . [Lin] gave [Scarpa] the address and he told him that he leaves his house like around four in the morning, and there's some kind of a gate that he's got to open and close before he leaves."

That Lampasi was killed leaving his house at four in the morning is something that any number of people could have told Schiro. But the part about the gate, I thought, had to have been provided by somebody who really knew the facts of the case. Perhaps Mazza gave her that detail when they considered doing "a book-type thing" together. If not Mazza, I could make up a pretty good short list of suspects.

Consistent with Dades's chart, Schiro was firm about Lampasi's status "during the war . . . He was on the Orena side."

In an effort to derail Doug's cross-examination, Vecchione spent a dangerous ten minutes trying to get Linda to explain why she told so many conflicting stories, but his effort would only give Doug more to work with. For example:

Q: *Now, did you tell the OPR investigators everything that you told this court today about the relationship between Scarpa . . . and DeVecchio?*

A: *No.*

Q: *And tell the court why not.*

A: *Well, because I was—I couldn't understand why OP—I mean, not understanding OPR—but I couldn't understand why FBI agents are investigating another FBI agent . . .*

If anything, the OPR investigators overexplain what they are doing and why they are doing it. It's hardly likely that Linda was unable to understand.

I loosened up a little and laughed when she described the kind of book a female author wanted to write with her: "Well, she wanted a book with . . . a lot of sex in it . . . The Mob, my life . . . Only she expressed a lot of sex . . . Her book was, well, let's get a lot of sex in the book . . ."

On the other hand, Jerry Capeci wanted a book about "my life with the Mob . . . No sex, though." Jerry Capeci would be teased about this in the elevator.

The judge asked Linda a question that was repeated by Vecchione; the two instances when it was asked would stick in my mind at the end of the trial:

Q: *When you were talking to [the writers], were you telling them fact or were you telling them fiction?*

A: *I was telling them fact. What they wrote I never read.*

———

Q: *The judge asked you this question. I'm going to ask it one more time. What you told these three writers, was it fact or fiction?*

A: *I told the truth.*

According to Schiro, I met Scarpa in his kitchen two to three times a week in the house the couple lived in until 1986. Writing on a pad, I rounded that off to twice a week for fifty weeks for six years. I got six hundred visits. In their second house Linda reduced my supposed visits to one to two times a week until the war started in November 1991. After this, she said, I stopped visiting. I rounded that off to once a week for fifty weeks for five years. I got two hundred and fifty visits. My total was eight hundred and fifty visits, conservatively.

"That's a lot of exposure for an FBI agent in Bensonhurst." I showed the pad to Ginnine. "No wonder Favo didn't tell me what was going on. I was never in the office."

The judge looked over at us. The hardest part for me during this ordeal was having to be silent.

Schiro didn't need me visiting that many times in order for me to conspire to commit four murders. Her first statement, in 1994, that I'd been to the house maybe ten times in twelve years was the truth and would have still worked, if she'd stuck to it.

In case you're wondering why no one in the Mafia neighborhood was worried about an FBI agent being spotted in the house, before I arrived, Linda said she pulled all the blinds. The second house had a glass window in the front door over which she taped a piece of construction paper every time I came. Although a lie, that blind pulling and taping made her an accomplice to Scarpa's and my alleged conspiracies.

On cross-examination, she told Doug that every time I visited, Scarpa gave me money. Whoever helped her construct this fantasy was very careful. Schiro had to say that my visits stopped when the war started because Scarpa's house was under intense surveillance for the first five months of the war and then under periodic surveillance as the war wound down. Whoever helped her construct her testimony knew this, and knew that with surveillance logs I could easily disprove any claim that I visited the house once or twice a week after the war started.

Doug got under Schiro's skin on this topic of home visits, and since she had trouble telling a story the same way twice, she changed her testimony and said that I stopped coming to the house once or twice a week not after the war began, on November 18, 1991, but after Scarpa got arrested, on August 31, 1992. This meant that a glance at the surveillance logs would show that she was wrong. The importance of this deviation from the script could not have been lost on Vecchione.

At the close of her first day of testimony, Schiro explained that OPR asked her about a tray of lasagna I admitted she had made for me.

Schiro: *They said it was lasagna. I said no, it was eggplant . . . It was eggplant Parmesan.*

The Court: *When you say "they" . . .*

Schiro: *OPR. They said it was lasagna and I said no, it was eggplant . . . He says well, I thought it was lasagna. I said no, it was eggplant. Because that's what I made good. Was eggplant."*

On the walk home, Carolyn did a dead-on imitation of Linda Schiro talking about the eggplant.

The next day was to be the first full day of what likely would be two or three days of cross-examination.

To throw her off balance at the start, Doug confronted Schiro with an affidavit she'd signed for Gregory Jr. in his 1998 RICO murder trial. In the affidavit she said that for years I paid Scarpa regularly for information, not that Scarpa paid me, as she had testified the day before. She accused me of revealing the names of "potential rats," but she couldn't name a single one. She claimed I got Gregory Jr. transferred from the federal jail in San Diego to Lewisburg in Pennsylvania as a favor for Scarpa, but then, later, she said, "I don't recall San Diego, no." By the time she made the latter statement, she'd been tipped off that San Diego was a pretrial prison and Gregory Jr., a sentenced prisoner, was not eligible to spend even a day there.

Q: *Well, you signed this affidavit?*

A: *I know. But, I don't recall saying San Diego.*

Doug took her through her efforts to secure a portion of Scarpa's loan-shark "book" with Little Allie Boy's help in the fall of 1994. He skillfully established a pattern of her spewing negative stories about me in order to please the Persicos while she was vainly trying to get some of this money. When she lost hope, the pattern turned to positive stories about me in the hope of getting money from the FBI. As she talked, Doug was able to weave the various things she told the authors into the testimony.

Schiro told Doug: "Greg was a gangster. I never paid taxes." As for Tommy Dades, she said, "I trust him with my life."

Doug got her to contradict the part of Team Vecchione's opening statement where it was said I had given Scarpa the "exact same wrong address" of Orena's girlfriend's house:

Q: *And did you call Special Agent Gabriel and tell him that where [the newspaper] claimed that DeVecchio had told Scarpa that Vic Orena was staying at his girlfriend's house was also a lie because that information came from Carmine Sessa?*

A: *Yes.*

Q: *You told [Gabriel] that DeVecchio never provided Scarpa with any information about where Colombo Family members were hiding during the war?*

A: *Yes.*

Toward the end of the second hour of cross-examination, Schiro couldn't tell the Nicky Black Grancio story the same way twice within a minute. When she realized she was giving two contradictory versions of the same story—neither of which incriminated me in any way—she said, as if making a mistake on a memorization test: "I got it wrong." The judge replied: "You are confusing me."

Doug confronted her with her grand jury testimony. At the grand jury it was Lorenzo Lampasi's work address that I allegedly provided, not his home address. Schiro answered: "Greg wanted information on Larry Lampasi, the exact times he left his house, where he worked, everything . . . [Lin] came in. He said that he got what Greg wanted. He told him the exact time Larry Lampasi opens or closes wherever he worked, the address, and he gave him the time."

Some sick joke, I thought. Before her grand jury testimony, she'd been coached to say that there was, in fact, something that Lampasi opened and closed, but she just couldn't seem to remember that it was a gate. So she made it the opening and closing of his office and she was stuck with that at trial: "opens or closes wherever he worked."

As the cross-examination proceeded, Schiro stopped moving her hands around. Her voice flattened and weakened. She began to fumble with the lines of her script:

Q: *How many homicides did you tell the D.A.'s office about in your first meeting?*

A: *Four of them.*

———————

Q: *What were those four?*

A: *The Mary Bari, Patrick Porco, Larry Lamp—what's his name again? Larry Lampasini [sic] and Carmine, and oh, and Joe Brewster?*

Carmine? As the judge had put it earlier: "We got a lot of Carmines."

Doug pointed out to her that when interviewed by two different book authors promoting her story she implicated an innocent boy named Chris Barrett in the Dominick Masseria murder in place of Craig Sobel. Chris Barrett was the ex-boyfriend of her son Joey's girlfriend. He was expendable.

Schiro's quintessential Mafia answer came when Doug asked a question that the judge followed up on: "And did you ever have any remorse or concern about what this man was doing that you were living with?" To which

Schiro replied: "I grew up with Greg. I met Greg when I was a kid. This was his life."

She repeated this answer when the judge said, "The question is, did you have any remorse about what he was doing?" Schiro replied: "I don't know what you mean by 'remorse.' Could you explain? Like, in other words, this is the way I grew up with him."

The day drew to a close. Doug had barely scratched the surface of his notes. It was going to be a long night for Schiro and Vecchione. I couldn't wait to see the haggard expressions on Schiro's and Vecchione's faces in the morning, knowing as they did that they had another day of this in store for them.

Jerry Capeci hurried to our table and called Vecchione over.

"Tom Robbins and I have tapes of Linda Schiro," he said.

"Tapes?" Doug and Mark said at the same time.

"They're from 1997. Tom and I interviewed her for a book. Tom just posted a story about the tapes on the *Village Voice* Web site. We will not fight a subpoena for these tapes. Linda Schiro, in our opinion, forfeited her protection under the press shield law by her testimony."

"In other words," Doug said, "you're withdrawing your original objection."

"Correct," Capeci said.

As Vecchione heard these words, his eyes narrowed.

CHAPTER THIRTY-FIVE

"TALL TALES OF A MAFIA MISTRESS"

Mark had a BlackBerry. When we finally got away from the media circus and into the bright sunlight, he began reading the article to us as we walked. The title was "Tall Tales of a Mafia Mistress."

The lead was: "Linda Schiro, the key prosecution witness in the startling murder trial of former FBI Agent R. Lindley DeVecchio, took the stand on Monday, and it was hard not to find her deadly story convincing."

That was scary to hear. Tom Robbins and Jerry Capeci were courtroom-savvy guys. Had I misjudged the impression Schiro made? Thankfully, no. Robbins was talking about the impression Schiro made before "the first break of the day" on the first day of her testimony, her easiest hour.

Mark read on: "In the eight days of testimony before

Schiro took the stand, a parade of mob cooperators and investigators testified about their suspicions . . . But suspicion is all anyone offered . . . The D.A.'s case appears to rest on her."

When Capeci and Robbins had interviewed Schiro on tape in 1997, they promised they would never disclose anything she said. However, Robbins wrote: "The threat of a life sentence trumps a promise."

Motivated by this belief, Robbins rummaged through a box of old material until he found the Schiro tapes. He explained that many were missing and some were inaudible, but the ones on which she spoke about the murders of Joe Brewster and Lorenzo Lampasi had survived in good condition.

Because one of their interviews took place the day after Gregory Jr.'s testimony during a 1997 trial implicated me in these two murders, they asked her about each one.

Schiro described the Mary Bari murder, but "she made no mention of DeVecchio at all in connection with the slaying."

"We asked Schiro whether Lin DeVecchio had had anything to do with the death of Joe Brewster. She seemed briefly confused by the question. 'No,' she said. 'He never met Joe Brewster.'"

As he continued reading, Mark's face was like a boy who received a pony for Christmas. I guess mine was like that, too.

Mark read on: "Schiro raised the subject herself back

then. 'There's another thing, too, with Larry Lampasi,' she told us. 'See, when Lin is right, I give him right. He didn't tell Greg about Larry Lampasi.'"

Instead, she blamed Greg's niece Rosemarie, a driver who worked for the school-bus company. Rosemarie complained about her boss, Lampasi, at a Thanksgiving dinner six months before the murder. Rosemarie had a lousy route and wasn't allowed to drive her bus home while other drivers were. This was interpreted as disrespect directed at Scarpa.

"We were sitting there," Schiro said, "when she told Greg all about Larry Lampasi. Lin did not tell." Schiro had no knowledge about the imprudent note from Lampasi that accused Scarpa of informing. "No," Schiro said. "I told you about Greg's niece."

"Greg's attitude at this time was he was going to fuck everybody. He don't give a fuck who he kills." Schiro said that as his illness grew worse, Scarpa turned into a maniac. I have since read about AIDS-related dementia. In the case of most sufferers, it produces lethargy, but in some it produces mania. That would be Scarpa.

Finally, she put me in the Patrick Porco murder, as she had done with two other book authors. To them she said that Scarpa and Joey killed Patrick. To Capeci and Robbins she said Joey shot Patrick with Johnny Loads Sinagra as his driver. At my trial she said Sinagra pulled the trigger with Joey as his driver.

Robbins believed that because she put me in the Patrick Porco murder and also accused me of receiving stolen jewelry, she would never be able to claim that she had

merely been protecting me when she said I wasn't involved in the Bari, Brewster, and Lampasi murders. So
that part about framing me for Porco—that was a good
thing.

We arrived at the courthouse the next morning and a
grinning Chris Mattiace greeted us with, "Trick or treat."
It was Halloween, the twenty-second anniversary of the
slaughter of Dominick Masseria on the steps of Our Lady
of Guadalupe.

In court, the subpoena was returned and Capeci turned
over the tapes. It was agreed that we would spend the day
together listening to them at the D.A.'s office.

"If the quotes in the article are accurate," Vecchione
told the judge, "the district attorney's office will enter a
dismissal on all charges."

"Please bring the witness in," Judge Reichbach said.

Linda Schiro calmly walked in and sat down in the
witness chair.

"There are tapes with your voice on them that have
surfaced that appear to contradict your direct testimony
in this trial. Don't say anything, please. I need to advise
you that if the tapes portray your voice saying the things
that have been alleged that you said, I am referring this
matter to the district attorney for a perjury investigation. That is all. You may step down and you are free to
leave."

Tommy Dades had left this very courtroom in disgrace
six months earlier. Now it was Linda Schiro's turn.

We listened to the tapes. There were no surprises. Robbins's article was accurate. We reported to the judge that the D.A. would enter a dismissal in the morning.

Only in America could an FBI agent be cleared by the lefty *Village Voice* in the courtroom of a campus radical with an FBI file labeling him "dangerous."

On November 1, 2007, after navigating through the sea of reporters outside the building, I submitted to the wanding ritual for what I knew would be the last time. Carolyn and I expected to walk into court, hear Vecchione enter a dismissal, hear the judge tell me I was free to go, and then get the damn thing off my ankle.

"On the record, Your Honor," Vecchione said, "the district attorney enters a dismissal as to all charges against the defendant."

But Judge Gustin Reichbach kept me in my place.

"Friedrich Nietzsche," he began, "sagely observed at the end of the nineteenth century 'that he who fights with monsters might take care lest he thereby become a monster . . . '"

Who was he talking about? I wondered. Who became a monster?

Favo?

Schiro?

Dades?

Vecchione?

No, that would be me. And the FBI.

While I sat there wrongfully imprisoned in my anklet, this judge told me that I lacked "probity"—integrity, honesty. Yet he delivered this judgment without ever hearing me utter a single word.

He told me I'd made a "deal with the devil" and had given Scarpa "criminal immunity for close to fifteen years."

All I ever did was go to bat for Scarpa at his sentencing in a credit-card case at a crucial time during our championship season when we needed him for cases like the Mafia Commission Case. And incidentally, to alert us if any prosecutors or judges had become targets, as had happened to Rudy Giuliani.

The judge compared my handling of Scarpa with "the current mind-set of some in the government who argue that the practice of terror and torture can be freely employed . . . that it is permissible to make men scream in the name of national security."

Will I ever get out of this unreal world? I thought.

And then, back to the real world: "There was no evidence presented at this trial," the judge said, "save the now-discredited testimony of Linda Schiro, that the defendant committed any of the acts as charged in the indictment. On the other hand . . ."

"Oh, man!" I almost said out loud.

"On the other hand, credible evidence was presented that indicated that the defendant was so eager to maintain Scarpa as an informant that he was willing to bend the rules, including sending misinformation to headquarters in order to reopen him as an informant."

Misinformation? You never heard my side of this,

Your Honor. I *still* haven't had a fair trial. When I sought to reopen Scarpa as an informant, I told as much of the truth as Favo had allowed me to know. Favo was the one who knew better, not me.

The reporters' pens were working rapidly all the while the judge spoke.

I was aware that he was keeping me in the pillory, in silence, making a public mockery of me. The next day the *Daily News* ran an editorial that said: "DeVecchio now returns to retirement pronounced not guilty. But he is guilty of plenty . . . He stained the FBI . . ." The editorial, as did every article for weeks, pilloried me with the judge's language.

The editorial did call Schiro "a flat-out liar." I thought a perjury charge would be a cinch. She said more than once under oath that what she told all of the potential authors of her book was "the truth." That made the Capeci and Robbins tapes the equivalent of sworn testimony. She contradicted that sworn testimony in the grand jury room and in the courtroom.

"They'll never charge her," Jim Kossler said, referring to the Brooklyn D.A.'s Office. "It would open up their own wrongdoing."

As always, Jim was a few steps ahead of the game. Dades immediately went public, threatening Vecchione and Hynes that he would testify that Schiro had leveled with them from the beginning. The special prosecutor they appointed, Leslie Crocker Snyder, would be running for D.A. in Manhattan at the next election and couldn't afford to make political waves. She issued a report in which she unjustly criticized my two surprise witnesses—my personal heroes Jerry Capeci and Tom Robbins—and declined to prosecute the perjurer Linda Schiro.

Vecchione and his team are immune from lawsuits or I'd have brought one against them. Vecchione told the press that he still thought I was guilty. Hynes called my case "nothing more than a bump in the road." A couple of weeks later a jury returned a not-guilty verdict for Craig Sobel in the Dominick Masseria murder case. Craig had been in the white limo as a member of the team in the shot-gunning of Dominick Masseria.

Dades and Vecchione kissed and made up once the Schiro perjury matter was resolved. With the help of publicity from my corruption trial and Reichbach's public humiliation, they managed to revive their Mafia Cops book deal, but with a new title.

Chuckie Russo, encouraged by Judge Reichbach's decision to paint the cop dirty, had his lawyer file a motion to unseal the record of my case, but we blocked it. Another judge dismissed the civil lawsuit against me for the Nicky Black Grancio hit.

The most unbearable part of that final day in court was having to listen to Judge Reichbach say to me, as I sat in court as his prisoner, and not permitted to speak out: "The court would be remiss if it did not single out for praise Special Agents Favo, Tomlinson, and Andjich. In the face of what must have been enormous institutional pressure to turn a blind eye when they grew increasingly concerned that the defendant had lost the necessary perspective and had grown too close to his informant, they stepped forward, risking the opprobrium of their colleagues."

When the judge was done accusing me and I was finally given permission to stand up, have the anklet taken off, and walk out of court a free man with Carolyn at my side, my colleagues, my FBI brothers, who knew the truth and never wavered in their support, burst into a very long standing ovation for me—and for themselves, for all we did together to destroy one of the most dangerous enemies America has ever had.

CHAPTER THIRTY-SIX

ONE MORE WITNESS

Months after the trial, what continued to nag at me was that Favo gave credibility to whatever anyone did to me or said about me. Even Linda Schiro could say, okay, I'm lying, but he's guilty anyway.

A couple of my supporters suggested I'd feel better if I talked to Kenny Steiger. I knew Kenny's reputation, but I'd never worked with him. I knew the bang-up job he did in Melville, Long Island, on Little Vic Orena, or I thought I did.

"I wondered whether you'd call," Kenny said. "My dealing with Favo had nothing to do with your criminal charges and it predates your OPR by a couple of years. When your OPR came up, Don North already knew the misery Favo caused me."

"I'm sure it wouldn't have been relevant to my legal

issues. Let me tell you where I'm coming from with this. I flat-out view Favo as the cause of it all."

"All right," Kenny said. "All right. A lot of things that transpired with him made my life miserable. My biggest problem with Favo had to do with an accusation about me and an informant."

"For some reason that doesn't surprise me," I said.

"He turned the Eastern District against me, too."

"I'd like to hear about it."

"Let me take a look at my notes, get the chronology down. I'll call you."

When we hung up I wrote down what I already knew and what I'd found out about Kenny. He grew up in Babylon, Long Island, and dug clams to earn money for college. His family tree went back to the Dutch in the 1600s. Nostrand Avenue is named after one of his ancestors. Kenny was a Villanova grad. He got his master's and he taught at St. John's University. Kenny was a key player on the Colombo squad in New York in the 1980s, at the heart of our championship season.

Shortly before I got the Colombo squad, Kenny moved to our Melville, Long Island, office, where he continued to do Colombo Family work. A lot of the Colombo wiseguys had moved to the Wild West of Long Island. During the war, there was a lot of action out there. The attempt on Orena by Carmine Sessa's crew. The Russo cousins' work on Johnny Minerva and Mike the Plumber. The acting Boss of the family, Vic Orena, was based on Long Island.

Kenny became the Orena case agent in the summer of

1990. Because of the Long Island connection, I signed the Reassignment Memo transferring the Orena case from our squad to Kenny's. By the fall of '91, the war caused me to lose touch a little with what Kenny was doing on Orena, but I knew that his squad had gotten a wire on Chubby Audino's car and that he arrested Orena in April '92.

"I want to be careful," Kenny said when we spoke again, "so I'm going to disguise my informant."

"Damn right," I said. "I won't reveal any information about your informant in my book."

"Okay. A good year before the war, it got back to me that Favo complained on the floor in the squad that I got the Orena case instead of him. He complained that Kenny Brown gave me an informant on Orena and not him."

"Maybe Favo accused Kenny Brown of leaking to an informant, maybe to get back at him for giving you his informant."

"Favo," Kenny said.

"I think he wrongfully accused Joe Simone."

"So did the jury," Kenny said.

"I remember," I said, "you were looking into Dennis Pappas as part of the Orena case."

"Right. Pappas, the financial consigliere. Pappas was a lawyer. His law office was a front that Orena used to collect vig. Frankie the Bug brought bags of money in every day. Kenny Brown gave me a lot of information on Pappas."

"Frankie the Bug," I said. "Scarpa was supposed to have been planning a jailhouse hit on him."

"He was about five four. A real bug."

"Kenny, my father was a financial officer in the military. I was always curious about Pappas."

"Well, what he'd do, for instance, is get zoning changes and permits to build a development. He'd go to a bank or to private investors, get his hands on the money to finance the development, but he wouldn't build anything. He'd put his sham corporation out of business and stick the bank or the private investors. If the private investors complained, his leg breakers would pay them a visit and they'd be happy just to lose their money and not their lives. Remember the Whitestone Savings Bank that went belly-up? That was Pappas's doing."

"These people did so much damage the public never knew about."

"Orena threw the third largest electrical contractor down the stairs and broke his arm in three places. It scared the sixty-five-year-old man almost to death. He just walked away from his multimillion-dollar company. Pappas took over the company for Orena and cleaned out the employee pension fund. Pappas grabbed all the money from the contracts the guy had and then put the company out of business. At the same time, Orena and Pappas killed racehorses for the insurance."

"Sweet."

"They'd fix races so their horse would win a few. That allowed them to syndicate the horse and sell shares. If a horse is syndicated, you can get insurance on it; otherwise you can't. In one instance they syndicated a horse named Finns. They insured Finns for four million dollars. Then a vet, who was on the Colombo Family payroll, injected the horse with deadly heartworms. The insurance company sent in their vets, who confirmed the heartworms and authorized that Finns be put down. The insurance company paid the four million to the lawyer Pappas. The rich racing people who invested in the syndicate asked for their share of the insurance. Orena sent a couple of strong-arm guys around to scare them and he kept the whole four million. Getting back to Favo . . ."

"By all means."

"When you made him Colombo coordinator . . ."

"Oh, man."

"Aw, you couldn't know. We were all used to banding together, sharing information. That wasn't Favo. He was going to take credit for everything."

"For trial, Andy Kurins interviewed a cop on our task force. He said Favo took a lot of credit for things others had done. The squad secretary said the same thing."

"Let me tell you how he did it," Kenny said. "He used the job you gave him as Colombo coordinator to skim the cream that passed through. A little over a year after he complained about me being the Orena case agent, he got a call from an agent on the Lucchese squad who had a former informant who was in the Nassau County Jail on drugs and who wanted to become a cooperating witness. The Lucchese agent was doing the right thing, wanting to turn the guy over. The guy helped bury a body for Orena. The guy could put Orena directly in the murder and he was willing to testify. As coordinator, does Favo pass this guy along to me like he's supposed to do? He never told anybody about the guy. Favo drove out to the jail."

"Let me guess. Without calling the Long Island office?"

"That's what I was getting to. Before he sets foot in Nassau, he's got to call and tell us why he's coming. Favo just sneaks in."

"I gave him hell for doing that in Jersey."

"If he called us, he'd have to turn over the source to me. Instead, Favo had the guy in jail tape-record a second guy who helped him bury the body. After getting taped, the second guy cooperated, too. He also put Orena directly in the murder. These two showed Favo where the body was. Favo came out and dug it up. Orena heard about the dig and quickly whacked a third guy who helped bury the body, Jack Leale. I would have protected Leale if I'd known what was going on. I'd have tried to use him as a cooperating witness against Orena."

"Scarpa told me Leale was whacked for a sloppy burial job."

"I don't know of anything Favo did to try to protect Leale. The body was Tommy Ocera. He used to go to Pappas's office every day. I was so close to solving that murder of Tommy. There are five New York Bosses and I had one of them and I had no idea what was going on. Favo was carrying all this information to the Eastern District."

"Favo," I said.

"But wait, there's more. End of November, the war

started. Don North put a premium on getting a bug in a hit squad car. Three months after the war started, we got a bug up on Chubby Audino's brand-new Pontiac. We stole the car to put the bug in."

"I remember that bug. I asked you what took you so long."

"Right." Kenny laughed. "My informant, call her Joan—who's the informant in question with Favo—gave us a nice chunk of the probable cause for the Pontiac. Chubby picked Orena up every morning. The Pontiac was Orena's headquarters for the war. What could be better than that?"

"That was a productive wire," I said. "Orena did a lot of talking in that Pontiac. As I recall it was only up a short time."

"It was up three weeks, but it should have been up longer. Favo jumped the gun. Behind my back Favo was running to the Eastern District with verbal reports with great evidence from my tapes as if he were the case agent or a supervisor. Armed with my tapes, with the work I did on Pappas, and with the two witnesses who buried Tommy who should have been my witnesses, like a claim jumper Favo got an indictment on Orena and Chubby Audino and other members and associates in the Orena faction. I couldn't believe it when I heard secondhand there was an indictment on my case and that my squad's wire had come down. I went right to my supervisor. That's when I found out what Favo had done. My supervisor insisted that the arrest, at least, was mine and my

Melville squad's. We made the arrest, but Favo ended up with the case and the trial. Favo sat at counsel table, not me, the real case agent."

"When you're done, Kenny, you need to hear my story."

"Wait, there's more. I'm working. I'm trying to put this behind me. My main source was Joan, but I had many cooperating witnesses in the street wearing wires. I made a lot of cases from my investigation of Orena and Pappas. I had one where the IRA tried to buy surface-to-air missiles from the wiseguys. I had Scotland Yard come over. We got the guy here and they made an arrest in Ireland."

"I worked the IRA undercover for Lou Stephens. They wanted to blow helicopters out of the sky."

"The IRA was very ambitious. Anyway, months went by after the arrest on Orena, and one day I got a call to come in to the Eastern District. I walked into an office where for years I'm treated royally, like a celebrity. I put my hand out. Gleeson just stands there glaring at me. He's holding up a piece of paper in his hand. That's a strange feeling I'll never forget. I know you know the feeling."

"That I do."

"A while before this day, Joan had told me that just before Tommy disappeared, Orena took a few people aside and told them to be careful not to go out drinking with Tommy because something was going to happen to him. Bingo, Tommy's gone. I had put that conversation into a 209. Gleeson stared through me and insisted that they wanted Joan to testify about Orena's warning. I figured Gleeson was holding up my 209. I asked him, politely, what are you doing with my 209? He didn't say anything. I said I was working on her to cooperate and testify, but she's not ready yet to become a witness. I gave him a laundry list of reasons she wouldn't cooperate."

"Don't worry, I won't reveal them," I said. Kenny then gave me a heartbreaking list of reasons that I can't repeat because it could identify his informant.

"Let's just say she was in grave personal danger and extremely afraid," Kenny said. "For herself and for her family."

"That's putting it mildly," I said.

"So then, out of left field, Gleeson raised his voice and literally yelled at me, 'You're having an affair with her.' I could barely believe my ears. You know how careful we have to be with all our informants. I yelled back at him, 'Are you crazy? Or do you think I'm crazy? An affair?'

"He said, 'That's right, you're having an affair with your informant.'

"I yelled back at him, 'That's a total lie. Don't ever say that again. Who told you that?' He didn't say a word. 'What are you doing with my 209?' I yelled. I pointed at the paper in his hand.

"He said, 'It's not a 209. It's a 302.' I grabbed it and read it.

"'I can't believe this shit,' I said. The 209 had Joan's real name in it. Favo had taken my 209 almost verbatim and typed it into a 302 with her real name in it so he could take credit for the source. Naturally, Gleeson saw a 302 and they wanted the witness for trial. To this day I don't know how Favo got her name or whether he guessed it. He didn't get it from my partner. When Gleeson insisted Favo produce her as a witness, Favo claimed they couldn't get her as a witness because I'm having an affair with her. Now they want to bang me. This was Gleeson who worked with Giacalone when they outed Willie Boy Johnson."

"Oh, I remember it well."

"I yelled at Gleeson, 'Where the hell do you get off accusing me of having an affair with an informant?' He admitted that Favo told him.

"I said, 'This 302 you've got in your hand is a fraud. Favo just retyped my 209. This woman isn't a cooperating witness; she's a confidential informant. I'm putting an OPR on Favo for converting my 209 into a 302. You want to talk to Joan. Bring her in.'

"It was bad enough that Favo stole our Chubby Audino wire and our years of work that went into that wire; now he wanted my informant on the wire. I got back to Melville and my supervisor talked me out of reporting Favo. If we traded accusations, I had more to lose with his accusation than he had with mine. The Eastern District brought her in and interviewed her twice. I was there the first time. She could barely talk. All she did was cry. She knew she'd be signing her own death warrant and that Gleeson couldn't protect her. They treated her like dirt. After her second debriefing, she took off before the trial. I didn't lay eyes on her for five years. She seemed scared, not working, worn out."

"Of course," I said. "Fear of the Mafia doesn't go away overnight."

"I'll tell you one about Ellen Corcella," Kenny said. "My name became mud at the Eastern District."

"Caproni had me thrown out of the Eastern District after my OPR was opened."

"I understand what you went through. It's emotional. So much of your life you work so hard, trying to do the right thing. You walk into the Eastern District to shake hands and they're looking at you like you're dirty. And Favo's poisoned the well before you even got there. Ellen Corcella told me she wanted me to testify that a particular wiseguy told me he had a gun. I said, 'The guy never told me he had a gun.'

"She said, 'Favo told me you'd hold this back because you're mad at him.'

"I said, 'That's nuts, where's the 302? What do you think, I anticipated Favo might someday need this, and so I didn't write a 302? If I had that conversation [with that wiseguy], it would be on paper.'"

"Damn right."

"She threatened to charge me with obstruction of justice if I didn't testify. I told her, 'Go ahead. I would never testify to something that didn't happen. Even to put a bad man in jail. I don't play by those rules. If it happened, I would gladly testify.' Corcella told me Favo told her that he overheard the fictitious conversation—a total fabrication. Lin, I hope you let everybody know about Favo."

"Anybody who will listen, my friend."

"Favo," Kenny said. "And he hasn't paid anything for any of this. I know it cost you plenty."

"Every month I open an envelope with a bill in it from my lawyers. The last one was for $630,904.55. They did many many hours of outstanding work for me they never charged me for and I can't make a dent in their bill. There's no pressure, but believe me, it's pressure. Favo feels none."

There was a long pause. I could hear Kenny exhale. What could he say?

"I hate to complain," I said.

"Favo's at headquarters now," Kenny said softly. "In the Integrity Section."

AFTERWORD

And that was the end of the story for me. The Colombo Family appeal strategy to make me the bad guy was dead on arrival. Caproni was chief counsel for the FBI. Favo was in the Integrity Section.

Since my trial, Vecchione has again been accused of withholding material information that would have benefited the defendant in a trial. Rather than submit to a full hearing, the Brooklyn D.A. dropped the charges. (Charlie Brandt and I decided not to waste any words on it. But anyone interested can Google "Vecchione.")

We submitted the manuscript of this book. Now, finally, it was my turn to be heard, and hopefully be able to put this all behind me.

Or so I thought.

While the manuscript was being edited, Chris Mattiace sent out a mass e-mail. He had gotten word from a

Bureau source that sometime after the dismissal of my murder charges, Director Robert S. Mueller III quietly gave the Bureau's Ethics Award to Favo and his three followers for what Favo did to me and to Detective Joe Simone.

Normally, the giving of Bureau awards includes publicity and fanfare. But not this one. None of us had even heard any announcement that it was forthcoming.

I boiled over when I read the language that accompanied the award:

The Manuel J. Gonzalez Award recognizes ethical conduct. The FBI benefited from AD Gonzalez's keen investigative abilities, leadership, high standard of integrity, and, above all, his unwavering commitment to ethical principles.

From 1991 to 1994, SSAs Christopher Favo, Howard Leadbetter, and Jeffery Tomlinson and SA Raymond Andjich led a series of investigations into the activities of more than one hundred members of the Colombo La Cosa Nostra (LCN) family, and almost half of the suspects were convicted or pleaded guilty.

I got up from my seat in disgust. From 1991 to 1994 these four FNGs "led a series of investigations into the activities of more than one hundred members of the Colombo . . . family"? A hundred members is the whole Colombo Family! I was the supervisor of the Colombo Family squad during this time period. It was in 1994 after the investigations were over that Favo got rid of me. Except for Kenny Steiger's part, I was the one who led the investigations.

I sat back down to face the music by reading on.

About halfway through the trials, the four agents found evidence that a detective and their own FBI supervisor each passed law-enforcement-sensitive information to members and associates of the Colombo Family.

"The four agents found evidence . . ." What evidence? Hadn't anyone in authority read the OPR file? This award read as if some other nation's FBI made the 1996 OPR decision. It read as if Detective Joe Simone had been found guilty of the charges against him, not innocent.

The agents displayed exceptional moral courage and resolve in the face of personal and public ostracism by reporting and then assisting in the subsequent investigation.

Now I was laughing out loud. Three of the four agents who "displayed exceptional moral courage and resolve in the face of personal and public ostracism" ended up having the designation "SSA" put before their names. That means they attained the rank of supervisory special agent. They got the same rank I had when I retired. They commanded agents. They trained agents.

The Colombo trials resumed successfully, pleas were obtained, and prior convictions were not reversed.

"The Colombo trials resumed successfully . . ." Caproni had her hands full in the Eastern District; she knows the damage the leaked OPR did to the trials and appeals.

The recipients were as follows: SSA Christopher M. Favo, Office of Integrity and Compliance; SA Raymond Andjich, Miami; SSA Howard Leadbetter II, Legat Ottawa; and SSA Jeffrey W. Tomlinson, Human Resources Branch . . .

Once again, the outpouring of support from my friends

and former colleagues outweighed the repugnance I felt as I read the words that turned these men into saints. On December 18, 2009, the Society of Former Special Agents took the unprecedented step of lodging a protest with Director Mueller.

But that Ethics Award turned out to be a blessing in disguise. Out of the blue, a member of Kenny Steiger's former Orena squad, the retired SA Joe Fanning, reached out to me. Joe had no idea Charlie and I had interviewed Kenny, with whom he hadn't spoken in years.

"The Ethics Award," Joe said. "That's what got me so worked up again. My fingers were typing faster than my mind was thinking. Shame on whoever came up with this award. Shame on the current Director. How can the Bureau give someone an award for something that a Bureau investigation had proved didn't even occur?"

Joe, a second-generation agent, retired in 2003 at the age of fifty-one after a productive and respected career. His dad was one of those cigar-chomping old-time agents who made a lifelong impression on me when I entered on duty, a tough bird, and no doubt he was proud to have Joe follow in his footsteps.

"I put the affidavit together and managed the bug in Chubby Audino's car," Joe said. "It was Long Island's blood and sweat that got approval for the bug, but Favo—who wasn't even a supervisor—wanted to grab that wire for himself and work it out of the New York office. Don North said no, it was Long Island's bug to be worked in Melville. That bug was solid. We had Orena—the Boss—on tape talking about guys they would kill if he saw them.

"After the Orena indictment came down, Don North ruled that the arrest was ours in Long Island, not Favo's. But to arrest Orena we had to find him and that wasn't going to be easy because he was hiding from the Persico faction. You know how they move around. Dennis Collins's surveillance squad did a great job locating the house belonging to Orena's girlfriend, Gina Reale."

"Gina?" I asked. "Like Gina Lollabrigida?"

"Right, but better-looking. She was one of the most stunningly beautiful women I ever saw and seemed like a very nice person. I could never figure her being with Vic. Anyway, we knew Orena might stay at Gina's from time to time, but if we hit her house and missed him, he'd go into the wind. He'd know we were looking for him with an indictment. We had to know for dead certain he was in there when we hit Gina's or he'd be gone forever.

"Gina lived in a cul-de-sac. It was hard to keep an eye out for Orena there without being made. It was freezing outside. I bundled up with a lot of clothes and wore a hood. I took my dog Tasha and walked her along the creek bed across the street from Gina's. Remember Frank Polite, one of Orena's main bodyguards?"

"Oh, yeah," I said.

"Around nine-thirty at night Frank Polite's car pulled into the cul-de-sac with its headlights pointing right at me. Polite knew me. But I had my hood on and all these clothes, plus I was walking Tasha. We knew that Polite often put Orena to bed. I'm hoping he's dropping Orena off. But Polite was alone. Polite pulled into Gina's. Then

I heard male voices, but couldn't make out the words. When Polite left I could see he was still alone.

"Off of that, seeing Frank Polite there that night, I said we should go. In my gut I knew Orena was there in that house. Around five that morning, George Stamboulidis's OC supervisor in the Eastern District got me on the phone and warned me: 'If you're wrong, it's your ass.' Can you imagine being talked to like that? All the work I did and my Bureau career is on the line.

"Well, we finally went in at six a.m. and the place looked empty. My heart sank. We saw loaded shotguns at every door. Then Kenny started down a spiral staircase to the basement with George Connell, a former marine captain, behind him and me picking up the rear. I don't have to tell you, going down a flight of stairs is a good way to get blown away.

"Especially during a shooting war," I said, "with a house full of loaded shotguns. Even when you yell 'FBI' they don't trust that you're not Persicos trying to fake them out."

"Kenny was yelling 'FBI, FBI' on the way down. Orena was yelling 'no problem, no problem.' Still, we didn't know who was down there with him or what he had in his hands. Anyway, there was Orena in his underwear. We got him. We let Orena put on his pants and took our prisoner upstairs.

"Meanwhile, Favo and other agents with him waited outside. Then, following prior orders, they came in the house and Favo walked our prisoners out of the house and took over from there. It was weird. Kenny was bumped off the case that we made. Kenny was not even allowed to walk Orena out of the house.

"Lin, I got to know Favo better when the trials started. I was on the stand in Orena's trial for about a week, giving testimony on the tapes and the terrific evidence we found at Gina's. I was tasked to be in the war room by North for the whole trial."

"I testified in Orena's trial as an expert," I said.

"I remember," Joe said. "Spending time in that trial war room, I got to see Favo in action. I heard Favo openly knock you all the time to his little clique. Being younger, I didn't know you well, Lin, but I knew that old-time agents that I respected thought the world of you. One day, and this was before the OPR was known, Favo uttered four words talking about you that I will never forget. Favo said: 'I will get him.' I can still hear him saying that."

"Can I use that in my book?" I asked.

"Absolutely. Anything I say, you can use. After Orena's conviction, the next trial to come out of the Chubby Audino wire that I was involved in was the crew that included Orena Jr., Frank Polite, and Chubby Audino himself. Again the evidence was overwhelming and a conviction was a foregone conclusion. Ellen Corcella and George Stamboulidis were the prosecutors. This time I was tasked to sit at the prosecutors' table in the courtroom every day with Ray Andjich.

"Lin, almost every day there was a miserable day.

"Favo ran around as if he was a prosecutor running the show. I called him AUSA Favo. By this time there was some publicity about your relationship with Scarpa, but I had no idea what was going on.

"I sat at the prosecution table with Ray Andjich when Ellen Corcella rose to give her opening statement to the jury. At one point she began to talk about you, that you were a corrupt agent, that you had given information to Scarpa, trying to win the war for his faction. I couldn't believe my ears. How could she do that? The case was lost right there in her opening statement. You could see the jury's expression and the defense lawyers had to love what they were hearing.

"At that point Ellen Corcella turned and looked directly at Ray Andjich and me. She said words to the effect '. . . and it was young agents under him that turned Lin DeVecchio in for his misdeeds.'

"I was incredulous. I thought about getting up and walking out. I wish I had, but you can't do that."

"No, you can't do that," I said.

"At the end of the day I went into Corcella's office, closed the door, and screamed at her for not letting me know they were going to take the tack that Lin was a corrupt agent and for insinuating that I had turned against him. How could they do that to the case? Were they nuts? Who does that, and how could she put me in the middle of something I knew nothing about? Nobody had even showed me the affidavits against you. When I walked out, Ellen Corcella was sitting in her chair in tears.

"On my way back to the war room, Stamboulidis started yelling at me, accusing me of not supporting the trial, using some pretty unflattering words. I started yelling back at him in the middle of the office. I walked toward him in a rage. Thank God for Laura Ward."

"She's a judge now," I said. "The best."

"For sure. Laura rushed out of her office and got me out of there. I'm afraid I would have hit Stamboulidis if I got to him. Lin, to this day I can still hear Favo saying, 'I will get him.'"

"Favo," I commiserated.

"I'm surprised Jeff Tomlinson accepted that award," Joe said. "In the war room, during one of the subsequent trials, Jeff and I were talking about the situation with you and he told me he knew he was a young agent who'd been manipulated by Favo. He regretted getting involved with Favo against you."

"Did he use the word 'regret,' Joe?"

"He sure did."